CAMBRIDGE STUDIES IN LII

General Editors · W. SIDNEY ALLEN · C. J. FILLMORE
E. J. A. HENDERSON · F. W. HOUSEHOLDER · J. LYONS
R. B. LE PAGE · F. R. PALMER · J. L. M. TRIM

Foundations of linguistics

In this series

* Issued in hard cover and as a paperback

FOUNDATIONS OF LINGUISTICS

DIETER WUNDERLICH

Professor of General Linguistics
University of Düsseldorf

Translated from the German *Grundlagen der Linguistik*
by Roger Lass

CAMBRIDGE UNIVERSITY PRESS

CAMBRIDGE

LONDON · NEW YORK · MELBOURNE

Published by the Syndics of the Cambridge University Press
The Pitt Building, Trumpington Street, Cambridge CB2 1RP
Bentley House, 200 Euston Road, London NW1 2DB
32 East 57th Street, New York, NY 10022, USA
296 Beaconsfield Parade, Middle Park, Melbourne 3206, Australia

Originally published under the title of *Grundlagen der Linguistik* in the series
Rororo Studium, general editor Ernesto Grassi

First published in English 1979

Printed in Great Britain at the
University Press, Cambridge

Library of Congress Cataloguing in Publication Data
Wunderlich, Dieter.
Foundations of linguistics.

(Cambridge studies in linguistics; 22)
Bibliography: p.
Includes index
1. Linguistics. I. Title. II. Series.
P121.W9313   410   77-82526
ISBN 0 521 22007 6 hard covers
ISBN 0 521 29334 0 paperback

Contents

One of the most fruitful means of discovery – compared to which the old *Quis, quid, ubi* is scarcely a rival – is to say to yourself, as soon as you hear anything: 'Is that so?' The rule that one should not speak or write before thinking shows a lot of good will on its author's part, but very little reflection; and the good man cannot have considered that – to speak judiciously but strongly – one cannot follow the rule without breaking it. For unless they avoided thinking, many men would never speak at all – wherefore I maintain the opposite opinion. How many men have finally, in desperation, said something wise, because they had to justify an unreflecting statement? And to assert is to philosophize. I except the few identical propositions that Euclid has pointed out for us, together with all others that derive from them through permissible deductions.

> A leg of mutton is better than nothing,
> Nothing is better than heaven,
> Therefore a leg of mutton is better than heaven.
>
> G. C. Lichtenberg

Foreword

This book is an attempt to outline the foundations of a science. But my chosen field – linguistics – is at present in a process of stormy development, and presents a picture of competing theories, opinions, principles and interests. Given the current state of the discipline, the goal I have set myself can be achieved only fragmentarily; its total achievement would transcend the personal ability and knowledge of an individual author – who besides is in any case bound to be the prisoner of the very questions he has formulated about his subject. It follows from this that any particular attempt to carry out such a programme will soon be out of date; and, indeed, it is my hope that this will be the case.

It is not even clear exactly what we should understand by 'the foundations of linguistics'. One approach would be to try answering the following three questions, and unifying the separate answers into a coherent whole:

1. What are the various aspects of language ? And what different (partly interdisciplinary) orientations for linguistics do they motivate ? (E.g. toward psychology and physiology of speech and comprehension; the physics of the acoustic signal; the three classical disciplines of the *Trivium* – rhetoric, logic, and grammar; possible connections with act-theory, theory of institutions, and socialization-theory; the incorporation of the historical dimension; practical problems in areas like data-processing, media-analysis, language pedagogy and language planning.)

2. What presuppositions (in terms of philosophy/theory of science and methodology) do we need in order to argue for or against particular scientific positions in the field ?

3. What are the fundamental categories, principles, and methods in linguistics ?

The answer to any one of these will set the standards for answering the others.

I will try here mainly to answer the second question; and in the course of this attempt I will discuss some of the central problems involved in it, especially that of the concept of meaning. In my view the usual conceptions of the theory of science cannot simply be transferred unreflectingly to linguistics. Rather we have to clarify anew the status of our linguistic knowledge, our reflection and argumentation about language in language – and thus the empirical status of linguistics itself. At least we must do this unless we want to run the risk of holding on to certain dogmatic preliminary decisions. All the essential methods of elucidation in science are modelled on procedures we use in our everyday lives; in science they are merely worked out more clearly and precisely, with a view toward more specific (and limited) goals. But our theoretical orientation basically determines the ultimate direction of our methodology; and therefore we also need some understanding of the status and function of theories.

All the above issues are problematical; and I readily admit that many sections of this book are rather like conversations with myself. What counts is not the definition of a firmly delimited universe of knowledge, concepts and procedures that can be confidently taken away by the reader, but rather the attempt to stimulate discussion and achieve an awareness of problems.

To this extent then this is not so much an introduction to particular linguistic theories and methods as a general introduction to linguistic inquiry and its characteristic modes of thought and argument. I assume as little as possible in the way of initial preparation; in particular, I do not assume much formal knowledge of linguistics. But of course a certain familiarity with linguistic problems (especially in semantics and syntactic analysis) is necessary: it is hard to see what the fundamental problems of a science are if you approach it as a stranger. Thus the best time for the student to read this book would be after the completion of at least an introductory course in linguistics. (The more difficult sections are marked with a preceding asterisk.)

I am grateful to my colleagues Renate Bartsch, Manfred Bierwisch, Walther Dieckmann, Konrad Ehlich, Jochen Rehbein, Helmut Schnelle, Christoph Schwarze, and Arnim von Stechow for their comments on early drafts of several chapters. I am also especially grateful to Karin Pols for her clerical assistance.

D.W.
Düsseldorf, Summer 1973

Foreword to the English translation

I am delighted that the Cambridge University Press has decided to make this book available for the English-speaking reader, and that they have found, in Roger Lass, such an able translator. This version has been slightly altered in a number of ways: a few passages have been omitted, and – not least through the kind advice of the translator – I have corrected a number of errors. I have also, as far as possible, brought the bibliography up to date. No one linguist, of course, can completely survey the current state of research in the field, so I have retained some sections that do not do justice to the most recent developments. I also realize that in some areas – notably phonology, dialectology, and historical and comparative linguistics – the theoretical basis has been worked out in much more detail than my treatment here would suggest. In syntax and semantics as well I have discussed only the basics, not the most recent theories (e.g. Extended Standard Theory, Montague Grammar, Transition Network Grammar, Frame Theory). For some more recent and precise treatments of the theory of linguistic inquiry by myself and others, see my *Wissenschaftstheorie der Linguistik* (Kronberg 1976c).

Since 1973 my own work has been mainly in the fields of speech-act theory and discourse analysis; for this see my *Studien zur Sprechakttheorie* (Frankfurt 1976b), where the position adumbrated here in §9.29 is more fully worked out.

Readers of the German edition frequently criticized me for taking a neopositivist position, and obscuring the fundamental distinction between the natural and the human sciences (like linguistics). I do not believe, however, that there really is this kind of fundamental distinction; if there were it would make interdisciplinary discussion impossible, which would be disastrous for the further development of human society, to which every science has a contribution to make. But on the other hand I do think that every science has its own problems; and we have to investigate these in detail before we can establish its precise status (e.g. in the light of a general theory of science).

I hope that the reader will be prepared to follow me in my rather complex and multi-layered argument; and I would be grateful for any comment and criticism. I thank Roger Lass for his painstaking and distinguished work as translator.

D.W.

Düsseldorf, December 1976

Translator's note

The task of turning a German book into a reasonably English one – as anyone with some knowledge of both languages will realize – is not an easy one. I am not sure whether I have succeeded in producing a book that does not 'read like a translation'. I hope at any rate that whatever infelicities of style remain, I have been faithful to the author's intention. Any success I have achieved in this is due in no small part to the author himself, who painstakingly went over an early draft, and provided assistance far beyond the call of duty on problems of finding English equivalents for German terms, as well as patiently answering my innumerable (and mostly illegible) marginal queries. So at least part of whatever is good in this translation (even *qua* translation) is due to Dieter Wunderlich; the mistakes are mine alone. I am also grateful to the many native speakers of German who helped me on various points, especially Dr H.-H. Speitel; and to my wife Jaime for stylistic advice.

R.L.
Edinburgh, March 1977

Mathematical and logical symbols

<	less than
⩽	less than or equal to
>	greater than
⩾	greater than or equal to
a o b	concatenation of the elements a and b
a b	connection of the elements a and b
⟨a, b⟩	ordered pair of the elements a and b
(a, b, ...)	ordered series of the elements a, b, etc.
{a, b, ...}	collection of the elements a, b, etc. into a set
$\{a_j : P(a_j)\}$	set of elements a_j with the property P
a ∈ A	a is a member of the set A
$[a\ b\ c]_A$	the string a b c is of the category A
A ∩ B	intersection of the sets A and B
A ∪ B	union of the sets A and B
A × B	product of the sets A and B
A ⊂ B	the set A is included in the set B
= df	the same by definition
&	logical conjunction
∨	logical disjunction
~	logical negation
⊃	material implication
≡	logical equivalence
⊢	logical derivability
⊩	logical consequence
≺	strict implication
→	strong inference; or assignment of a value to a function
(x)...	For all x, it is the case that ...
(Ex) ...	there is (at least) one x, such that ...
⇒	transformational derivability
a → bc	replace a by the string b c (production rule)

I Introduction

1.1 Matters of course and problem-cases

Speech and other forms of self-expression (like gestures, mimicry, writing) are part of everyone's daily life. Communication in general is a well-defined human activity, embedded in a series of other activities. For the most part we have no problems with communicative activities; we simply learn them as natural forms of human interaction in specific contexts. They are, however, complex; they require very complex capabilities, like observation, cognitive processing, memory, anticipation, interpretation of social situations and other people's capacities for understanding and action, control of socially recognized procedures. These capabilities are partly interdependent, and we learn them together.

Accordingly, there is something paradoxical about reconstructions of human communication that start from a view of man as a self-contained being, and take communicative competence as self-initiating. It is difficult to imagine how to treat the situation that would arise when two such solitaries met. This of course does not happen, so it is virtually meaningless to interpret human communication as a solitary and self-initiated activity: men are constantly engaged in manifold relations with one other. In the same way it is absurd to ask what language a child would speak if it were brought up in total isolation. Such a creature (if it survived at all) would simply die when it reached its purely biological maturity. The possibility of living as a grown human being is inextricably bound up with communication.

Every communicative act presupposes that the participants have a set of COMMON INTERESTS. If these are lacking, they must be created, i.e. the participants must enter into a common learning-process. It is by means of such consistently mutual and self-completing processes of learning and cooperation that we achieve both 'common knowledge' and common convictions, values and orientations ('common sense'). Each participant has these common possessions; and it is with reference to them that he engages in the exchange of information and proposals for action, and expresses a further 'conjectural knowledge'. What is held in common can be assumed without question: there are normally no alternatives. He expects both that he will be understood, and that the other person will carry out certain appointed actions; and he also anticipates the expectations of others. This MUTUALITY OF EXPECTATION is guaranteed by the fact that the expectations are not merely private, but are based on social knowledge and attitudes, and on a socially defined interaction range.

This building on common interests is not of course absolutely reliable. If the basic presuppositions are not met in particular cases, difficulties in comprehension, and ultimately discrepancies of judgement and problems in sustaining the interaction, arise. These are often eliminated through further inquiry, correction and supplementary discussion. If this fails, if the expectations that had been built up are disappointed, then the act of communication is essentially meaningless. In real life, indeed, meaningless actions are generally eliminated; at least in the sense that disappointments lead to new orientations, and one learns to avoid them while at the same time modifying one's expectations.

As long as difficulties in understanding can be resolved in obvious ways there is no need for explicit reflection about communication. It is when failures, either in the detail or fundamentals of communication, are relatively frequent that particular aspects of communication and communicative competence first appear over the horizon of the obvious. When this happens the participants have to make these aspects conscious (or perhaps only make them conscious again) in order to clarify and explicate the problems, and to look for ways of explaining the failure.

Disturbances in the normally problem-free course of communication occur on various levels, and on each of these we have to look for specific causes and explanatory principles. In part these disturbances can be treated as deviations from the normal and expectable, for which the individual is to blame: one can demand that he justifies them ('You should have known...', 'You have to...'). In part they can be treated as deviations that must be cooperatively resolved.

Disturbances of the first kind are mainly due to individual (or sometimes group-specific) transgressions against accepted communicative norms; disturbances of the second kind often have physiological, psychological and social causes; often indeed exclusively physical ones. Examples would be pronunciation difficulties due to hoarseness, cleft palate, missing teeth, faulty breathing rhythm (e.g. in spastics); hearing difficulties due to deafness, static, environmental noise or simultaneous speech; dyslexia, stuttering, etc.; aphasia following brain damage, schizophrenia (systematically contradictory speech), expressive difficulties in states of anxiety or depression; articulatory problems in foreign languages or dialects, and so on.

Other difficulties stem from vague, ambiguous, contradictory, elliptical, or over-complex language, from the use of terms inappropriate or irrelevant to the situation, from the omission of expressions signalling non-comprehension or non-acceptance, and so on.

Austin (1962: lecture II) has classified some typical failures, or infelicities, of speech acts as the starting point for his theorizing on the nature of speech acts. He distinguishes:

(a) MISINVOCATIONS. There is no convention for performing the speech act in question (e.g. I cannot normally amaze someone by saying 'I hereby amaze you'); or the convention does not allow the act to be carried out under particular circumstances. (This is naturally more common: I should not thank someone for a reproach; if someone tells me the time I shouldn't ask what time it is; etc.)

(b) MISEXECUTIONS. Specified procedures are incorrect or not fully carried out. Here we have all kinds of vagueness, ambiguity, grammatical mistakes, and above all transgressions against the obligations imposed by preceding speech acts (if I start an argument I have to conclude it; if I start off saying 'first' I have to continue at least to 'second'; I have to answer questions, respond to greetings, etc.)

(c) ABUSES. Dishonesties are possible within the speech act itself (all kinds of cheating, lies, etc.), and there are speech acts that are practically non-functional, since the expected consequences fail to materialize (if someone accepts my request he ought to carry out the corresponding action). Abuses of this kind do not generally lead directly to communication problems, but rather to divergent assessments of the results of communication; and conflicts can arise later because of this.

(d) ERRORS. One can make an assertion that is true to the best of one's knowledge, but later turns out to be false. Here too problems arise in the subsequent assessment. But an error as such is generally pardonable; it is not a transgression against communicative obligations, and therefore does not lead to conflict.

This classification, though theoretically sophisticated, is imperfect, but cases like those mentioned here do motivate us to look for causes and explanatory principles. Even given the matter-of-courseness of communication, we can ask questions about the very unproblematicalness of its achievement. What is this matter-of-courseness really based on? Why do we get problems in some cases but not in others? What in fact are the specific conditions and presuppositions for communication?

Specific types of disturbances also point to SPECIFIC ASPECTS OF LANGUAGE AND SPEAKING. Corresponding to each of these we can have a scientific activity whose goal is the clarification of its precise meaning. I am not claiming that this is always specifically a task for linguistics: thus it is not primarily for linguists to study the influence of harelip or cleft palate on articulatory capability, or to concern themselves with how errors can be avoided. In most cases in fact we need an interdisciplinary approach: other disciplines have their part to play even in linguistic inquiry. I do not think we can define, *a priori*, the boundaries of a field reserved only for linguistics. Whenever one of the problems mentioned above becomes acute according to accepted social standards (and, moreover, problems connected with language-teaching or data-processing arise), there is a corresponding social interest in a specific form of linguistics.

The scientist's mental horizon, like other men's, is bounded by common knowledge and common convictions. The truth of common knowledge does not really have to be established; but this knowledge nonetheless can and must be analysed in order for problem cases to be solved. For it often turns out that what we have is only apparent or superficial knowledge; deeper analysis brings deeper principles to light. We must then show how it comes about that exactly these particulars and not some others are established as common knowledge. Common convictions are socially certified; they are certainties for the individual at least partly because he believes that they are also certainties for everyone else. But the scientist who accepts these common convictions unreservedly is being uncritical about his own presuppositions. Because of this, he has to cultivate a critical, sceptical attitude toward common knowledge and convictions at a specific phase of analysis. If he makes a few points into problems, he will support himself on others with these common acceptances, and seek to defend them. At bottom however none of them is immune to criticism.

The scientist uses a set of argumentative procedures in his search for a STABILIZATION OF SOME SPECIFIC PART OF HIS PRELIMINARY UNDERSTANDING. His theoretical designs are in fact plausible only insofar as they acknowledge certain aspects of it. Scientific understanding has to support itself partially on plausibilities; otherwise every theoretical design would exist in a vacuum. But the plausible is often merely a kind of prejudice. The extent to which the scientist perpetually questions his own positions will be an index of how radically he problematizes. This questioning of positions also requires acute argumentative techniques, and these are an indispensable part of scientific method.

1.2   Conventions

Problem-free communication presupposes common knowledge and convictions. But these do not have to be explicitly recognized or attested, i.e. we are dealing with normally implicit knowledge and commitments. The 'normality' of our expectations and modes of behaviour in fact depends largely on just such implicitness.

Each participant in a communication has his own particular interests, related *inter alia* to his convictions and needs; but in a given situation the interests of all participants (however divergent they might otherwise be) are also partly the same. For there must be an agreement to give the interaction a specific direction, to carry it on or break it off at a given point. So to this extent at least communication is COOPERATIVE ACTIVITY. Each participant carries out specific procedures (e.g. articulation of particular sequences of phonemes); he assumes (and expects) that the others will understand their intersubjective meaning, and will perform (or be able to perform, circumstances permitting) the corresponding procedures.

These are conventional. If someone performs them we can say that he is, as it were, following SOCIAL RULES. (We must always remember that social rules are never isolated, but are always connected to other rules.) The nature of a social rule first becomes apparent when one is broken. In the debate that follows some deviant ('not normal') behaviour, rules first begin to be made explicit. For example, in order to justify a reproach ('but you should have done X') we must utilize a criterion that allows a particular behaviour to be judged as deviant.

Naturally STATEMENTS or reconstructions of social rules can be false or inappropriate, e.g. it could be that the behaviour is not really properly characterized as deviant. Thus grammatical rules in the traditional sense (e.g. as used in schools), or in the sense of scientific theories, are only particular reconstructions: it clearly makes no sense to say that THESE are being followed. But it is possible that someone might follow them in the future, because they presumably mirror what was up to now done unconsciously.

I have referred to these communicative procedures as conventional: but what are we to understand by a convention ? David Lewis (1969) has attempted a general clarification of this notion, particularly in regard to arbitrary regularities arising in the course of human cooperation.[1] It is based on a cooperative games model, in which one participant can secure an advantage only when the others can also secure one (an advantage is thus not – at least not primarily – achieved at someone else's expense). The basic considerations are roughly these: fulfilment of one's own interest does not depend only on one's own actions, but also on those of others. Therefore, in order to fulfil his own interests, every participant has to coordinate his actions with those of the others, i.e. he must always select his actions in such a way that he anticipates what the others are going to do. But since the actions of others derive in turn from THEIR expectations of the actions of others, he must also be able to anticipate the others' expectations. Thus whenever mutual expectations are not disappointed, and others act as expected, he has reason to expect and to do the same under similar circumstances.

A regularity developed in this way is a CONVENTION, if each individual conforms to it, and expects everyone else also to conform; and if he prefers to conform under the condition that the others will; but if the others were to conform to other regularities, he would do so as well. Only if he coordinates actions directed toward the fulfillment of his own interests in this way with the actions of others can he rationally (and legitimately) expect his own interests to be fulfilled.

It is also possible, of course, to solve a coordination or cooperation problem by means of an EXPLICIT AGREEMENT: the participants negotiate among themselves as to what they will do; they make promises, assume obligations with respect to their future actions. Such a behavioural regularity, however, can be called a convention only when the power of the original promises has vanished – perhaps because of the advent of new participants who orient themselves only to the existing regularities, or because the (original) participants themselves do not treat their actions as directed by the original promises.

---

[1] On first consideration, one might understand 'behavioural regularities' in terms of the frequency of specific behaviour; but there are obviously conventional regularities determined not only by their frequency but by their normality – and this can be specified in terms of expectation.

A convention serves to coordinate the actions and behaviour of various persons (e.g. the sequence of speech acts as in questions and answers). The opinions, attitudes and convictions of a speaker and his hearer are likewise coordinated – namely in the processes of understanding which precede or accompany sequential actions. THE COORDINATION OF SPEAKING AND UNDERSTANDING is on the one hand a presupposition for the COORDINATION OF SPEAKING AND SPEAKING (in general, the actions of different persons); on the other hand it is possible only on the basis of normal, everyday coordination of actions. These two coordination problems are not identical, but they are connected. Lewis clarifies only the problem of the coordination of various speakers or actors; the second problem, which is the fundamental problem of meaning, is taken as clarified or clarifiable through the other. I will not discuss at this point either the correctness of this view or what further considerations of the meaning problem might be necessary.[1]

Here is Lewis' complete definition (1969: 78):

A regularity R in the behavior of members of a population P when they are agents in a recurrent situation S is a *convention* if and only if it is true that, and it is common knowledge in P that, in almost any instance of S among members of P,

(1) almost everyone conforms to R;
(2) almost everyone expects almost everyone else to conform to R;
(3) almost everyone has approximately the same preferences regarding all possible combinations of actions;
(4) almost everyone prefers that any one more conform to R, on condition that almost everyone conform to R;
(5) almost everyone would prefer that any one more conform to R', on condition that almost everyone conform to R',

where R' is some possible regularity in the behavior of members of P in S, such that almost no one in almost any instance of S among members of P could conform both to R' and to R.

It is not entirely clear what condition (3) means; possibly it is to be understood as uniformity of interests relative to specific communication situations (the type of procedure depends on the type of interests, but they are all decided on here in the same way). Condition (4) applies to stabilization of conventions, and (5) to change of conventions.

Lewis' definition has been criticized by Schnelle (1973a), mainly on two points:

---

[1] Cf. ch. 9.III below. Also Bennett (1973· 141–68), especially 150ff.

1. Lewis assumes that all participants show the same behavioural regularities. But it is merely necessary, in order for them to understand each other, that the regularities be SIMILAR, e.g. that the participants speak 'neighbouring' language varieties. A participant can never say with certainty that someone else follows exactly the same conventions he does; he can at best say that the other follows conventions very similar to his own, and reconcilable (compatible) with them. In order to have a convention it is sufficient that the members of a speech-community be CONVINCED that a convention (in Lewis' sense) exists; but the actual content of the convention can be something different for each one.

2. Not all members of a speech-community can be judged to have identical command of the language. But with regard to both the stability of conventions and their susceptibility to change we must consider the degree of linguistic competence that a given member of the community judges the others to have. For under the appropriate conditions we can tolerate the linguistic behaviour of members who do not completely follow the conventions, or who follow certain related (but perhaps irreconcilable) ones.

On the basis of these criticisms Schnelle (1973a: 302) proposes a new definition, specifically restricted to linguistic conventions:

A set M of regularities in speech behaviour of interactants of a speech-community P is a set of CONVENTIONS FOR A LANGUAGE L if and only if for each interactant X in P and for at least one regularity R in M such that X commands R, it is the case that

(1) X makes himself understood by means of R to a degree of sufficiency K in practical situations S to almost all Y in P whom he communicates with.

(2) X assumes that almost all Y in P who must be reckoned with likewise command R. Occasional contra-indications like misunderstandings are due to accidental or situation-bound misuses of competence – either X's or Y's.

(3) X assumes that what applies to him under (1) also applies to almost all Y who must be reckoned with.

(4) X assumes that almost every Y who must be reckoned with has roughly the same preferences (and aversions) regarding all possible speech-forms and their use.

(5) X assumes that almost everyone prefers that if almost all speakers who must be reckoned with conform to R, those who have not done so up to now will finally also conform to R.

(6) X assumes that almost everyone would prefer that if almost all those who must be reckoned with should conform to R', then those who had not yet done so would do so.

Aside from a few small differences of verbal detail, and a restriction to practical communication situations, Schnelle's main departure from Lewis is this: that all the observations that Lewis gives here count only as ASSUMPTIONS of the interactants. But this is particularly to be rejected.

1. Schnelle's first objection could be dealt with in the framework of Lewis' definition: either we understand a behavioural regularity R as sufficiently abstract (as an abstraction-class of all similar and mutually reconcilable regularities), or we introduce FAMILIES of related CONVEN-TION-SYSTEMS (cf. ch. 11 below), which are mutually tolerated (without shifting these conventions into the speaker's assumptions). In each case we would have to make clear what we meant by 'reconcilable' and 'irreconcilable'.

2. Schnelle's conception suggests that the speaker (like the linguist) makes assumptions in some explicit sense. But this is normally the case only if he has a motive, e.g. if the existence of a particular convention becomes a problem. In general speakers assume the existence of con-ventions only IMPLICITLY: i.e. they have learned to do one particular thing and nothing else in order to behave in accord with their interests. There is no sharp boundary for them between the conventional and the non-conventional. (Within a given domain such boundaries, even once assumed, are always variable.) Because of this the problem of reconcil-ability or irreconcilability in the strict sense never arises: these notions have a precise sense only for the linguist, and only in relation to particu-lar explications.

3. The existence of conventions as conditions for communication is not simply a useful fiction for the speaker, but a FACT. Speakers do not merely assume that there are conventions in Lewis' sense, and then behave only as if there were such conventions. Speakers learn (by and large) to make themselves successfully understood – and in general there are alternative ways of doing this – and they do not simply learn to develop assumptions about the possibilities of communication, even if these are pertinent. In cases of conflict they ask for, and may accept, the judgements of others; and these judgements are not taken as deriving from their assumptions, but rather as judgements about the factual content of conventions. The sanctions that can follow non-observation of conventions are realities for the speaker.

4. Within the framework of the notion 'convention', it is hard to know how to take the persons 'who must be reckoned with'; such per-sons are primarily authoritative only when a judgement is required in a

conflict situation. On the other hand another person can assume the right to be 'reckoned with' directly in a POWER SITUATION; but here the subordinate person merely adapts himself to circumstances, without regarding his behaviour as conventional. In any case it is problematical to connect cooperative situations with possible power situations or the demand for tolerance, in the way Schnelle does.

Schnelle's introduction of tolerance regarding the behaviour of others makes it clear, moreover, that both his and Lewis' definitions miss an important point. Tolerance means not only the possible recognition of other conventions that are irreconcilable by nature, but likewise (and perhaps primarily) recognizing that certain deviations even from a valid convention do not incur sanctions. For all conventions there are also IMPLICIT COMMITMENTS: under particular circumstances certain procedures have to be carried out, and certain others do not. The circumstances also involve particular procedures having already been carried out: therefore the carrying out of procedures relative to the given situation imposes commitments relevant to proceeding further with the situation. If these commitments are not fulfilled (e.g. if these or certain alternative procedures are neglected, or inappropriate ones performed), we have to reckon with SANCTIONS (non-attainment of goals, being called to account, penalties, etc.). Here we can see clearly the intersubjectivity and reality of conventions: sanctions are experienced immediately.

In addition sanctions can be partly accepted, as is shown by corrections and excuses. Neither commitments nor sanctions remain solely in the realm of judgements and assumptions. It is only when the commitments which are bound up with conventions are partly acknowledged that we can speak of communication as cooperative.

Implicit commitments are of course not to be equated with EXPLICIT PROMISES or EXPLICIT BEHAVIOURAL NORMS (commands and prohibitions). They are similar, however, at least insofar as transgressions against commitments by the other participants can be treated exactly like transgressions against norms, or unfulfilled promises. But implicit commitments are just as unclearly defined as implicit conventions.[1]

In this sense EVERY LANGUAGE IS A PRAGMATIC LANGUAGE: there are

---

[1] Schnelle's criticism of Lewis may be based on something like this: if implicit conventions are unclearly defined, there can be a set of different clarifications, each precise in its own way, and each a possible basis for fully rational action. There can also be differing (and perhaps competing) judgements as to what the conventions are. Each clarification – taken as a speaker's judgement – is in fact only an assumption; a clarification that deviates from it is not necessarily a mistake.

obligations or normative regulations that determine – relative to the situation, and especially to preceding actions – when any speech acts are necessary, when they are permissible, and when they are not permissible. There is also a second pragmatic factor which is not necessarily binding on all languages or varieties of a language. Utterances are judged according to the extent to which the circumstances of the situation of utterance must be brought to bear in determining their interpretation as speech acts and as expressions of particular states of affairs. If the kind of speech act performed depends on both the uttered phonemes and the circumstances of utterance, we have a pragmatic language in the second sense (natural languages are generally of this type).

If the utterance itself defines the type of speech act performed, we can speak of a SEMANTIC LANGUAGE (certain explicit forms of natural languages are of this type, but they are still pragmatic in the first sense). In such a language, however, deictic expressions, elliptical expressions, etc., can be used, and their factual reference is specifiable only with respect to the circumstances of utterance. If there are no such expressions, i.e. if all interpretations can be determined solely by the utterance itself, we can speak of a SEMANTIC LANGUAGE IN THE STRICT SENSE (e.g. the usual types of logical languages).

Mathematically oriented linguistics often deals with formal languages emptied of all possibilities of interpretation; these can be called SYNTACTIC LANGUAGES. But here it is inappropriate to speak of 'languages' in the literal sense, because we cannot communicate with formal languages alone; a means of communication must always have both form and meaning (content, sense).

1.3 Linguistic tradition

A science does not continually begin anew with as it were original or natural problems, even if these represent an important motivation for the individual scientist. The evolution of every science – as a social institution – is controlled by three types of influences: its own tradition, the dominant scientific conceptions of the time (which are often oriented toward some other particular science: so one science can model itself on the image of another), and current social tasks and commitments. These global orientations are necessary not only for the further development of a science, but also its social recognition (financing, etc.). To this we must add a reconciling function with respect to the individual's experiences and problems, which always have an innovatory character. (We could put this the other way: experiences and problems that are new for the individual must be worked out and clarified in the light of the three influences mentioned above.)

Each science has its own history: its problems and formulations of questions have a more or less long tradition. It is a subject in the universities, where different 'schools' have their own conceptions and pedagogical ideas, and therefore many of its problems, concepts and solutions have already been enshrined in a canonical form. It is therefore especially important for a science to recognize its own historical stages and to decide their value for present work. The subject matter of linguistics is in part its own history.

The question of AUTONOMY is often a central problem for a science: what are the grounds for distinguishing it from neighbouring disciplines? Is not linguistics really a branch of psychology or sociology or even human neurophysiology? The history of linguistics provides various answers to this:[1] some that explicitly assign it to one of the neighbouring disciplines (e.g. for Chomsky it is a branch of cognitive psychology, for others it is a social science); and others that maintain autonomy, and have characterized exactly where this autonomy lies (e.g. in the investigation and comparison of the grammars of individual languages).

I take the problem of autonomy to be unimportant, and certainly peripheral to my purposes here (though I do not deny that there are certain central questions in linguistics – especially problems of grammatical theory – that do not have the same importance in other disciplines). Let me justify this briefly:

1. Answers to the autonomy question are primarily JUSTIFICATIONS, mainly with INSTITUTIONAL REFERENCE: how do we introduce and delimit specific subjects, e.g. in the development of curricula? How can we get money and personnel for working on specific problems? What institutional classification is desirable and necessary? Naturally as a science is actually being established very central questions about what that science understands itself to be have to be raised and answered. One distinction that can be understood only in this context is that between 'philology' (*Sprachwissenschaft*) and 'linguistics' (*Linguistik*): the increasing use of the term *Linguistik* in Germany was directed against the previously dominant historical orientation which endeavoured mainly to understand earlier language states, and the 'humanistic' (*geisteswissenschaft-*

[1] For a very useful discussion of this theme see Heeschen & Kegel (1972).

liche) orientation (especially the Weisgerber school). Conversely, the proponents of *Sprachwissenschaft* have argued against the linguists' substantive and methodological contraction of the concept of language.[1] The terminological point of a conflict is naturally always something extrinsic. In this case I will attach myself to neither party (both are partly right), but will equate the two terms. What is central is the concept of language, and the way the discipline understands itself – not a label, behind which the most disparate positions can always conceal themselves.

2. But however we define the subject matter and methodology of linguistics, its INTERDISCIPLINARY ORIENTATION is fundamental. What matters is that we recognize that potentially similar problems face both linguistics and other disciplines, and that the distinction is only a matter of emphasis. And that, on the other hand, those problem areas to which linguistics lays special claim are hardly ever unitary (compare the problems of phonetics with those of semantics). Particular aspects of language are significant not only for linguistics, but just as much for logic, rhetoric, psychology, sociology, etc. If these sciences adhered strictly to their autonomy, an incoherent proliferation of research could easily result, which would prevent us from recognizing common reference points.

Discussion of its own history is not equally relevant for all sciences. For linguistics this problem is quite different from what it is for physics. Over the past two hundred years, physics has accumulated a canonical body of knowledge. Descriptive methods and certain epistemological attitudes have changed; after a period of stabilization few fundamental doubts remain about the statements of mechanics, thermodynamics, and atomic physics. In linguistics there is much less canonical (i.e. generally accepted) knowledge; certainly not on the level of theory, at most perhaps on the level of facts and specific methodological operations. Thus in linguistics it is possible for old or rejected positions to be taken up again. Chomsky invokes Descartes, Humboldt and the Port Royal Grammar of 1660; other contemporary linguists ally themselves explicitly with Hermann Paul or Bloomfield in preference to Chomsky. But it would surely be a mistake to see this as merely a kind of oscillation – the grandchildren taking up their grandfathers' ideas. This shift of positions could be due at one point to the changing extrinsic conditions of the

---

[1] One can get some idea of these discussions from Weisgerber (1970), and the rejoinders of Wienold, Baumann, and Schnelle (*Linguistische Berichte* 10, 11).

science, at another to the greater clarification of certain theoretical positions.

The individual scientist is rarely familiar with his own tradition, i.e. his scientific self-consciousness is not clear and explicit. Particular modes of argument and conceptual distinctions are simply part of the set of presuppositions that he learned more or less unconsciously during his apprenticeship. These presuppositions are no doubt at work in his scientific activity, and they often take on the character of dogmatic basic convictions. In a sense a given tradition is rather a Procrustean bed for the further development of the discipline. Old, ostensibly proven procedures and concepts are no longer questioned; they develop as it were a life of their own in the scientist's thinking. His problems follow from these procedures and concepts, not from an original confrontation with his own experience; new problems either fail to develop, or are rejected at the outset by appeal to the received views.[1]

For this reason the history of linguistics shows periods of particular sterility, where fossilized basic principles are adhered to and the only development is in the refinement of argumentation; the courage needed to discover radical new orientations seems to be lacking (e.g. among the Neogrammarians, the American structuralists, and the 'orthodox' MIT school). Present-day theory has its own characteristic dogmas, such as strict separation of language-system (*langue*) and language-use (*parole*); an underlying uninterpreted syntax with semantics and pragmatics added only by interpretation or extension; abstract assumption of metatheories that are only later given empirical content; the attempt to establish a universalist viewpoint in the form of a universal grammar; the requirement that the set of sentences of a language be recursively enumerated; the claim that it is possible to make a strict distinction between grammatical and ungrammatical; the unreflecting extension of the notion 'grammar' to texts; the requirement of a strict extrinsic order for grammatical rules. Each of these principles may be relatively justified insofar as it can help in the elucidation of particular questions: but none of them is absolutely tenable.

---

[1] In this connection Kuhn's notion of a scientific paradigm becomes important. Cf. Kuhn (1962), and the various articles collected in Diederich (1974) and Wunderlich (1976c).

1.4 The outward orientation of linguistics

Although individual problems in linguistics have a long history, they are nevertheless tackled again from time to time, and not only through ignorance or reservations about the tradition. If the general epistemological and theoretical climate has changed, specific questions may indeed arise which seem to be similar to those raised in the past; but they are never identical. The history of linguistics can be regarded as the sequence of its different THEORETICAL ORIENTATIONS. These are rarely the product of the science itself, but are nearly always developed in conjunction with other sciences. To this extent we are justified in talking about an outward orientation. I will not go into these individual relationships in detail, since I am not writing a history of linguistics: I will merely give a brief sketch.

Nineteenth-century linguistics can be seen primarily in the light of a programme of historical reconstruction (we can understand what we are, and occasionally justify what we will be, if we unfold the past events that have necessarily led to our present situation). This tended more and more towards the mere collection of past facts. The influence of positivism can also be seen in the general outlook of the Neogrammarians (sound changes have the character of 'natural laws') and of the physiological phoneticians (Sievers, etc.); there is also a strong psychological orientation.

In this century, behaviouristic notions were dominant at one point, as in all the social sciences (speech as a set of behavioural dispositions describable in terms of stimulus and response): here we might especially note Bloomfield and the semioticians influenced by Morris. At other times, often along with behaviourism, we find positions committed in various ways to Vienna Circle logical positivism (logical reconstruction of language, the attempt to reduce theoretical concepts to observational ones: there are striking examples of this in Glossematics and other structuralist schools). Both orientations were developed further under the impress of subsequent criticism, and in their more advanced variants represent a good part of the contemporary outlook in linguistics. Logical semantics and Chomsky's transformational grammar are based on partially similar positions of this advanced type; both use sophisticated algebraic representations.

Meanwhile a new 'pragmatic' orientation was developing, thanks in part at least to the English tradition of analytical philosophy (developed largely under Wittgenstein's influence). And in addition to this there was a growing interest in language on the part of Soviet psychologists (Vygotsky, Leontyev, Rubinstein; 'psychology' here is to be understood in a broader sense than is usual in Western countries).

There is no theoretical unanimity in present-day linguistics; positions have developed from nearly all the orientations I have mentioned, in the most varied combinations. Even my own position is not fully homogeneous, partly for practical reasons (the problems linguists have to face are not all of the same kind), and partly because one's own standards can only be developed by the criticism of others' positions.

Every science, as a non-private undertaking, has SOCIAL FUNCTIONS, even if these are often only indirect (i.e. not productive in the economic sense, but productive for the self-consciousness of particular social groups). The social function is often assessed differently by the scientists and by non-scientists; this seems to be the case particularly (a) when the science has an 'alibi-function' in the context of a particular ideology (e.g. under labels like 'scientific pluralism' or 'disinterested research'), which the scientists do not or will not acknowledge; and (b) when scientists (who are often sceptical about such matters) fail to share society's expectations about potential applications of their science.

A science's social functions largely derive from its achievements, as it were by hindsight. But the scientist is often given tasks connected with social interests, from which results of a particular type only are expected. This expectation can be based on factual knowledge of scientific possibilities, on the need to solve particular problems which on this account are assigned to the science, on the attempt to restructure institutions to make them more practicable (e.g. for educational purposes), or on the commitments of politically influential proponents of the science. The ongoing conduct of a science, in terms of finance and personnel, is always the expression of specific tasks and/or expectations. We already have part of the answer to the question 'Who has what interest in this kind of science?' when we have discovered the sources of financial support for a particular institute, and analysed the kind of contracts it has.

Scientists can (and should!) also determine the social tasks of their science themselves: e.g. social criticism and enlightenment are tasks which they are presumably not encouraged to engage in, but which nevertheless fall into their proper province – insofar as they take the requirement of radical doubt seriously.

A comprehensive history of linguistics should also concern itself with the social or partly social significance the discipline has had at various times, and what its appointed tasks and actual functions have been. In Ancient Greece, for instance, the development of rhetoric was connected with the solution of social problems; there were (as to some extent there still are) economic, political and administrative motivations for developing unified common (e.g. national) languages and writing systems; in the Renaissance the Humanists' concern with vernacular languages also involved an opposition to ecclesiastical influence, and served to support the development of middle-class self-consciousness and the expansion of manufacturing and trade. The investigation of foreign languages (beyond Europe and the Near East) that has developed since the seventeenth century was, among other things, necessary for colonialism and missionary work. The present-day relevance of this is apparent if we think of the orientalist establishments in Britain and France, the US army's foreign language programme during and after World War II, the needs of international business and industrial research in foreign countries, and the training of missionaries and technical assistants for undeveloped countries.

The rise of German philology in the nineteenth century (Humboldt, Grimm, etc.) can partly be seen in the context of the Romantic vision of the arts and their role in nationalistic ideology. Again, American and Soviet linguists in this century have concerned themselves with very concrete problems: in the US with the Indians (cultural and administrative integration of the Indian tribes), and more recently with Blacks, Puerto Ricans, etc.; in the USSR with the nationality problem (especially with regard to the Asiatic and Caucasian Soviet Republics, as well as the Karelians, Estonians and other minorities). Similar problems can be seen today in West Germany with foreign workers. In addition to foreign language instruction, the teaching of supraregional or prestigious dialects has always been important, and not only with respect to written communication: verbal communication in public has begun to be considered a skill that should be taught in the schools. We should also add the claims of data-processing technology and all organizations interested in it; these are demonstrated most clearly in the expansion of formally oriented grammatical research areas like automatic translation, automatic information-analysis and retrieval and man–machine communication.

1.5   On the notions 'science' and 'theory'

Science is an outgrowth of a particular kind of division of labour, only indirectly concerned with the fulfilment of material needs. Through its models and analyses it attempts to elucidate, understand and formulate men's possible relations with one another and with nature. SCIENCE IS A CLASS OF HUMAN ACTIVITIES DIRECTED TOWARD THE ELUCIDATION OF EXPERIENCE. It leads to knowledge, i.e. to an objectivized human understanding of man and the world, which permits man to pursue his practical activities. 'Objectivization' can be defined as follows: the special knowledge, opinions and ideas of the individual are transformed into the acknowledged, proved, established knowledge of many men. In this way man and his behaviour can be thrown into relief as an object of thought; but this object must be reapprehended by the knowing subject. Science is not a class of individual activities, but the common activity of many. Whatever an individual's special motivations, interests, institutional affiliations and modes of action may be, they remain marginal (even eccentric) if they are not reconciled with common interests and the demand for objectivization. An individual can neither found a science nor stop its development.

Institutions secure the objectivizing character of sciences. INSTITUTIONS GROW OUT OF DIVISION OF LABOUR; and within them the individual's activities are controlled by norms (or at least conventions). This also means, among other things, that they are exempted from arbitrariness and unnecessarily repeated decisions. It is not that repeated decisions are in principle unnecessary, but rather that certain decisions do not have to be repeated to fulfil their function; the scientist is freed from superfluous activities by virtue of the existence of his science and its tradition. Outside these institutions he cannot be a scientist, nor can he be one outside the framework of traditional systematics, methodology and problem areas. Traditional knowledge, however, becomes meaningful for the individual scientist only when he adopts it as his own. The critical acquisition of knowledge is itself a part of scientific activity; when the questions change, the relevance of traditional knowledge has to be tested, and its oversimplifications and falsifications corrected.

The propounding, justification and criticism of theories is at the heart of scientific activity. THEORIES ARE SETS OF SENTENCES (or STATEMENTS) defined in terms of both form and content.[1] (Alternatively, it has been

---

[1] Sentences always represent particular statements; and statements are not just arbitrary kinds of conceptual entities, but only those things that can be represented in

proposed that we understand theories more abstractly as set-theoretical predicates from which theoretical statements can be drawn.)[1] Theories are, however, not to be equated with knowledge in a science. There are four reasons for this separation:

1. Knowledge is what has already proved itself to be relatively justified; theories have yet to be justified. This does not mean that already accepted knowledge does not enter into theories, it does, but they nevertheless also transcend it. They claim a conjectural knowledge, and develop it constructively. Theories are thus always STRUCTURALLY designed (so that they also partly restructure existing knowledge), and they always contain explicit HYPOTHETICAL ASSUMPTIONS (at least with respect to the possibility of structuring knowledge). In their constructive proceedings, theories base themselves on logics.[2]

2. Knowledge is independent (or invariant) with respect to the forms in which it can be represented (we could perhaps define knowledge in terms of equivalence-classes of theories); theories, however, are always formally defined. In order to develop, justify, and criticize them we need (*inter alia*) objective TECHNIQUES FOR DEFINITION AND DEDUCTION; but we can (at least to some extent) speak of knowledge without having such techniques.

3. Theories are GENERAL AND ABSTRACT; they transcend individual experiences and cover those experiences generally possible in a given domain. Knowledge embraces singular experiences (individual facts), and it is the main job of theories to reduce this to generalities. SYSTEMATIC ANTICIPATION of experience is only achieved in theories.

sentences. Conceptually the language of sentences is identical to the language of statements. But if we allow, for instance, that the same theory can be formulated in German as well as in English, then we give preference to the language of statements. We must of course then assign a formal characterization to statements in order to take account of the fact that the various formulations of a theory are intertranslatable. But this objection can be weakened by a sufficiently abstract definition of 'sentences of a theory': these will then be formulated in a logical language, and thus neither in English nor German.

[1] This conception has been introduced by Sneed (1971). It is particularly useful for comparing theories and investigating their development.

[2] I do not propose a sharp dichotomy between theory and logic. The distinction is roughly this: a logic constructs relations among items of possible knowledge of a particular form, whereas knowledge itself is relatively arbitrary. A theory structures knowledge in relation to a totally determined and circumscribed domain of experience.

Structural coherence in theories, moreover, does not have to correspond to the process of setting up theories. Even an individual can design a theory; what he has to justify is the theory itself, not the way he discovered it. To this extent the process of research is less important than the RESULTS. This does not mean however that scientific ACTIVITIES are of secondary importance: justification of a theory and its requirements and deduction from a theory are not optional activities.

4. Knowledge in a science includes more than what is structurally worked out in theories; it also includes knowledge of problems, formulation of questions, methods, standards, definitions, successes and failures. This knowledge itself, however, can be worked out in theories of science.

We must clarify what kinds of objects the sentences (or statements) of a theory are (or should be). I have already narrowed the field by referring only to statements; thus the contents of questions, justifications, etc., are not part of theories. But a theory does give answers to questions, and it does serve as a basis for justifications. A theory is therefore largely defined through the type of activities that lead to it, and that can and should be based on it. These activities motivate the particular demands made on theories. The sentences of theories are for the most part (often exclusively) DESCRIPTIVE: they describe classes or types of events, circumstances, actions, valuations, norms, etc. (at least we interpret whole theories, if not their individual sentences this way). But the sentences of a theory do not necessarily have to be descriptive: they can also EXPRESS VALUE-JUDGEMENTS OR NORMS, which is not the same thing as describing them (e.g. 'It is good/useful, etc. to do p', 'In the circumstances x one ought to do p').

A distinction is often made between empirical sciences, which describe the content of experience, and non-empirical sciences, which express value-judgements or norms. The natural sciences in particular are considered to belong to the first group, and jurisprudence, philosophy of science, as well as constructive sciences like mathematics and logic to the second. But this is not an absolute distinction: value-judgements and norms are also expressed in theories of measurement and observation, and jurisprudence and philosophy of science also describe what men do in particular circumstances and what counts for them as acknowledged fact. But there is a logical distinction between descriptive and evaluative propositions: one cannot be derived from the other.

How is one given theory to be distinguished from others? We can classify theories according to (a) THEIR SUBJECT MATTER, (b) THEIR METHODS, (c) THEIR GUIDING EPISTEMOLOGICAL INTEREST and (d) THE SCIENTIST'S ATTITUDE TO THEM. These are all inter-connected, especially with respect to the problems the science deals with. Every theory, if only because of the division of labour between a science and its sub-disciplines, has a closely circumscribed domain; but these domains are not subject matters; they are, rather, particular aspects of subject matters as they appear in the formulation of questions.

The subject 'language' appears under many aspects; by itself it does not suffice to distinguish linguistic theories from psychological ones, for example. Each kind of question-formulation demands specific methods for answering it; some of these methods will be useful for other sciences as well, while others are highly specific and dependent on particular theory-forms. The guiding interest is not something extra, but is part and parcel of the formulation of questions. The scientist's attitude toward theories shows itself in general in the demands he makes of them, and in his activities relative to them ('Why do I produce this theory? What do I do with it?') Even purely descriptive theories are not value-free; they have a specific place within scientific activities, and must be evaluated with respect to this. Methodology, theory and philosophy of science derive from the fact that sciences exist and have acknowledged procedures and principles; they also clarify the function of these procedures and principles, and ultimately indicate what these ought to be if the tasks of sciences are to be properly accomplished.

In a critical attack on the established sciences, Habermas (1968) proposes the following classification, in which he employs the notions of subject matter, method, interest and attitude in terms of a pair of oppositions.

He divides the empirical–analytical sciences from the historical–hermeneutic sciences; and ultimately proposes a third type: critical theory, which transcends the shortcomings of both. The EMPIRICAL–ANALYTICAL sciences are empirical in terms of their subject matter, they are concerned with the hard facts, laws and structures of some reality; methodologically they are as much analytical–deductive as observational–inductive; their interest is directed toward technical mastery over nature or reality; and the scientist's dominant attitude is value-free – he is concerned with the description of facts, not their evaluation.

The HISTORICAL–HEREMENEUTIC sciences have a historical subject matter, they are concerned with the history of human societies and cultures and the unique manifestations of this history; their methods are hermeneutic, i.e. they seek to understand their subject matter or to stabilize their preliminary understanding of it; their interest is in the practical need for understanding among men. The scientist's attitude is oriented toward values, where possible toward value-norms.

CRITICAL THEORY is not primarily definable in terms of its subject matter or methodology, but by its interest, which, unlike the other two kinds of sciences, it explicitly recognizes as a factor in its theory-construction. Its interest is emancipatory: freeing men from their natural limitations by enlightenment and making self-reflection possible. It therefore embraces criticism of false and limited consciousness. For Habermas, the prototype is psychoanalytical theory. Along with this goes the demand that at least all social theories see themselves in this way as critical, and thereby develop a practical dimension which the empirical and hermeneutic sciences do not have.

While I agree that enlightenment and ideological criticism are tasks that sciences should carry out (especially in relation to their dominating self-understanding), I have grave doubts about both the logical coherence and value of Habermas' analysis.

1. Is critical theory like a theory of science, or like a putatively all-embracing philosophy and theory of society, which can be used to call scientific division of labour into question? Does it supersede all other sciences, or are there individual critical theories with specific tasks and subject matters? If critical theory is a theory of science or a general social theory, then it should be compared with other theories of science and general social theories, and not with individual theories about particular empirical domains; but postulates relevant to individual theories or the activities of scientists in individual disciplines must be derivable from it. If there are a number of individual critical theories, then we must ask why empirical and historical theories cannot be critical, and why they should be denied an emancipatory interest.

2. The empirical–analytic/historical–hermeneutic opposition yields an inadequate typology both for existing sciences and the theories that dominate them; it singles out at most only those practitioners who display that limited self-understanding discussed above. And this is probably not a true picture of the sciences overall. All scientists have to be explicit and ANALYTICAL in their argumentation; all sciences require UNDERSTANDING of arguments and of their subject matter. It is obvious that the question-formulations of medieval history are not identical to those of linguistics, that those of linguistics are not identical to those of biochemistry. But their common methodology, insofar as it is not already tied into the formulation of questions, is not necessarily divergent in just the same way; and the scientists' attitudes toward the tasks and methods of their subjects and their roles in society can be essentially similar. Scientists' critical or uncritical attitudes do not stem from the characteristics of their disciplines.

The EVALUATION OF THEORIES must always be accomplished through argument, and this often has to be done over and over again. First, we must justify the demands of the theory, as well as the delimitation of its domain. (Are the demands reasonable ? Are the goals appropriate ? Can they generally be achieved ?) Then we must establish how far the formulated theory justifies these demands: whether it is generally meaningful, so that people can agree on it (so that its presuppositions are accepted, its formulations are not vague or ambiguous, its premises not purely tautological); whether it makes significant generalizations and makes genuine new knowledge possible (i.e. gives answers to questions); whether it is manageable and conceptually clear; what scope it offers for further research, where it is incomplete or inadequate. Theories themselves must thus be justified, tested, criticized and developed. Their function is often purely instrumental: the theory that guides more activities to successful conclusions is the better theory. In this way even inadequate theories can lead to the advancement of knowledge.

1.6 Aspects of language

There are so many aspects to human languages and their manifestations, their individual and social function, their psychic and physical connections, their acquisition and history, that it is difficult (if not hopeless) to establish connections among all of them. At the beginning we can only state the various aspects, and to a certain extent study each one for its own sake. We claim indeed that such connections do ultimately exist, but we cannot derive any productive questions from such a global assertion. We have to state concrete problems and formulations of goals; some aspects will come into the foreground relative to these, while others will remain subordinate. I do not believe that everything that has anything, however remote, to do with language must in consequence be a subject for linguistics. A linguistics like that would be a universal science, in which scientific division of labour would be completely neutralized. In any case nobody today is in a position to follow, even roughly, all research in all areas that have anything to do with language. We can probably agree that some aspects, especially those related to social communication processes, are preeminently subjects for linguistics, while others belong preeminently to neighbouring sciences.

I use 'preeminently' here to stress that the isolation should not go so far that we lose sight of the significance of the neighbouring aspects for human understanding. We must ensure that we do not propose opinions in one scientific domain that are fundamentally incompatible with knowledge in others. This is the only guarantee of meaningful scientific cooperation. All the individual aspects of language are thus from one point of view or another relevant to linguistics, without all of them necessarily leading to the development of aspects of linguistics. The enumeration that follows is admittedly both arbitrary and merely additive; its only purpose is to give some kind of clearly bounded outline of our knowledge of language.

CONSCIOUSNESS

Consciousness is primarily something that we ascribe to the individual. He is conscious (if often only vaguely) of himself and his surroundings, and he has available to him (not only in an isolated form, but in a continuum of memory) certain psychic representations of his environment, which he develops in his thought-processes, and which decisively control his behaviour. His thoughts are not necessarily always couched in language, but language is a precondition for consciousness proper (as distinct from prelinguistic types of experience), i.e. the awareness of an 'I' who is conscious relative to other 'I's'. Language is the form in which consciousness develops during social life, and in which discursive concepts and the thought-processes that utilize them (cognitive activities) develop. Language, as the means for social interaction, likewise represents the social (common) consciousness of a community, i.e. its general capacity for controlling actions and attributing meanings. The individual in his daily life is inescapably bound up with this common consciousness (even if, as a scientist, he is to some extent engaged in questioning it); it is the primary basis for the differentiation of the individual's knowledge, commitments, and opinions.

COMMUNICATION

A society as a whole develops, stabilizes and changes on the basis of individual relations and their continually changing realizations. It is in innumerable collective situations that appropriate means of communication are fabricated and changed; this is done in such a way that they are suitable for innumerable other similar situations. Insofar as we do not have to recreate the society we are born into, we also do not have to recreate the means of communication; to begin with we only have to reconstruct them, i.e. acquire them for ourselves. Into each situation we can bring experiences from other situations; in Mead's words (1934), we can construct 'the generalized other' for ourselves. Beyond this, we can use reports, reported speech, predictions, etc., to refer expressly to any number of other communicative situations. Only in this way can we explain the extent to which a community's common language and common consciousness can be developed together.

ACTION

Communication is above all functionally connected with particular collective forms of work. In simple kinds of work (e.g. fishing, hunting, house building, etc.), simple forms of communication are sufficient to coordinate individual actions. But if the individual's role is complex, and problems develop over the direction that the collective labour should take, a need develops for more complex forms of coordination and communication. In planning, communications precede the real work, they do not simply accompany it; they are to a certain extent trial actions as it were. The linguistic utterances of an individual often merely represent substitutes for particular actions, which he could possibly carry out himself should their objectives lie within his reach (a result of division of labour). Thus I can use a request to get someone else to perform an action for me. These verbal substitutes, however, are also actions – not actions on natural objects, but intersubjective actions. Linguistic utterances are also actions insofar as they require justification, are controlled by commitments and norms, and can even create new commitments.

The variety and strength of these commitments derive from the character of their institutional context. In all known societies there are institutions for the safeguarding of authority; so that linguistic communication cannot be taken as detached from the existing relations of authority and power. Linguistic obligations are partly determined by power, and linguistic instruments are also used to secure it (political propaganda, transmission of ideology, publicity).

THE ORGANIC–PHYSICAL BASES OF SPEECH AND HEARING

Speech is a physical activity; if there were no human organs to produce and receive the appropriate stimuli, there would be no contact between men. We can distinguish three complexes:

1. THE MOUTH AND EAR (we can make this restriction if we leave out derived forms like writing, braille, or sign-language). Among the matters to be investigated here are the productive limitations of the vocal apparatus, the role of monitoring in the control of speech (especially in language learning), and the processes of speech-perception.

2. THE INTERNAL BASIS. Language is not metaphysical, but is represented in the human brain. The neurophysiological foundations of 'the possession of language' and the various activities bound up with it have been relatively little explored; no linguist today would claim that he could describe neurophysiological conditions and processes of this kind in any reasonable way. On the other hand, observation of speech deficits due to brain damage, and the attendant neurophysiological research, can provide important indications of the extent to which given linguistic models can or cannot be adequate in principle. In addition, certain changes in the brain are accompanied by characteristic difficulties in communication. We can no longer maintain the notion of a unitary 'speech-centre' in the cortex; other parts can take over important speech functions, even if only after protracted learning-processes (cf. Whitaker 1971).

3. THE EXTERNAL BASIS. Speech sounds are carried by oscillation-patterns in the air. Acoustic differentiation, however, does not run quite parallel to what the human ear does. Because of this, acoustic characterizations can only reflect very imperfectly the function of particular oscillation-patterns for the discrimination of linguistic meaning. The phenomena of transition between speech-sounds pose special problems for speech-synthesis; the same holds true for automatic speech-recognition. To a certain extent linguistic concepts like phonological features are interpretable in terms of articulatory as well as acoustic and auditory phonetics (or at least the possibility of such an interpretation is taken as a criterion for introducing them); one could even imagine the results of studies in aphasia and neurophysiology being used in a similar way, for the interpretation of other theoretical linguistic concepts. This can hardly be achieved today, but it could doubtless impose crucial requirements on linguistic theory. We would then be able to characterize

the material basis of speech and hearing more clearly than has been possible up to now.

THE PSYCHIC MEDIATION OF THOUGHT AND SPEECH

It is much easier to find connections between the concepts of linguistic theory and those of the psychology of language. There are many studies of verbal planning processes and verbal perception and understanding, and of verbal memory (including the analysis of errors in repetition of heard or read utterances), as well as the familiar word-association studies. Some of these studies have been undertaken with the express purpose of proving the psychological reality of structures and rules proposed in particular grammars (e.g. transformational grammars); as far as this goal is concerned they have generally been failures. This is not surprising, since it is not the job of theoretical grammars to reconstruct the cognitive processes of the individual speaker (in which many factors are at work), but solely to reconstruct one of these factors in isolation: namely the relations between linguistic elements on the basis of our knowledge of these relations. In psychological investigations we predicate a complex set of abilities of individual speakers (the activation of particular capabilities in test situations), but we do not directly predicate knowledge to which the speakers orient themselves if they consciously carry out specified speech procedures (they know – at any rate partially – the structure of these procedures, but not how they are individually realized). Thus knowledge of procedures and their performance cannot be equated, even when they are interdependent. If we want to work this interdependence out precisely, we have to confront the results of psychological studies with those of grammatical studies, and look for interpretations relevant to both. We can certainly require at least that the respective results be reconcilable with each other (even if we still have to work out more clearly just what we mean by 'reconcilability'). The development of verbal planning and understanding in childhood will also be significant.

SOCIAL PROCEDURES IN SPEAKING

I have already argued that this aspect of language is central to linguistics. But I take 'procedures' in a more inclusive sense than other linguists: I include those procedures that are relevant to the functioning of speech in specific situations, which are often taken to be the province of text-linguistics or discourse analysis. We can distinguish them as follows:

1. PERSUASION AND INFLUENCE, whose elucidation is the province of rhetoric. Of special importance here are the choice and presentation of data and value-judgements, and modes of argument in specific contexts of action.[1]

2. RATIONAL JUSTIFICATION AND ARGUMENT, to a certain extent also the province of rhetoric, and in their more explicit forms the province of logic. But not all forms of argument can be reconstructed in logic, only those that are in some sense already standardized; so we must reach agreement on what is to be understood by 'rational'.

3. THE FACTUAL REFERENCE OF UTTERANCES, to be elucidated especially by logical semantics, with the aid of notions like 'truth', 'interpretation' and 'logical consequence'.

4. THE FORMS OF SOUND-MEANING CORRESPONDENCE, which are the province of grammar (grammatical theory).

5. DERIVED MANIFESTATIONS, especially writing-systems; these are dealt with by graphemics, as well as grammar and phonology. We have to distinguish (a) historically developed writing-systems of various cultures (logographic, syllabic, alphabetic), evolved mainly for economic, administrative and religious reasons; (b) special-purpose writing-systems (like shorthand), visual sign-systems of other kinds (flag-codes, sign languages for the deaf), tactile systems (Braille), and systems of electronically mediated signs (Morse Code, etc.); (c) phonetic transcription systems for scientific purposes; and (d) other scientific notational systems (e.g. for stating formal or semantic relations).

It would be useful at this point to introduce some of the notions commonly used in the description of these procedures. Every verbal procedure results in concrete and generally unique events (if we except mechanical reproduction): speaking produces UTTERANCE-TOKENS (acoustic events or sound-patterns), writing produces INSCRIPTIONS (marks on a surface, or script-patterns). The concepts 'utterance-token' and 'inscription' are often extended in such a way that they intersect: thus 'speech' and 'writing' are lumped together as 'utterance' or 'utterance of...'. The procedures are always general communication-processes, and are thus defined relative to general abstract forms, not to individual concrete patterns. Whenever a specific degree of abstraction is

---

[1] For a comprehensive standard coverage of this field see Perelman & Olbrechts-Tyteca (1958).

assumed, we speak of UTTERANCE-FORMS or of EXPRESSIONS (e.g. sentences) or of EXPRESSION-FORMS.[1]

In every linguistic procedure some of these forms of expressions are realized (or INSTANCES of forms or expressions are uttered, in short, expressions are uttered). We will often express it this way: in an utterance-token there are particular OCCURRENCES of instances of expressions, and in a complex expression there are particular OCCURRENCES of simpler expressions (note that these are two distinct senses of 'occurrence').

A communicative procedure is naturally not to be treated as detached from the process of communication itself: it exists only insofar as it does actually lead to communication. Active or passive command of a procedure involves the ability to produce or recognize realizations.

We need certain theoretical assumptions in order to represent procedures: there is a distinction between (a) minimal realizing units (e.g. sounds, letters) and their combination into individual meaningful expressions, and (b) minimal meaningful expressions (lexical units) and their combination into larger (up to maximal) meaningful expressions (sentences, texts, discourses). Some derived manifestations (flag-signals, ideograms, logical languages) lack this distinction; they have only the combinatory level (b). If we speak of expression-forms, we are concerned only with kinds of combination (sequence, inflexion, intonation).

RECONSTRUCTION OF PROCEDURES

If we want to talk about procedures (e.g. present them verbally in order to learn them, or take note of transgressions), we have to represent them linguistically. In doing this we are always implicitly or explicitly utilizing generalizing and abstracting (to this extent theoretical) concepts. Thus school grammars for instance contain a wealth of theorizing. In linguistics the structure of procedures is worked out in a much more abstract way. For the structural aspect alone linguistics makes use of mainly mathematical (algebraic) means of representation; for the connection of the formal and conceptual aspects it uses a combination of such devices, especially in relation to explicative logical languages. For the processual

---

[1] There are a number of degrees of abstraction that have to be distinguished (cf. 4.3 below): e.g. abstraction relative only to the spatiotemporal coordinates of utterance-tokens (⟨a⟩ and ⟨a⟩ are two instances of the same form), or relative to an aspect of form irrelevant to language (⟨a⟩ and ⟨ɑ⟩ are two instances of the same letter, but of different forms).

connections linguists often use abstract automata as well as other special mathematical models. Some of these can be realized as computer programs, which allows the simulation of linguistic processes. (Simulations do not describe linguistic processes, but they do show us something about their structure.) I will deal more thoroughly with the problems involved in reconstruction in chapters 5–7 below; so these brief remarks will suffice for now.

THE GENESIS OF THE EGO IN THE SOCIAL FIELD

The concept of socialization in child development is misleading, since it implies that an original individual merely has to 'become socialized'. One could equally well say that an original infant moved only by innate drives and reflexes merely has to 'individualize'. In psychoanalytic theory, and later in various theories of socialization, there has been at least a preliminary working out of the interdependence of socialization and individualization. The development of an ego-consciousness implies the development of an ability to sublimate drives, of social insight, and of the ability to accept social obligations. Many linguistic theories make the mistake of treating human beings as if they only acted and spoke consciously; this creates the oversimplified picture of a totally rational being: speech-act theory in particular runs this risk. But the problems that a psychotherapist or psychoanalyst faces, which are at least partly mirrored in communicative behaviour, make it clear that the way experiences are processed (even quite early) and the interaction of unconscious, preconscious and conscious processes are crucial for human communicative behaviour. Those interactions must be considered in a precise analysis of factual communication processes.

LANGUAGE INSTRUCTION

There is already some language training in the child's primary communicative relations, in the form of explicit corrections and reprimands, and reflections on what is linguistically possible and necessary. Thus even before the child goes to school he has a number of immature ideas about language. These ideas are stabilized in social institutions (especially the schools) mostly at the expense of other, competing ones; many original speech-forms are suppressed (especially for dialect-speakers) in favour of supra-regional variants recognized as 'higher'. The problems involved here become clear in attempts at 'compensatory' language instruction for children with particularly poor command of these recognized (middle-class) speech-forms; such attempts are often bound up with untenable hypotheses about the influence of formally elaborated speech on thinking ability.

THE HISTORICITY OF COMMUNICATION PROCEDURES

The historicity of language manifests itself in many ways: from a social point of view in the way individual consciousness and its changes are represented in language change. Everyone can use communicative procedures creatively, i.e. process new situations, modify the procedures, etc.; many procedures themselves already have built-in productivity, i.e. they permit analogical extension (making new word-formations possible, etc.); in language conflicts other conflicts often come to light (not only between generations, but also between different social classes); languages can be standardized for various purposes (technical, administrative, scientific); new forms of division of labour lead to new forms of language, and conversely these new forms make possible the stabilization of the new relations. Every language at a particular time is changeable in many ways, and thus at the same time is also unstable; it contains elements that are left over from earlier stages and can easily disappear, as well as elements in which the possibilities of future change are already represented. The fact that over long stretches of time a language changes so that it can barely be understood by its speakers' descendants is thus only one aspect of this historicity. Historical linguistics has for the most part been concerned only with this one fact, and has tried to analyse it in detail from the documents of preceding centuries – but without being concerned until recently with the social motivation of language change.

LANGUAGE POLITICS

Language politics can be defined as the active influencing of linguistic change. (The school is only one place – though an important one – where this happens.) There has been a robust language politics as long as there has been military confrontation between tribes and peoples. At certain times this has led to the extermination of whole tribes and peoples, and thus to the extermination of their languages; at others it has led to full integration, but for economic and administrative reasons language extermination has again resulted (or as historical linguists say, the superstratum is imposed on the substratum – even if it perhaps absorbs some substratum elements). This kind of policy has been pursued up to the present, e.g. against the Indians in North and South America, and against the native tribes in Australia, Polynesia, and to some extent in Africa.

In some nations there is now an increasing attempt to take into account both the need for a supraregional commercial language and the interests of cultural and linguistic minorities through LANGUAGE PLANNING. This is especially true in the emerging nations of the Third World, in which many tribes have to be integrated. There are also special problems involved in the introduction of compulsory writing-systems that can be mastered by the bulk of the population (e.g. in China).

THE TECHNOLOGIZATION OF COMMUNICATION

The invention of printing made possible for the first time the reproduction of any desired number of written works; we all know what a change in communications (and concurrently in the whole social structure) this produced. One's audience could be extended virtually *ad libitum*. Printing was also responsible for the first mass medium – the newspapers. In more recent times, and perhaps with greater effect, radio and television have been added; the preschool child is already subject to their influence. The power of these media for serving economic, political and ideological ends is massive and obvious to everyone; the political responsibility arising from this is all the more important.

This is also true for another technological sector, namely the automatic processing of language-data in information-systems (analysis, storage and retrieval), which has been developed and organized largely for marketing purposes.

1.7 Linguistic methodology

We can interpret linguistic methodology in a narrow sense, by first restricting the subject matter of linguistics (perhaps to the form and content of grammatical processes), and then only discussing the specific procedures and methods relevant to this subject matter: e.g. special procedures for analysing utterance-tokens, the description of grammatical relations, the testing of linguistic claims. I will however take methodology in a wider sense, and include under it all of the scientist's relevant activities. Much of what I say in this book will be methodological in this wider sense. I justify this on the following grounds:

1. Since (or insofar as) linguistics is an empirical science, it faces the same problems of observation, explanation, abstraction, etc., as other empirical sciences. It is therefore reasonable to go beyond the subject-specific procedures.

2. Linguistic phenomena are many-sided, and this means we need an interdisciplinary orientation; therefore it makes no sense to restrict ourselves from the outset to a very narrow conception of the subject matter. The possibility of pursuing new lines of inquiry is partly dependent on success in superseding the current division of labour among the sciences. The procedures of the social sciences, psychology, logic and even mathematics must at times complement each other; as a linguist one should at least be aware of them. I will, however, be restricting myself to the fundamental problems, since among other things I do not feel sufficiently competent to discuss specific methods of investigation, testing and procedures of evaluation in the social sciences and psychology.

3. Methodology must be concerned with all kinds of approaches to linguistic problems, whether they arise in our everyday use of language, are already at hand in a standardized form, or actually arise through our following specific methodological principles.

4. Insofar as science is a corporate undertaking, it presupposes argumentative techniques. The individual must not only be able to use methods of analysis, description and testing, but must be capable of unambiguous communication. Knowledge must be established, justified, and passed on to others, and learnable by them. These purposes are served by standardization of concepts, forms of expression, and modes of argument. I will go into this in more detail below.

In the framework of methodology we generally encounter four types of expressions that have to do with scientists' behaviour: first DESCRIPTIVE STATEMENTS ('The scientist does a if he wants to achieve g'); second, EVALUATIVE STATEMENTS ('It is good/reasonable/necessary to do a if one wants to achieve g'); third, NORMATIVE STATEMENTS ('One ought to do a to achieve g'); and fourth, INSTRUCTIONS FOR ACTION ('Do a if you want to achieve g').[1] These are logically distinct; we cannot deduce

---

[1] Cf. the comparison of descriptive and normative statements in 5.8; also the discussion of Hare in 9.26.

one kind from another without additional information. They are never-theless mutually supporting, in the sense that a scientist carrying out a particular activity or giving particular instructions justifies them by reference to normative or evaluative statements, and under some circumstances justifies these by reference to those descriptive statements which determine that the results of actions are successful. But justifica-tion is a practical and not a logical or semantic issue.

'To do a' in the statements above can be fulfilled in various ways. Wittgenstein has shown that it is mainly a matter of asking the right questions. Thus the following could be necessary, meaningful, and productive (based on Schmidt 1968: 152f.):

(1) What does it mean to say X ?
    What can I replace X with ?
    What does an explanation of X look like ?
    How have I learned the meaning of X ?
(2) What can I compare X with ?
    How can I compare X with Y ?
    When can I substitute Y for X ?
(3) Under what circumstances do I say X ?
    (In what situations, in what cases, in what context, in what sense do I say X ?)
    What role does the utterance of X play here ?
(4) What use is X ?
    (What good is X; what can I get with X ? What happens when I use X ?)
(5) How can I know X ?
    What criteria determine the use of X ?
    How do I use X legitimately ?
(6) What examples of X can I adduce ?
    What (stylized) situations will make the use of X clear to me ?
    How can I learn X ?

One could replace 'X' with just about any particular expression or expression-form; but it makes no difference whether these are colloquial or scientific. (The questions can be asked in both cases.) These are basically clarifying questions; we still have to look for procedures for getting good answers.

A somewhat different position from Wittgenstein's is taken by Popper. (This is not the place for a properly detailed treatment of their ideas, so I can do justice to neither of them.) Popper regards it as a subjectivist error to assume that science consists of going beyond common everyday knowledge and convictions, to gain the most certain knowledge possible (and perhaps also the most certain convictions possible). For him scientific knowledge is always only conjectural, theoretical knowledge, in the sense that it is fundamentally fallible and therefore open to criticism. Science does not begin so much with doubt (which always contains a certain private element), but with criticism. Only criticism is truly productive, because it has to declare its reasons and criteria. Popper gives the following as representing the scientist's characteristic activities (1972: 140f.):

> '*S* tries to understand *p*'.
> '*S* tries to think of alternatives to *p*'.
> '*S* tries to think of criticisms of *p*'.
> '*S* proposes an experimental test for *p*'.
> '*S* tries to axiomatize *p*'.
> '*S* tries to derive *p* from *q*'.
> '*S* tries to show that *p* is not derivable from *q*'.
> '*S* proposes a new problem *x* arising out of *p*'.
> '*S* proposes a new solution of the problem *x* arising out of *p*'.
> '*S* criticizes his latest solution of the problem *x*'.

Obviously the first three activities at least can be regarded as cases of seeking answers to questions. (It is clear that wherever the questions come from, they can also arise from a problem-situation relevant to everyday life or commonly held beliefs.) Popper also covertly acknowledges the argumentative character of scientific activities (in the notions 'criticize', 'propose'). To this extent the difference between the position Popper criticizes and the one he supports is, methodologically speaking, not as great as he suggests.

From a general point of view we have to distinguish between linguistics itself and the theory of linguistics whose subject matter consists of linguistic theories and the various scientific activities of linguists. In the theory of linguistics the general principles of the theory of science are reflected, applied and concretized within the field of linguistics; on the other hand, it may well be the case that we can abstract from the theory of linguistics more general points which might be useful for other sciences, as well as for the theory of science itself; for the theory of science cannot be developed without the knowledge of what individual sciences do (particularly in as much as theory of science was, I believe, almost entirely oriented to the natural sciences in the past, but is now aware of a need to be oriented to the social sciences and humanities also). It is possible to divide the theory of linguistics into the theory of linguistic inquiry and the theory of linguistic descriptions. The latter is concerned with the logical form of linguistic descriptions and theories,[1] while the former can be equated with the methodology of linguistics.[2] One has, however, to be aware that both parts of the theory of linguistics are interdependent, for the logical form of linguistic theories partly determines the way investigations can be carried out, and it is the purpose of an investigation that leads to the choice of a particular form. The logical form of a theory even reflects in part the inner structure of its subject matter; thus the theory of linguistic descriptions is not independent of particular aspects of language and language behaviour.

In linguistics – as the subject matter of the theory of linguistics – we have, besides the several sciences of particular languages and language groups, (general) Linguistic Theory. It is concerned with the different aspects of natural languages in general; thus we have as parts of it Phonological Theory, Grammatical Theory, Sociolinguistic Theory, Language Acquisition Theory, etc.

In this book I am mainly concerned with the theory of linguistic inquiry; some conclusions are drawn that are equally relevant to Linguistic Theory as well – though there is no attempt at a concise, systematic presentation of a particular linguistic theory.

In the following chapters I will be looking mainly at some of the characteristic ACTIVITIES OF SCIENTISTS. Their procedures derive in a systematic and specialized way from the PROCEDURES OF EVERYDAY LIFE; therefore I will look at these first, and attempt to show how they serve as a pattern for the development of scientific activities. The scientist of course is simultaneously oriented toward the PROCEDURES OF EVERYDAY LIFE and toward THEORETICAL MODELS; so their status as well as their relations to theory (relative to a specific domain of knowledge) and logic (as a schematic reconstruction of modes of argument) will have to be clarified. In what follows, then, I will not be concerned specifically with linguistics in a narrow sense – or if I am, it will rather be as an example than for its own sake. But I will be demonstrating some significant

[1] Lieb (1970: 6ff., 14ff.) considers Grammatical Theory to be a part of the theory of linguistic descriptions; this I think is a misleading use of the notion 'Grammatical Theory'. I would myself consider Grammatical Theory to be that part of Linguistic Theory which is concerned in general with grammatical aspects of natural languages.

[2] For the whole relationship of theory of linguistics and Linguistic Theory I refer to Lieb (1976a); observe, however, the objection in note 1 above. The notions of scientific discipline and scientific investigation have been clarified in Lieb (1976b).

aspects of language, especially scientific language, and its derivation from ordinary language. To this extent language is the basic theme of this book. But given this conception it will not always be possible to distinguish strictly and systematically between Linguistic Theory and the theory of science; even language itself incorporates concepts that are already theoretical – or should we say pretheoretical – namely those of everyday knowledge. The demand for a stricter distinction will become intelligible only when we are clearer about the relations between the two.

2 Knowledge and argument

2.1 Assertions of knowledge

We will assume that all knowledge – individual or collective – can be expressed by acts of assertion. This presupposes command of a language. Since the acquisition and processing of knowledge are human intellectual activities, the structure of knowledge is determined by the structure of thought processes (in the widest sense, e.g. including conscious perception). If we assume that all knowledge can be expressed verbally, then the structure of knowledge must be connected with the structure of language (and both connected with the structure of thought processes).

Knowledge is always asserted in some specific situation – and whoever makes the assertion usually claims to be making a relevant contribution: e.g. he is answering questions, giving reasons for his behaviour, information about solving problems, or information serving as a guide for particular actions. The participants usually turn their attention only to particular segments of their knowledge: they adduce only what is relevant to a specified domain, and – usually – what is not already known to all the participants.

What is knowledge about? A possible answer might be that all knowledge is about events or sequences of events (including actions) or facts in a particular WORLD, or – in its more abstract forms – about connections, relationships, regularities, social rules relating to events and facts. We can take 'world' as a relatively neutral but undefined basic concept.[1]

A world is constituted by a particular thematic context, and a particular segment of our knowledge corresponds to it. We conceive our knowledge in connection with particular worlds and we speak about them when we assert it. Every world is a temporal or spatial or spatiotemporal manifold in a particular context. We can speak about the world we live in, and divide it into different subworlds (e.g. worlds of momentary

---

[1] On the notion 'world' cf. Ballmer (1972: 183–206), especially 188ff.

perception, particular institutions, the whole of our assumptions about the interests and intentions of particular persons, etc.); we can talk about past and future worlds (past cultures, plans we are trying to realize); we can talk about worlds not directly accessible to us (distant galaxies, the atomic nucleus, strangers' lives); we can even talk about worlds we imagine for ourselves, worlds on which we bestow attributes of our perceptual worlds and value-systems, but which we do not really believe exist (fairy-tale worlds, etc.).

We utter assertions in the form of assertive (or declarative) sentences. Here are some examples of categorial assertion sentences, where specific knowledge is expressed without qualification:

(1) The word *memme* used to be used in German for the mother's breast.

(2) The question 'Do you have the time?' should not be answered merely with 'Yes'.

(3) When Peter said 'Oh go to hell' he wanted to be left alone.

(4) *Weitgehendst* is ill-formed, *weitestgehend* is correct but ugly. [Superlative of 'extensive'.]

(5) In the future the verb-form *sog* will be superseded by *saugte*. [3 pers. sing. pret. of 'suck'.]

The class of possible assertions is thus quite extensive, and contains a number of subcategories: e.g. descriptive judgements, statements of values, normative statements, prophecies, etc.

Knowledge is often not asserted categorically, but qualified in certain ways. The content of an assertion sentence p is expressed in conjunction with a sentential operator (or modality) – characteristically an adverb like *possibly*, *perhaps*, or one of the verba sentendi like *assume*, *know*, with a first-person grammatical subject. Below I give a few kinds of non-categorical assertions of knowledge, without connecting them to any further theoretical model:

I. DEGREES OF CERTAINTY OF KNOWLEDGE

Certainty or uncertainty of knowledge can be expressed explicitly:

(6) a. I conjecture p.
b. Perhaps p.
c. I believe p.
d. I am sure that p.
e. I know that p.

If someone says (6d), there is still some possibility of error; if he says (6e) error is excluded, e.g. because he is relying on immediate evidence. The distinction becomes clearer if we substitute third for first person:

(7) a. Nina is sure that p.
    b. Nina knows that p.

Someone who says (7a) is reporting Nina's ostensible knowledge, without committing himself to it (he can deny that p); while someone who says (7b) commits himself to taking Nina's knowledge as his own (he can no longer deny that p).

2. DEGREES OF PROBABILITY OF KNOWLEDGE

(8) a. It is rather improbable that p.
    b. It is very probable that p.
    c. It is more probable that p than that q.

Carnap has shown that we have to distinguish several uses of the word *probable*.[1] In the subjective sense it expresses only the speaker's relative certainty; but there are also two possible objective uses, where we can not only compare probabilities, but make quantitative statements about them: statistical probability treats statements on the basis of observed frequencies or theoretical computations; inductive probability treats the degree of confirmation of hypothetical statements on the basis of empirical knowledge.

3. JUDGEMENTS OF KNOWLEDGE RELATIVE TO ALTERNATIVES AND CONSEQUENCES

(9) a. It is possible that p.
    b. It could be that p.
(10) a. It is impossible that p.
     b. It cannot be that p.
(11) a. It is necessary that p.
     b. It must be that p.

If someone says (9), he admits that not-p is also possible, or that q or r are possible instead of p; there are alternatives to be considered. If he says (10), he admits that affirming p would lead to unacceptable consequences. If he says (11), he admits that the non-affirmation of p leads

[1] Carnap & Stegmüller (1959). Cf. also the account in Kutschera (1972: ch. 2).

to unacceptable consequences (contradictions, sanctions, etc.). We can evaluate alternatives and consequences from various points of view: physical, physiological, conceptual, mathematical–logical, terminological, juristic, etc. (cf. Toulmin 1969: 23).

4. HYPOTHETICAL ASSERTIONS

In many contexts of discussion we assume certain events, actions, or relationships, and base arguments on them. If we are considering alternatives, for instance, we consider them first as competing – but potentially defensible – assumptions. Scientific procedure in particular can be singled out as hypothetical: general and abstract statements always transcend factual knowledge, but the knowledge they express is not certain, but conjectural: it has to be tested by argument, perhaps by experiment, and is to be regarded as fundamentally revisable. Even explicit particular statements can be understood as hypothetical:

(12) I assume that p.

(13) I suppose that p.

(12) is to be understood as: 'I start from the assumption that p, without really knowing it to be the case.' Occasionally (12) can also have a demand component: the speaker expects or demands that p, in the sense that p is to be established. (13) is to be understood as: 'I believe that p, since it could be the case that p, but I have no certainty about it.'[1]

5. TRUTH CLAIMS

(14) a. It is correct that p.
    b. It is true that p.
    c. 'p' is true.

These are equivalent. A speaker generally expresses truth claims only when the justification of such a claim is called into question, perhaps through questions like 'Is it really true that p?' A person who merely wants to express his knowledge will certainly intend this claim, but he will not formulate it explicitly. Someone who, instead of saying 'p' or 'I know that p', brings his knowledge into discussion by saying 'It is

---

[1] It is worth noting that in an utterance of (12) or (13), the speaker himself explicitly mentions assumption or supposition; so it is not possible for (12) to express his (covert) assumptions, or for (13) to express (wilful or false) assumptions that he has made.

true that p', thereby suggests to his hearers that he has some special reason for formulating the truth claim explicitly; and this reason could very well be that he really cannot justify it at all.

6. CORRECTIONS OF KNOWLEDGE

Knowledge always exists at some particular time. It can later be forgotten and, most important, it can be re-evaluated and corrected in the light of later events and experiences. Old knowledge may turn out to be only apparent knowledge, or subjective opinion. This is why formulations like (15) below are hardly acceptable, but are replaced by ones like (16):

(15) $\begin{Bmatrix} \text{It was possible} \\ \text{I knew} \end{Bmatrix}$ that p, but I was mistaken.

(16) $\begin{Bmatrix} \text{It seemed possible} \\ \text{I thought I knew} \end{Bmatrix}$ that p, but I was mistaken.

In corrections of knowledge we can also distinguish between excusable error and inexcusable carelessness or even fraud:

(17) Nina thought she knew that p, but she was mistaken.
(18) Nina claimed she knew that p, but she didn't know it at all.

While (17), like (16), only corrects some earlier knowledge that was perhaps justifiable at the time, (18) embodies the reproach that the knowledge was not warranted even then: in the light of later events and experiences it turns out that even then Nina could have produced no warrant for her claim, and therefore that she spoke carelessly or even with intent to deceive.

2.2   The justification of claims to knowledge

Anyone who makes a sincere claim to knowledge also claims to direct his hearer's attention in a particular way, and makes a commitment to provide evidence or sureties that the hearer can trust. So if he wants to do justice to his pretensions, he must also be prepared to adduce acceptable grounds for his claim. This means that the process of adducing grounds must correspond to some accepted STANDARD. When a speaker produces the assertion-token 'p', he conventionally entitles his hearer to conclude that he believes that p, and authorizes him to say that p, or to trust that p (Toulmin 1969: 11). An assertion 'I know that p' is distinct from 'p' only by its explicitness and the fact that the hearer can conclude that the speaker is very certain that p.

If a hearer wants to demand justification for an assertion of knowledge, he can ask, for instance,

(19) How do you know that p ?

(19) does not generally call the speaker's truth-claim into question, but rather presupposes it; what the hearer wants to know is what it is based on. But the following is very different:

(20) Is it really the case that p ?

Here the truth-claim itself is being questioned. At the same time this can mean that grounds for the justification of the claim have to be invoked; therefore (19) and (20) can perhaps both be answered in the same way ('I was there', 'I heard it on the news').

There are various kinds of answers to (19) (cf. Toulmin 1969: ch. v):

(a) The speaker invokes BIOGRAPHICAL GROUNDS: his own experiences, his own controlled observations, communications from others that he trusts.

(b) The speaker invokes COMMONLY ACCEPTED GROUNDS and assumes that they are also known to the hearer: known facts, notions of the course of events, regulations, norms of behaviour. The goal of the argumentation is to make clear to the hearer the connection of these acknowledged things with the speaker's assertion of knowledge.

In (a) only the modes of connection between biographical grounds and the assertion of knowledge have to be recognized; elements of the speaker's personal biography obviously cannot be known or assumed to be known. They only have to be plausible, i.e. the hearer must be able to be convinced that someone could actually have experiences like those the speaker claims to have had.

(c) Finally there is IMMEDIATE EVIDENCE, stemming from direct contact with something. This cannot be justified by other evidence: one can only say 'It's so.'

On this basis we can give some examples of questions that make no sense:

(21) How do you know you're tired ?

(One can only establish that it is possible for someone to become tired; one cannot prove that he is tired.)

(22) How do you know your brother's name is 'Peter'?

(23) How do you know that 3 times 9 is 27?

(One can only say that he has simply learned it, that his brother could be called something else, but is not; one can give no justification for why he has not forgotten what he has learned.)

(24) How do you know it says 'Exit' there?

(One can only say that he uses his eyes, i.e. he has eyes and has learned how to read; naturally there could be something else over there, but there is not; one could give reasons WHY it says 'Exit' over there, but no proof THAT it says it.)

So not all knowledge can be justified by argument. These primary, unquestionable pieces of evidence (unquestionable at least in everyday life) are thus to some extent 'ultimate justifications': they belong to the realm of self-evident experience. But these pieces of evidence from everyday life are not to be confused with the 'ultimate justifications' of the empiricists, namely sense-perceptions (and perhaps controlled observations). There may even be some doubt whether I can perceive my own tiredness; and I certainly do not know my brother's name, the product of 3 and 9, or the words of my language, on the basis of sense-perception.

The justification of claims to knowledge leads to an ARGUMENT. The simplest forms are:

(25) a. p, therefore q.

       b. q, because p.

The PREMISS (or conjunction of premisses) p is already certain or acknowledged or believed to be certain; the CONCLUSION q still has to be certified, and we want it to be believed. Therefore we assert q in relation to p. The degree to which q can be accepted depends on the extent to which p itself is already accepted.

The following comments may help to delimit this definition of argument more precisely.

1. The term 'argument' is used in two different ways, though it is not necessary to adhere strictly to one or the other use (they are easily inter-translatable): on the one hand we can call a whole expression like 'p, therefore q' an argument; on the other, we can say that p is an argument for q. The second formulation is used especially when we are considering alternatives, and evaluating the arguments for one or the other. Let p_1 be an argument FOR q and p_2 an argument AGAINST q. If p_1 is more

certain than p_2, and both the transitions from p_1 to q and from p_2 to not-q are equally accepted, then we can claim q rather than not-q; if p_1 is just as certain as p_2, but the transition from p_1 to q is more acceptable ('better') than that from p_2 to not-q, one can likewise claim q rather than not-q.

2. There are many expression-forms which establish the relations between individual assertions of knowledge, but which do NOT have the character of arguments, e.g.

(26) a. p, and also q.
   b. p, and especially also q.
   c. p, but nevertheless q.

But implicit reference is made here to certain arguments, e.g. in (26c) to 'normally not-q, because p'.

3. The expressions 'because' and 'therefore' are AMBIGUOUS: we are not always conducting arguments when we use them. In colloquial usage the boundaries are not always clear; it is only in the context of a scientific reconstruction that we can clearly distinguish between arguments and non-arguments. Compare the following statements:

(27) It's cold in here because the heating is defective.
(28) Max is in the library because he has to write an essay.
(29) Max is in the library (I know this) because I saw him there.
(30) Max is in the library (I conclude this) because his bicycle is outside.
(31) Close the window (I ask you to) because I'm freezing.

The explanation in (27) is causal, while that in (28) is finalistic. The justifications lie in the facts themselves, not in knowledge of the facts. In (29) and (30) on the other hand, the explanations given are rational; the possibility of adding 'I know this' or 'I conclude this' shows that we are dealing with arguments which purport to justify certain factual knowledge. In (31) it is a particular speech act (a request) that is justified, not a particular piece of knowledge. The structure of the various explanations and justifications is similar in many respects, e.g. we could also say:

(32) From the fact that the heating is defective I conclude that it is cold.
(33) I justify my claim that Max is in the library with reference to the fact that I saw him there.

Causal explanations can thus be given in the form of an argument; and arguments can be given in the form of justifications. In the following chapters I will discuss the similarities and differences in more detail. But initially we can agree that only justifications in the form of (29) and (30) will be treated as arguments.

4. Many arguments are COMPLEX, i.e. they can undergo a definite development. On the one hand the premisses of an argument can be justified anew, i.e. they can appear as conclusions in other arguments, and the argument as a whole can be analysed into several subarguments. On the other hand we can compare and evaluate competing arguments (especially arguments for and against).

5. In scientific argumentation especially we often find HYPOTHETICAL ARGUMENTS, where the premisses are purely conjectural. One therefore does not say

p, therefore q

(since this presupposes that p is already established), but rather

Provided that p, one may conclude that q

or

If p, then q

(where there is no assumption about whether p itself can be asserted or not).

The particulars of any argument lie in the transition from premisses to conclusion. In an undifferentiated colloquial sense we can use various expressions: e.g. the premisses IMPLY the conclusion; the conclusion FOLLOWS FROM the premisses; it is permissible to CONCLUDE from the premisses. The schematizations of logic are an attempt to define this transition precisely; they give a precise sense to notions like 'imply', 'follow from', 'conclude'. The schematizations likewise establish in detail which expression-forms can be used for 'p' and 'q'. Only if language is standardized in this way can we reconstruct arguments schematically, and formally separate valid from invalid arguments. In colloquial argumentation we make only occasional and partial use of logical schematizations. The main question is not what structure the subarguments and the whole argument must have for the argument to be valid, but what criteria we should use in general to evaluate arguments as 'good' or 'bad'. Hamblin (1970: 224–52) has characterized three types of EVALUATION CRITERIA FOR ARGUMENTS; they concern respectively the truth of the assertions involved (alethic criteria), the knowledge that the assertions are true (epistemic criteria), and the acceptance of the assertions (dialogic criteria).

I. ALETHIC CRITERIA

    (A1) The premisses must be true.
    (A2) The conclusion must be implied by the premisses (in some suitable sense of the word 'implied').
    (A3) The conclusions must follow reasonably immediately.
    (A4) If some of the premisses are unstated, they must be of a specified kind.

(A1) gives no particular criterion for truth; we have to proceed at first on the basis of our everyday understanding (e.g. 'It is the case that p', 'It is correct that p'). Hypothetical arguments are excluded, since they say nothing *per se* about the truth or falsehood of their conclusions, but only about the appropriateness of the transition to the conclusion. The truth requirement however can be relativized so as to make it possible to characterize even hypothetical arguments as 'good'. For example the truth requirement could be replaced by the following: every hypothetical element in the premisses must be indicated; the premisses must be meaningful in a particular context of discussion; a procedure must be specified by which the truth of the premisses can be established. The notions 'imply' and 'follow' in (A2) and (A3) can be made more precise in various ways; but the transition from premisses to conclusion should be easily comprehensible (it should not be difficult to show that an argument is 'good'). According to (A4), for instance, it is permissible to leave premisses unstated where they follow from the extraverbal context or were produced earlier or are self-evidently part of the theme of discussion.

2. EPISTEMIC CRITERIA

    (E1)   The premisses must be known to be true.
    (E2, 3) The conclusion must follow clearly from the premisses.
    (E4)   Premisses that are not stated must be such that they are taken for granted.
    (E5)   The conclusion must be such that it would be in doubt in the absence of the argument.

For an argument to be meaningful in a given discussion, not only must the premisses be true, but the participants must know them to be true; in this sense (E1) is a stronger requirement than (A1) Requirements

(E2, 3) together form the counterpart to (A2) and (A3): all the participants must be able to know that the conclusion follows immediately. Therefore there must be no failure in producing premisses that everybody acknowledges. (E4) requires that it be taken for granted that the omitted premisses can be guessed to be premisses FOR this kind of argument. The additional condition (E5) says that an argument should be adduced only when the conclusion is in doubt; otherwise it would be superfluous, i.e. useless for the advancement of our knowledge, and hence 'bad'. The notions 'known', 'taken for granted', 'be in doubt' refer in general to all participants; but in certain contexts they can refer to the speaker alone, the addressee, possible hearers, or a whole group.

We can generalize the epistemic criteria by establishing degrees of knowledge or doubt: we can then replace the conditions (E1) and (E5) by the following probability conditions:

(P1) The premisses must be reasonably probable.

(P2) The conclusion must be less probable *a priori* than the premisses.

3. DIALOGIC CRITERIA

(D1)   The premisses must be accepted.

(D2, 3) The passage from premisses to conclusion must be of an accepted kind.

(D4)   Unstated premisses must be of a kind that are accepted as omissible.

(D5)   The conclusion must be such that, in the absence of the argument, it would not be accepted; or: the conclusion must be such that, in the absence of the argument, it would be less accepted than in its presence.

In (A1) or (E1) the requirement is that the premisses be true or known to be true. The alethic criterion in particular could suggest that there are absolute standards for evaluating arguments, which an observer can avail himself of. But in the normal course of things it is the participants themselves who make these judgements; they end a disputation, for example, when they are convinced – though it can always be reopened. If we want to characterize the way the arguers themselves evaluate their arguments, we have to consider their acceptances. An argument is 'good' when it is believed or accepted.

In the sense of dialogic criteria every argument is an *argumentum ad hominem*: it is directed toward particular persons and must therefore take account of their acceptance.

2.3 The structure of arguments

Logic attempts a schematic reconstruction of the structure of certain especially commonly used argument-types. The aim is to make possible an EVALUATION OF ARGUMENTS SOLELY ACCORDING TO THEIR FORM, i.e. to disregard the particular content of the component assertions. Arguments that display one of the permitted forms are called formally valid. Logical investigation often has a further goal, the formal derivation or deduction of all possible conclusions from given premisses. Therefore we speak in this case of deductive arguments. The formal argument-schema achieved in this way also gives us an indirect insight into the structure of various colloquial arguments. There are two crucial preconditions for this:

1. It must be possible to translate the assertion sentences actually used into canonical logical forms, without destroying their essential meaning.

2. It must be possible to subdivide the whole argument so that it can be seen as a complex of simple arguments in canonical form.

In traditional logic arguments are reconstructed in the form of syllogisms or categorical syllogisms. These however do not include all deductive arguments, but only a few particularly typical ones. In chapter 5 I will show that the notion of deduction in a formal logical system is more far-reaching than the notion of syllogism: for this reason modern logics do without syllogisms (at best this notion is fully included in other logics). I will nevertheless sketch out the syllogism concept briefly, as an illustration of argumentative structure (what follows is based on Copi 1968: chs. 5–7).

All assertions occurring in arguments are expressed in one of the following STANDARD FORMS:[1]

All S are P.	(abbreviated as A
No S is P.	E
Some S are P.	I
Some S are not-P.	O)

---

[1] These standard forms are also called 'categorical propositions'. We can explicate them fully in the framework of a quantified predicate-calculus, which shows that the theory of syllogisms is fully contained in predicate logic. (The abbreviations derive from the two words '*Affirmo*' and '*nEgO*'.)

The predicates 'S' and 'P' refer to classes of objects or properties of objects. Under the assumption that these classes are non-empty (i.e. there are objects that are S or P or not P, e.g. S = politician, P = liar), the following direct inferences (among others) are valid:[1]

Premiss	Conclusions
A is true.	*E* is false, *I* is true, *O* is false.
I is true.	*E* is false, *A* and *O* are undetermined.
A is false.	*O* is true, *E* and *I* are undetermined.
I is false.	*A* is false, *E* is true, *O* is true.

Further immediate inferences are possible if the predicates are reversed, or if we introduce negation:

Premiss	Conclusions
All S are P.	Some P are S.
All S are P.	No S is not-P.
All S are P.	All not-P are not-S.

A syllogism, in contrast to the direct inferences just cited, is an argument with TWO premisses and a conclusion. A further restriction is made in the case of CATEGORICAL SYLLOGISMS: the premisses and the conclusion must be in one of the standard forms. In addition, there must be exactly three distinct predicates included, two of which appear in each component sentence, e.g.

(Premisses)   All linguists are egotists.
               Some linguists are idiots.

(Conclusion)   Some idiots are egotists.

The grammatical subject of the conclusion ('idiots') is called the major term S, the grammatical predicate of the conclusion is called the minor term P, and the term which is missing from the conclusion is called the middle term M. Altogether, according to the distribution of S, P and M, there are four syllogistic FIGURES, namely:

$$
\begin{array}{cccc}
M - P & P - M & M - P & P - M \\
S - M & S - M & M - S & M - S \\
\hline
S - P & S - P & S - P & S - P
\end{array}
$$

In addition there are $4^3 = 64$ different MOODS, according to the sequence of the standard forms *A, E, I, O* in a figure (the example above belongs

---

[1] On the basis of these inferential properties it is clear that *A* and *O* or *E* and *I* are respectively contradictory, and *A* and *E* or *I* and *O* are contraries.

to the third figure and is in the mood *A, I, I*). The validity of a categorical syllogism depends on the distribution of the standard forms in a
figure, i.e. given mood and figure, we can tell absolutely whether an
argument is valid or not. To avoid enumerating all valid forms, we can be
guided by particular rules which allow us to establish whether or not the
syllogism is valid. If any syllogism is established as valid or invalid, then
every argument of this form is valid or invalid (regardless of the predicates involved). This often allows us to use logical analogies, to convince
someone of the validity or invalidity of a particular argument. Let us say
that someone asserts:

> All socialists are for cooperative organizations.
> Some ministers are for cooperative organizations.

Therefore: Some ministers are socialists.

We could reply that in that case the following conclusion must also be
valid:

> All rabbits run fast.
> Some horses run fast.

Therefore: Some horses are rabbits.

It is obvious that not many everyday arguments are in the form of
classical syllogisms. But we can often translate them into this form, e.g.
we can replace synonymous expressions, describe verbs in the form of
predicate terms, replace quantifiers like 'only', or 'no-one except' by
other quantifiers, reformulate 'there are'-sentences;[1] if there are more
than two premises we can try to subdivide the argument. But many
arguments are not reducible to one of the syllogistic forms, e.g. if their
assertions cannot be interpreted in one of the standard forms (this is
especially true in complex sequences with 'or', 'if...then'), or if we
have restricted universal statements ('nearly all', 'almost everyone',
'normally', etc.). So syllogisms do not reproduce the general structure
of arguments.

Toulmin (1969: 113f.) has raised a central objection to the undifferentiated treatment of various kinds of premises. In his view some
premises (especially particular statements) are to be taken as attested
data or information, while others (especially general statements) are to be

---

[1] E.g. 'Only citizens may vote' → 'All those, who may vote, are citizens'; 'There
are no blue elephants' → 'No elephant is blue'; 'Wherever people have picnicked, there
are tin cans lying around' → 'All places where people have picnicked are places where
tin cans lie around.'

taken as theoretical claims. But the functions of data and theoretical claims in arguments are different: claims must be justified themselves. Universal premisses in this view are often ambiguous: 'All linguists are egotists' can express an assumption by means of which particular inferences can be justified; but it can also express a general empirical fact ('every individual linguist has proved to be an egotist'). In the second instance the conclusion that a given linguist L is an egotist is already included in the premiss: the argument produces nothing new. Toulmin calls such arguments 'analytic'.

Theoretical assumptions are totally different in character; they can be refuted by single instances. Toulmin calls arguments with theoretical assumptions 'substantial'.

On the basis of this criticism Toulmin develops a general structural schema for arguments, which assumes no special assertion forms. Every argument proposes a particular claim, in relation to specific data. The transition from DATA to CONCLUSIONS requires a special justification or WARRANT, generally theoretical. Warrants are normally in the form of universal sentences ('all...', 'every...', 'whenever...then'); all theoretical premisses are thus counted as warrants. Warrants themselves are BACKED by a set of further data (similar to the given data), through procedural considerations, or general theoretical principles. Here there may be a set of REBUTTALS (even if the warrant is produced in a categorical form, like 'all...', etc.), i.e. competing warrants, leading to alternative conclusions. The conclusions are therefore often provided with a restricting QUALIFIER: an uncertainty factor, a degree of probability or possibility ('presumably', 'perhaps', 'certainly', etc.). The general layout (henceforth: the Toulminian schema) is shown in figure 1 (Toulmin 1969: 104).

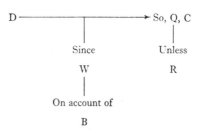

Figure 1   (D = data, C = claim, W = warrant, B = backing,
Q = qualifier, R = rebuttal)

D: a set of observations   →So C: the claim (5)
on the hitherto accepted use of
sog and *saugte*, that they
have the same meaning, the first
represents a strong, and the second
a weak preterite, etc.

Unless

R: a meaning distinction
were to develop between
sog and *saugte* (like
that in *schliff* vs.
schleifte, bewog vs.
bewegte)

Since

W: general theses about the historical evolution of
languages as well as the current use of German, e.g.
whenever two forms A and B with the same meaning are
in competition, A will supersede B if:

   (a) the derivation of A follows a more productive
rule than that of B;

   (b) in cases of doubt speakers prefer A;

   (c) children learn the rule for constructing A first.

In present-day German conditions (a)–(c) hold for *saugte*
as against *sog*

On account of

B: the mass of statements on usage up to the present,
grammatical and historical data on preterite formation
in German verbs, as well as similar competing forms
(as in D) in the realms of syntax, morphology, and
phonology.

Figure 2

I will illustrate the schema (figure 2) with the claim given above
(2.1, (5)):

(5) In the future the verb-form *sog* will be superseded by **saugte**.
The Toulminian schema incorporates the assumption that the exhaustive
justification of all the elements appealed to in the schema will be presented (or ought to be presented) in context. To make this assumption
more plausible, I will illustrate the schema with a fictional dialogue:

A. In the future the verb-form *sog* will be superseded by *saugte*.

B. How do you know?

A. I have established that both forms have the same meaning, and are used concurrently. The important distinction is that *saugte* belongs to the weak conjugation, but *sog* is strong.

B. I know that, but how do you justify your claim?

A. That's tied up with the weak conjugation. There the rule for preterite-formation is very simple, whereas in the strong conjugation the preterite-form has to be learned separately for each verb.

B. Fine, but how is that relevant to your claim?

A. If you give me some novel verb, I can say with certainty that it will be weak, e.g. *haschen – haschte*. And when a child learns the language, he learns this weak inflexional rule first: he begins by saying *laufte* instead of *lief*, and if he figures out at some point that Ablaut is usual here, he will still often produce forms like *liefte*, i.e. he follows the rule for weak inflexion in addition. So I conclude that *saugte* follows a more productive rule than *sog*, and can be learned more easily. Now it's common knowledge that forms that follow productive rules and are easier to learn supersede other equally correct forms that follow less productive rules and are harder to learn. Therefore *sog* will be superseded by *saugte*.

B. O.K., you've shown me that *saugte* follows a more productive rule than *sog*, and in addition (or therefore?) it's easier to learn – though you haven't shown it for these particular forms, you've only given me an analogy. However, I'll let that pass. But then you brought up something else that you call 'common knowledge', and you applied this to *saugte* and *sog*. What is the status of this common knowledge? Isn't it merely an assumption of yours?

A. You're right, strictly speaking it is an assumption. But I find it an entirely plausible one, at least much more plausible than its inverse. In addition I can give you lots of examples that back up my assumption. Does anyone nowadays say 'Nach dem Essen *pflog* er zu schlafen', or 'Sie *buk* einen Kuchen' instead of *pflegte* and *backte*? If you want I can give you lots more examples of competing expressions from the history of German or some other language to support my assumption. If there are apparent counter-examples, I've at least succeeded so far in showing that there must be other circumstances involved that have to be considered. But we'd have to enter into a course in language history, if all this won't convince you.

B. All right, I'll admit that there are reasonable grounds for your assumption. But another question: you've made a direct inference from present and past data to a process that has to occur in the future. Is that generally – I mean in principle – allowed? Couldn't something else happen in the future, something that you can't foresee today, that would upset this conclusion?

A. First your second point: my original claim is in fact justified only if I assume that the meanings of *saugte* and *sog* will also be the same in the future. A differentiation in meaning at some point in the future – which I can't foresee – would make my inference meaningless. Because there are cases where both the weak and the strong forms of a verb remain, because they belong to different meanings of the verb. Think of 'Er *schliff* sein Messer' and 'Er *schleifte* den Sack über den Boden', or 'Er *bewog* mich zu gehen' and 'Er *bewegte* seine Hand'.[1] Now to the basic question: the content of my claim is precisely that this inference from past to future is permissible. Something that follows from this general assumption is proven only when the future becomes the actual present, so I can't prove my assumption now. But I don't want to PROVE my original claim to you, only to JUSTIFY it. I hope you understand the distinction: I'm sure that things will turn out as I've predicted, and I rely on that, but I can't give you any demonstration of it. I think that in principle we can't do without assumptions like that. We always have to make them if we set ourselves any goals for the future.

B. I must take up again the distinction you made between proof and justification. You think you could prove your original claim if your assumption were proved. But since – in principle – you can't prove this assumption, you can't prove your original claim either. As far as justification goes, you now go two steps further: first, you justify your original claim by means of the assumption you've made, and second, you justify this assumption by means of other data, and by general principles, such as that, since we must orient our action toward the future, we therefore always have to have such general assumptions. Have I understood you correctly?

A. Yes, exactly.

We can get a clearer idea from this dialogue of just what the distinction is between the Toulminian schema and the syllogistic schema.

---

[1] 'He sharpened his knife' vs. 'He dragged the sack over the floor'; 'He induced me to go' vs. 'He waved his hand' [Trans.].

1. In the syllogistic schema a conclusion is derived or 'proved' formally from exactly two premisses, which in addition have to be expressed in a standard form. 'Formally' means here that only the terms that appear in the premisses have to be appropriately arranged. This syllogistic schema is included in the Toulminian one, to the extent that e.g. we identify one premiss with D and other (universal) premisses with W, or even subsume both premisses under D. But the Toulminian schema goes beyond this: it not only characterizes formally valid arguments, but also other kinds, for instance where the transition from premisses to conclusion is justified on grounds of plausibility.

2. The syllogistic schema represents only simple arguments, while the Toulminian schema also embraces very complex ones. In the latter there are always at least two stages of argument involved:[1] namely first argument from data and a justifying warrant to the conclusion, and second argument from other backing data (plus certain empirical principles) back to these justifying principles. The backing generally includes data of the same or a similar type as that used directly for the conclusion, while the conclusion can be of a different type. (In our example, data and backing data referred to the past and present, while the conclusion referred to the future.)

3. The syllogistic schema uses logical entities expressed in sentences of a normalized standard language. In the Toulminian schema the conclusion is understood as the content of a temporally localized assertion. The validity of an argument is not timeless and universal, but time-dependent; and it further depends on whether or not the standards employed (in the justification and supporting data, and the relations between them) are accepted. These standards change, even according to the empirical domain in question; they can include the use of a normalized standard language, but they do not have to.

4. In the Toulminian schema, we can substitute for the content or claim contained in an assertion a claim which is bound up with any other kind of action. The justification of any action can in principle be embraced by the schema. In this way the special status of acts of assertion is neutralized – although this does not have to mean that there are no other grounds for singling out assertions as against other kinds of speech acts (e.g. every justification is an act of assertion).

---

[1] This is somewhat obscured by Toulmin's treatment. He does indeed distinguish arguments that use warrants from those that first have to establish their warrants, but appears not to notice that both types are already united in the schema, namely as the first and second steps of a complex argument.

2.4 On the classification of arguments

There are, no doubt, many possible ways of classifying arguments: according to the evaluation-criteria used, according to the empirical domain, according to the type of assertion made in the conclusion and premisses. I will mention here only the one Toulmin proposes, which is based on specific requirements for 'strong' arguments (Toulmin 1969: 135f., 148f.). Several of these demands can be met simultaneously (e.g. requirements 1–3 are met in the categorical syllogism).

1. The justifying assumption must be so constructed that the conclusion can be stated unequivocally: such an argument is NECESSARY.

2. The conclusion must result only from the appropriate arrangement of terms in the data and the warrant (more generally: it must follow solely from the form of the premisses). Such an argument is FORMALLY VALID (or deductive).

3. Data, warrant and conclusion are to be expressed in terms of a LOGICAL LANGUAGE; in particular only logical quantifiers (for 'all', 'some') and logical connectives (for 'not', 'and', 'or', 'if...then') are to be used.

4. The conclusion must follow logically from the data and supporting data together (in a semantic sense of 'follow'), which is as much as to say that the conclusion is already contained (explicitly or implicitly) in them. Such an argument is ANALYTIC.

Toulmin calls all non-analytic arguments SUBSTANTIAL. In a substantial argument the data are logically of a different type from the conclusion; it is thus impossible to argue solely from data to conclusion. Therefore we need a JUSTIFYING ASSUMPTION, which will allow us to surmount this difference in logical type. This is a THEORETICAL assumption: it does not arise solely from the data and is in principle subject to revision. Given the appropriate theoretical assumptions, substantial arguments too can be formally valid; the goal of all theoretical work, in fact, is precisely to find appropriate assumptions of this kind, and to make them plausible. In most empirical domains all significant arguments are substantial, and therefore theoretically oriented.

In the examples (1)–(5) below I give some assertions that cannot be justified on the basis of observational data alone (because they are not observational judgements themselves); let us look at them briefly (cf. Toulmin 1969: 222):

(1) The word *memme* used to be used in German for the mother's breast. (No collection of statements about what is written in Middle High German texts can logically imply an assertion about what medieval men meant or referred to by a given word.)

(2) The question 'Do you have the time?' should not be answered merely with 'Yes'. (No collection of descriptive statements about contemporary usage, the consequences of our actions, the moral concerns of our contemporaries can logically imply a conclusion about our commitments (a normative assertion).)

(3) When Peter said 'Oh go to hell' he wanted to be left alone. (No collection of statements about a person's utterances, gestures, reactions and the circumstances of these utterances, etc. – no matter how exhaustive – can logically imply a conclusion about his wishes, feelings or intentions.)

(4) *Weitgehendst* is ill-formed, *weitestgehend* is correct but ugly. (No collection of statements about usage can logically imply the certainty that a grammatical rule has been broken, and no collection of statements about usage and grammatical rules can logically imply a stylistic or aesthetic judgement.)

(5) In the future the verb-form *sog* will be superseded by *saugte*. (No collection of observational and empirical data from the past and present – no matter how large – can logically imply a prophecy about the future.)

The notion 'data' here must be rather strictly defined. A datum is something established on the basis of observation, not on the basis of our everyday knowledge. In our normal experience, reaching the conclusions (1)–(5) is unproblematical; indeed all our everyday knowledge is (pre)-theoretical, and already incorporates the necessary general assumptions. The examples show the need for explaining and working out this (pre)-theoretical knowledge, if we want to reach similar conclusions in science. For example we can uphold (5) by logical inference if we add to the two facts

(a) *saugte* is the weak form of the verb *saugen*
(b) *sog* is the strong form of the verb *saugen*

the theoretical assumption

(c) the weak form of a verb will replace the strong where no difference in meaning develops.

3 *Perception, description and explanation*

3.1 Reprise: problem situations

Let us recall briefly the kinds of situations which we might say constitute the beginnings of science, in that they motivate the scientific formulation of questions (whether they lead to the initial recognition that a problem as such exists, or to the reformulation of a question in the context of a scientific institution).[1] These are situations that previously have typically been treated as unproblematical: men have developed control over the circumstances of their daily lives, and become dependent on practical knowledge developed not by them but by others; they have come to depend on generalizations, abstractions, value-judgements, prejudices, stereotypes, without asking how certain or how justified they are. A PRIMARY PROBLEM SITUATION arises when this unproblematical context is disrupted in some specific way. There are three characteristic types of disruption:

1. NEW EXPERIENCES which cannot be incorporated with previous ones: they are strange, astonishing, puzzling. It may be a matter of entirely new phenomena, or of already known ones arising in unexpected contexts.

2. MUTUALLY CONTRADICTORY EXPERIENCES, which cannot be treated consistently. The individual cannot evaluate his own experiences without a sense of conflict and does not know how to behave. This contradictoriness is often only apparent, especially if the situations in which the experiences occur have not been properly analysed, though in many cases it can express deeper social conflicts.

3. PRACTICAL PROBLEMS which arise in situations where it is difficult

---

[1] This is of course an idealized reconstruction. For the individual science does not begin directly with such problem situations: the student gets many problems at second hand (ones that have already been structured through the development of the science), and new ones arise out of the scientific work itself. Dissertation and research projects are often motivated by coincidences, the interests of financial backers or publishers, the predilections of supervisors, etc.

to satisfy immediate needs, or perform tasks designed to do this. We do not know how to remedy a pathological condition (like stammering, schizophrenic behaviour, hysteria, aggression, partial aphasia); we do not know how to argue convincingly, confirm a suspicion of dishonesty, learn a new language rationally and quickly, structure a large set of linguistic data, etc., so we must explain the new, unexpected or contradictory phenomena, or find ways of handling the unsatisfactory practical situation. We have to reorient our behaviour: in one case we need new information and techniques to do this, in another we need principles on which to base our future behaviour. This will require cognitive, communicative and practical exertions.

From the beginning we will attempt to work out and control the problem through argument. We will seek to assure ourselves that it is not merely private, but that others also confront or can confront it. We will perhaps try to get the necessary information from others, or at least listen to their experiences; and these individual experiences will have to be systematically classified and organized. We will discuss possible explanatory hypotheses and solutions: what general connection is there between the new experience and other, familiar ones ? If we were to admit some particular hypothesis, what would follow from it ? What are the arguments for or against a proposed solution ? In this argumentative process we isolate and standardize individual questions, and propose them in an explicit form. At the same time we develop systematic methods of problem-solving, enabling people to work cooperatively on the same problem.

In working out a problem we repeatedly encounter PRIMARY EXPERIENCES: someone perceives a particular event, experiences particular phenomena and processes himself, has learned to master particular situations in a certain way, feels himself to be in a certain state. Such primary sensory (perceptual) experiences, which we process in everyday life, are the basis of EMPIRICAL SCIENCE. Perceptions always relate to everyday life, and are socially controlled. We learn to make particular perceptions; we learn to distinguish relevant perceptions from irrelevant ones; we even learn to accept some perceptions as merely apparent, and others as veridical. Thus empirical science does not merely build on primary experiences without influencing them; it in fact determines, by the ways it processes particular aspects of problems, what should (within its own domain) count as primary experiences.

3.2   Perceptions of language

If we are to regard linguistics as an empirical science, we must be able to state what kinds of everyday experiences it can or ought to be based on, and how we should go about systematically looking for new experiences. Now that we have established that very different aspects of language and speech can be thematized, we have been led to a particular understanding of the content and tasks of linguistics; correspondingly linguistics will also base itself on various experiences and phenomena. The perceptible (or directedly perceptible, i.e. observable) LINGUISTIC PHENOMENA are:

(a) The results of the activities of speaking and writing: sequences of speech sounds or written texts and their structural organization.

(b) The external (visible or audible) surroundings of communication situations.

(c) The activities of speaking and hearing (or reading) themselves; these are particularly open to self-perception by those performing them, but they can also be identified by others on the basis of accompanying phenomena, and of course also by results and reactions. (Linguistic phenomena of type (a), together with contexts of type (b) can also be called LINGUISTIC EVENTS.)

These perceptions are an indispensable part of our everyday communicative activities. But they are largely unconscious; they focus only on those features relevant for a particular speech-community, and are mainly concerned with the meaning of utterances. It is only with foreign languages that this is not the case – and then we have considerable trouble constructing and stabilizing consistent perceptions. These difficulties can only be removed when we have at least partially learned the language ourselves, or constantly back ourselves up with informants who have mastered it. This is not surprising; we know from the psychology of perception that perceptions are always active reconstructions, in which a selection of information-bearing elements fixes the structure of the phenomenon to be constructed (cf. Klix 1971: 265ff.). Every perception already represents an isolation and foregrounding of particular features, and a segmentation, classification and establishment of invariants on the basis of those features. Speechperceptions – where the structural arrangements of speech-sounds are only carriers for meanings – surely belong among the highest forms of invariance-achievement. Psycholinguistic experiments have shown clearly that the structure of an utterance will be held in short-term memory only until the utterance can be assigned a particular meaning; after that, it is mainly the meaning that is retained. After some time this can be reproduced relatively correctly, while there are many more errors in reproducing the verbal form.

One of the central tasks of linguistics is CAPTURING THE RELATION BETWEEN THE FORM AND MEANING OF UTTERANCES. If we restrict ourselves to a narrow notion of sense-perception, it is only the form of an utterance that can be perceived, and not its mean'ng – though the perception is guided by a search for possible meanings. The relation between form and meaning underlies social rules (conventions); only insofar as we control and follow these rules can we mediate and understand intentions, information, etc.

Thus, if we take 'empirical' in a narrow sense (referring solely to sense-perception), linguistics would be empirical only insofar as it studied linguistic phenomena, not the relation of the phenomena to their social meaning. I will discuss this problem in more detail later on (see especially 7.5). Here I will simply indicate that 'empirical' can be taken in a more comprehensive sense by demonstrating that, pre-scientifically, it is quite plausible to say 'I know from experience that these rules apply in language L, and that failure to observe them can produce misunderstanding and perhaps other consequences'; 'I know from experience that when a child learns the language he learns this rule later than others'; etc. Such experiences are at least based on perceptions. The same holds for statements like 'Person X has a linguistic competence of such-and-such a kind.' Here we have an assertion about the presence of a particular DISPOSITION. (In one sense assertions about linguistic rules can also be taken as assertions about certain dispositions present in a speech-community – i.e. dispositions toward social understanding.) Now it is obvious that dispositions as such cannot be directly perceived or observed; but they can be established on the basis of perceived SYMPTOMS. Particular utterances or reactions under particular conditions can be taken as symptoms.

Even if the linguistic phenomena mentioned above are often not directly represented in the formulation of questions in linguistics, they are usually evaluated as symptoms of the existence of a disposition. Linguistics can be regarded as an empirical science at least in this indirect sense.

But contrary to what is normally the case in problem-free daily communication, the linguist's attention is not solely directed to the meaning of utterances: he is also concerned with their possible form and structure, and aspects of communication situations. In order to clarify the relationship between symptoms (linguistic phenomena) and dispositions (ability to speak and understand), and in order to explain further which relationships hold in a given case, the linguist has to deal with linguistic phenomena themselves more clearly and consciously than those who only use them as a means of communication. He has to learn a new kind of controlled and differentiated perception, in order to reconstruct how it is possible for understanding-, communication- and perception-processes to be carried out. I emphasize this point here since the beginner often has special difficulties in developing his ability to observe linguistic phenomena which he learned long ago to perceive unconsciously.

As soon as there is a heightened attention to linguistic phenomena, there is a CHANGE IN THE STRUCTURE OF PERCEPTION. This is in fact already the case if one's attention is directed to the EXACT MEANING of utterances.

Some of the properties of altered perception are:

1. Accentuation of individual features and aspects, according to what motivates the new perceptual orientation.

2. A selective reduction of the stimulus-threshold of the sense-organs, so that those stimuli that mediate crucial or relevant features are perceived more easily.

3. An articulate cultivation of expectation with respect to identical or similar phenomenal features under identical or similar conditions.

4. A stepwise classification of phenomena according to their relevant features, and concomitant abstractions which organize particular feature-bundles into complex features.

5. A heightened receptivity to impressions: in order to achieve a steady and concentrated attention we have to retain the relevant features firmly in our memory.

3.3 The investigation of linguistic data

Linguistic phenomena can be perceived (or observed) in three kinds of situations; these are the situations where linguistic data – what we will call primary data – can be investigated.

1. EXTERNAL OBSERVATIONAL SITUATIONS: from a non-participant

standpoint we register how others say things, what they say, how they react – linguistically or non-linguistically – to the utterances of others. When the observer stands outside a communicative situation, we can speak of the EXTRACOMMUNICATIVE investigation of linguistic data.

2. INTUITIVE REPRESENTATION OF COMMUNICATION SITUATIONS (or situation-types): we imagine how someone else would speak in a particular situation and what he would say, how we ourselves would behave, etc. This representation may be retrospective (reconstructing experienced situations) or prospective (anticipating situations). This is made possible by the fact that everyone who has learned a language has also learned to process experienced communication situations after the fact, and to prepare himself for future ones by anticipation. This kind of linguistic investigation can be called REFLEXIVE: it is both outside the imagined situation and inside another one – since the representation places the investigator in a situation of communication with himself and his reconstructed or anticipated partners.

3. THEMATIZATION OF COMMUNICATION SITUATIONS (or situation-types): we can distinguish two types, (a) METACOMMUNICATIVE and (b) ARGUMENTATIVE-REFLEXIVE. In the first case we consciously perceive ourselves and our communication partners within a situation whose primary concern is understanding; but this perception takes place on levels only indirectly related to understanding and normally perceived only unconsciously. We also attempt to speak about those perceptions. In this way a communication situation is partly thematized within the situation itself. This thematization is often possible only for one partner – since carrying it further would destroy the original situation. In the second case the partners discuss experienced or possible linguistic phenomena, and thus both of them represent these phenomena within an imagined situation. Such situations can be initiated by directed questions or assertions, which aim respectively at agreement or contra- diction. An indirect thematization by only one partner is also possible, where he does not thematize the linguistic phenomena themselves, but only seeks to discover his partner's disposition toward particular modes of linguistic behaviour (e.g. to react to particular questions or assertions). In particular, we can use techniques here that are similar to those used for investigating sociological data, e.g. people's attitudes toward parti- cular facts, value-systems, etc.[1]

---

[1] Structuring of problems, description of modes of behaviour, and investigation of data are always theory-directed. I make no assumption about particular types of theory.

The investigation of linguistic data is fundamentally different from the investigation of physical or physiological data in only one main respect: LINGUISTIC data are LINGUISTICALLY determined; the things one is speaking about are the same in kind as speaking itself: we speak ABOUT communication situations IN them. We must therefore have learned the distinction between perceiving a situation in order to understand it, and perceiving it in order to thematize it. Physical and physiological data however are different in kind from the situations in which we communicate about them: these latter are determined linguistically, not physically or physiologically. The investigation of physical or physiological data consists mainly of observations, often aided by supplementary instruments (if the phenomena cannot be directly or precisely perceived by human sense organs).

Even in this respect, however, linguistics is not fundamentally different. In the first place, instrumental means can be appropriate, e.g. in establishing the structure of speech-sounds or hearers' reactions. In the second place, even physical or physiological data can be reflected on or questioned; we can remember what we do on a bicycle or on ice-skates to keep our balance, the sensations in the different phases of a three-metre jump, the sensations resulting from drinking too much alcohol, the distortion of perspective that arises from seeing two objects at different distances the same size, etc. One can in fact say that the praxis of physicists and physiologists has largely abandoned this everyday realm of experience, while that of physicians, say, derives mainly from anamnesis, i.e. from questioning the patient about this or that symptom-perception. The real distinction between physics and linguistics is in their differing levels of development – e.g. everyday consciousness of human behaviour in the natural world scarcely plays a role in modern physics, but everyday consciousness of human linguistic behaviour does play an important role in contemporary linguistics. There is no principled distinction in the way primary data are obtained.

3.4 Descriptions

If we want to make experiences in general (phenomena and perceptions, connections between symptoms and dispositions) accessible to scientific investigation, we have to represent them linguistically, i.e. describe

In particular, I do not adhere to any strict operationalist programme (i.e. that observational concepts are to be given theoretical status in a strong sense, and that we allow only those investigative procedures that guarantee this).

them. Scientific work is at least partially the devising and standardizing of meaningful and coherent descriptive systems, so that others can depend on descriptions without having had the corresponding perceptions.

I have argued that in systematic perception we expect particular features, and therefore bring them into prominence, while we down-grade others; and, further, that perception always includes a particular classification of phenomena. This holds *a fortiori* for description, where language determines which features and feature-complexes are fore-grounded: any particular descriptive system also assumes an abstract classificatory system for the phenomena to be described.

The CONCEPTUAL CLASSIFICATION of a phenomenon includes above all answers to these questions:

What individual properties are most perceptually salient?

What is the internal organization of constituent parts?

How does the phenomenon contrast with others; in particular, what are the environmental conditions for it?

How does the phenomenon change over time?

When does it appear, what precedes it, and what follows it?

What does it indicate (e.g. is it to be taken as symptom, signal, or intentional expression)?

What human activities is it connected with, how is it connected to them, what does it mean for them?

The act of classifying allows us to obtain a general view of situations and the events, actions, etc. that occur in them; it allows a stable orientation toward them, and guarantees the recognition of identical or similar situations. Linguistic description also guarantees that the general view, orientation and recognition are not merely individual achievements, but the achievements of a group or even a whole scientific institution.

Ordinary language offers the most varied descriptive possibilities for an individual phenomenon; the descriptive point of view can change from case to case, it is oriented more toward practical needs than to the task of formulating questions relevant to a comprehensive theory of a whole realm of phenomena and its systematics. Therefore all sciences develop their own descriptive systems, which lead to a standardization of ordinary-language concepts, the introduction of new concepts, a reduction of the possibilities of syntactic combination for these concepts, and, ultimately, to the introduction of a constructed abstract language. The adequacy of a scientific description is thus always measured by wider theoretical interests and requirements.

A distinction is often made in the linguistic literature between observational and descriptive adequacy, especially with reference to grammars (as theories of individual languages). We can state this distinction in general as follows: a representation is OBSERVATIONALLY ADEQUATE if it includes all features of a phenomenon or a number of selected phenomena which in their actual organization are significant with respect to a given question. This by itself, however, would allow us to choose particular descriptive procedures (which might be inapplicable to other cases) *ad hoc* for just these selected phenomena. We therefore try to achieve a higher type of adequacy, descriptive adequacy. A representation is DESCRIPTIVELY ADEQUATE if it rests on a system of procedures that can capture a whole field of related phenomena, i.e. not only those phenomena actually observed,[1] but all potential observable phenomena in a particular field. For a linguistic description this means not only those sound-sequences uttered at a given time in an observed speech-community, but all those sequences possible on the basis of the existing linguistic rules. A description of this kind must thus already have classified the individual speech-sounds according to the generating rules.

The justification for this – for systematically marking out a whole field of connected possible appearances, and referring to general regularities or rules – does not derive from observation and description of phenomena, no matter how comprehensive these are assumed to be. It derives from a particular explanatory and theoretical requirement, and from the general problem-situation as seen by a science at a given time.

The distinction between observational and descriptive adequacy can be formulated in another way: a representation is observationally adequate if it describes the DATA correctly (e.g. notates particular accentual distinctions correctly, and notates them in the same way whenever they appear); it is descriptively adequate if it describes the FACTS correctly (e.g. that in certain syntactic constructions in German the accent falls on the last full verb or noun). As long as we do not know how a fact is distinguished from a datum, this is merely a terminological novelty (the parenthesized examples are only pointers toward a proper distinction). Crudely put, data are established through individual observations, but facts are established by generalization and abstraction – never merely by observation and certainly not by individual observations.

---

[1] Following 3.3 we can more generally substitute 'phenomenon included in a primary datum' for 'observed phenomenon'.

3.5   Observational and descriptive adequacy in Chomsky

I will here briefly introduce Chomsky's notions of observational and descriptive adequacy; these depart somewhat from the definitions given above (especially in their relation to a particular theory), and have led to a long-lasting controversy (which I will not go into here).

Along with observational and descriptive adequacy, Chomsky sets up a third type: explanatory adequacy; I will discuss this in detail below (3.9). Observational and descriptive adequacy are required primarily of GRAMMARS (as theories of particular languages); explanatory adequacy is required of linguistic (or grammatical) THEORIES, which specify the form of individual grammars. A theory of grammar is explanatorily adequate if on the basis of primary data it succeeds in selecting a descriptively adequate grammar (Chomsky 1965: 25–6). Chomsky writes (1964: 28):

we can sketch various levels of success that might be obtained by a grammatical description, associated with a particular linguistic theory. The lowest level of success is achieved if the grammar presents the observed primary data correctly. A second and higher level of success is achieved when the grammar gives a correct account of the linguistic intuition of the native speaker, and specifies the observed data (in particular) in terms of significant generalizations that express underlying regularities in the language. A third and still higher level of success is achieved when the associated linguistic theory provides a general basis for selecting a grammar that achieves the second level of success over other grammars consistent with the relevant observed data that do not achieve this level of success. In this case we can say that the linguistic theory in question suggests an explanation for the linguistic intuition of the native speaker.

He supplements this in a note (p. 28, n. 1):

What data is relevant is determined in part by the possibility for a systematic theory, and one might therefore hold that the lowest level of success is no easier to achieve than the others...The problem of determining what data is valuable and to the point is no easy one. What is observed is often neither relevant nor significant, and what is relevant and significant is often very difficult to observe.

We can also speak in an extended sense of observational and descriptive adequacy in reference to theories of grammar; in this case these criteria refer not to individual languages but (in principle) to every language.

For Chomsky, observational adequacy in reference to a theory of grammar means that the theory must be able to provide a procedure for enumerating the class of possible sentences of any language, and further, a procedure for assigning corresponding structural descriptions (and meanings) to these sentences.[1] Sentences are understood here roughly as strings of phonemes, corresponding to possible sound-sequences. This definition of observational adequacy naturally is not immune to false interpretations and misunderstandings. We must above all understand clearly that we cannot observe the sentences of a language; we can only observe utterances (i.e. temporally extended sequences of speech-sounds) and then interpret or understand them in a special sense as (realizations of) sentences of a language. It would perhaps be useful to distinguish here – as Carnap proposes (1956b: cf. 8.3 below) – between THEORETICAL LANGUAGE and OBSERVATION-LANGUAGE: the term 'sentence' belongs to the language of linguistic theory, while 'utterance' can be regarded as belonging to the corresponding observation-language. The terms of both languages now have to be systematically related (Carnap does this by means of so-called correspondence rules): only in this way can a theory be called observationally adequate. Chomsky however fails to do this – apparently for two reasons.

First, he considers both perceptions (especially observations) and the classifications and abstractions derived from them to constitute one domain, in essence pretheoretical, but not in itself systematizeable: to put it crudely, it does not matter how you arrive at a theory as long as you can justify it afterwards. (Here above all we will have to refer to perceptions.)

Second, Chomsky believes (correctly) that in all descriptions of phenomena, test-procedures and data-interpretations, the norm that in the last analysis makes interpretation possible is the linguistic knowledge of the linguist or the participants. This linguistic knowledge cannot be mediated by strict and completely objective testing proce-

---

[1] Cf. Chomsky (1965: 24). Chomsky thinks that the assignment of meanings is not strictly a task for grammatical theory; that is why I have put the reference to meaning in parentheses. In *Aspects* Chomsky does not, as he did in earlier works, speak explicitly about observational adequacy; I have however taken his conditions (1965: 30; 12.i, ii) in this sense, since they correspond approximately to the earlier notion.

I refrain here from any more detailed consideration of Chomsky's conditions (e.g what do 'sentence of a language', 'structural description' mean?). See chapter 8 below, where I discuss his 1957 *Syntactic structures* in some detail. Even if individual ideas changed between 1957 and 1965, the basic position has remained unaltered (especially with respect to the role of grammatical theory: cf. 8.3 below).

dures; there are in fact very few tests that give any reliable information
at all. Chomsky however takes the essential subject matter of linguistics
to be the possible linguistic knowledge of speakers and hearers. He
therefore pays little attention to observation and perception; the relevant
facts (the possible expressions and sentences in a language and their
structural properties) are rather to be obtained through the linguist's
intuition.

This is not without its problems:

1. The individual can become intuitively aware only of his own
linguistic knowledge, i.e. he runs the risk of absolutizing his own
idolect (or dialect). No one is in a position to control even the most
important variants of his own language.[1]

2. It is not easy to represent the pure sentences of a language: this
demands at least some training. It is much easier to represent for oneself
possible utterances in situational and linguistic contexts. If we characterize such utterances by means of concepts like 'sentence' or 'subordination', we must not forget that these are already theoretical
concepts.

3. It is very easy to import into intuitive judgements – just as
into observational claims – a whole set of unreflecting theoretical or
pre-theoretical premises. But explicit or implicit knowledge about
language does not have to correspond in any way to actual language
ability or language behaviour, and given intensive enough reflection
the object often enough shifts toward what we want to find, without our being aware of it. (Judgements of linguistic impossibilities
are for instance often contradicted by the judger's actual utterance:
'You can't say "X"' – but he nonetheless says 'X'.) Intuitive
judgements should therefore at least be supported by the observations
of others, so the linguist can make sure he is not just pursuing his own
fancies.

Chomsky's remarks on observation, description and linguistic data
are on the whole relatively vague and unsatisfactory; they encourage
all sorts of false interpretations and speculations. The relations between
intuitive judgements and observations and the possible connection
between theoretical concepts (like 'sentence', 'structural description')

---

[1] In discussions based solely on intuitive judgements, we often find that in disputed
cases the linguist falls back on his own idiolect (dialect); this amounts to abandoning the
claim to be saying something about a language rather than about merely his own
idiolect, which can have various idiosyncratic properties, even those solely produced by
the linguist's inquiry itself.

and observational concepts are quite unclear.[1] In order to relate grammatical theory in Chomsky's sense to the phenomena of linguistic behaviour, we have to establish some connection between the formal reconstruction of linguistic knowledge and the possible premisses and results of empirical testing procedures.

For a grammatical theory to have descriptive adequacy, Chomsky insists that, in addition to observational adequacy, it must provide (a) a procedure for enumerating the class of possible generative grammars for the organization of the sentences and structural descriptions (plus meanings) of a language, and (b) a function that will assign a structural description to each sentence generated by each grammar.[2]

We must note that this definition is exclusively synchronic – which sentences with which structural descriptions are possible means of communication at a given moment? There is no consideration of the fact that every language contains the seeds of its own future modifications: from a historical point of view, and in comparison with related dialects, not all dialects have the same status – i.e. the same degree of productivity, extensibility, mutual comprehensibility with other dialects, etc. If we take this into consideration, then grammatical theory must provide in addition at least a procedure for enumerating possible extensions (i.e. modifications of grammatical units or rules: see Kanngiesser 1972, and cf. 11.5 below).

3.6 Explanations

Observational and descriptive adequacy together define the external adequacy of descriptions and theories (by which we can specify how theoretical concepts relate to perceptual ones). 'External adequacy' means adequacy with respect to the experiences, perceptions and facts

---

[1] Perhaps Chomsky thinks he can make this problem disappear by using concepts with *systematic ambiguity*: they can be taken as either observational or theoretical (e.g. 'grammar', 'sentence', 'rule'). One can object that e.g. rules (as procedures internalized by speakers) are unobservable, though they can indeed be established by intuitive judgements. One might therefore claim that an intuitive judgement is equivalent to an observational one. But this is contradicted by the general assumption that in observational judgements only individual statements are possible, whereas in intuitive judgements we can make general statements as well. Intuitive judgements are thus potentially more strongly theoretical by nature.

[2] Cf. Chomsky (1965: 31; 13.iii–iv, 14.iii–iv). A descriptively adequate theory thus characterizes not only (isolated) sentences and structural descriptions, but a whole class of hypotheses (generative grammars) about the overall possible structural descriptions of sentences.

the scientist confronts. Along with this however we must aim for a second, as it were internal, type of adequacy, which is connected with the demand for explanation. Even if we have described something adequately, we have still not achieved very much – although the description may have gone beyond actual experience, by specifying particular possible or expectable experiences. We have produced only data, without saying anything about their mutual dependencies. However, it is precisely this that we need to know about if we are to find a strategy for problem-solving. We need to refer to general and recognized explanatory principles (principles that permit us to explain a datum by means of other data). In addition we have to certify the descriptive and explanatory principles for individual data, so that we can refer to other, independently obtained knowledge.

We must, however, observe that an explanation only allows us to answer questions that arise because certain unexpected, strange or contradictory experiences occur; it does not itself give a direction for action. Nevertheless when we explain why a particular action will probably have results that will satisfactorily change a practical situation we are also justifying particular instructions or proposals for action; and the steps taken in accordance with them may solve the problem.

In spite of these complexities we should first discuss the colloquial (prescientific) sense of 'explanation'. To begin with, there is a PRAG-MATIC NOTION OF EXPLANATION, which is illustrated in the following expressions (cf. Stegmüller 1969: 138ff.):

(1) For person B, x is explained by y.

(2) Person A explains the fact x to person B by means of y.

We will call x the EXPLANANDUM ('what is to be explained') and y the EXPLANANS ('that which explains'). Explanations of this kind are special types of argument (x is to be identified with the content – or claim – of an assertion, and y with the data and/or warrant). According to Passmore (1962) a 'good' explanation has to meet the requirements of comprehensibility, adequacy and correctness: the connection between the proposed explanans and the explanandum must be of the usual (i.e. generally accepted) kind; the conditions given in the explanans must be truly sufficient in the concrete situations in which the explanandum arises; and we must make sure there are no errors or deceptions. From the pragmatic concept of explanation we can derive an OBJECTIVE, impersonal (or LOGICAL) NOTION OF EXPLANATION; this will be utilized especially in science, but also in everyday life. In this way we can say that a particular explanation is clear to all knowledgeable people, i.e. those supplied with the requisite information:

(3) y explains x.

In other words, an explanation should be convincing for further potential (rational) men. As we will see, the logical notion of explanation relies on the logical concept of consequence, with the addition that empirical regularities appear in the explanans. In developing the logical concept of explanation we must assume that there are objective procedures for verifying these empirical regularities; but that is just what is normally assumed or required in empirical science anyhow (on the logical or scientific concept of explanation see 3.8 below).

Explanations are generally provoked by 'WHY'-QUESTIONS, e.g.

(4) Why is this so (and not something else)?

But there are also related question-forms, e.g. 'How is it that...?', 'How was it possible that...?'. It is typical of these questions that they make no necessary reference to the hearer: in this respect they are different from the 'How do you know that...?' questions treated in 2.2.

Let us look at some examples of 'why'-questions:

(5) Why did you call me an idiot?
(6) Why did A say 'Idiot' when a driver spattered him with mud?
(7) Why did A say 'I have to work now'?
(8) Why did A say 'I have to work now' when he's only going to watch TV?
(9) Why does A always say 'Thanks' when I accidentally step on his foot?
(10) Why does he say 'Go to hell' when he obviously doesn't mean it?
(11) Why shouldn't you merely answer 'Yes' to the question 'Do you have the time'?
(12) Why is *weitgehendst* ill-formed?
(13) Why doesn't German have the words *xlrox* and *fratteln*?
(14) Why do we write /o:/ sometimes *oh*, sometimes *oo*, and sometimes just *o* (as in *Mohn, Moos, Mode*)?
(15) Why do we say *gloves* in English but *Handschuhe* in German?
(16) Why do German adjectives come before their nouns, but French adjectives usually come after?

(17) Why does *Nicht Otto kommt* mean something different from
Otto kommt nicht ?

(18) Why does German have so many irregular verbs ?

(19) Why are some words inflected and others not ?

(5) demands a pragmatic explanation: the addressee either has to
justify or excuse himself; in (6) and (7) there is a problem-situation
concerning the momentary interests, motivation and grounds for
behaviour of a person A – but this is not a linguistic problem-situation.
Cases (8)–(10) are slightly different: here linguistic problems can arise.
We can generalize them thus: Why do we have to use excuses or
non-literal modes of speaking, and how are they to be understood ?
(11) refers to a normative assertion; so (in a somewhat different way)
does (12). In both cases the problem is already formulated generally,
without reference to observable linguistic phenomena.

In all the examples (13)–(19) we presuppose linguistic expressions,
their orthographic forms, their meanings, particular classifications or
even linguistic concepts like 'adjective' and 'inflected'; these 'why'-
questions are only indirectly connected with actual linguistic phenomena. (We might say that they assume general linguistic facts.) It is
obvious that questions requiring explanation in terms of linguistic
theory will be posed in this general way.

But behind all this there can be practical problems as well: How can
you teach orthography ? Can you get by without irregular verbs ? How
can I learn and teach the meaning of word-order distinctions ? And in
reference to questions (8)–(10): How can I recognize excuses ? Is it
necessary for me to behave ironically in certain situations ? And so on.

We can sum up this way: a linguistic problem or the demand for an
explanation in terms of linguistic theory must have a particular DEGREE
OF GENERALITY; we do not refer to an individual linguistic phenomenon,
in fact we often refer only indirectly to linguistic phenomena at all.
We do not expect or accept answers involving only individual motivations and biographical information; we presuppose concepts of linguistic
theory (even if only in colloquial form); we likewise presuppose normative assertions about proper linguistic behaviour: the explanations will
then refer to linguistic rules.

Questions (13)–(19) refer indirectly to linguistic phenomena. Let us
consider (17) for instance. This presupposes a set of unproblematical
facts: among others that utterances like *Nicht Otto kommt* and *Otto*

kommt nicht can be produced on occasion by speakers of German, that both types are comprehensible, but give rise to different expectations or reactions (e.g. *Who is coming instead of Otto?* in the first case, and *Then we'll be alone* in the second), that they will have different intonation contours, etc. Thus in case of misunderstanding we could clarify the essential difference and even, by means of an appropriate generalization, abstract specific rules for negative placement in German. These rules will be able to explain the semantic distinction between the two sentences, and also explain why the utterance of one or the other might be appropriate in a given situation.

Concrete linguistic events (phenomena in context) are thus made explainable by virtue of the fact that individual expressions, their combinations, intonation, orthography, meaning and function can be represented on another level by means of rules.

These rules must be understood as social rules, otherwise we could not call on them in practical situations for purposes of reproach, admonition, or justification. The linguist can assume that the normal speaker is capable of explanatory interventions of this kind, and thus also capable of the necessary generalization and abstraction. He cannot however assume that all such explanations will have the same result: the more generally a problem is put, the more individual judgements, if not controlled, can deviate from each other.

The concepts I have introduced can be summarized briefly:

LINGUISTIC PHENOMENON: perceptible (observable, directly experienceable, intuitively presentable) speech-sounds or written texts, the external constellations they appear in, the activities of speakers and hearers.

PRIMARY LINGUISTIC DATUM: a linguistic phenomenon established in a perceptual judgement and thereby already classified.

LINGUISTIC DISPOSITION: the tendency or ability of a person to produce particular linguistic phenomena and to recognize, understand, and react to them.

LINGUISTIC EVENT: a speech-sound or sequence in its context.

LINGUISTIC FACT: what can be or is actually established in generalizations about language (there are such and such rules, expressions, possibilities for communication, etc.).

LINGUISTIC DATUM IN THE WIDER SENSE: an established linguistic phenomenon or event, an established linguistic disposition or linguistic fact.

3.7   Concepts of explanation

In prescientific colloquial usage we can distinguish various non-pragmatic concepts of explanation:

1. A datum in the wider sense is explained if we can adduce another datum that counts as its CAUSE, OCCASION, SYMPTOM or DISPOSITION. An event A is the cause of an event B if there is a causal process that leads directly from *a* to *b*. An event A is an occasion for B if it triggers a causal process leading to B (e.g. because of the existence of a particular disposition). An event B is a symptom of the existence of a disposition C if there exists another event A that triggers a causal process leading to B. A disposition C exists if there are events A and B and A triggers a causal process leading to B.

These definitions can be applied only in a limited sense to the explanation of linguistic data, namely where we are concerned with the external or internal foundations.

We can then understand causal processes as physical, physiological or neurophysiological. We must therefore make two modifications, if we want to explain linguistic data in the wider sense:

(a) We must replace 'cause' by 'motivation'. For a speaker an event A can be the MOTIVATION for producing an event B (uttering something, carrying out a particular action): this is an action that follows conventional and intentional specifications (a state of interest, a goal-orientation and its social mediation).

(b) We must replace 'event' in many cases with 'fact'. We can then say for instance that a particular linguistic fact A is to be regarded as the cause of another linguistic fact B (we refer here to the causal processes of speech perception, linguistic localization, learning and retaining of linguistic abilities). Likewise we can say that a particular linguistic fact A can be regarded as the motivation for another linguistic fact B (in which case we refer to conventional and intentional performances).

2. A datum in the wider sense is explained if its GENESIS is established. This notion is largely built on the preceding one: e.g. if we make a collection of individual explanations in the above sense into a chain of explanations, or analyse such an explanation more precisely so that it becomes such a chain. This procedure is either purely systematic (a unified process is divided into various phases) or historical (in the sense that for each individual explanatory step we enlist further – independent – data: cf. Stegmüller 1969: 131). This conception of

'historical' embraces the history of an individual as well as the history of institutions, human groups and languages.

3. A datum or the connection between data is explained by adducing similar (known and familiar) data and connections. This can be called ANALOGICAL EXPLANATION. Stegmüller considers the claims for this type somewhat exaggerated, since it depends basically on a psychological effect, and therefore cannot count as a scientific explanation. He justifies his view as follows: familiarity with something is a purely subjective matter; the experience of familiarity may in fact be based on prejudice and be unable to stand the test of verification. Further, familiar things still require explanation: the hypothetical character that scientific explanations should have is obscured here. Given a strong interpretation of 'science' this is indeed partly justified. But on the other hand this view oversimplifies the way a science is established: prescientific and scientific explanatory possibilities are in fact interdependent. It is actually impossible, in establishing a science, not to rely on the familiar (though the familiar must be more than subjective: it must be guaranteed through the argumentative process by which the science itself develops). There is also at least an implicit hypothetical element even in the claim that we can rely on the familiar, and in the claim that we can set it up as an analogy to the unfamiliar.

Stegmüller also mentions explanations by means of ANALOGICAL MODELS. He considers them to be heuristically valuable for uncovering new laws and practically valuable in often being easier to handle. We often demand the same properties from theories; at least if we have to distinguish between two otherwise equally adequate theories, and if the theories are constructed with practical aims in mind. There is thus no principled distinction between theoretical explanation and the search for practically useful explanation.

4. A datum in the wider sense is explained if we can point to a general structural and functional connection between data such that it logically follows or at least can be made plausible that this datum (necessarily) is as it is. This is the type of explanation mainly pursued in the sciences.

3.8   The Hempel–Oppenheim schema

Many philosophers of science are of the opinion that all strict scientific explanations follow (or ought to follow) the schema for logical explanation proposed by Hempel and Oppenheim (cf. Hempel & Oppenheim 1948; Hempel 1965; Stegmüller 1969: 86ff.):

Explanans $\begin{cases} C_1, \ldots, C_n & \text{(sentences describing antecedent conditions)} \\ L_1, \ldots, L_r & \text{(general laws)} \end{cases}$

Explanandum E (description of event to be explained)

The following conditions should hold:

C–1. The argument leading from explanans to explanandum must be CORRECT. (In explanations of this type – called 'deductive-nomological' – the explanandum must be a LOGICAL consequence of the explanans.)

C–2. The explanans must contain at least ONE GENERAL LAW (or sentence from which a general law follows logically).

C–3. The explanans must have EMPIRICAL CONTENT.

C–4. The explanans sentences must be TRUE.

(In the case where it is laws that have to be explained, no antecedent conditions are necessary.)

In addition, scientific PREDICTIONS always have the same logical structure as scientific EXPLANATIONS; the only distinction is that in one case the temporal locus of the explanandum is the future, while in the other case it is the past.

If we want to use the Hempel–Oppenheim schema for linguistic explanations, we must – in the light of the preceding discussion – first make some alterations:

1. The term 'sentence' is to be understood basically in the sense of 'statement', i.e. what counts is the meaningful content.

2. The statements describing antecedent conditions are to be understood as data in the wider sense.

3. 'Event' in many cases is to be replaced by 'fact'.

4. 'General law' in many cases is to be replaced by 'description of a general rule' (if we take 'rules' as something that men follow intentionally and conventionally).

If we do this, however, we cannot distinguish clearly between the assertions C_i and L_i; for we have said that an established rule can also count as a datum in the wider sense. This problem in fact appears in a similar form in the natural sciences, in the distinction between data and natural laws.[1]

5. The truth-requirement in C–4 needs special discussion (see 5.4 below). In particular we have to clarify the sense in which one can say that the description of a rule is true. (It is no less necessary to clarify what we mean by saying that a general law is true, especially because laws are understood – even by Stegmüller – as hypotheses).

Dray (1957; cf. Stegmüller 1969: 379ff., esp. 384) has objected to the Hempel–Oppenheim schema on the grounds that it cannot handle what he considers an important explanatory type: RATIONAL explanation. A rational explanation asserts that a man's activity is rational, insofar as one accepts his goals and convictions as given (regardless of whether one accepts them as meaningful or not). According to Stegmüller, however, a rational explanation in Dray's sense can be represented by the following NORMATIVE RATIONALITY SCHEMA:

D (a) Person X found himself in a situation of type C.
   (b) In a situation of type C it is appropriate to
      do Y (...Y ought to be done).
_____
   (c) In the situation in which X found himself, it
      would have been appropriate to do Y (...X must have
      done Y).

Here the premiss (Db) is a normative assertion. Hempel and Stegmüller both deny that this schema can explain why person X acted in a particular way in the situation in question (we should add that the schema in fact explains only why it was appropriate for X to act in a particular way, and to this extent it furnishes a justification for X).[2] Hempel attempts to reformulate this so that it corresponds to the general explanatory schema; Stegmüller calls this version an APPROXIMATIVE RATIONALITY SCHEMA (1969: 396):

---

[1] Externally (i.e. linguistically) the distinction is easy: laws are general statements; data (e.g. observation-statements) are singular (existential) statements. General statements are not directly verifiable (at best they can only be inductively confirmed); singular existential statements are directly verifiable. But in terms of content the distinction is problematical, since even in existential statements we use general concepts; they can therefore not be made fully independent of individual general statements.

[2] Presumably we should replace 'would have been' in (Dc) by 'is', otherwise the schema would rather furnish grounds for rebuking X for not doing Y.

H   (a) Person X found himself in a situation of type C.
    (b) Person X was a rational agent.
    (c) In a situation of type C every rational agent
        will do Y.

    (d) Thus X did Y.

The distinctive difference between this and Dray's schema is that instead of the normative assertion (Db) we have the descriptive statement (Hc). In this reformulation we have to specify more precisely the class of men who follow a norm (here it will be defined as the class of rational agents). In addition Hempel adds the explicit premiss (Hb). A similar premiss ('X always acts appropriately') could in fact also be added to Dray's schema, and we would then likwise be able to conclude the statemenʈ (Hd).

We can obviously restate normative statements FORMALLY as descriptive ones. The norm lies then only in the word 'rational'. This means that as far as content goes the problem of verification is unchanged; we have the same difficulties with both formulations. We cannot establish by observation alone (from an extracommunicative standpoint) what a rational action is, and what every rational agent would do; this must rather be tested under practical conditions and learned or defined through explicit norms. Rationality is judged by the following of particular rules, which express particular explicit norms or implicit conventions, and generally have social meaning.

Since linguistic explanations often include reference to socially meaningful rules, they pose the same fundamental verification problem: we must refer to practical (linguistic) knowledge and experience IN communication situations. Even if we use the Hempel–Oppenheim schema in these explanations, we must not let this obscure the fact that our descriptive statements are to be understood either as reformulations of particular normative statements or as judgements of experience – which are not pure observational judgements.

In the Hempel–Oppenheim terminology, (Hb) must be understood as a cause of (Hd). For Hempel a person's rationality is in a wider sense a dispositional feature (comparable in fact to properties like 'magnetic' or 'breakable'). On this view, an explanation following the approximative rationality schema is a dispositional explanation.[1] For Hempel,

---

[1] According to Stegmüller (1969: 126), dispositional explanations have the following form: [cont. p. 81]

most explanations in the human sciences (especially psychology and sociology) come under this heading. Against this, however, Stegmüller claims that in many cases an agent's dispositions (e.g. his convictions) cannot be established in a conceptually comprehensive form; therefore the assumed type of explanation is in a strict sense impossible (cf. Stegmüller 1969: 415). This means that many 'dispositions' in this sense cannot be established precisely, since this would require precise test conditions and reactions. 'I perform particular actions' is clear, but the analysis of actions in terms of test conditions, reactions, and corresponding dispositions is not.

The reader will have noticed that the Hempel–Oppenheim schema for explanations is simply a special argumentation schema, in which we can dispense with the persons of the arguers (i.e. it is assumed that this kind of argument is universally valid). The explanans corresponds to the data and warrant in the Toulminian schema, the explanandum to the claim of an assertion. In addition, the warrant is assumed to be backed in a particular scientific context. If we understand an explanation as being concerned with the justification of an explanandum claim, then an explanation is produced just as soon as this is accepted – where 'acceptance' is to be understood in a particular objective sense, namely as measured by the standards of particular sciences. What is intended is not acceptance by some arbitrary persons, but the agreement of persons who accept or have learned particular standards. The standards of course do not have to be the same for all sciences, since not all sciences have the same problems; but the scientist does have to discover whether or not the standards of another science might also hold for him.

3.9 Explanatory adequacy in Chomsky

For Chomsky (in contrast to Hempel–Oppenheim and Stegmüller) the central question is not so much the possible form of a linguistic explanation, but rather how linguistic descriptions and explanations can be justified. Here he introduces the notion EXPLANATORY ADEQUACY OF A GRAMMATICAL THEORY.

In 3.5 above a grammatical theory was said to be explanatorily

A_1: a was in situation B.
A_2: a possesses the property D.
L: Every object that possesses the property D will
    react in the manner R in a situation of kind B.

E: a reacted in manner R.

adequate if on the basis of primary linguistic data it could select one descriptively adequate grammar from a set of alternative ones.[1] It is assumed that the given alternative grammars are compatible with the primary linguistic data (in the sense of descriptive adequacy). An explanatorily adequate grammatical theory must thus include an EVALUATION PROCEDURE FOR GENERATIVE GRAMMARS. Chomsky now requires that we specify a function m which assigns to each alternative grammar provided by the theory a natural number as its value (Chomsky 1965: 31); the higher this value, the greater the explanatory adequacy of the corresponding grammar.

Chomsky gives no more precise information about what this function m looks like and how it is to be established. Nevertheless there are further general discussions which suggest the direction in which explanatory adequacy (and thus in principle the evaluation-function m) is to be defined.

Each individual rule of a language, as well as the whole rule-system, has to be learned by speakers before they can control the rules. A particular group of speakers, assumed to be homogeneous,[2] can in this sense be said to follow uniformly a system of rules (in short, a linguistic

---

[1] The problem of assigning sets of relevant linguistic data to particular generative grammars is treated by Peters under the heading of the PROJECTION PROBLEM; he follows *inter alia* various pronouncements of Chomsky's on this theme (Peters 1972: 171–87). I will merely outline Peters' position briefly here, and otherwise concentrate on Chomsky's.

For Peters, the projection problem consists in providing a general schema for specifying a particular grammar or grammars that human beings can learn when confronted with a possible set of basic data (172). Let D_1, D_2, ... be a recursive enumeration of all sets D_i of basic data (or of representative corpora), and let G_1, G_2, ... be a recursive enumeration of formal grammars G_j of all possible natural languages (including all descriptively adequate grammars). Then we must specify a projection-function π (from the set of data-set indices onto the set of grammar indices) such that $j \in \pi$ (i) just in case there are human beings who can learn G_j if they are confronted with D_i (for any i, j – Peters 1972: 173). If there were a procedure for computing π, then this would be identical to a discovery procedure for grammars; a weaker requirement would be that we find an empirical evaluation for the specific proposed function π.

From this illustration it is clear that the projection-function (or in Chomsky's terminology the grammatical theory) must have empirical content. This raises three important questions: (a) What are the data-sets on the basis of which a language can be learned, and how are these to be formally enumerated? (b) How are the grammars of all possible languages to be formally enumerated? and (c) How is the condition that human beings learn grammars through confrontation with data-sets to be understood in detail, and what assumptions about the acquisition process do we need? These are extremely difficult questions. In order to obtain even an approximate answer we need rigorous constraints on the possible form of grammatical rules, and thus less freedom in the choice of the features of formal grammars (indeed, according to the principle that the FORM of a rule corresponds to its semantic function, i.e. is to be established on the basis of substantive considerations – Peters 1972: 183).

[2] For criticism of the homogeneity assumption, cf. 11.3 below.

system); we will define a part of this system more precisely and call it grammar. The individual generative grammars provided by the theory should serve to describe this grammar. It is clear that such a description can be adequate only if it agrees with our knowledge of how this grammar is learned – or better, how it can be learned. Let a generative grammar G_i describe particular linguistic rules in some form F; and let this form F entail that the linguistic rules in question (under normal conditions, over a few years at most) cannot be learned. Then G_i is inconsistent with the claim that grammars describe something that is actually learned. The grammar now does not reconstruct in any way the process of language-learning (let this be the general task of a theory of language acquisition); but it should (a) be compatible with the final RESULT OF LANGUAGE-LEARNING PROCESSES, and (b) accord with our knowledge (which is largely abstract and generalizing) about these processes – insofar as we have any. The evaluation-function operates on any specific generative grammar in both these ways.

This raises two problems:

1. If the evaluation-function for generative grammars is to express exclusively particular empirical facts (in relation to the class of all learnable languages), it would be reasonable to assume that grammatical theory must precisely enumerate those generative grammars that are the best; if however we demand only compatibility with empirical facts, there could be several equally highly-valued generative grammars (in practice this is usually the case: cf. Peters' examples, 1972: 180). If we are dealing with numerical values, we assume that the set of alternative generative grammars can be ranked along a value-scale. We do not permit varying evaluation-criteria, since otherwise there would have to be several scales. But criteria like complexity of a language, relatedness to other languages, universality of rules, details of learning processes, do not necessarily lead to the same evaluation. With the exception of a few attempts in phonology and morphology concerning the generalizability of rules (cf. Chomsky & Halle 1968; Matthews 1972), there have been no concrete proposals for an evaluation-function.

2. Generative grammars characterize the end-product of language-acquisition processes. If it is claimed that grammatical theory, in order to achieve explanatory adequacy, should consider evidence from language acquisition, then this can only be in the sense that the whole acquisition process is understood as instantaneous, with all the relevant data simultaneously available – and not as a multi-stage development

(cf. Chomsky & Halle 1968; Chomsky 1976). This assumes that the presentation of data, their temporal sequence, even the presentation of irrelevant or defective data, corrections, various presentation situations, etc., have no influence on the final result of the learning-process. This assumption itself is both empirical and problematical. (The relevance question is especially difficult: Which data are relevant, and how can the learner know? Is a particular frequency of use part of relevance? etc.) We could assume, for example, that given different sequences of data-presentation, learners would internalize different grammars.

Chomsky now develops two ideas, in order to meet at least the second problem. The first – which is in fact an old one – is an ANALOGY: that THE PROCESS OF LEARNING A LANGUAGE ESSENTIALLY CORRESPONDS TO THE PROCESS OF DEVELOPING A THEORY OF THIS LANGUAGE (cf. Chomsky 1965: 25). Just as in the case of a theory it is the results that are interesting, and not how the theory came about, so in language-acquisition only the result is interesting. More specifically, the analogy means that a child has at his disposal, on the basis of his perceptions, a quantity of primary data (which may include corrections of his own utterances by his mother or others); from these he must be able, within a few years, to develop the complete language-system, including the grammar. To do this he needs specific abstracting and generalizing procedures, which he utilizes actively and in reference to already given basic theoretical principles and patterns. This has a certain similarity to the scientific process that leads to the formation of theories.[1]

But we should be careful of pushing such similarities too far: (a) Chomsky for the most part bases his empirical arguments not on perceptual judgements (which one must assume for the child), but on his own knowledge of linguistic facts. He elucidates what he already commands intuitively, while a child first has to develop a knowledge of linguistic rules (i.e. reconstruct what others command). (b) In develop-

---

[1] This analogy permits the systematically ambiguous use of notions like 'grammar', 'linguistic theory', 'rule', etc., referred to above: grammar for Chomsky is both a system of linguistic rules which human beings have learned and follow (a construct of human beings who know a language), as well as a system for describing such linguistic rules (a construct of scientists). I use 'grammar' here exclusively in the first sense, as against 'generative grammar', 'categorial grammar', etc., which I use exclusively in the second sense. This does not, to be sure, prevent all possible misunderstandings, but it does have the advantage of allowing me to follow Chomsky's usage at least to some degree while avoiding conceptual ambiguity. I treat 'rule' in the same way (a 'linguistic rule' is something that men follow in their everyday life; 'substitution rule', 'transformational rule', etc., are prescriptions for scientific activities or relations that scientists set up); while 'linguistic theory' is reserved solely for scientific constructs.

ing theories the scientist uses a fully developed language that he himself already commands – often a standardized or even formalized language – while the child does not yet command any language at all, but has to learn one.

On the other hand Chomsky's analogy allows us to see the scientific processes of classification, abstraction and deduction as not fundamentally different from our normal everyday activities. Scientific activities merely follow more powerful and conscious principles, and are finer and more highly differentiated. Beyond this, Chomsky's analogy could lead to a rethinking of the relation between theory and its subject matter (for Chomsky the subject matter of linguistic theory is already 'theory'): this relationship does not have to be one of description, but could also be explication or reconstruction (cf. chapter 7 below). Further, the contention that linguistics is not a science that DESCRIBES empirical facts could be based precisely on this point of Chomsky's: if a human language-system is already a theory, then the linguist's work would consist primarily of the reconstruction of a pre-existent theory. But in this case, as I have argued, the work would be only partially achieved; for the linguist would still have to show how human beings, operating with a linguistic system, use it to regulate their daily lives and to understand their experiences, actions, etc. We must therefore demonstrate the empirical–theoretical character of a linguistic system with reference to everyday communication; and this can only succeed, I think, if linguistic theory itself is taken as an empirical theory. It is only by taking an abstract syntax as the centre of a linguistic system (as Chomsky does), and largely neglecting the physiological–physical conditions and the meaning-constructive side of language, that grammar can be seen as not tied to experience and simply as a system of formal constraints; a theory of grammar, therefore, simply represents such formal constraints on the combinatorial possibilities of linguistic units.

Chomsky's works provide few considerations of this kind on the methodological consequences of the analogy between scientific theory and language systems (as 'everyday theory'). While he obscures the difference between theory and its subject matter terminologically, he re-establishes it with notions like 'observational adequacy' and 'descriptive adequacy'; but this is only an adaptation to the usual usage of the empirical sciences, and not a genuine distinction, since he does not clarify the precise empirical sense of 'observation' and 'description'.

Chomsky's second idea is already partly contained in the first: the child develops his own grammar on the model of the grammars that are followed by those he communicates with (elders, playmates, etc.); but the child uses A PRIORI THEORETICAL PRINCIPLES to do this, just as the scientist does.[1] Every child is born with a disposition to acquire a language – not a specific one of course, but any language at all (namely the one in his environment). This inborn disposition (Chomsky speaks in a quasi-Cartesian sense of 'innate ideas') is identical with the general human capability for language. According to Chomsky, it corresponds to 'UNIVERSAL GRAMMAR', as the class of all grammars that human beings are capable of learning. The language-learning process leads from the total set of perceived linguistic data to a restriction to exactly one grammar (out of this class) and the elimination of all other initially possible grammars.

Here the second problem is eliminated in a radical way: the evaluation of generative grammars is not done on the basis of any knowledge about the language-learning process, but on the basis of a HYPOTHESIS ABOUT THE PRECONDITIONS FOR LANGUAGE-LEARNING PROCESSES, namely some 'universal grammar' or set of innate dispositions.[2]

A theory of grammar is explanatorily adequate if it refers appropriately to this universal grammar. In this way a very abstract hypothesis, divorced from any observational possibilities (and thus very difficult either to verify or falsify), is presented as the proper explanatory hypothesis.

If we now try to reconstruct Chomsky's notion of explanation in the framework outlined by Hempel and Oppenheim, we can get first the two schemata (A) and (B), according to the twofold notion of grammar (as the innate grammar of the child, and as the linguist's grammar):

(A)   Explanans

The child's primary linguistic data
$D = \{A_1, ..., A_n\}$
Universal grammar $\Sigma = \{G_1, ..., G_r\}$

Explanandum

G_i (that grammar which is best compatible with the given data – there may be several such grammars)

---

[1] Chomsky developed this idea mainly in polemics against behaviourist learning theory (cf. his review of Skinner 1957: Chomsky 1957a). He tried to show that this theory cannot explain how a child can reconstruct a system as complex as a grammar in a few years on the basis only of primary data.

[2] The connection with the evaluation measure mentioned above can perhaps be seen this way: the RESULT of an instantaneous learning-process is fully derivable from the PRECONDITIONS for language-learning processes, together with a set of primary data; but the individual phases of the learning-process are not derivable.

(B)   Explanans

The linguist's linguistic data

$D = \{A_1, ..., A_n\}$

Universal generative grammar

$g\Sigma = \{gG_1, ... gG_r\}$

Explanandum gG_i

These schemata do not correspond to the requirements of Hempel and Oppenheim: the explanandum is not an event but a grammar (i.e. at best a general law, or, according to the alterations I have introduced, the description of a complex general rule); in this case, however, there did not have to be any antecedent conditions, whereas (A) and (B) include linguistic data. (It is problematical, by the way, whether the Hempel–Oppenheim schema is applicable to the explanation of general laws (or rules).)

We can get another explanation schema if we consider the explanandum of (B) as a hypothetical law (or rule) that has explanatory force in itself. We can then say that an individual linguistic datum A_j (which is not already included in the given data) is explained by a generative grammar if it can be derived as follows:

(C)   Explanans

Linguistic data $D' = \{A_1, ..., A_m\}$

Generative grammar gG_i

Explanandum A_j

For Chomsky, however, the generative grammar in such a case would be only descriptively adequate, unless it has itself already been proved to be explanatorily adequate. Thus Chomsky's notions of explanatory and descriptive adequacy coincide with the single Hempel–Oppenheim notion of explanation. Even if we accept the schema (C) it is not clear how we should interpret it. Weydt (1975), for instance, has proposed interpreting the explanans data as some given utterance-tokens, and the explanandum datum as the reaction of an informant (rejection or acceptance). This would certainly correspond with the requirements of Hempel and Oppenheim, but what we should like to explain is not so much the reaction of an informant but rather a particular linguistic phenomenon or event that has been produced under normal circumstances.

The schemata (A) and (B) above are fully analogous. In the case of (B) there must be as part of the universal generative grammar some evaluation-procedure for establishing the highest degree of compatibility of the chosen generative grammar gG_i. To expound the analogy, Chomsky now extends his innateness hypothesis: the child also must already have an evaluation-measure at his disposal, so that he can establish that certain grammars are to be excluded on the basis of the primary data, and determine which of the remaining ones is most compatible with them. Thus the analogy is complete; every human being is assumed to have an evaluation-measure just like the one the scientist uses in his theoretical activity.

Leaving aside the difficulty of fitting Chomsky's notion of explanation into the notion common to most theories of science, the main substantial problem with schemata (A) and (B) is the notion of universal grammar they employ:

1. Universal grammar cannot be the class of all grammars that human beings can learn, since the human being also learns the specific features of a specific language, and these are *per definitionem* not universal. On the basis of universal grammar, every individual grammar is determined only with respect to its necessary features (those common to all languages), but not its sufficient features (those specific to this language or group of languages). Therefore the language-acquisition process cannot properly consist in the selection of an innate language from a large class of languages.

2. If under the rubric of universal grammar we wish to understand only the class of all features common to languages as a whole, the use of the term 'grammar' is misleading:

(a) It suggests that there are human beings who communicate by means of universal grammar (which is dubious if we consider that communicative exigencies are specific, not universal).

(b) It could be supposed that this grammar guarantees the inter-translatability of languages. But *per definitionem* universal grammar does not include the specific features of individual languages, and thus cannot guarantee translatability.

3. In order to use the universal grammar (or better LANGUAGE UNIVERSALS) hypothesis in an explanatory schema, we must give it some empirical meaning. There are three methodological approaches to this:

(a) An *a priori* theoretical speculation on the conditions of human communication and the structure necessary in principle for means of communication. Such reflections are transcendental in the sense that they are not directly based on empirical research, but can precede it (in any case they transcend its results).[1]

---

[1] Habermas' sketch of dialogue-building universals (1971), for instance, belongs to this class, as do other linguistic–philosophical studies: cf. e.g. Schnelle (1973a: ch. 1).

(b) Investigations of many (genetically, sociogeographically, typologically) different languages, in connection with the search for generalizations.[1] In this case the language universals hypothesis is meaningful only if it is applied to hitherto unknown languages; since if a particular language has already been taken into account it is self-evident that this hypothesis is already applicable to it.

(c) The acquisition of independent empirical knowledge about the human substrates of language capability: memory, perceptual abilities, articulatory organs, thought, human social action, etc. While in case (b) above there is no immediate reason for tracing the universal properties of languages back to innate dispositions, here this is quite possible. Indeed, this does not prove that all these dispositions must show a unitary organization (beyond the fact that every normal person has them all together); consequently the use of the term 'universal grammar' in this connection is also entirely out of place.

In what follows the aprioristic-transcendental formulation will not be considered, and we can then specify two areas of importance for determining the explanatory adequacy of a linguistic and grammatical theory:

1. Determining language universals on the basis of the investigation of various languages (as hypotheses that can be tested by means of additional languages).

2. Determining whether statements in linguistic and grammatical theory are compatible with statements in INDEPENDENTLY developed theories: we can use these theories in evaluation. For example, the theory of language-acquisition in my opinion is just such an independently available theory.

All these theories can also contain statements about innate human dispositions of one kind or another; so to this extent we can take up Chomsky's claim that explanatory adequacy has to refer to such dispositions. Only we can hardly use these dispositions directly in a simple form like 'innate ideas' for the evaluation of linguistic theories: this must take place through the mediation of the individual theories. The evaluation of a particular empirical theory can be considered here as well: it must be in agreement with other empirical theories. Only in this way can we guarantee that our knowledge as a whole is free of contradiction.

---

[1] In this connection see the Stanford University Universals Project Publications (*Working Paper in Language Universals*), and Greenberg (1963).

3.10   Model of a linguistic system

We have up to this point used a rather imprecise notion of grammar. Every grammar is a system of procedures that the speaker of a language uses (or follows) in various communicative situations. Particular utterances (phonic or graphic patterns) carry meanings relative to an existing situation, especially with regard to its continuation. It is therefore important that the speaker be able to distinguish typical and atypical features of utterances and situations together; by typical I mean, among other things, expected and (under the given circumstances) capable of being carried out. The speaker and hearer understand concrete utterances as realizations of sentences (or sentence-like expressions, sentence-sequences, etc.) of a language, i.e. as arrangements of lexical units in particular constructions. The lexical units in each case have a particular phonological structure and a particular meaning (in the sense both of factual reference and relation to other meanings). Correspondingly, sentences also have phonological structures and meanings, which among other things derive from the lexical units and their formal arrangement and modification (e.g. inflexion). The meaning of typical utterances in a given typical situation arises *inter alia* from the meaning of the uttered sentences. I will discuss this notion of meaning in more detail in chapter 9; here I will only note that we have to distinguish between designations (direct factual reference) and conceptual meanings (often called intensions).

The notions 'understand as', 'have phonological structure and meaning', 'derive from' are in each case to be understood in such a way that we are dealing with particular socially valid conventions, which we can reconstruct in the form of rules. We can identify a linguistic system as a whole with a system of rules which operate on certain units and allow the possible manifestations (utterances) of the language in question to be produced and understood. To begin with, I make no assumptions about the form of these rules; I assume only that some of them can be grouped in specific subclasses, because they operate on similar elements; in each process of utterance or understanding, in general, we require rules from each of these subclasses. We can summarize this in the MODEL OF A LINGUISTIC SYSTEM (figure 3).

A certain part of a linguistic system can be called its GRAMMATICAL SYSTEM, namely that structure which does not contain the components 'Situational meanings' and 'Utterance-tokens/Phonetic structures';

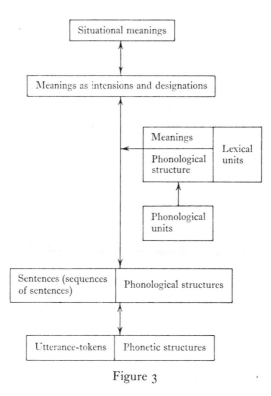

Figure 3

but I will not adhere strictly to this usage. It is necessary to keep it in mind, however, if we want to compare this scheme with Chomsky's SCHEMA FOR THE COMPONENTS OF A GRAMMAR (figure 4).

According to Chomsky, the LINGUISTIC COMPETENCE of speakers and hearers resides in the fact that they make use of a grammatical system; the central part of this is a syntax (rules for generating base structures, filling these with lexical units to produce deep structures, transformational rules for converting deep structures into surface structures); semantic and phonological structures are obtained by interpretation of syntactic structures. The utilization of competence results in situations of action and utterance (performance).

There are two fundamental criticisms of this schema (cf. also the comments in Bartsch & Vennemann 1972: 6–10):

1. There is no basic schematic coordination of phonological and semantic structures – which we should expect, as a characterization of the interpretability of sound patterns and the realizability of meanings.

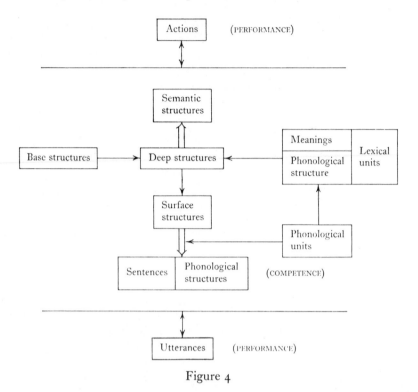

Figure 4

Instead of this we have 'in the middle' a basis of abstract and at first purely formal SYNTACTIC STRUCTURES. These structures are to be interpreted both phonologically and semantically,[1] i.c. they EXPRESS SIMULTANEOUSLY THE FORMAL CONSTRAINTS ON BOTH THE PHONIC AND SEMANTIC ASPECTS OF LANGUAGE. The transition from phonological to semantic structures is stated only indirectly. In addition there is the methodological problem of whether the primary focus should be meanings or sounds. This problem is the source of the deep structure/ surface structure distinction: the former is oriented toward possible meanings, the latter toward possible arrangements of words.

The realization of the grammatical model in the work of Chomsky and his followers shows clearly that the latter is always dominant: there is a separate phonological theory attached to grammatical theory, where

[1] 'Interpretation' here is to be taken in the theoretical sense: giving a formal structure a concrete meaning. This must be distinguished from the interpretation of sound patterns (which are already concrete).

the possible sound structures of a language are worked out (partly in reference to their phonetic realization); a semantic theory is envisioned, but mainly in principle, without really being developed. There are indeed a few attempts to take syntactic deep structures or something very like them as semantic representations (e.g. in the work of the so-called generative semanticists like Lakoff, McCawley, etc.); but this is not Chomsky's view; all of these proposals are based on familiar developments in logic (cf. chapters 5, 9 below).

Taking syntax as a point of departure has consequences for the notion of language universals: if men innately possess the principles for organizing language in the process of acquisition, these are for Chomsky primarily syntactic principles, and not perceptual, intellectual and social-behavioural dispositions, which are later integrated at a particular stage in the child's development. For Chomsky the unity of all factors relevant to speech and understanding is given at birth (and this unity is grounded in syntax); therefore all these principles can be collected under the heading of universal grammar.

2. Chomsky maintains a STRICT SEPARATION OF COMPETENCE AND PERFORMANCE. Though he claims to represent a natural and partly innate human capability, he makes an abstraction from all processes of expression and understanding, which amounts to an effective denial of any direct psychological interpretation of competence. It remains unclear how and in what context this abstract linguistic competence is relevant for human communicative behaviour, and what results (if any) from psycholinguistic and acquisition research could be brought to bear on the evaluation of a grammatical theory.[1]

3.11 Language universals

I turn now to the language universals hypothesis. Universals serve to effect a general characterization of human language ability, and are therefore a primary subject for general linguistic and grammatical theory.[2] The development of this theory, however, must also be oriented toward individual languages. We must follow two complementary lines of inquiry:

---

[1] LINGUISTIC COMPETENCE for Chomsky is a theoretical construct and not an actual property or capability of human beings. But the question still remains as to how this construct can be understood in relation to human properties and capabilities, and the perception and observation of human communicative behaviour.

[2] For general information see Greenberg (1963), especially the 'Memorandum concerning language universals'; for a more sophisticated discussion see Lieb (1975).

(a) What are the consequences for general linguistic theory of the fact that particular phenomena occur in particular languages ?

(b) What are the consequences of the assumption of specific universals for the description and explanation of individual phenomena and facts in individual languages ?

A distinction is often drawn between formal and substantive universals. FORMAL UNIVERSALS characterize the forms of possible linguistic systems, while SUBSTANTIVE UNIVERSALS characterize their content. The first hold necessarily and unconditionally for all languages at all historical periods, while the second do not have to be present in all languages; but if they are present in a particular language, then they are so only under specific conditions, i.e. the language must simultaneously display certain other properties. It follows from this that languages do not have to be intertranslatable at all stages of their existence, e.g. if language A has the substantive universal U, but language B does not; correspondingly B might have the substantive universal V, while A has nothing corresponding. Each language thus utilizes only a part of the total set of possible structures.[1] But each can be extended, in the sense that it can adopt a larger part of the set of possible structures, so that intertranslatability could be achieved between languages A and B.

We can imagine stronger formulations of the substantive universals hypothesis;[2] thus we could assume that a particular set of structures is actually present in all languages, or even that certain central structures (e.g. Chomsky's deep structures)[3] are actually present in all languages at all historical periods. This second assumption – according to the proposed relationship between deep structures and semantic representations – would perhaps imply the actual intertranslatability of all languages; we should therefore be somewhat sceptical about it.[4] In addition, it contradicts the view that not only do languages show substantive differences from one another, but also individual languages

---

[1] We understand substantive universals here as substantive STRUCTURES (in the same way as we talk of semantic structures beside phonological ones). They are thus not isolated properties, like individual sounds or word-meanings, but always clusters of properties in mutual relations (e.g. if a language has voiced obstruents it will have voiceless ones; if there is an expression for marking the speaker, then there is always one for the addressee, etc.).

[2] These are discussed by Kanngiesser (1972: 120–8, 140–1).

[3] Chomsky's notion of universal grammar is perhaps to be understood in this sense.

[4] Naturally translations are often possible if we choose particular paraphrases; but we are then very often dealing with other underlying deep structures.

show substantive internal differences (and not only on the lexical level), which is one of the main reasons why languages change.

The FORMAL UNIVERSALS hypothesis is closely tied up with the possible structures of descriptive systems for languages (whereas the substantive universals hypothesis is connected rather with the possible structures of explanatory systems); what is necessarily true for every language should be reflected in the manner in which all languages are described. It must be emphasized that on this view the FORM OF THEORIES (e.g. descriptive systems for individual languages) is not a matter of arbitrary choice, but in itself expresses a testable EMPIRICAL HYPOTHESIS in relation to language universals.[1] The proposed formal universals are therefore nearly always oriented toward particular linguistic and grammatical theories and their concepts, precisely in the sense that even the forms of these theories have empirical content.

Given this interpretation, the concepts that Bloomfield (1926) introduced into his axiomatization of linguistics (morpheme, word, phoneme, sentence, constructional meaning, form-class, etc.) can be taken as expressing formal universals. The same is true of the distinctive features in Jakobson's (or Chomsky and Halle's) phonological theory – insofar as they are understood as points in feature-matrices for the characterization of sound-sequences;[2] of the form and existence of transformations in Chomsky's theory, or of extension-rules in Kanngiesser; of the principle of cyclic rule-application in transformational grammar; of the form and existence of serialization rules in Bartsch and Vennemann, etc.[3] We already have a formal universal in the general assumption that phonological structures are always understood as temporal, whereas semantic or cognitive structures are time-independent (it is only the cognitive processes operating on these structures that occur in real time), and in the assumption that we can distinguish hierarchically interrelated levels in semantics that are gradually disassembled in the transition to phonological structures (the principle of serialization). We also assume formal universals when we

[1] This view is opposed to that of many philosophers of science, who consider the form of empirical scientific theories to be irrelevant: theories are to be selected according to particular goals and relations to observational concepts (i.e. it is primarily the relation to observational concepts that has empirical content).

[2] Against this, any alphabet of distinctive features, together with their relationships, must be taken as a set of substantive universals (cf. Jakobson & Halle 1956; Chomsky & Halle 1968).

[3] Chomsky (1957a: 34–48); Kanngiesser (1972: 106, 110, 114, 118); Chomsky (1972: 24ff.; on cyclical application); Bartsch & Vennemann (1972: 118ff.).

distinguish exocentric and endocentric constructions, or argument–predicate and operator–operand relations.

SUBSTANTIVE UNIVERSALS are to be assumed primarily in phonetics/phonology and semantics. This conjecture is based on the one hand on the fact that human articulatory and perceptual capabilities are organically determined, and on the other hand by the fact that possible sentence-meanings are determined by general human intellectual and perceptual structures. This holds for possible lexical structures as well, though not for the individual words or morphemes of a language: since the verbal concepts necessary for a speech-community depend on its characteristic modes of production, its culture, etc., and not on the general biological and social conditions of human life.

If substantive universals are assumed on the syntactic level, this is always with reference to the connection with possible meanings. Classifications are often proposed in which languages are grouped as belonging e.g. to SVO or SOV types (where S = 'subject', O = 'object' and V = 'verb'). This assumes that all languages can have sentence structures that incorporate S, O and V.

Such motivations based on human activity are of course not compelling, and many linguists reject them. Similarly the cases posited by Fillmore (1968, 1971), insofar as they are taken as substantive universals, are semantically motivated by reference to the fact that certain further differentiations in the description of activities, processes or circumstances are needed. The set of possible cases will not of course be utilized by all languages in the same way; but this is also true, analogously, for the set of possible phonological features.[1]

Let us now return briefly to the two language-system schemata introduced in 3.10. The first schema represented the EXTERNAL AND INTERNAL BOUNDARY-CONDITIONS which control the possibility and need for speech; a grammatical procedure connects the external conditions (what sounds can one produce that are both perceptible and discriminable by the hearer?) with the internal ones (in what situations will it be necessary to mediate what intentions and information?). All substantive universals are imposed on languages by these boundary-conditions. Thus even individual linguistic phenomena and facts can be explained by reference to them; we can evaluate a linguistic or grammatical theory according to independently constructed theories of these conditions. On the phonological level we have available a relatively good theory of

---

[1] It is not clear anyhow whether the set of possible cases is to be taken as finite.

this kind in physiological, articulatory and auditory phonetics (which are drawn on to some extent in recent phonological theory, especially that of Chomsky and Halle); nothing like this can be said for semantics. As we have seen, logic, theory of action and psychology alone are not sufficient (and considering the demands of linguistics, even they are in a primitive state of development); we also need theory of socialization, theory of institutions, etc. The interdisciplinary context in which linguistics must develop thus results from its subject matter, and the notion that linguistic EXPLANATIONS presuppose knowledge of the boundary-conditions on human language (cf. the discussion of this problem in 1.6 above).

In Chomsky's schema and its developments, on the other hand, only the phonological boundary-conditions are considered; and this is one-sided, since syntactic structures are only INTERPRETED phonologically. The schema itself already incorporates a hypostasis of the concept of syntax, since this is understood as the creative centre of a linguistic system, and totally removed from the proper task of syntax, namely the constitution of procedural connections between sound-patterns and sense-patterns (meanings). Still further, we find a hypostasis in the very place where the explanatory adequacy of a theory is determined: here a hypothesis of innate universal grammar is introduced, which I suspect can be neither falsified nor confirmed empirically. Hypotheses should not be judged only according to how speculative or abstract they are, but according to whether they can open the way to new empirical research.[1]

[1] In the form in which Peters gives the hypothesis (namely as a problem of projecting between sets of primary data and grammars), it is less speculative. But at the same time Peters' discussion makes clear that this hypothesis allows for too much freedom, so that he seems himself led to the conclusion that possible grammars must be constrained on the grounds of further substantive considerations. This corresponds to my insistence on more detailed consideration of the boundary-conditions for speech and understanding.

4 *Abstraction and deduction*

The relation between empirical observation and description and theory is often defined in terms of INDUCTION and DEDUCTION. These complementary inferential procedures are characteristic of scientific argumentation. Induction leads from individual phenomena and facts to limited hypotheses, and from them to more inclusive hypotheses about possible new expected phenomena and facts. It eventually permits theory-construction, at least in the limited sense of systematic collection and generalization of individual hypotheses. Deduction is in principle the reverse, i.e. the derivation of individual hypotheses from a presupposed theory. A refutation of one of these individual hypotheses is a refutation of the relevant part of the theory, which is thus shown at least to require partial correction. Conversely, if the derived hypotheses are not falsified, the theory is still usable – even if we cannot say with any certainty that it will not be refuted later by new facts.

The transitions from individual hypotheses to theories and vice versa are not without their problems: individual hypotheses refer directly to statements of phenomena and facts (which as we have seen are already partly theoretical); while theories always refer only indirectly to such statements. In order to get from individual hypotheses to a theoretical construct or vice versa, we have to re-coordinate and adjust our concepts appropriately: in Carnap's terms, the concepts of the observation-language must correspond to concepts of another kind in the theoretical language, and vice versa. In linguistics this raises the question of whether the concepts used in data in the wider sense (statements of facts not deriving immediately from perception) should already be considered theoretical. The answer to this is probably yes; but we must always establish clearly what level of abstraction our theories are operating on, and modify the answer from case to case.[1]

[1] Cf. the levels of abstraction in the examples in 4.3 and 4.4 below. Many of these concepts are indeed theoretical in character, but are not explicitly connected to any particular theory: these 'pretheoretical' concepts require explication. On conceptual explication see 7.4 below.

The 'theoretical language'/'observation-language' distinction is not absolute; it is always possible to theoretize part of a given observation-language and coordinate it with the concepts of another observation-language. As I pointed out earlier, even the simplest concepts used for describing perception are already (pre)theoretically controlled.[1]

In what follows I will concentrate on a few components of inductive procedure – mainly the role of (stepwise) abstraction. In connection with this we must also consider the implications of a precise consideration of deduction for the form of theories and the statements derivable from them (cf. chs. 5–6). We must also clarify the relation of deduction to the requirement that theories be explanatory; and finally answer the question: in what sense and to what extent can proposals for action be based on theories? We will also consider the axiomatization of theories: Can we fix theoretical statements precisely in relation to one another? Does this protect us from errors and misunderstandings? Can theories be uniquely evaluated with respect to empirical adequacy? And do theories deliver new knowledge, i.e. is it appropriate to use them as means of knowing?

4.1 Induction

Several distinct aspects of the construction of knowledge are usually conflated under this heading.[2] They all necessarily presuppose particular goals; this allows us to determine what points of view are relevant and will therefore decide how the induction is to proceed. It is impossible to specify any strict procedures for induction, even when we have formulated the goal precisely: approximative procedures (e.g. statistical ones) are certainly conceivable, but only in reference to the second of the components to be mentioned below. Further, we must stress that induction is already part of the everyday construction of knowledge, and thus is not uniquely characteristic only of scientific procedures. I take the following as components of induction:[3]

[1] I will discuss the relation between theoretical and observational concepts more fully in 6.4 below. I will consider Carnap's position and criticize it on particular points (e.g. in regard to the search for an absolute demarcation between theoretical and observation languages). The concept of OBSERVATION-LANGUAGE turns up in the literature in two forms: (a) it is the everyday language in which we formulate observations; it therefore also contains some concepts that occur in theories (and which might better be called pretheoretical); (b) it is itself a formal (or formalizable) language, and we can establish exact criteria for using it; the criteria depend partly on the theory in question.

[2] I will not go into the extensive philosophical and epistemological literature on the concept of induction. See for instance Kutschera (1972: ch. 2, §5: 189–251).

[3] Each of the terms used refers both to a particular kind of activity and to its result. These are conceptually distinct, but methodologically should be treated together: the

1. ABSTRACTION
2. CLASSIFICATORY GENERALIZATION
3. HYPOTHETICAL ASSUMPTIONS.

The central concept is abstraction. This is in fact already involved in perpetual processes, which means that the possibility of induction is itself already established there. We use classificatory generalizations to extend the domain of our knowledge. We speak of generalizations if for instance we draw conclusions about all languages (or possible language universals) from the study of individual languages; but here there is a hypothetical and abstractive factor as well: we go beyond the observations of individual languages, and disregard their individual particularities. Thus the domain of any true generalization is not restricted to finitely many subjects, and this gives it a necessarily hypothetical character. Hypotheses can also be contained in formulations like

It could be the case that...

Let us assume that it is the case that...

We must then ask:

What are these assumptions based on?

What follows from them?

A theory as a whole can be regarded as a global hypothesis; thus the central question is that of CONSEQUENCES: what can be derived from the theory; what follows logically from it; is this compatible with our experience and factual knowledge or not?[1] For justificatory purposes the answer to this question is more important than (say) the answer to 'How did we arrive at this theory?' – since we can arrive at theories through fantasy, intuition and spontaneous inspiration, which can scarcely be 'justified' in the usual sense. (This is why there are no strict inductive procedures, but at best procedures for testing the results of an induction.)

activities are related to their results, and the results belong to particular activities. As long as we refer to everyday perceptions, descriptions, etc., we are dealing with the individual's cognitive-psychic activities. They are at least a partial model for the development of the scientist's systematic activities – though these latter are more objective and theoretically directed: i.e. we are dealing in this case not with the cognitive activities of an individual person (which are of no interest for the result of a research programme), but with systematized operational activities.

[1] For critical purposes it is often demanded that we reflect on the ASSUMPTIONS of a theory before we use the theory itself. It is questionable whether this is generally possible. The explicit assumptions are given in the answer to the first question (what are these assumptions based on?); but the implicit assumptions involved can only be discovered if we examine the implications and consequences of the theory, i.e. if we treat it to begin with as an assumption. In this sense 'reflection on the assumptions of a theory' is nothing more than 'examination of the consequences of assuming the theory'. It is precisely the critic of particular theories who cannot avoid examining their consequences in just this way.

4.2 Abstraction

It has often been pointed out that notions like 'language' or 'linguistic knowledge' (as compared for instance to primary linguistic perceptions) are products of higher degrees of abstraction – let us say that they mean the cognitive abilities behind linguistic concepts (manifested in learning processes), linguistic rules or the facts that go into linguistic rules (combinations of expressions, their possible meanings, etc.). Because of this the linguist has to ask questions like: To what extent should he assume these abstractions? Should he reconstruct them theoretically? Should he, in his scientific work, abstract appropriate goals totally independently of them? Should he assume or reconstruct abstracting ACTIVITIES or only their RESULTS, while he assumes products of a different degree of abstraction and connects these to one another solely through logical (abstraction) relations? There is no single answer to these questions: it depends on the coverage and particular goals a linguistic theory aims at. Certainly every linguistic theory has to take at least some account of abstractions as capabilities of natural-language speakers and hearers; thus it either assumes them or at least reconstructs their results, i.e. relates statements about languages to statements about linguistic knowledge and its attainment.

Many traditional grammatical theories confine themselves to treating language on a single level of abstraction, and thus skirt the abstraction problem itself; but the procedures of American structuralism, for instance, which can be taken as inductive procedures for theory-construction, can be interpreted as simultaneously reconstructing certain abstracting abilities of speakers and hearers.[1] The idea that levels of abstraction have to be identified is also laid out explicitly in Chomsky's theory of transformational grammar: syntactic deep structure characterizes a level more abstract than that of the surface forms of sentences, and even more so than that of utterances; though this level is not described as the result of abstractions, but as depending on inborn dispositions.[2] Some of Chomsky's followers adopt a particular interpretation

---

[1] This interpretation can be found in the work of various linguists (e.g. Hockett). It is also what Chomsky is thinking of when he turns his criticism of behaviourist learning theory against the procedures of the American structuralists, and criticizes their methodology on the grounds that it cannot explain how anyone is able to learn a language.

[2] The criticism of Chomsky's notion of 'innate ideas' could now be accommodated by saying that it is not the case that a more abstract level is given at birth, but only the disposition to construct such levels for the organization of speech and understanding.

of the abstractness of deep structures, where this means at the outset that the level of concern is semantic.[1] This interpretation however has no real content, since for the speaker the meanings of utterances often refer to fully concrete and particular practical situations; particular expressions describe things in their perceptual environments, etc., and these things are at least as concrete as the sound-patterns themselves, which they understand as expressions of a language. It is not the meanings themselves (compared to the sound-patterns) that are abstract, but rather the organization of the relation between sound-patterns and semantic structures (i.e. the syntactic processes) that is abstract in comparison to sounds or meanings.

Every abstracting activity involves a number of closely interconnected factors, which I shall specify under three headings (on this and what follows cf. Klix 1971: 593ff.):

1. ISOLATION
2. COMPRESSION (TYPIFICATION AND INTENSIONAL GENERALIZATION)
3. IDEALIZATION.

1. ISOLATION takes place on the sensory as well as cognitive levels. Significant features are singled out, insignificant ones ignored. What counts as significant or insignificant depends on one's orientation at the time. In the case of speech perception Bühler already tried to show, with his PRINCIPLE OF ABSTRACTIVE RELEVANCE, that the perception of individual sounds is governed by their meaning-discriminating function within a language-system (1965: 42ff.). Within methodology we can treat isolation as a conscious procedure: we separate out (often step by step) the factors irrelevant to the problem, and from this we get a collection of factors that can lead to a more inclusive theory. If a linguist wants to confine himself to so-called 'clear cases', this demands considerable isolation.[2]

The existence of clear cases furnishes an argument for making a distinction between them and unclear cases. But the boundaries often remain vague, i.e. there are unclear cases where various factors are intimately mixed, and where the disregarding of any particular factor (in order to refer the case in question to one or another group of clear cases) is arbitrary. For this reason theories developed on the basis of

[1] For a satire on (among other things) this notion see Emmon Bach (= Čabnomme, 1971).
[2] The clear cases often become standard cases, especially when a particular isolation-procedure becomes standardized.

clear cases should furnish arguments for the treatment of unclear cases as well (i.e. enable us to make non-arbitrary distinctions). If we cannot do this, we must re-examine the various factors that led to the distinction in the first place, and develop a more inclusive analysis.

2. COMPRESSION can be understood as a higher degree of classification, which is intimately connected with the formation of (intensional) concepts. In a classification we group objects or events on the basis of their possessing one or more common features; in a compression we conflate one or more feature-bundles into a single complex feature. This procedure allows us to encompass a whole correlation IN A SINGLE CONCEPT, which in turn facilitates recognition of other correlations of the same kind. In the same way we can encompass a multitude of phenomena, differing in details, in one concept. Most concept constructions (especially those with verbal equivalents) are based on one or more degrees of compression. These are not, at the outset, scientifically controlled, but are the everyday achievements of a social group (society), aimed, for example, at producing conveniently brief forms for the necessary descriptions of their environment.[1] These ready-made concepts are already available to the individual in their verbal equivalents, and it is the task of scientific conceptual analysis to reconstruct possible processes of compression. This also holds for those concepts which we use for characterizing the properties of languages or features of linguistic competence, e.g. in the description of linguistic facts.

Successive compressions often lead to a hierarchization of what we might call levels of abstraction. Structures on different levels display different degrees of abstraction; but this does not mean that their logical status is different (e.g. in the sense of higher-order predicates). Thus *the language my friend Wilfred uses*, *Saxon* and *German* represent different levels of abstraction; but we can still say 'this is an expression that my friend Wilfred uses', 'this is a Saxon expression', as well as 'this is a German expression'.

Every abstractive compression is also a TYPIFICATION: it conflates features that have a particular pragmatic sense-connection, and the characterization of the whole sense-connection defines a TYPE. Individual phenomena and facts are typical cases if they represent, in a relatively clear and pure form, the sense-connection belonging to the corresponding

---

[1] In terms of information-theory, every compression leads to a reduction of information-content. Since the information-capacity of short-term memory is limited, this allows a larger domain of phenomena to be present to it at one time, which in turn allows a wider general view.

type. A typical case will then be one that is also suitable for clearly distinguishing one type from others.

A complex CONCEPTUAL CONTENT generally leads to a greater CONCEPTUAL RANGE. Thus every compression implies a GENERALIZATION. But since ONE concept is available, we are dealing not simply with an intensional class-construction, but with an intensional generalization, which is bound up with the conceptual content – though this generalization also has an extensional interpretation. Thus we can say (irrespective of the more precise relations of conceptual and factual analysis) that more organisms will be subsumed under the concept 'mammal' than under 'solid-hoofed mammal' or 'ape'; more expressions will be subsumed under 'nominal expression' than under 'noun'; more sociolects will be subsumed under 'the German language' than 'the Saxon language' (or 'Saxon dialect').

3. Every abstraction entails a certain IDEALIZATION. If for instance we reduce a fact to its typical features and separate out certain properties, the fact will be represented only in an idealized form, and we will be faced only with an idealized version of the problems associated with it. But this is precisely the purpose of abstraction: an idealized question is easier to answer than one involving all the contingent factors as well.

The following distinction, I think, holds between idealization and typification: we idealize in reference to what is theoretically necessary or attainable – we thus direct ourselves toward a particular theoretical form, which seems to have a chance of providing a solution for a problem; we typify solely in reference to particular pragmatic sense-connections, independently of whether the type is theoretically accessible or not. Strictly speaking no real case has to correspond (except approximately) to an ideal; what real cases correspond to is a type. One could perhaps say that ideals are formulated in a theoretical language, but the corresponding observation-language (or our ordinary language) only contains particular corresponding types.

When we idealize, however, we run the RISK OF EXCESSIVE ABSTRACTION. Let us say that a question is so complex that a high degree of abstraction seems necessary. The problem that has been idealized in this way can perhaps be solved; but there may be no inference from the solution back to the original concrete problem. Such an abstraction will be useless or empty; it actually contributes nothing to the solution of a problem, but provides only pseudo-solutions, which often lead to new pseudo-problems. This danger has been amply demonstrated by the history of science. Global concepts, fundamental conceptual distinctions and systematizations are set up, and these determine the subsequent development of the science; but they cannot be related to real experience, and only disguise the real original problems. Certainly at each stage of its development every science requires idealizations and, at a later stage, finds them confining; it is the criticism of these idealizations that leads to a new scientific self-consciousness. The history of linguistics provides the following examples: Hermann Paul's conception of language history, Saussure's synchrony/diachrony and langue/parole distinctions; Chomsky's assumption of an ideal speaker–hearer as the representative of an homogeneous speech community.

I must also refer briefly to another common conception of abstraction, according to which abstraction is the tracing back of a particular phenomenon to its causative or conditioning factors. The origin of this notion seems clear: phenomena are concrete and perceptible, causes and conditions can be very complex and abstract. Here one should speak rather of the search for an explanation than of an abstraction; abstractions are in fact generally presupposed in explanations.

For instance, transformational-generative theory frequently makes use of the notion 'underlying': some deep structure or other 'underlies' a particular surface structure. On the one hand the particular deep structure serves as the typification for a class of possible surface structures while, on the other, it maintains a particular place in the explanation of particular syntactic surface facts.

In what follows I will discuss two examples of abstraction in language and their corresponding abstractions in linguistics. The first concerns the relation of utterances to sentences, the second the relation of individually controlled means of communication to a language as a whole.

4.3   Abstraction, example 1: utterances and sentences

Let us begin with Schnelle's view of how we get – stepwise – from linguistic phenomena to linguistic expressions. This is concerned solely with linguistic form. Schnelle distinguishes five levels (1973a: 121ff.):

   A. Phonetic and graphic events as products of particular utterance-acts.
   B. Properties or similarity-classes of phonetic and graphic events; properties or similarity-classes of actions.

C. Standard-classes of phonetic and graphic events; standard-classes of actions.

D. Phonetic and graphic expression-forms (= properties of the standard-classes); standard dispositions to produce and identify occurrences of these forms.

E. Syntactic expression-forms, neutral with respect to phonetic or graphic manifestation.

Every expression of a language can now be characterized by a statement of its syntactic expression-forms, and its possibilities for phonetic and graphic manifestation.

The transition from A to B is a class-construction, that from B to C a typification; at the same time utterance-acts are isolated from their products, and acts of understanding from their objects. In the transition from C to D we perform an abstraction (postulating the properties of a standard): phonetic and graphic events are understood as realizations (or manifestations) of phonetic or graphic expression-forms; actions are traced back to specific standard dispositions toward them. This abstraction is theoretically oriented. In the transition to E we disregard the fact that every expression of a language appears either in a phonetic or a graphic event; we are concerned only with expression-forms, without reference to special properties of their realization (whether actual or postulated in a standard). The idea behind this is that from the point of view of linguistic form we can disregard distinctions of realization. This can be carried further – we can say that speaking and writing (or the understanding of something spoken or written) in principle follow the same rules. The availability of linguistic rules of this kind then corresponds to the standard dispositions of level D.

We should note that even on level A we have performed a very significant isolation: we regard individual events as products (or objects) of actions. We have abstracted away from the action situation as a whole, i.e. what actions have preceded, and what actions follow, as well as from the fact that the individual actions are performed by different persons. This isolation naturally continues on all succeeding levels. In order to neutralize it (or more precisely to reduce the degree of isolation), we could substitute on level A:

A′. Phonetic and graphic events as products of particular persons in an action situation.

For 'phonetic and graphic events as products of actions' we can also substitute 'utterances' (actions and their results). By typification we then get

C′. Typical utterances of typical persons in a typical action situation. Typical persons here can be normal mature speakers of a given language, representatives of a particular social group, etc.; in borderline cases it would be a question only of the distinction of persons, with one of them at any point taking his turn as speaker, while the rest count as addressees. Those actions that normally precede an utterance of that type and those that normally follow it as a consequence form part of the typical action situation; the term 'normally' must then refer to particular typical expectations, especially those based on conventional sequence-schemata for actions.

Theoretizations that do not undertake more significant isolations with respect to level C′ can be called pragmatic. But we do not have to abandon further abstraction, e.g. in respect to 'phonetic and graphic events'; such abstractions are necessary for various reasons. But the process should be carried out so that the utterances are based on particular linguistic rules:

C″. Typical utterances of expressions (e.g. sentences) of a language according to the rules of this language, by typical persons in a typical action situation.

It is clear by now that we have to consider particular situational conditions on linguistic rules; for at least some of the rules are concerned with schemata for expectable sequences of actions (e.g. question–answer relations).

For Schnelle, theoretizations on levels D and E are syntactic, since they contain only syntactic expression-forms and their phonetic and graphic manifestations. Semantic theoretizations are possible, if we include the situational relevance of utterances or their meanings (referential and intensional). In this case every expression of a language would be characterized by a statement of its syntactic expression-form, its phonetic and graphic manifestation possibilities, AND its possible meanings. The standard dispositions for production and understanding can then be taken as restricted to meaningful occurrences. In syntax as well as semantics we dispense with typical utterance-acts, typical persons, and typical situations; in syntax we dispense with even the possible meanings of expressions. To this extent we would be justified in speaking here of degrees of abstraction; but the abstraction is only a further isolation, not an increasing typification and generalization. Even in

pragmatics it is meaningful (in relation to typical situations) to speak
of the utterance of an expression a (with the meaning b), i.e. we employ
concepts on the same level of abstraction as syntactic and semantic
concepts. Pragmatics therefore includes syntax and semantics and is
not itself on a lower level of abstraction, only a lower level of idealization
and isolation.

On the surface it might seem for example that the concept of logical-
semantic inference arises by abstraction from that of pragmatic consequence: in semantics one of our tasks is to clarify which other sentences
a given sentence follows from logically and which others follow from
it; in pragmatics one of our tasks is to clarify what other actions a given
action can be derived from as a consequence, and what others can or
should be its consequences. But deriving a practical consequence is no
more concrete than drawing a logical conclusion – it just contains
something extra. In order to be able to derive practical consequences,
we must already have drawn logical conclusions for the purpose of
understanding a situation or a previous utterance. Drawing a logical
conclusion is a cognitive operation (an intellectual activity and not an
intersubjective action); deriving a practical consequence is an action.
Making up one's mind to such an action is of course based on cognitive
operations, but is itself a deliberate act.

4.4   Abstraction, example 11: sociolects and languages

I will keep discussion of this example fairly brief, since I will return to
it in more detail in chapter 11. Linguists have always been concerned
with the question of what the relation is between individuals' linguistic
capacity and a language as a whole. This breaks down into two
subquestions:

1. A PROBLEM OF ABSTRACTION. The ability to produce and understand
single utterances is part of the individual's linguistic capacity; from
single observations we can get only an inference about individual
linguistic capacities. How then can a speaker who learns a given
language know what the individual properties and capabilities of all
individual speakers are, and what are the properties of a supra-individual
linguistic system that all these speakers participate in? And how can
the linguist adequately reconstruct this learning process?

2. A PROBLEM OF DEMARCATION. On what level of abstraction can we
say that a particular language exists, and that it contrasts, synchronically

and diachronically, with other languages? (Is Middle High German a different language from New High German, or are both simply stages of the same language? If we take the second view, must we say that Italian is only another stage of a language one of whose earlier stages was Latin? Is Low German a different language from High German, Provençal a different language from French, or are both dialects of a single language?)

The abstraction problem is clearly more important. It must be solved to some extent by any speaker who wants to communicate with speakers from other places or social groups, etc. And this requires that his expectations with respect to understanding be justified. In contrast, the demarcation problem concerns various political, national, cultural and historical motivations, but not the need for understanding; it is pretty much a matter of indifference for the individual speaker whether he confronts a speaker of another language or only another dialect, so long as the two can communicate.

In considering the problem of abstraction we can assume the following stratification:

A. An individual linguistic system.

B. A homogeneous linguistic system for a group, relative to particular situations of use (sociolect).

C. A family of simultaneous homogeneous linguistic systems (sociolects), i.e. a dialectal or diatypic variety of a language at a given time.[1]

D. An individual language at a given time.

E_1. A dialectal or diatypic variety of a language in all its historical stages.

E_2. An individual language in all its historical stages.

F. A language family (with apparent genetic relationship: a mother language with its daughters, a set of coexistent daughters, etc.).

G. A language type.

H. Human language (universal properties of languages).

[1] DIALECTAL varieties are primarily defined by particular groups of speakers, and include geographical and social dialects, etc.; DIATYPIC varieties are defined by particular purposes and include different manifestations (written, oral), professional dialects, styles (e.g. public vs. non-public), etc. (The terms 'diatopic' and 'diastratal' are used parallel to 'dialectal' and 'diatypic' also (cf. Heger 1969, 1971).

Diachronic variation is often taken as a third dimension, alongside diatopic and diastratal variation; but in this case it would be specified on another level, i.e. Heger uses 'dialect' as a cover term for variation in a language along any of these three dimensions.

There are two difficulties involved in taking individual linguistic systems as the lowest level of the hierarchy: (a) individuals participate in languages, but they do not represent them for themselves alone (this would be tantamount to claiming that there are private languages, which would conflict with the conception of language as the condition for social life, and as conditioned by it); (b) individuals can participate in very different languages (e.g. bilinguals), but nobody would want to collapse these participations into a single linguistic system. We will therefore assume that the lowest theoretically relevant level is B, the SOCIOLECT.

The speakers of a sociolect belong to the same social stratum, are of comparable age, live in the same region, use language in comparable situations, have comparable interests and experiences and frequent contacts with one another, and so on. These largely sociological facts should not be taken as the demarcation criterion for a sociolect (for this we would use the approximative identity of the individual linguistic systems or parts of them, i.e. the linguistic homogeneity of a group); they should rather be taken as explaining why a nearly homogeneous linguistic system is able to arise in such groups (relative to linguistic activity IN the group). This is a narrower notion of sociolect than the usual one, which is on the same level as that of dialect (i.e. sociolects in this sense can display internal variation). One person's share of a socio-lect can be called an IDIOLECT.[1]

It is often claimed that only an idiolect can be truly homogeneous, i.e. have a unitary system. But we do not understand a sociolect as characterizing ALL the linguistic activities of a group. Correspondingly a sociolect-group is not a mere collection of persons; these are relevant only insofar as they follow the rules of the sociolect, and only with respect to those activities in which they do.

In all the abstractive steps we get typifications, generalizations and isolations (*vis-à-vis* other linguistic systems or sets of linguistic systems). Up to level D it may be possible to represent the result of an abstraction (a language-variety or individual language at a particular time) through individual typical speakers or sociolects – though this can easily obscure the important point of the internal non-homogeneity of the varieties

[1] The term is Bloch's: 'The totality of the possible utterances of one speaker at one time in using a language to interact with one other speaker is an *idiolect*' (1948: §1.7). Lieb (1970: 63) discusses this in connection with other common terms, like 'individual language'. For a further discussion of the notion of idiolect see Weinreich, Labov and Herzog (1968).

and individual languages. But this is no longer possible from level E on, and we need considerable idealization here. Certainly on level F we can no longer speak of a unitary 'linguistic system', but at most of a 'system-aggregate', i.e. it is impossible to characterize a language family with a single self-consistent grammar.[1] The best we can do here is to specify the common features of several grammars. The same holds *a fortiori* for G and H.[2]

In Chomsky's theory the LINGUISTIC COMPETENCE OF AN IDEAL SPEAKER–HEARER is described by means of a transformational-generative grammar. This involves a threefold abstraction: first, what is described is only the capacity for producing and recognizing the sentences of a language, not its utterances (and to this extent the ideal speaker–hearer is already an idealization, since no real speaker has an isolated capacity of this kind); second, the ideal speaker–hearer is taken as a representative of a homogeneous speech-community (which is on level D);[3] and third, an inner capacity of the speaker is assumed – namely his linguistic competence – which is to be specified more precisely in psycholinguistic or acquisition studies, etc.[4]

We can criticize two aspects of this view:

1. The hypostasis of the notion of COMPETENCE. The capacity for language must have an internal basis; but this is a property only of real speakers and not of the ideal representatives of a speech-community. So what would be the organic basis of the competence of a whole speech-community? There is none (cf. Lieb 1970: ch. 11, 177ff., 228 n. 20).

2. The construct of the HOMOGENEOUS SPEECH-COMMUNITY that the ideal speaker–hearer represents. This makes it impossible to describe and explain the processes of linguistic change (which *inter alia* derive from the existence of various characteristic varieties and sociolects of a language) in any rational way (cf. Kanngiesser 1972: esp. 37ff.; Lieb 1970: 11).

[1] In a precise treatment of non-homogeneity we can no longer speak of exactly ONE grammar from level C on. Only if we grant that there are typical speakers and sociolects can we single out one of several possible grammars as typical.

[2] This is one of the reasons why the notion of universal GRAMMAR should be rejected as misleading.

[3] We can make the following distinction *vis-à-vis* the typical speaker: along with a real typical speaker we admit other equally real but less typical speakers; no real speaker actually corresponds to the ideal speaker, but there is roughly the same gap between him and all real speakers.

[4] But studies of this kind can only be undertaken with real speakers, not with an ideal speaker (who is a theoretical construct).

4.5 Deduction and proof

The working out of the concept of deduction is closely tied up with the development of formal logic. A scientific argument is DEDUCTIVE if its conclusion follows SOLELY FROM THE FORM OF THE PREMISSES, regardless of their content. The argument is valid if the transition from premisses to conclusion follows from the unequivocal use of general RULES OF DEDUCTION (or deductive schemata); only the form of an expression counts in a deductive rule. The primary subject of logical studies is deductive rules of this kind (together with the statement forms they are based on). These studies also have an empirical aspect, in the sense that the deductive rules RECONSTRUCT particular colloquial or scientific FORMS OF ARGUMENT:

1. The statement-forms must be able to express the wealth of assertions needed in arguments in colloquial or scientific language.

2. The only meaningful deductive rules are those that correspond to argument-forms in colloquial or scientific argumentation.[1]

The use of deduction in the empirical sciences therefore requires a thorough logical orientation; the contents of particular statements are relevant only to particular sciences. But since the contents are empirical, we must judge this as well as validity, i.e. we have to determine whether and how far particular premisses can be asserted. If the premisses are empirically true and the argument is valid, then the conclusion is necessarily also empirically true. If however the conclusion is empirically falsified, then either the argument is invalid, or (at least) one of the premisses is empirically false.[2] The use of deductive logic assumes the possibility of empirical confirmation or falsification of premisses (and conclusions); but this is not itself the subject of deductive logic, but rather of a logic of induction.[3]

Empirical theories considered as classes of universal sentences

---

[1] Not all accepted argument-forms of course have to be reconstructed as or reconstructable as deductive rules, for instance if we also allow content-oriented as well as formal standards (i.e. there is no pure deductive argument in the logical sense), or if they are regarded as complex arguments (i.e. divisible into several subarguments).

[2] If we put our trust in logic – and the more explicitly we base ourselves on a developed logic, the more we can do this – we will make the second assumption: i.e. we will look for the error first in the premisses, not in the argumentation. This is only one of the advantages of using logic.

[3] An attempt has been made to include the form of inferential procedures for empirical confirmation (e.g. according to degrees of probability) in the inductive logic developed by Carnap and others (see Carnap & Stegmüller 1959; Kutschera 1972: ch. 2). On the whole such logics have not been developed very far; I will therefore be concerned in this book only with some forms of deductive logic.

(statements) are generally set up in such a way that the sentences are deductively related – depending on the theoretical language and certain basic statements of the theory.[1]

Deduction from the universal sentences of the theory to individual cases is possible if we add singular statements as initial conditions to the premisses; we must then include these in the theoretical language.[2]

In 2.4 I sketched out briefly the traditional THEORY OF SYLLOGISMS; every valid (or permissible) syllogism corresponds to a particular rule of deduction. The further development of the concept of deduction in FORMAL PROPOSITIONAL AND PREDICATE LOGIC will be described in chapter 5; the achievements of syllogism theory are fully included in these forms of deductive logic, but with greater clarity and generality. In this section I will only make some general comments on the relation of deduction to the concept of proof.

We must ask first what the colloquial meaning of 'proof' is, and how we can give it a logical interpretation. A PROOF serves to show that the content of an assertion utterance is true, valid, correct, permissible, etc., either absolutely or relative to certain assumptions. A proof is generally the outcome of an argumentative act – though not necessarily: I can prove my assertion that I can walk on my hands by walking on my hands; I can prove my assertion that a lake is frozen by taking someone there and showing him the ice; I can prove my assertion that it will be cloudy tomorrow by waiting for the next day and looking (though I could perhaps prove or at least substantiate this on meteorological grounds); I can prove my assertion that Ludwig told me he wanted to go to Paris by asking Ludwig myself, or getting someone to ask him, whether this is true. In all these cases assertion and proof are temporally separated; it will therefore be necessary either to announce the proof in advance or mention it afterwards. This will also happen in argumentative or quasi-argumentative acts.

The CONCEPT OF PROOF is similar in some respects to the CONCEPT OF JUSTIFICATION: proofs, like justifications, are supposed to convince. Whether or not they succeed depends (among other things) on the expected or even institutionally prescribed standards in a given domain. We can however establish this distinction: justifications are given when

[1] To this extent deduction accomplishes more than the mere 'reversal' of induction. The relatively trivial case of reversal of a generalization is permitted by the following deductive inference: If for all x of the class K it is true that $A(...x...)$, and a is a member of K, then it is the case that $A(...a...)$. ('$A(...u...)$' symbolizes a statement about u.)

[2] On this cf. the Hempel–Oppenheim schema for scientific explanation (3.8 above).

WFD

in the course of an argument specific reasons are cited for arbitrary acts (*inter alia* assertions); proof is required only for the contents of an assertive utterance, but this may be adduced in other ways than in an argumentative act, primarily by demonstration.

If an appearance or the testimony of a witness is to count as PROOF OF AN ASSERTION, we need an ARGUMENTATIVE ASSESSMENT of the appearance or testimony. We can therefore develop a stronger or concept of proof, where a proof is identical with this argumentative assessment.

In jurisprudence, for example, judges' rules lay down what kind of assertions require proof, who has to bear the burden of proof, and what can count as proof; there are immediate proofs (by direct evidence, current documents, perhaps even confessions) and indirect proofs (by circumstantial evidence, depositions, witnesses and expert testimony). The legal definition incorporates many things that play a role in the everyday notion of proof; it is also normative, and thus feeds back into our ordinary language understanding of proof.

In particular jurisprudence always prescribes the assessment of a proof: this depends not so much on the subjective factor (conviction), as on the objective factor (validity). Whatever statements a judge makes in reference to one of the parties (whatever his subjective motivations may be), they gain weight and recognition mainly because they are based on an assessment of proof (and on the statements of the law). Every legal judgment must be substantiated, and part of this substantiation is a weighing of the various proofs.

OBJECTIVITY and VALIDITY are also decisive for scientific proofs. No matter what subjective reasons and ideas and what lines of intellectual development have led a scientist to a particular statement, he must be able to adduce acceptable reasons and stage them in an acceptable argumentative sequence.

When we request that someone should prove his statements (but not acts), and exclude any subjective impressions we may have, we are operating on the level of logic. Every proof is thus a SCHEMATIC REGULAR CONSTRUCTION in a language, which in principle can be carried out by anybody (and therefore ought to be accepted where the principles of the schematic construction are accepted). The constructive activity of proof itself (and only this is to be assessed and taken as objective) must be distinguished from heuristics or strategies or real activities of the persons doing the proving. We often disregard this constructive aspect, and understand a proof solely as a RELATION BETWEEN STATEMENTS (or classes of statements), i.e. we prefer a static to a dynamic terminology; but these are just two sides of the same coin.[1]

I will be concerned below only with proof in the sciences. Where does the constructive factor reside in this kind of proof? First, in the fact that it must be as explicit as possible, and formally unequivocal and compelling. In many arguments (even scientific ones) not all the steps are stated, premisses (especially general ones) are left implicit and only expanded if this is required. Proofs on the contrary must make all their steps explicit and formal; this is the only way they can also be schematically verifiable. Second, proofs often reverse the natural direction of argumentation. The natural direction of an argument would be to start from the statement to be proved, p, and to state a ground for proof q_n, and if need be prove q_n by q_{n-1}, etc., until we finally arrive at the undoubted initial statement or at a certain initial hypothesis q_1:

p because q_n, because, ...because q_1.

Many proofs proceed in exactly the opposite way: from undoubted initial statements or certain initial hypotheses q_1, they derive the statement p schematically in several steps (or deduce p); if this is successful, then p is proved (relative to q_1):

p is to be proved.

q_1, therefore, ...therefore q_n, therefore p (QED).

This kind will be called DIRECT PROOF. It demands particular strategies for selecting the appropriate initial statements and derivational steps. Even if we admit only a few fixed basic statements and rules of deduction, and set up the rules so that they are almost mechanically applicable, there is still no guarantee that we will discover a proof: we need a PROOF-STRATEGY, and there are only a very few cases in which even this is mechanically applicable. Every proof of this kind is a goal-oriented activity; the goal is defined by the assertion p to be proved.

There are other forms of proof as well. One that should be mentioned is the PROOF BY CONTRADICTION (or INDIRECT PROOF). Here we assume hypothetically the negation of the statement to be proved, i.e. $\sim p$; and then deduce from it some statement r as well as its negation, $\sim r$. Assuming the principle of contradiction (r & $\sim r$ is logically false), and the principle of the excluded middle (p $\vee \sim p$ is logically true), the statement p to be proved must be correct.

---

[1] The difference between proof and justification will now be clearer: in proof only objective standards count, but in a justification subjective ones may also. A justification is never viewed as merely a constructive activity, and certainly never as a relation between statements.

In case p is a disjunctive statement or generalization, we can undertake an INSTANCE-ANALYSIS, and prove each instance separately; the construction of a single counterinstance is sufficient for a refutation. A typical example of instance-analysis is the so-called proof by induction; here the way the language itself is defined tells us in advance what the analysis must look like (see 4.6).

In instance-analysis the whole proof is put together out of the conjunction of partial proofs. There are also other forms of SUBORDINATION OF PROOFS. Just as we frequently discuss subproblems in everyday argumentation, before returning to the main problem, so here each individual premiss requires its own proof. Likewise we often make auxiliary assumptions, which serve as the basis for additional deductive steps; but the result is independent of these auxiliary assumptions, if it can be shown that they were purely arbitrary, i.e. that they have not reduced the generality of the original statement.

*4.6 Proof by induction

The so-called proof by induction is also in fact a deductive process. Its name is misleading, but it has nevertheless become established in logic and mathematics. It obviously has nothing to do, however, with empirical induction. It is based on an INDUCTIVE (or RECURSIVE) definition of the following kind:

> The elements of a class K are successively constructed by means of an operation f (often several operations, f, g, h, etc.) out of one or more initial elements x_0; i.e. the construction is an enumeration of the class.
>
> (a) Beginning: x_0 is a member of class K.
> (b) Expansion: if x is a member of class K, then f[x] (i.e. the element that arises from x by the operation f) is also a member of the class K.
> (c) Closure: only those elements defined in (a) or (b) are members of K.

This definition is always used if the class K contains a potentially infinite number of elements, where we cannot specify each one individually; but it allows the elements of K (and only these) to be constructively characterized. Only the inductive definition allows a constructive approach to a POTENTIALLY INFINITE MANIFOLD. Formal languages (including those of formal logic) generally contain expressions that can be introduced by means of an inductive definition.

The simplest use of this kind of definition can be seen in the definition of natural numbers: we assume that o is a natural number, and that there is an operation of addition, which given a particular natural number allows us to construct its successor:[1]

Beginning: o is a natural number.

Expansion: if x is a natural number, then the successor of x is a natural number.

Closure: only the elements defined according to (a) or (b) are natural numbers.

The construction obviously begins with the initial element, i.e. we define the successor of o (i.e. 1), then the successor of 1, etc.

A PROOF BY INDUCTION can be established relative to the manifold of objects introduced by an inductive definition. We must prove that all elements of the class K have the property P, and we do it thus:

(a) x_0 has the property P.

(b) (Let $x = x_n$ and $f[x] = x_{n+1}$, with $n \geqslant 0$:) If x_n has the property P, then x_{n+1} also has the property P (weak induction).

If x_n has the property P, and it is also assumed that all x_j where $0 \leqslant j < n$ have the property P, then all x_{n+1} have the property P (strong induction).

---

[1] This operation – as we know – is addition of 1. The concept of 'successor' still has to be further clarified, as it is for instance in the axioms of Peano or Russell (cf. Carnap 1958: §44).

5 *The development of deductive argumentation: logic*

5.1 Formal inference in a logical system

Every proof is a CONSTRUCTIVE ACTIVITY IN A LANGUAGE; this means that FORM and CONTENT are equally important. The construction is of course partly controlled by the forms of the language; but these forms must be able to present the content appropriately. It is the connection of these two factors that gives the proof its value for working out problems of content.

The development of logical systems is an attempt at explicit reconstruction of deductions and the rules governing them. We still need appropriate strategies; but these are generally not stated explicitly – they remain more or less intuitive. Explicitness and unequivocalness of deduction require a FORMAL RECONSTRUCTION, i.e. one based entirely on the forms of the language; this can only be achieved if we have an appropriately constructed LOGICAL LANGUAGE. But this language must also be understood conceptually, and we must take this into account when we set it up. Content can also be handled later, by means of specific interpretations and evaluations. In what follows I will refer to 'proof', 'inference', or 'deduction' when I am not making any distinction between the formal and the conceptual; when only the formal (syntactic) aspect is under consideration I will speak of 'derivation'; when only the conceptual (semantic) aspect is under consideration, I will speak of '(logical) consequence'.

Formal logical systems were at first developed mainly for mathematical purposes: logic was the FOUNDATION SCIENCE OF MATHEMATICS. Many problems were treated only from the mathematician's point of view, and this led to an overemphasis of the constructive–formal aspect. Mathematical subjects, moreover, are notable for their extreme abstraction and reduction; even the most complex structures derive their special properties via their construction out of a very few simple structures.

A language that utilizes only a minimal set of simple but multiply combinable means of construction is particularly suitable for a subject like this. Logical systems (like e.g. that of predicate calculus) formulated in such a language are the simplest and most basic; we can use them as a basis for studying the general properties of logical systems and the general requirements on such systems.

Things are rather different in the empirical sciences: their subject matter does not lend itself to free abstraction and reduction. The formulation of empirical theories has to be guided by a preliminary understanding of their subjects and problems. If we took this as an essentially dispensable informal understanding, it would lead to our assigning an independent status to the deductive–constructive procedure in the empirical sciences – but the formulation of empirical theories is not merely a field for the application of mathematics and formal logic. On the contrary: here the nature of the logical system to be developed (and thus the logical language as well) must be responsive to the requirements of the particular science, instead of the science being oriented only toward existing logical systems. It is not only the content of empirical theories that represents an empirical problem, but sometimes even the form as well: How rich does the logical language have to be to express the specific facts of the science in general terms? What kinds of properties, events, processes, situations, attitudes, etc., have to be distinguished? What kinds of deductive rules are relevant?

Since formal logic is to be understood as the reconstruction (in particular sciences) of natural-language argumentation, this necessarily includes an analysis of the colloquial or standardized language used. This is where logic and linguistics meet. For linguistics, the development of logical systems is not merely the development of a theoretical apparatus, but of an ANALYTICAL TOOL: the meaning of colloquial sentences and sentence-complexes can be elucidated by reconstructing them in an appropriate logical language. This leads to the requirement that all possible natural-language distinctions should also be to some extent represented as possible distinctions in the logical language (e.g. not all adjectives and common nouns can be treated in the same way; adverbs, articles, aspect, tense, etc., all pose their particular problems; and so on).

The following are basic requirements for a logical system:

1. Establishment of a constructed logical language: definition of vocabulary with respect to individual categories to be distinguished (individual expressions, predicating expressions, function-expressions,

quantifiers, connectives, etc.); definition of sentences. More significantly, construction of the language so that the subsequent requirements can be relatively easily met.

2. Specification of an informal procedure for translating or explicating expressions of a natural (possibly standardized) language into the formal language. This is important because it is in natural language that we first communicate about problems; we should be able to 'bequeath' comprehensibly to the formal language any natural-language under-standing we may already have achieved. Or conversely: the expressions of the formal language should be comprehensibly paraphrasable in the standardized language.

3. Specification of possible formal modes of representation for the various types of natural inference. This guarantees in advance our familiarity with and ability to handle the chosen formal language – even before we have actually begun to work with it.

4. Treatment of syntactic concepts like derivability and provability.

5. Treatment of semantic concepts like satisfaction, satisfiability, universal validity and logical consequence.

6. Proofs of the system's soundness (freedom from contradiction) and completeness (on requirements 4–6 cf. 5.3–5.5).

Some further specifications:

1. The number of VOCABULARY ITEMS is to be RESTRICTED, and each item used in only one sense: thus as logical connectives we will restrict ourselves to the conjunction 'and', the disjunction 'or', the negation 'not' and the material implication 'if...then' (symbolized respectively as '&', '∨', '~', and '⊃'). Each of these will be used in only one of its meanings (and we could even do without two of the connectives), while 'but', 'not only...but also', 'as well as', etc., will not be used.

2. The form of the logical language will be so defined that THE STRUCTURE OF ITS SENTENCES WILL REFLECT AS CLOSELY AS POSSIBLE THE STRUCTURE OF THE STATEMENTS MADE WITH THEM. The structures of sentences are to be read off formally from the symbols, brackets, etc., used in them, but they will also show how the meanings of parts are to be combined into the total meaning. Deductions from statements can now be treated as formal operations on sentences, i.e. we can apply individual deductive rules mechanically, and we are thus certain that the results represent the desired statements.[1]

[1] This is crucial for theoretical linguistics. Since the meanings of expressions can only be stated in language, we have to choose a language which represents the structures of sentences as well as their meanings. Since languages of this kind have been developed

3. All deductions are so analysed that we end up with a minimal number of RULES OF DEDUCTION.

4. We establish several BASIC STATEMENTS (axioms) whose universal validity cannot or ought not to be doubted.

5. We establish a comprehensive (deductive) procedure for THE ENUMERATION OF ALL UNIVERSALLY VALID LOGICAL STATEMENTS (theorems)[1] IN A LOGICAL SYSTEM (consisting of logical language, rules of deduction, and axioms) – and only these, so that we can establish whether the logical system as a whole is sound and complete. In addition, theorems can be introduced at arbitrary points in a deduction as premises, which makes many deductions significantly easier.

The simplest systems are those that come under the heading of PROPOSITIONAL LOGIC. There are a number of equivalent ones, differing only in the way the language is defined (through the selection of basic sentence connectives) and in their axioms. Every axiom or theorem of one system (or its translation) is universally valid in every other system. The internal structure of the elementary sentences is not considered: all expressions are sentences of the language. The following is a possible system of propositional logic (I am not differentiating here between syntactic and semantic aspects; this will come later):

ELEMENTARY SENTENCES (statements): p, q, r, …

SENTENCE CONNECTIVES: $\supset$ (material implication), $\sim$ (negation).

in logic, we should use them as a basis – though they will generally be inadequate, as logical languages normally do not have the expressive capabilities of natural languages.

I refer to 'p ∨ q' etc. as statements, because the sentence 'p ∨ q' also represents the statement (or proposition) 'that p or that q'. We could of course try to focus the difference between a string of symbols and a statement by some special notation, but this seems superfluous. In logic we are never concerned only with uninterpreted strings of symbols, but simultaneously with the statements they represent. A logical language is not to be identified with a formal language in the sense of an algebra (cf. 10.5 below).

Once we have introduced formal derivational conventions, we can prove particular sentences formally, without a previous understanding of their conceptual consequences. This is often of great heuristic value: we have no occasion to doubt the 'correctness' of a sentence (relative to the selected premises), and are therefore compelled to interpret it appropriately from the conceptual point of view, which can lead to new and productive questions (e.g. with respect to the richness of the chosen logical language and its applicability to particular problems). In this sense the formal procedures embody a productivity that transcends the scientist's conceptually determined intuitions; though this productivity is ultimately valueless unless it is made a part of the scientist's understanding. This is why it is in principle correct to say that every proof is a constructive activity in a language, determined by both form and content.

[1] A logical statement is universally valid if it is true in all situations (interpretations); it is universally invalid if it is always false. E.g. 'p $\supset$ p ∨ q' is universally valid, and 'p & $\sim$ p' is universally invalid; 'p ∨ q' on the other hand is neither. If 'p' and 'q' are particular empirical statements, then 'p $\supset$ p ∨ q' is true no matter what statements we choose, but the truth of 'p ∨ q' depends on the truth of these empirical statements.

DEFINITION OF SENTENCES:

(a) p, q, r, ... are sentences.

(b) If A and B are sentences, then A ⊃ B is also a sentence. If A is a sentence, then ∼ A is also a sentence.

(c) Only expressions constructed according to (a) or (b) are sentences.

'A' and 'B' are used here as metavariables: they stand for any elementary or complex sentence. We must add that in any formula in which for example 'A' appears more than once, each occurrence of 'A' stands for the same sentence; conversely, 'B' can also stand for this sentence. Such a stipulation is often called a constitution rule; according to this rule the formula 'A ⊃ (B ⊃ A)'[1] can stand for 'p ⊃ (q ⊃ p)', 'p ⊃ (p ⊃ p)', '∼ q (p ⊃ ∼ q)', etc., but not for e.g. 'p ⊃ (q ⊃ q)' or 'p ⊃ (q ⊃ ∼ p)'.

We can now introduce other sentence connectives by definition, e.g.

A & B = df   (A ⊃ ∼ B)
A ∨ B = df   ∼ A ⊃ B
A ≡ B = df   (A ⊃ B) & (B ⊃ A)

These connectives, however ('&', '∨', '≡') are only abbreviatory devices, and do not belong to this logical system.

The single elementary RULE OF DEDUCTION is the *modus ponens*:

$$\frac{\begin{array}{c} A \\ A \supset B \end{array}}{B}$$

From A and A ⊃ B we can conclude that B. Let A and A ⊃ B be the premisses which (depending on the circumstances) are taken as true, hypothetically true, or universally valid; then B is a permissible conclusion and true relative to the premisses. The 'converse' of this rule is known as *modus tollens*: from ∼ B and A ⊃ B we can conclude that ∼ A. On the basis of the properties of material implication, which are fixed as axiomatic, the *modus tollens* is not however an independent rule of deduction; it is therefore not to be considered an additional rule. All rules used in deductions can be defined by means of *modus ponens*.[2]

---

[1] The parentheses indicate the applicational sequence of (b) in the definition of sentences. We would have to make this explicit in a more precise definition of the language.

[2] The so-called rule of substitution in a wider sense is often considered to be one of the elementary rules of deduction. Let A be any sentence, and let A ≡ B; then we can substitute B for all occurrences of A in a given formula. This rule however is metalogically definable (cf. Thomason 1970: 8of.). The rule of substitution in a strict sense, where the requirement that A ≡ B is dropped, is not a rule of deduction.

In order to obtain the class of universally valid sentences (theorems), we compile a small set of mutually independent universally valid basic sentences (axioms, postulates, principles), and derive all other theorems deductively from them. But there is a difficult question here: whether ALL theorems can be obtained by means of these axioms (the problem of completeness); whether ONLY THESE theorems can be derived, and not for example others that might be false in particular situations (the problem of soundness); and, finally, whether the axioms are in fact independent of one another (this one is less important). All the axioms of our system should correspond to the following AXIOM-SCHEMATA:

AS 1. $(A \supset (B \supset A))$
AS 2. $(A \supset (B \supset C)) \supset ((A \supset B) \supset (A \supset C))$
AS 3. $(\sim A \supset \sim B) \supset (B \supset A)$

Since any sentences whatever can stand for A, B and C, and since according to part (b) of the definition of 'sentence' there are infinitely many sentences, there are infinitely many axioms.

DEFINITION OF THEOREMS

(a) Every axiom is a theorem.
(b) If all the premisses of a rule of deduction are theorems, then the conclusion is also a theorem.[1]
(c) Only sentences obtained according to (a) or (b) are theorems.

The systems of propositional logic are not adequate for the purposes of mathematics (much less for those of any empirical science); they make no reference to the internal structure of the sentences (statements) p, q, r, etc. In particular utterances we will want to state the identity of two structures, in others that we can predicate particular properties of particular structures, that particular structures stand in certain relations, that we can obtain other structures by particular operations. There are particular and general statements (the problem of quantification), there are statements about what is possible, impossible, and necessary (the problem of modalities), etc. Corresponding to ideas of what should be representable in a logical system we will thus introduce PREDICATE LOGICS (with identity and quantification), MODAL LOGICS, etc. The procedure in principle follows that of propositional logic, except that non-sentential expressions have to be defined first in order for the sentences to be defined. Additional axioms are also added; and with quantification and modality we need an additional elementary deductive rule.

---

[1] Here we need to refer only to the *modus ponens*, since all the other rules of deduction can be defined by it.

Various logicians (especially Gentzen) have noted that natural inference in general does not stem from a number of self-evident axioms, but from assumptions that lead to inferences; and through further inference the result of the original one can (under certain conditions) be made independent. In general, every theorem-schema whose form is an implication can be rewritten as a rule of inference;[1] thus for the schema AS 3 we have the corresponding rule of inference:

$$\frac{\sim A \supset \, \sim B}{B \supset A}$$

(from $\sim A \supset \, \sim B$ we may conclude that $B \supset A$); and for the *modus ponens* there is the theorem-schema

$$(A \, \& \, (A \supset B)) \supset B$$

A proof of contradiction is based on the theorem-schema

$$(\sim A \supset (B \, \& \, \sim B)) \equiv A$$

or on the rule of inference

If from $\sim A$ we can conclude that $B \, \& \, \sim B$, then we may conclude that A.

A proof by instance-analysis is based on the theorem-schema

$$((A \lor B) \supset C) \equiv (A \supset C) \, \& \, (B \supset C)$$

or on the rule of inference

If it can be concluded from A as well as from B that C, then we may conclude that $(A \lor B) \supset C$.

In this case, as in the foregoing ones, the rule of inference is reversible.

Instead of constructing an axiomatic logical system, we can therefore develop an equivalent calculus of natural inference, with no axioms, but many more rules of deduction.[2]

5.2 Metalogic

If we want to study the general properties of a logical system (logical language, axioms and rules of deduction), especially if we want to prove completeness and soundness, it is usual to introduce, in addition, a

---

[1] Cf. Hasenjäger (1962: 78): 'Sentences are as it were "frozen" rules and rules are "thawed" sentences.' In 'rewriting' a theorem as a rule of inference we must be careful to avoid the paradoxes of material implication discussed in 5.6 below (a theorem is not equivalent to a rule of inference); the one is a sentence (or statement), the other a constructive prescription. Given a theorem in the form of an implication, the first part can also be false; when we use a rule of inference we assume the (relative) truth of the premisses.

[2] A calculus of this type was first developed by Gentzen (1934/5).

constructed metalanguage. The metavariables A, B, C, etc., that we have used belong to this metalanguage – though in general we have up to now only used English for speaking about logical systems. In the constructed logical language – as in any other language – the formal and semantic aspects are united; the sentences of this language represent certain statements, while the deductions in the system lead to changes in the form of sentences, and this leads to other statements.

On the level of metalogic these two aspects are treated separately: the formal–schematic properties[1] in the syntactic metatheory (SYNTAX for short) and the semantic properties of the system in the semantic metatheory (SEMANTICS for short). Deductions in the logical system, then, are to be regarded on the one hand as formal derivations and, on the other, as semantic consequences. At first this may seem to be merely a terminological distinction: in many logical systems formal derivations and semantic consequences lead independently to equivalent results (e.g. in the propositional logic discussed above and in first-order predicate logic); but this is not always the case (e.g. in higher-order predicate logics, where we have predicates of predicates). Here semantic and syntactic considerations have to be complementary, because under certain conditions a non-derivable statement can nevertheless be obtained as a semantic consequence. In natural languages it is obvious that we need syntactic considerations (in the sense of formal properties of strings of expressions) as well as semantic ones, since the forms of strings of expressions rarely make the connections of their constituent meanings directly visible.

The term 'metalanguage' can only be understood in a RELATIVE sense, i.e. a language L_1 is not a metalanguage *per se*, but only in relation to some language L_0. In L_1 we speak about what is done in L_0 (or in a formulation that escapes any imputation of psychologism, we characterize the properties of expressions and their relations in L_0). In our case, deductions are carried out in the logical language and spoken about in the metalanguage – e.g. there are names for what is involved in a deduction ('deduction' for instance is one of these names). This terminology has a precise meaning only if the languages are precisely defined: for only then can we distinguish strictly between L_1 and L_0.

This is of course impossible in natural languages: they are not established by constructive definitions, but have developed in the practical

---

[1] A syntactic metatheory was first developed in studies of the foundations of mathematics as a metamathematics or theory of proof. (The term 'theory of proof' suggests the centrality of mathematical proofs from the beginning.)

contexts of everyday life; and their richness is such that most of what is done in them is also describable by them. Thus 'assertion', 'promise', 'question' are names for certain types of acts that are performed in natural language. But these names are not outside of the natural language; and they are not used exclusively as names, but also for explicating the meanings of actions while they are being performed (e.g. in performative formulae, commentaries, etc.). Though of course there are differentiations in natural languages that correspond to the language/metalanguage distinction, e.g. in the utterances

Berlin has two million inhabitants.
Berlin has six letters.

In the second utterance, the fact that the reference is to the name of a city rather than to the city itself can be shown in writing by inverted commas or a different type-face; but these differentiations do not allow us to define a systematic distinction.

When we speak of introducing constructed languages or metalanguages – about why we do it, how we do it, what it accomplishes, etc. – we obviously use a natural language comprehensible to each of us; we could therefore say that this is the 'metalanguage' with respect to the constructed language (the inverted commas indicate the transferred sense). At the same time we construct logical languages on the model of certain aspects of natural language; i.e. we only reconstruct an already highly standardized scientific language. It is thus always possible to say that the constructed language 'stems from' a natural language. In this way the natural language is also a metalanguage with respect to the languages 'stemming' from it, ultimately its own 'metalanguage'. This makes it clear that the term 'metalanguage' in its use in natural languages cannot be defined. These relationships are clarified in figure 5.

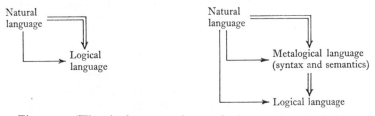

Figure 5   (The single arrows denote the 'stems-from' relation; the double arrows the 'meta-' relation)

*5.3 Logical syntax

The concepts of proof and (formal) derivation have to be distinguished in the syntax; only theorems are proved, but sentences that are not theorems are also derived. The concept of derivation is thus the more general one. Let us assume a logical system H (what follows is based on Thomason 1970: 63ff.):

(1) A PROOF in H is a sequence $A_1, ..., A_n$ of sentences in H such that every entry in this sequence is either an axiom in H or is derivable from preceding entries by *modus ponens*. In other words, for all i where $1 \leqslant i \leqslant n$, A_i is either an axiom in H, or there is some $j < i$ and some $k < i$, such that A_j is identical to $A_k \supset A_i$. For any sequence $A_1, ..., A_n$ which is a proof, we can also say that it is a proof for its last entry, namely A_n.

(2) A sentence A in H is PROVABLE in H (or is a theorem in H) if there exists a proof for A in H. In this case we can write: $\vdash_H A$, or in short: $\vdash A$.

(3) Let HYP be a set of sentences in H. A sequence $A_1, ..., A_n$ of sentences in H is then a DERIVATION of A_n from the hypotheses HYP, if for all i where $1 \leqslant i \leqslant n$ it is the case that: either A_i is an axiom in H, or A_i is an element of HYP, or there is some $j < i$ and some $k < i$, such that A_j is identical to $A_k \supset A_i$.

(4) A sentence A in H is DERIVABLE from a set of sentences HYP in H, if there is a derivation of A from HYP in H. In this case we can write HYP $\vdash_H A$ or in short: HYP $\vdash A$.

It is clear that the concept of derivability is more general: provability can be defined as the case where the set HYP is empty.

The reason for a more precise definition of provability and derivability is this: under certain conditions we can be convinced of the non-existence (impossibility) of a proof, without actually having to carry out any proof; in many cases this knowledge of the existence or non-existence of proofs is entirely adequate. In addition we can find strategies that will reduce a difficult proof to a number of easier ones. For this purpose we can, for instance, use the following DERIVATION THEOREM (which is thus a metatheorem): if to the set HYP we add a sentence A, and then B is derivable, then $A \supset B$ is derivable from HYP:

(5) If HYP $\cup \{A\} \vdash B$, then HYP $\vdash A \supset B$.

This theorem means that a set of hypothetical but assumed to be true sentences can be reduced stepwise, since it is not individual sentences but their implications that will be derived.

From the proof of the derivation theorem we can easily obtain the following metasentence as valid:

(6) If $A_1, A_2, ..., A_n \vdash B$, then $\vdash A_1 \supset (A_2 \supset (... \supset (A_n \supset B)...))$.

In other words, to every derivation in H there corresponds exactly one theorem in H.

*5.4 Logical semantics

In syntax we elucidate concepts like provability, derivability, and others that are built on them; in semantics we are concerned with concepts like satisfaction, satisfiability, validity, and logical consequence. In semantic analysis sentences do not count as mere strings of symbols; they contain or make statements, and something will be said about these statements. Even if this is not explicitly stated, in what follows 'sentence' will always be understood in the sense of the contained statement.

Here, as before, we will treat only the simplest form of propositional logic. We will begin from the assumption that all simple sentences (statements) are either true or false, and that this can vary in different situations (interpretations). The truth-values of complex sentences are fully determined by the truth-values of their constituent simple sentences, according to their particular mode of combination. To every SYNTACTIC CONSTRUCTION there thus corresponds a TRUTH-FUNCTION, whose arguments are the truth-values of the constituent sentences, and whose value is the truth-value of the complex sentence. In propositional logic we are concerned only with sentence connectives as means of syntactic construction; the truth-functions corresponding to them can be represented in truth-tables:

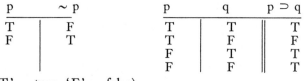

p	~ p
T	F
F	T

p	q	p $\supset$ q
T	T	T
T	F	F
F	T	T
F	F	T

(where 'T' = true, 'F' = false).

The main point of constructing a logical language so that the structure of sentences reflects their meaning is to enable us to compute the meaning of a complex sentence (in this case its truth-value) from the meanings of its parts, according to the syntactic structures in which they occur. The same procedure in principle is used in other types of logic, e.g. predicate logic where the internal structure of simple sentences is also considered (only in this case the meanings of the component parts are not defined by truth-values). It is clear anyway that a truth-value only constitutes part of the meaning of a sentence; sentences with the same truth-value are for the most part distinguished by their intensions (cf. 9.3ff. below). Obviously not all sentences of a natural language can be assigned a truth-value; this is possible only for declaratives, and only insofar as these are formulated independently of their situations of utterance.[1] We can say that these are formulated in a NON-PRAGMATIC LANGUAGE; the meaning of an utterance-token of such a sentence derives completely from the meaning of the sentence itself.

This in itself does not constitute an objection to the logician's procedure, since truth-values are assigned as meanings, not to the sentences of a natural language, but to those of a constructed logical language. The logician's goal is not to reconstruct ALL of the sentences of a natural language (even our best developed logical languages are too poor for that), but only those (already standardized) sentences that play a special role in scientific argumentation. Such sentences are in fact often formulated in a non-pragmatic language (in the above sense), because they must be as explicit as possible, as independent as possible of situations of utterance; and for the most part they are declarative sentences.

The assumption (or requirement) that all the sentences of a logical system should be EITHER TRUE OR FALSE under a particular interpretation raises a problem – though this is less a problem for logic than for individual empirical sciences wanting to formulate their statements in a logical language. The problem is simultaneously epistemic (when do we know that particular statements are true or false?) and connected with the type of classification, typification and idealization (how do we treat the unclear and atypical cases, and those that correspond only marginally to an idealization?). We can reduce this problem to a certain extent by first treating only the clear cases, and drawing conclusions from them which can apply to the unclear ones. We can also assume certain truth-value judgements hypothetically, provided that we examine their possible consequences. Otherwise we can deal with epistemic and methodological problems in the appropriate extended logics (e.g. with epistemic modal operators). We could also explain vagueness or indeterminacy by

---

[1] The truth-values of sentences with deictic expressions (like *I*, *here*, etc.) are definable only relative to the situation of utterance.

using the notion of partial intension or by constructing a multi-valued logic (with other truth-values besides 'true' and 'false': cf. 9.9 and 9.10 below).

Another problem is posed by the question of the general conditions for saying that a particular statement is true or false. We could imagine, for instance, that certain extralinguistic criteria would have to be met: that certain observations should be possible, certain actions successfully performed, a statement be acknowledged by others, etc. These however are CRITERIA OF ADEQUACY, and they are the province of the individual sciences, not of logic.[1]

Here the concept of truth can be defined only RELATIVE TO AN ESTABLISHED LANGUAGE. Of course it cannot be defined only through the forms of sentences: this is possible only for logically true (universally valid) statements. But all other statements must be capable of being assigned a precise truth-value. Tarski (1935; reprinted in Berka & Kreiser 1971: 453) therefore proposes a SEMANTIC CRITERION OF TRUTH:

(T) X is a true statement if and only if p.

In a particular case an individual statement can stand for 'p', and a (metalinguistic) name for this expression for 'X', e.g.

(T_1) 'It is snowing' is a true statement if and only if it is snowing.

This does not define when it is permissible to say that it is snowing, but only when it is permissible to say that 'it is snowing' is a true statement.

(T) is not to be taken as a definition of truth; but nonetheless all equivalences of the form (T) must follow from such a definition. Tarski stresses that (T) is in agreement with the classical Aristotelian conception of truth[2] – which does not however mean that (T) is identical to it. In particular, (T) assumes NO ONTOLOGICAL INTERPRETATION of the type that the truth of a statement inheres in its agreement (correspondence) with reality. Tarski's conception of truth, which is generally acknowledged nowadays by logicians, is language-relative, but also extensional: a statement is not called true because it represents a particular sense in the frame of connections in everyday life. Competing conceptions of truth, of course, may require just this: then they must replace language-relativity with some kind of practical relativity.

In the semantic theory of truth it is the linguistic function of statements that is foregrounded. At the same time, a distinction is often made

---

[1] For linguistics cf. for instance 3.5 and 3.9 above, and 7.4 below.

[2] 'To say that the existent does not exist, or that the non-existent exists, is false; conversely, to say that the existent exists, and the non-existent does not exist, is true' (Aristotle, *Metaphysics* IV, 7).

between a correspondence theory and a consensus theory of truth.[1] In the one, we are concerned with the EMPIRICAL TESTING OF STATEMENTS, in the other with their SOCIAL VALUE. These are connected: in order to be able to apply particular tests for adequacy, we must ourselves assume that they are generally acknowledged; in order to facilitate the acknowledgement of particular statements, we must employ particular tests or justification procedures. The semantic theory of truth clarifies only the conditions on truth, not the truth of individual statements; in individual cases it has to be supplemented by testing and acceptance. On the other hand it assumes the social value of language, i.e. conditions on communication in general. But the social value of language is not to be equated with the social value of individual statements: to this extent they can be elucidated neither in the correspondence theory nor in the consensus theory of truth. For many individual statements testing and acknowledgement are hardly possible; but these statements can nevertheless be taken as true, precisely because the language being used and the semantic truth-conditions are known (or learned). We can demonstrate this with the simple sentence *I'm hungry*.

SEMANTIC THEORY. *I'm hungry* is true if and only if I am hungry (or if the speaker is hungry at the time of utterance). The identity of the expression *to be hungry* must be equivalently understood in all cases (and this holds for all sentences which are inferred from the given sentence and use the expression *to be hungry*): we do not state HOW this expression is to be understood. (It is understood on the basis of certain everyday experiences; but the basic problem of course is whether everyone understands it the same way. The key to this is whether the same intensional inferences are valid for everyone).

CORRESPONDENCE THEORY. *I'm hungry* is true if and only if the sentence

---

[1] Thus Habermas (1971: 124) argues for a consensus theory: 'The condition for the truth of statements is the potential agreement of *all* others. Each other must be able to convince himself that I am correctly attributing the predicate p to the subject, and must then be able to agree with me.'

Traditionally, a distinction is usually made between correspondence theory, coherence theory, and pragmatic theory of truth (cf. White 1970: ch. 6).

According to the coherence theory, a statement is true if it is connected with a system of statements on the basis of inferential relationships; truth is defined relative to a system of knowledge. I will argue for a variant of this in 6.3, from the point of view of interpretation through other theories. The semantic theory of truth can be regarded in part as a further development of the coherence theory; another direction in its development has been taken by Rescher (1973).

According to the pragmatic theory a statement is true if it fulfils its function (in practical human intercourse); the consensus theory of truth can be regarded as a further development of this one.

designates an existing fact. The existence of this fact is of course hard to test. We might perhaps clarify the function of this sentence in certain contexts by observation of reactions or physiological observations; but we do not know whether the speaker actually feels hungry.

CONSENSUS THEORY. *I'm hungry* is true if and only if all competent persons can agree with it. Obviously agreement is an inappropriate criterion in this case: it may clarify for others how (in a particular situation of utterance) they will judge the truth-value of this sentence (possibly on the basis of testing procedures); for the speaker himself such agreement is of no importance (even non-agreement cannot convince him of its falsehood). That the expressions 'I' and 'to be hungry' and their combination are understood by others can only be an assumption on his part.

The EXTENSIONALITY of the semantic concept of truth is shown in the following example, which sets up an interpretation in simple set-theoretical language:

Fido is white is true if and only if we can SAY independently that the object i referred to by *Fido* belongs to a CLASS I of objects with that property that we have referred to as *white*. In short:

$Fido \rightarrow i$

$white \rightarrow I$

Fido is white is true in case $i \in I$.

The class-assignments of the constant expressions *Fido* and *white* (symbolized by '$\rightarrow$') represent an arbitrary interpretation here, since i and I are not further specified. Such specification is not necessary for stating a truth-condition; the only necessary assumption is the form of the interpretation, i.e. i and I belong to a domain of interpretation D (which must be more precisely fixed for a particular interpretation); D can include additional objects, which may perhaps be necessary for the interpretation of other sentences.[1] This type of interpretation is language-relative; for 'i' and 'I' only REFER TO objects or classes of objects, and thus only the functions of expressions like *Fido* and *white* are clarified. The sentence *Fido is white* has to be judged in each case under a particular interpretation: it is true if and only if $i \in I$, otherwise it is false. In order to test the expression '$i \in I$' we have (according to circumstances) to invoke extralinguistic criteria; but these are not part of the truth-conditions.

---

[1] Interpretations of this type for classes of sentences are often called 'models': cf. 6.3 below.

Tarski's truth-concept (T) is trivial for the elementary sentences of propositional logic, since the simplest expressions in that language are elementary sentences. For predicate logic (T) is not trivial, since even the simplest sentences have to be constructed. (Our last example would be stateable in predicate calculus.) In all logics, however, the task of finding an appropriate DEFINITION OF TRUTH, i.e. characterizing the class of ALL true statements in the language, is non-trivial. The class of all true expressions, to begin with, is not the same as the class of all expressions formally derivable from other true expressions, since there might be true expressions that are not derivable from other true expressions (and in some logics these do in fact exist). Conversely, however, it probably makes sense to require that all expressions formally derivable from true expressions also be true; if this were not the case, the syntactic explication of the concept of deduction would be crucially defective.

For certain reasons the definition of truth in various systems of logic is transferred to the concept of satisfaction. In propositional logic we can proceed as follows. Let a basis M (often called 'morphology') in H be a fixed set of elementary sentences (statements). Let V be an EVALUATION-FUNCTION for M in H, which assigns every element in M a truth-value, namely either T or F. The value of this function for complex sentences is given by the truth-functions of the sentence connectives:

(7) If A is identical to $\sim$ B, then $V(A) = T$ if $V(B) = F$, and $V(A) = F$ if $V(B) = T$.

(8) If A is identical to $B \supset C$, then $V(A) = F$ if $V(B) = T$ and $V(C) = F$, and $V(A) = T$ otherwise.

Every possible evaluation of all sentences of a morphology M corresponds to a particular situation, i.e. a situation is something that determines the truth-values of all sentences in M. To this extent every evaluation implies an assignment to a particular domain D, in which the statements from M are made, and in which it is established whether they are true or false in reference to D. But the assignments to D in this case do not have to be specified in the evaluation-function, since the structure of the elementary sentences plays no role in propositional logic. If M includes a total of n sentences, there are thus 2^n possible valuations or situations.

The concepts of SATISFIABILITY and UNIVERSAL VALIDITY can now be introduced as follows:

(9) A sentence A relative to M is SATISFIABLE just in case there is a value V for M such that $V(A) = T$.

(10) A sentence A relative to M is UNIVERSALLY VALID just in case for all values V for M it is the case that $V(A) = T$.

The last definition must now be generalized so that reference to a fixed basis M is superfluous; I will not do this here, because it will raise additional problems which are not relevant to our discussion.

(11) A sentence A relative to M is TRUE relative to a valuation V just in case it is satisfied by V (i.e. $V(A) = T$).

This appears trivial only for propositional logic since the evaluation-function was to be formulated independently of the internal structure of sentences. But if we take this into consideration, the evaluation-function must always be defined relative to a domain D of objects and a basis M of expressions for these objects, classes of such objects and relations between them. In the above definition we then only have to substitute 'satisfiable in D' for 'satisfiable', and we can define V appropriately.[1]

In the definition of V we must take account of the fact that complex sentences do not consist only of simple sentences in combination, but often of even simpler SENTENCE-FUNCTIONS.[2] For example the statement *Barking dogs never bite* would be reconstructed in a quantified predicate calculus as '(x) (Dog x $\supset$ (Bark x $\supset$ $\sim$ Bite x))'; in this sentence three simple sentence-functions of the form 'Px' are combined, and the quantification ranges over the complex sentence-function.

Using the concept of satisfaction we can also define the important concept of semantic (logical) consequence:

(12) Let HYP be a set of sentences relative to M, and let A be a sentence relative to M. A FOLLOWS LOGICALLY from HYP (or HYP logically implies A, i.e. HYP ⊩ A) if and only if every valuation for M, which simultaneously satisfies all elements of HYP, also satisfies A.

---

[1] In Tarski's original treatment the concept of satisfaction was conceived of somewhat differently: it meant SATISFACTION OF A SENTENCE-FUNCTION BY OBJECTS. E.g. the sentence-function 'Bark x' (for 'x barks') can be satisfied by Fido. Here Tarski's notion is taken account of in the evaluation-function V.

[2] A sentence-function like 'Dog x' (for 'x is a dog') takes arguments from the domain of individual constants (a, b, c, ...) and has a value in the domain of sentences (Dog a, Dog b, Dog c, ...).

*5.5 Soundness (freedom from contradiction), completeness and independence in logical systems

The early development of what would today be called 'classical' logical systems (propositional logic, first-order predicate calculus, and the like) involved in each case the establishment of a few axioms as basic; it was expected or assumed that these would be free of contradiction, complete, and independent of each other. Different axioms were taken as basic, according to the language chosen; but logicians were not equally sure in all cases whether or not the relevant theorems and only these were derivable independently of the chosen axioms. These stipulations were not always free of error: e.g. Russell and Whitehead in their *Principia mathematica* used one axiom in their propositional calculus which was not independent of the others. The same thing has happened in the development of the newer logical systems, like modal logic, tense logic, deontic logic, etc. It is only in a second stage of analysis that the corresponding proofs are introduced on the metatheoretical level. In classical logic (and hence without invocation of a metalogic) an axiom system counted as sound (free of contradiction) if some arbitrary sentence AND its negation were not both derivable. We can now establish soundness more precisely by the use of a syntax or semantics; completeness and independence can generally only be treated on this level, i.e. meaningfully defined and proved. Let S be an axiom system for the logical system H; then the following definitions hold:

	Syntax	*Semantics*
Soundness	There are sentences in H that are not derivable from S[1]	Every sentence that follows logically from S is a theorem in H (i.e. universally valid).
Completeness	(weak) On the addition of a sentence not derivable from S, S becomes contradictory.	(absolute) All theorems in H and only these follow logically from S.

---

[1] 'Not derivable from S' means the same as 'not provable in S'. An axiom system is syntactically sound if in the associated logical language sentences can also be constructed which are not theorems; those are just the ones that are 'interesting' from an empirical point of view, namely those that are true or false according to situation. The invalid (logically false) sentences also belong to this set.

The requirement that there exist sentences not derivable from S is more general than the requirement of the non-derivability of an arbitrary sentence p and its negation. The first is however a consequence of the second: for if the first were not true, then e.g. both p and $\sim$ p would be derivable from S in H; this would contradict the second requirement.

	Syntax	*Semantics*
Completeness	(strong)	(relative)
(*cont.*)	Every sentence in H is either provable in H or refutable.[1]	All true sentences (statements) relative to a domain of interpretation D in H follow logically from S and the assignment-function between the constant expressions in H and D.
Independence	No axiom or its negation in S is derivable from the remaining axioms in S.	No axiom or its negation in S follows logically from the remaining axioms in S.

As I have already mentioned, propositional logic and first-order predicate logic are both syntactically and semantically sound and complete. It is only because of this that formal derivation and logical consequence give the same results; i.e. if X is any set of sentences and A is any sentence in H, then it will be true that

(13) X ⊢ A if and only if X ⊩ A.

5.6 Other concepts of consequence

In colloquial argumentation the *if...then* connection is regarded as expressing an entailment. It is however used in different ways;[2] these are specified and reconstructed in logic. In the classical logics discussed so far there are two explications:

1. In establishing whether a particular conditioning relation is present, *if...then* is explicated as MATERIAL IMPLICATION, either on the object-language or metalinguistic level. X ⊃ Y explicates the fact that X is a sufficient condition for Y or that Y is a necessary condition for X.

2. In inferences, *if...then* is explicated as a RULE OF DEDUCTION (syntactic derivability and logical consequence). As a general condition, it is the case that we cannot obtain a false conclusion from a true

---

[1] This means that the set of theorems is decidable.

[2] In addition to expressing entailment, *if...then* also expresses presupposition ('in case p, then q': this does not claim that there is a relation between p and q, but merely that q is the case under the assumption that p is), and as the expression of a counterfactual condition ('If Otto had driven more slowly, then he would have avoided the accident': we are given to understand that Otto did not drive slowly, and that he had an accident). Cf. the logical elaborations of Belnap (1973) and Lewis (1973).

premiss. This condition can be divided into two complementary basic principles of deduction:

(a) If Y follows from X and X is true, then Y is also true.

(b) If Y follows from X and Y is not true, then X is also not true.

The first principle is reconstructed in classical logic as *modus ponens*, the second as *modus tollens*; 'Y follows from X' is understood as an expression of material implication, for which it is the case that $X \supset Y$ and $\sim Y \supset \sim X$ are equivalent. This leads to the conclusion that the *modus tollens* is to be regarded solely as the inverse of *modus ponens*, i.e. either is sufficient as a basic rule.

Various attempts have been made to identify implication and derivability, i.e. to take them as mutually equivalent explications of the *if...then* connection. In the case of classical logic this leads to the so-called PARADOXES OF MATERIAL IMPLICATION. According to their definition (or axiomatic establishment) it is the case that:

(a) A logically true (universally valid) sentence is implied by any arbitrary (true or false) sentence (*verum sequitur quodlibet*), e.g.

$$q \supset \sim p \lor p$$

(b) A logically false (universally invalid) sentence implies any arbitrary sentence (*ex falso sequitur quodlibet*), e.g.

$$\sim p \,\&\, p \supset q$$

If we replace 'implies' by 'is derivable'. it must be the case that:

$$q \vdash \sim p \lor p$$
$$\sim p \,\&\, p \vdash q$$

This contradicts both basic principles of deduction.

There have been a number of proposals for getting rid of these paradoxes. For the explication of the relation of logical consequence we introduce another form of implication, in which sentences corresponding to those in (a) and (b) are not provable, i.e. in which there is no identification with derivability. These proposals lead to the introduction of a modal logic. C. I. Lewis (1914) defines a STRICT IMPLICATION. which is narrower than a material implication, as follows:

$$p \prec q = \text{df } N(p \supset q)$$

where the modal operator N = 'it is necessary that' (equivalent to the operator $\sim p \sim$ = 'it is not possible that not...'). It is obvious that even strict implication – if it is identified with the concept of derivation – has its own paradoxes: a logically necessary sentence is strictly implied by any arbitrary sentence; a logically impossible sentence strictly implies an arbitrary sentence. A further narrowing of the concept to get rid of these paradoxes leads to the concept of STRONG IMPLICATION or ENTAILMENT (Ackermann 1958; Kripke 1959; Anderson & Belnap 1962). The corresponding formal systems however are generally not very satisfactory; they exclude intuitively acceptable sentences as unprovable.

The most satisfactory system is that of Sinowjew (1970: esp. chs. 6–7). He does not seek primarily to get rid of certain sentences that seem intuitively paradoxical, but rather to construct a closed system that will suffice for certain previously established conditions on the sense of sentences. The basic idea is that sentences which stand in a relation of logical consequence must have certain elementary constituent sentences in common. A STRONG INFERENCE from p to q in Sinowjew's sense ($p \to q$) is present if in q there appear only such elementary sentences as appear in p, and if every truth condition for p is also a truth condition for q.[1] Paradoxical sentences like

$$q \to \sim p \lor p$$
$$\sim p \,\&\, p \to q$$

are therefore not provable.

In strong implication or strong inference we are dealing with an INTENSIONAL SENTENCE-CONNECTION (which relates to the sense of both sentences); it is not definable by means of a truth-function alone. Accordingly we have to consider, in the structure of sentences, not only the occurring predicates, quantifiers, and conjunctions with *and, or*, etc., but also other means of construction, especially the complements of intensional verbs.[2]

Consider the sentences

(14) Peter has given up smoking.

(15) Peter has arrived in Paris.

Reconstructed in the system of material implication, sentence (14) implies for example

---

[1] Sinowjew also distinguishes several other kinds of inference: in a weakened inference there is at least one identical elementary sentence in p and q; in a maximal inference the same elementary sentences appear in p and q; in converse inference only those elementary sentences appear in p that also appear in q (Sinowjew 1970: 93, 100ff.).

[2] This is supposed to be taken care of by Sinowjew in the construction of elementary sentences. Unfortunately, he gives no indication of what this construction would be like in the analysis of natural languages. The following discussion can therefore only deal with an intuitive consideration of natural-language examples.

(16) Peter has given up smoking or Peter has given up working.

(17) Peter is in Paris or Peter is not in Paris

and is implied by

(18) Peter and Fritz have given up smoking.

Sentence-relations like (14) ⊃ (17) are not generally regarded as inferences in natural languages; though (18) ⊃ (14) and (14) ⊃ (16) would, even if both cases would perhaps be regarded as trivial. Material implication therefore gives too broad an explication; it also fails to capture many relationships between sentences which ARE regarded as inferences. E.g. the following are understood as inferences from (14):

(19) Peter has smoked (before now). [Presupposition of (14)].

(20) Peter will not smoke any more (from now on).

And as inferences from (15):

(21) Peter will be in Paris (from now on).

(22) Peter was not in Paris (before now).

(23) Peter went to Paris (before now).

These inferential relations are not formally derivable in classical logic; an attempt should be made (by appropriate analysis of natural-language sentences into elementary constituent sentences) to derive them formally in the system of strong implication. But we must exclude a formal derivation of (17) from (14). In natural-language argumentation we make use of intensional inference-relations between sentences like those discussed above; the task of logic is to find appropriate forms of explication.

5.7 Modalities

The development that began with the invention of modal logics is important for scientific methodology for a different reason. Thus von Wright (1951) has established systems with various types of modalities, which allow us at least to begin to distinguish the various types of scientific statements:

1. ALETHIC MODALITIES: 'necessarily true', 'not possibly true', 'possibly true'. These correspond by and large to the classical modalities 'necessarily', 'not possibly', and 'possibly'. They do not characterize states of knowledge of or belief in empirical facts or the recognition of the content of assertions, but rather universal forms of knowledge (or belief) relative for example to the structural connections between statements.

Whatever special interpretation we want to give to the individual statement (i.e. whatever domain of knowledge or experience we refer to),
this statement will turn out, on the basis of its structure or the structural connections it stands in, to be always true, always false, or sometimes true/sometimes false.

2. EPISTEMIC MODALITIES: 'verified' (known to be true), 'falsified'
(known to be false), 'undetermined' (not known to be either true or
false). These modalities characterize particular states of knowledge with
respect to empirical facts: such states change through the acquisition
(controlled or uncontrolled) of new experiences. The progress achieved
in a discussion, experiment or test can be expressed in terms of epistemic
modalities. Above all we must distinguish among cases like 'something
is known to person X', 'something is known to be true by the group of
persons X' and 'something is known to be true'; in the last case we
assume that there are particular persons who possess this knowledge, but
the membership of the group for all practical purposes is arbitrary. It is
given if necessary by the context. Thus we assume that scientific knowledge can be acquired by anyone, and is not bound to the scientist's
person.

Alongside of epistemic modalities we must distinguish DOXASTIC
MODALITIES: here we refer not to knowledge but to belief, which we
could paraphrase as 'something is supposed to be unquestionably true
(accepted, correct, etc.)'. Correspondingly, something is supposed to be
unquestionably false or undetermined.

3. DEONTIC MODALITIES: 'obligatory', 'forbidden', 'permitted' (and
possibly – depending on the concept of permission established –
'indifferent'). These modalities characterize norms of action. They can
be implicit conventions (e.g. concerned with the 'normality' of an
action and only explicated by the scientist) or already explicit existing
norms. Even methodological statements in a science could be regarded as
normative: a particular mode of speaking introduced by definition means
'it is obligatory that this rule be followed'.

The deontic modalities are closely tied up with the concept of
SANCTION: if an action is obligatory, this means that failure to perform it
CAN (though it does not have to) lead to a sanction. The concept of
sanction must be defined in a sufficiently general way, e.g. as failure to
reach the desired results, or as employment of the actions of others
against those who have failed to perform the obligatory action (social
proscription, punishment, etc.). In the case of scientific activity, trans-

gression against norms at first leads only to the scientist not achieving the desired results; later it leads to his no longer being understood, being isolated from the development of the discipline and not receiving recognition. He can follow methodological procedures other than those generally acknowledged only as part of an explicit attempt to change scientific norms; otherwise he runs the risk of availing himself only of private methods of acquiring knowledge.

In interpreting statements with deontic modality, we can generally distinguish two aspects, which lead to different formulations of deontic logic: the aspect of HAVING-TO-DO (*Tun-Sollens*) and that of HAVING-TO-BE (*Sein-Sollens*). In the first case the doing of an action is required, forbidden, etc. (e.g. 'smoking is forbidden', 'it is obligatory to use the *modus ponens*'); in the second a state which was brought about by an action is required, forbidden, etc. ('possession of pornographic literature is forbidden', 'the examinee must have handed in an essay that he wrote himself').

Another development of modal logic is the introduction of RELATIVE MODALITIES: i.e. the modal operators are taken as two-place operators, whose second place specifies the conditions under which the modal statement is to be made. Thus P p/q is to be read 'p is possible in case q', or 'p is possible under the conditions q'.

In the case of the epistemic modalities the conditions include criteria for determining when something should count as verified or falsified; in the case of the deontic modalities, the conditions include criteria for determining whether an action is necessary, forbidden, etc. In this way we can refer to other obligations, prohibitions and so on; we can state for instance that particular actions are permitted only if possible alternative ones are forbidden.

The distinction between alethic and epistemic criteria is, as we have seen, also assumed by Hamblin in his discussion of the evaluation of arguments (Hamblin 1970: 224–52; cf. 2.2 above). An argument can be justified only if (among other things) (a) the premisses are true, and (b) they are also acknowledged to be true. But this is not enough: consequently Hamblin also proposes additional DIALOGIC CRITERIA. Thus an argument is justifiable only if (among other things) the premisses are accepted. Indeed, each discussant is free to accept or reject the whole argument. But if this were all there was to it, then it would be impossible to understand how it so often happens in the sciences that something is generally accepted (independently of a scientist's private acceptance).

The explanation can only be that there are rational standards for acceptance or non-acceptance, i.e. if certain conditions are fulfilled a scientist should accept. This 'should' can be described in terms of deontic modalities; acceptance is, however, a dialogic act (it is generally made clear by the utterance of particular expressions of acceptance or the omission of particular expressions of non-acceptance), and not only a cognitive act.

5.8   On the defensibility of statements

The classical logical systems reconstruct statements which are to be judged according to their truth. These can be seen – in relation to facts – as DESCRIPTIVE; they describe the way particular facts appear. What has to be judged is whether these descriptions are true in detail (in the sense of a correspondence theory of truth). Thus the only arguments that are reconstructed are those whose individual assertions are descriptive.

Sentences with modalities can also be understood as descriptive: thus a NORMATIVE statement is true where the norm described is actually valid. Normative statements, however, are also used in other argumentative connections. The demand 'Do a' can be justified with the statement 'It is obligatory to do a' ('One must do a'). Proof of the existence of a stable norm in a case of this kind serves as the criterion of truth. However in many cases we have instead of this a criterion of appropriateness or correctness: the normative statement is justified by saying that under given conditions it is appropriate to perform an action of type a (in short, an action a).

The APPROPRIATENESS OF ACTIONS can be assessed as follows: it is appropriate to perform an action a if the potential consequences in some particular case are more advantageous than the possible consequences of not performing a. Conversely, it is inappropriate to perform a if the consequences are more disadvantageous. The TRUTH OF STATEMENTS can also be judged similarly: a statement S is true if none of its consequences is false; S is false if there is a consequence of S that is false. But we must make the following distinction: 'true' is a metalinguistic predicate of statements, and thus a term of the semantic language; 'appropriate' is an object-language predicate of actions, and its application is governed by pragmatic criteria.

In order to work out the parallelism more clearly, let us agree on the following:

1. In the case where normative statements are justified by the appropriateness of performing particular actions, we introduce the metalinguistic predicate 'appropriate' for these statements.

2. The predicates 'true' and 'appropriate' will be understood pragmatically: they will be used in particular (standardized or stylized) argument situations; statements to which they are applicable in such a situation will be called defensible.

The following criteria, for instance, might hold:

(a) A descriptive statement S is true (defensible) under particular conditions, if none of the consequences of S under these conditions is false (i.e. not also defensible).

(b) A descriptive statement S is false (not defensible) under particular conditions if there is any consequence of S that is false (not defensible) under these conditions.

(c) A normative statement to the effect that the action a is permitted under particular conditions is appropriate (defensible) if the statement that none of the 'normal' consequences of a under these conditions is more disadvantageous than the consequences of not performing a is defensible.

(d) A normative statement to the effect that the action a is prohibited under particular conditions is appropriate (defensible) if the statement that there is a 'normal' consequence of a that under these conditions is more disadvantageous than the consequences of not performing a is defensible.

(e) A normative statement to the effect that the action a is obligatory under particular conditions is appropriate (defensible) if the statement that there is some 'normal' consequence of the failure to perform a that is more disadvantageous than the consequences of performing a under these conditions is defensible.

We can formulate similar criteria for the inappropriateness of normative statements, parallel to those for the falsehood of descriptive statements.

In these formulations we have adopted two terminologies that require further discussion. One is the expression that a particular consequence follows 'normally' from the performance or non-performance of an action. Unlike the logical consequence of a statement, the consequence of an action is not fully determined by the type of action: thus actions can 'miscarry' in various ways, without this being intended by the agents, or without their having to answer for it; and in intersubjective (especially communicative) actions part of the consequence is the conclusions that others draw from the action. They could however refuse to draw these conclusions, if they transgressed against existing conventions or obligations; therefore one could only say of them that it is normally to be expected that particular consequences should follow particular actions.

The second thing that has to be justified is the claim that the consequence of one action can be more disadvantageous than the conquences of possible alternatives. ONE kind of disadvantageousness is the possibility (or applicability) of sanctions; there are however other more general ones, relating to particular sets of interests and value-systems, which we use as the basis for the introduction of new norms or pleas for new norms.

The parallelism between (a) and (b) on the one hand and (c)–(e) on the other is this: in all cases we refer to the defensibility of a statement in an argumentative situation; from this pragmatic point of view the distinction – so obvious in semantics – between descriptive and normative statements disappears.

The notion of the defensibility of statements is doubly interesting for us:

1. THE TOTAL CONTEXT OF THEORIES which we regard as descriptive, their METHODOLOGIES, and their theory-based ACTIONS, must be elucidated. Proposals for action are based primarily on normative statements, and often only indirectly on descriptive ones. In order to make theories fruitful in terms of proposals for action, we must think of them in their wider argumentative context: in the methodology we must discuss both the normative requirements on theories (relative to particular goals), and the normative statements relating to further activities which refer to theories. Scientific activity as a whole makes it necessary for us to produce and at times to defend descriptive as well as normative and evaluative statements.[1] It is therefore necessary to consider criteria of the types (a)–(e) in the theory of science.

2. Some sciences consider themselves to be mainly descriptive. But only in a few cases do the relatively simple systems of propositional and predicate logic suffice for the task of description; we must generally at least introduce modalities. In the social sciences (including certain versions of linguistics) men's knowledge and convictions, as well as

---

[1] On the relation between descriptive, evaluative and normative statements cf. 1.7 above and 9.26 below.

social conventions and norms, play a role; therefore we have to use more highly developed logical forms (especially those based on a deontic logic).[1]

In this way we can still understand the possible statements in such a science as descriptive – even if this is often not fair to the claims of these sciences (think for instance of jurisprudence). Linguistics, in addition to its other tasks, has this special one: to develop THEORIES OF NATURAL-LANGUAGE ARGUMENTATION (which can be effective in a normative sense), and to develop them independently of the concrete context of these argumentations. Therefore the relation between descriptive, normative and evaluative statements in argumentation can be taken as an empirical problem. We will probably need pragmatic concepts like 'defensible' in order to handle this.

---

[1] It may also be possible to handle complex social facts like conventions and values in the framework of a predicate logic, and to reduce the conceptual conection, not formally to a correspondingly rich theory form, but only descriptively to a correspondingly rich axiom system. In this case, however, we will need a comprehensive metalevel in the theory (e.g. for treating the sense-relations between the descriptive predicates) – a level on which we must be able in principle to do anything we could do in a richer logic. This would not have any advantage, but would rather complicate and obscure the connections.

6 *The use of deductive arguments in empirical science: theories*

6.1 On the relationship between logic and theory

So far we have been concerned with LOGICS; now we will turn to empirical THEORIES, and look at them from the point of view of their deductive character. Logics attempt to represent processes of argumentation – especially deduction – in a consistent form. This is always, as we saw, a CONSTRUCTIVE ACTIVITY IN A LANGUAGE. 'In a language' means that every logic ASSUMES a particular language; and conversely the choice of a language INDUCES particular forms of logic. The activities are constructive in the sense that they follow precise rules, and in doing this they arrive at new sentences with particular syntactic and semantic properties which are unambiguously determined relative to the initial sentences. To speak only of mechanically applicable procedures, as logicians are sometimes reproached with, is misleading: first, sentences contain or represent particular statements, so that they cannot be understood as merely formal strings of symbols; second, the rules have both SYNTACTIC AND SEMANTIC aspects (while mechanical procedures are to be understood only syntactically, as manipulations of strings of symbols); and third, the strategies for applying rules are not precisely determined, e.g. the logical derivability relation is not decidable, so there can be no mechanical procedure for establishing it.

In logics, we disregard the fact that statements are made about a particular empirical domain. This means:

1. The choice of particular constant (meaningful) words of a language (individual, predicate, or functional expressions) is completely arbitrary, and not determined by any empirical goal.

2. Often only variables are used for particular words: either in the sense that the variable is always to be thought of as replacing an arbitrary constant, or in the sense that the variables themselves are to be understood as the basic expressions of the language, which can be used

in sentence-functions (statement-functions). The variables can also be thought of as items which give rise to sentences only if they are bound by universal or existential quantifiers: e.g. the way we can say in natural languages 'Someone must have done that', 'Someone did something to him with something', etc.

In theories we have to refer explicitly and systematically to the corresponding factual domain. The general idea is that a theory derives from a logic if all constant expressions are interpreted only with reference to a FIXED DOMAIN OF FACTS, i.e. if the arbitrariness of the constant expressions is neutralized. In practice this means that new constant expressions as well as basic statements (in the medium of the logical language) are established with reference to the factual domain, so that we can speak relatively exhaustively about these facts. This is because:

1. The empirical sense of theoretical statements derives primarily from the constant expressions of the language (the vocabulary) and from the relations established in the additional basic statements.

2. The standards of argumentation are established by the rules of logic.

This kind of relation between theory and logic is not without its problems.

(a) The form of possible theoretical statements is already fully determined by the form of the logical language. The choice of a particular logic therefore represents a prior decision about the types of statements possible in the theory. Statement forms, however, are not the same in different empirical domains; so even THE FORM OF THEORIES REPRESENTS AN EMPIRICAL PROBLEM. The development of empirical theories would indeed be tightly constrained if ALL theories could be based on only ONE kind of logical language; but this is impossible. If we wanted to speak only about properties and relations between objects, a simple predicate logic would be adequate; but if we wanted to speak about processes and events involving those objects, we would need a higher-order predicate logic, and probably even a tense logic; and if we wanted to treat human actions, we would have to develop action logic, preference logic, deontic logic, and use them as bases. These different logics cannot be developed independently of the empirical sense of the presupposed domain of the statements; a logic of action is, to a significant degree, already a theory of action (even if the type of action is not fixed in detail), just as predicate logic is, to a significant degree, a theory of attributes (properties and relations).

(b) The STANDARDS OF ARGUMENTATION are not totally independent of the empirical domain.[1] The goals of the argument determine not only the type of LOGICAL LANGUAGE, but also the type of LOGICAL RULES. Most logics are deductively oriented, yet only a fraction of scientific arguments (and, in a liberal sense of 'theory', theoretical arguments) are in fact deductive. Inductive arguments are also important (e.g. when arguing from statistical data or probabilities), and so are arguments referring to the 'normality' of particular behaviour sequences and expectations – without this 'normality' being expressed solely in frequency-expressions (but rather in terms of the existence of norms or the rationality of agents).

6.2 Symbolization, formalization and axiomatization of theories

The development of theories does not necessarily presuppose a formally constructed logic and theoretical language. It can often be achieved by an implicit acknowledgement of a certain form of logic, or a corresponding extension of language through theoretical concepts, where we depend on generally recognized forms of colloquial language and argumentation. In those cases where there is no certainty or agreement as to the precise type of formal logic to be used this is especially so. This procedure is justified insofar as theoretical understanding is oriented at first toward everyday-language interpretations and descriptions. If the concepts employed are then introduced in context by a constructive procedure they will become more precise. In addition a STANDARDIZATION of the colloquial forms used is required, together with a standardization of the employed (permitted) forms of argument:

---

[1] This will become clear if you try to imagine how each of the following assertions might be justified, and what would constitute a sufficient or acceptable standard:
Alfred was actually his wife's murderer, because...
Picasso became very famous, because...
Fröhlich's theory of superconductivity is inadequate, because...
Rousseau's theory of the state is inadequate, because...
The next tide begins at 5.32, because...
10,000 people won't fit into the Philharmonic Hall, because...
Charlton should play for England, because...
You can't reason with weak verbs, because...
You can't ask what fire weighs, because...
You can't smoke in the no-smoking compartment, because...
You can't trisect an angle with only a ruler and compasses, because...
Energy equals mass times velocity, because...
(Cf. also Toulmin 1969: 13, 14f., 23.)

the character of scientific (non-private) problems demands explicitness and lack of ambiguity. In addition, we can set up the following (partly independent) conditions on theory-construction:

1. REDUCTION OF THE LANGUAGE TO SYMBOLS. This allows us to make complex expressions shorter, clearer and easier to handle, as well as to get rid of misleading associations and connotations more easily.

2. FORMALIZATION of the language, i.e. constructive introduction of the expressions and their formation-rules. This gives us an overall view of the richness and the properties of the language and rules we are using, and we can see what is expressible, derivable, etc., and what is not. It is only at this stage that it makes sense to say that a theory RECONSTRUCTS particular pretheoretical knowledge and the modes of justifying it. Since in general even the simplest languages allow infinitely many distinct expressions, only the formal constructive method allows us to achieve an explicit and precise command of it.

3. AXIOMATIZATION of the theory. Certain basic statements are set down in the form of axioms. In addition to the logical axioms there are non-logical axioms; these formulate general laws (in the Hempel–Oppenheim–Stegmüller sense), which are assumed to be valid or at least valid in a particular theory. (This is where the hypothetical factor enters. It is through the non-logical axioms as a whole that we determine more precisely how far the theory we are developing represents a global hypothesis about some empirical domain.) The established axioms allow us to establish the class of all additional valid general laws.

Axiomatization is also possible in principle when we are using a standardized but not fully formalized language. Of course this does not allow proofs of soundness or completeness, but at best provides intuitive hints of the existence of such proofs. Since the class of valid non-logical theorems is in general indefinitely large, the constructive procedure alone makes it possible to characterize them completely; though we must of course admit that many theorems are simply transforms of others (which is often intuitively obvious), and many are irrelevant for practical purposes. The axiom system should therefore be so chosen that all relevant theorems are constructible in relatively few steps.

In the case of logic we have established that we can substitute for an axiomatically constructed logic a calculus of natural inference, which manages without axioms and instead uses a larger number of deductive rules. By the same token we can also imagine giving up non-logical axioms – but this produces worse difficulties. Logical regularities can in fact be understood as regularities of constructive relations with arguments, but empirical regularities can only partly be understood as regularities of constructive relations with nature; for the rest they are understood as regularities IN nature. We can make statements about such regularities in the theory, but we cannot reconstruct them in it; the theory reconstructs only our KNOWLEDGE (or our assumptions) about them. Knowledge, however, is not a schematic action, and therefore cannot be characterized by rules of inference.

The problem in relation to linguistic theory is somewhat different: do we reconstruct (and generalize) only our knowledge of language, or also our use of it ? The knowledge relates in large part directly to the nature of our linguistic activities,[1] and these are possible only if we possess certain (unproblematical) knowledge of language; i.e. ability and knowledge are interdependent. This touches on the problem of the source of the empirical status of a linguistic theory (I will go into this in 7.5 below).

Formalization of a theory is meaningful only when we make sure that we have a sufficiently 'rich' formal logical system available, i.e. one capable of the necessary statements and deductions. If we base a theory on a formal logic, we often try to axiomatize it at the same time (especially if the logic itself exists in an axiomatized form). The logical system L is then to be added to the theoretical system T as follows:[2]

1. Add the non-logical (theoretical) constants: this yields the expanded logical system L'.

2. Add a class of sentences AX_T as the non-logical (theoretical) axioms, which establish the relation between some of the non-logical constants (the axiomatic basic constants of the theory); this yields the theoretical system T.

Logical system L	*Theoretical system T*
Logical language	+ Theoretical constants
Rules of deduction	
Logical axioms	+ Theoretical axioms

[1] As we have already seen, this does not always hold: e.g. our knowledge of the acoustic properties of sounds or the psychological or neurological representation of language is not part of our everyday knowledge, nor do we require it in our normal use of language.

[2] Cf. Carnap (1958: §42). He discusses another version, where the theoretical axioms are not sentences in L', but sentence-functions in L, and contain axiomatic variables. In interpretation we substitute constants, each of which represents a particular interpretation, for the axiomatic variables.

A non-logical theorem Th is derivable in L' ($AX_T \vdash_{L'}$ Th) and is provable in T ($\vdash_T$ Th), but not provable in L'.

6.3 On the interpretation of theories

Every theory, whether expressed formally on the basis of a logical system or in colloquial or standardized-language form, is a class of systematically related sentences or statements.[1] At least some (if not all) of these are universal sentences, and employ abstract theoretical concepts characteristic of the theory. The interpretation of these theoretical concepts involves the possible interpretations of the theory as a whole. Theories are interpreted primarily with reference to the particular empirical domain for which they were developed; but they can often be interpreted in other similar domains. Many (often only implicit) analogical arguments in the sciences depend on this.

We can understand the concept of INTERPRETATION OF THEORIES in various ways:

1. General preliminary understanding bound up with the formulation of the theory; the implicit meaning of the theory for scientific activity.

2. Informal explanation of the concepts of the theory.

3. Statement of an explicit logical or mathematical interpretation.

4. Statement of an explicit descriptive interpretation.

5. Intensional interpretation.

6. Interpretation through other theories.

If we consider the sentences of a theory only from the syntactic point of view, we completely disregard their empirical interpretation; we are concerned with them only formally (in particular, deductively). From this point of view theories themselves can also be a subject for mathematics. But even in mathematics we are not only interested in abstract structures (represented through an axiom system) but also in more concrete objects, which can fill out these structures; such objects are called MODELS OF THE THEORY. A model comprises a domain of individual objects and an assignment-function between the constants of the theory and single individuals. It is a model of the theory in question if and only if all the non-logical axioms of the theory are valid according to the chosen assignment-function in the domain of individuals: i.e. if it is

---

[1] There is also a non-statement-view of theories, introduced by Sneed (1971), according to which each theory can be characterized by a complex set-theoretical predicate. Under further assumptions the theoretical sentences can then be drawn from this abstract theory. For the sake of brevity I will not consider this view any further here.

true that the structure of the domain of individuals – the more concrete object – is such that it is correctly reproduced by the theoretical axiom system. We can take the mathematical theory of groups as an example. In this theory the two following non-logical axioms hold:

$(x \circ y) \circ z = x \circ (y \circ z)$ Associativity

$(Ex) (y) (x \circ y = y) \& (y) (Ez) (z \circ y = x)$ Existence of an identity element and an inverse element for every element

If we take the concatenation sign 'o' as the addition of numbers, then for instance the set of natural numbers is a special model of group theory (the identity element is the number 'o', the inverse element is the corresponding negative number). If we take the concatenation sign as multiplication of numbers, then e.g. the set of rational numbers is a model of group theory (the identity element is the number '1', the inverse element is the reciprocal of any number). Many other mathematical objects – given the appropriate assignment – will satisfy the axioms of group theory (e.g. the set of rotations about a fixed point, the set of vectors of a plane, the set of all substitutions of n elements); group structures like this play a role even in the empirical sciences.

It has often been proposed that initially all theories are to be construed as purely syntactic calculi, in which all the basic constants can be taken as arbitrary; it is only later that they are given an interpretation by the introduction of models. But this is untenable even for the development of mathematical theories. First, we recognize particular objects and assign them to groups on the basis of their obvious relations. Then the task of the mathematical theory of groups is to work out the common properties of the groups, i.e. why it is correct to treat these different objects analogously. So far the theory is the result of abstractions. The various concrete objects that we perceive should thus turn out to be models of the theory. We can however find still further models, since once the theory is set up it can serve as a heuristic tool for the discovery of further objects which are related (in a strong sense, defined by the theory) to those already known.

Even in the empirical sciences the establishment of theories is always based on preliminary understanding, the problems of content already being clarified – usually in a standardized language. Some abstractions and generalizations are assumed, especially obvious relationships which, for instance, play a role in analogical arguments, and require clearer explication and analysis. Before we look at appropriately constructed forms for a theory, we already know something about what the theory is supposed to do, i.e. what it is to be used for and what it means in relation to some empirical domain.

Thus the logical language we choose must allow the necessary differentiations, particular concepts must be regarded as basic, the interesting general statements must be derivable stepwise from the possible axioms. General concepts as well as the specific experiential connections which interpret them must be theoretically reconstructed. The preliminary understanding is *implicit*, relative to the theory to be constructed, but at the same time it serves to give direction to the theory and to provide a point of departure for evaluation. It is the source of both general and special demands on the theory (e.g. that it should yield particular models in particular empirical domains whose form is as yet only partly established). It is only after this that we can give EXPLICIT INTERPRETATIONS of the theory, which in their turn are evaluated on the basis of our preliminary understanding. If the explicit interpretations are not valid reconstructions of particular preliminary knowledge, then the theory has failed. It is only later that we can interpret the theory from other points of view, and obtain meanings that were not already established at the beginning. The particular way in which the theory fails can also serve as a special source of information about more appropriate theoretical strategies.

The first stages of theory-construction involve the selection of particular concepts and statements constructed with them. We take these – to some extent in an experimental spirit – as basic. On the basis of our preliminary understanding we give these concepts (the axiomatic basic constants), and thus also the statements, an INFORMAL INTER-PRETATION, which serves to control the individual steps in theory-construction. If, on the basis of the reconstruction of the basic concepts (and statements), we fail to achieve an acceptable correlation with other concepts, or a clarification of unclear cases, we have to establish a new basis. In this way our preliminary understanding itself is refined and made ever more precise.

In the empirical sciences, LOGICAL OR MATHEMATICAL INTERPRE-TATIONS merely serve an auxiliary function. If a theory is semantically sound, there must at least be an interpretation of all the axiomatic basic constants such that all the axioms are true. In other words, there must be at least one model for the theory. This can best be shown if we construct a mathematical model for the theory, where the individuals are numbers, n-tuples, classes, or the like. If there is no model at all for a theory, then the theory is inconsistent. And conversely, we must be able to find at least one model for every sound axiom system. We assume that soundness is proved if the theory is interpretable, though this naturally does not guarantee that any particular interpretation will be relevant for the questions we are interested in.

We can also construct models under the explicit descriptive interpretation: though their individual domain encompasses, not mathematical models, but the relevant sort of empirical objects. The statement of the objects of a particular empirical domain is carried out through (constructive) enumeration: a corresponding model is called an EXTENSIONAL INTERPRETATION.

There are usually several possible descriptive models for any theory; the statement of the model is thus only a PARTIAL INTERPRETATION. We can say, in this sense, that theories are fundamentally only partially interpretable: if their function is to predict possible new experiences, then the class of actual models must be open. Every new model found (on the basis of new experiences) extends the class of models, and thus also extends the theory's domain of applicability and our understanding of the theory.

Let the function Int(T, i) be understood as an INTENSIONAL INTER-PRETATION of a theory T:[1] i is an element of a class of possible worlds of experience, and Int(T, i) has as its value a model of the theory T in the world of experience i. If we now find a new world of experience, in which a further model is assignable to the theory, the class of extensional interpretations is extended, and new values are found for the intensional interpretation (which up to now was only partially determined). We usually develop theories only when we already have a class of possible worlds of experience (or possible worlds of application, if these are not the same) in view, i.e. if the arguments of the function Int(T, i) are established. If this is the case, our general understanding of the theory is not altered by the fact that we now have actual models in some of these worlds of experience (as values of Int(T, i)); it is only made concrete. However, the class of possible worlds of experience can also be determined in some other way – and then the intensional interpretation changes. It is probably impossible to establish a complete class of possible interpretations of a theory in advance.

---

[1] On the concepts of extension and intension cf. the detailed discussion in 9.4–9.9 below.

Many philosophers of science (especially Carnap) understand the descriptive interpretation of a theory as the appropriate ASSIGNMENT OF DESCRIPTIVE CONCEPTS TO THEORETICAL CONCEPTS by means of correspondence-rules. This type of interpretation can also be called intensional, since we assign not objects but concepts applicable to classes of objects. The descriptive concepts can be reconstructed in a predicate logic; extensional models, especially the content of specific observations, can only be assigned to observational concepts. Thus a theory is only INDIRECTLY INTERPRETED by observational concepts.

Carnap further allows for some of the theoretical basic concepts not being assigned to any observational concepts; they derive their meaning solely from their use in theoretical statements together with other theoretical concepts which are assigned to observational ones. The theory as a whole – though not every individual theoretical concept – is then interpreted in terms of the observation-language. In this connection Carnap also speaks of partial interpretations of a theory (though 'partial' is not to be understood in the sense in which I used it above).

An explicit reconstruction of observational statements in a predicate logic is itself theoretical. Carnap and others, however, deny this: for them the interpretation of statements in the observation language – in contrast to theoretical statements – is totally unproblematical (we could perhaps concede that it is less problematical). In this sense a theory of observation might be on a lower theoretical level than other theories which only relate indirectly to observations. (One could say, for example, that the concepts of theories of observation fall into the realm of perceptual psychology, not say nuclear physics or semantics.)

In general we can say that theories are INTERPRETABLE THROUGH OTHER THEORIES, provided that these other theories are INDEPENDENTLY established. (Thus a grammatical theory could be specifically interpreted through theories of phonetics, language acqusition, the structure of human communicative acts, etc.) If theories can be reciprocally interpreted, this means that they are compatible. This would be an important requirement if we were interested in developing interdisciplinary studies. Theories should not be evaluated only in isolation, but also according to whether they are essentially compatible with theories of other aspects of our experience; this is the only way to achieve either theoretical integration or more comprehensive theories.

Interpretation by means of the statements of other theories plays a certain role in Chomsky's conception of grammar. A scientific grammar for him is a theoretical construct that exclusively characterizes the possible strings of symbols of a language and their syntactic structures. It is thus interpreted by means of the sentences and sentence structures of a natural language.[1] But the phonological and semantic aspects have to be taken care of too. Here Chomsky speaks of a phonological interpretation of the syntactic surface structures, and of a semantic interpretation of deep (as well as, in more recent work) surface structures.[2] These interpretations, though only rudimentarily outlined for semantics, are done via expressions of another theory, namely either phonological or semantic theory. (The expressions of phonological theory, in addition, are phonetically interpretable – in which case the language of phonetics can be taken as an observation-language relative to the language of phonology.) Syntactic theory is central to both these interpretations: the interpretations are essentially 'filters', which 'filter out' the uninterpretable syntactic structures (e.g. there are grammatical sentences which are meaningless).

Given this framework, if we compare natural-language syntax with the syntax of a constructed language, we can see that Chomsky is proposing a modified form of the view that a theory should be based on an uninterpreted calculus. This notion can be faulted on the ground adduced above (neglect of the role of preliminary understanding in relation to possible interpretations). We can also criticize Chomsky for defining the role of syntax for the connection of semantics and phonology only after the fact, as it were, and not laying it down in a unified theory of grammar (cf. 3.10 above).

6.4   Theoretical language and observation-language

In the early days of Vienna Circle philosophy of science, an attempt was made to find an exact criterion of meaningfulness for all theoretical concepts which would justify their scientific use. Such a criterion was held to be unproblematical for observational concepts, as they are used

---

[1] The fact that Chomsky's syntax is not stated in the usual form for axiomatic theories is probably unimportant. As J. Wang (1968, 1971) has shown, the syntactic base rules and the insertion of lexical items can be reformulated in such a way that they can be taken as the non-logical axioms of a theory. In this theory, then, all sentences meeting certain specifications are provable: i.e. sentences in which the terminal strings of a deep structure and certain of their parts have those predicates attributed to them that are expressed in the deep structure by category-names like 'S', 'NP', 'VP', etc. The transformational rules too can be described either as non-logical axioms or as special rules of derivation.

[2] See Chomsky (1970) and Jackendoff (1972) on surface structure interpretation.

in the description of individual spatiotemporal events (or the temporal behaviour of individual objects): the meaning of these concepts could be directly defined in relation to the observed events. All theoretical concepts were therefore to be encompassed completely in expressions of an observation-language of this type; only then would the meaning of these concepts be exactly and unequivocally established. The theoretical concepts were introduced either by means of explicit definitions based on observational concepts, or by means of reduction-sentences (a kind of conditional definition in terms of particular operations). All theoretical statements should therefore be translatable in principle into statements in the observation-language.

The original programme failed for two reasons: first, because of a misunderstanding of the character of theoretical concepts and, second, because even observational concepts turned out to be by no means as unproblematical as had been assumed. This failure led to the conclusion that theoretical concepts and observational concepts should be strictly distinguished. Theoretical concepts in principle transcend existing observations and their contexts, and it is only possible to relate them to observations in each individual case; thus the theory is given an indirect interpretation through so-called correspondence-rules.

The following programme was developed in an essay by Carnap (1956a): the total language of science, L, is to be taken as consisting of two parts, the OBSERVATION-LANGUAGE L_0 and the THEORETICAL LANGUAGE L_T. L_0 serves for the description of observable events and in this sense is to be taken as fully interpreted. It is assumed that L_0 is used as a means of communication by a particular speech-community, and that all sentences of L_0 are understood by all its members in the same way. L_0 can be reconstructed as a predicate-logic language, in which case the following should hold:

1. All basic descriptive terms are observable.
2. All derived descriptive terms are explicitly definable.
3. The values of all variables must be concrete, observable entities.
4. The set of models for L_0 is finite, i.e. the range of values of the individual variables is finite.
5. Every value of any variable of L_0 is designated by an expression in L_0.
6. All sentence connectives in L_0 are truth-functional; there are no terms for logical, causal, or other modalities.

The theoretical language L_T is first reconstructed as an empirically uninterpreted calculus: the theoretical-descriptive terms represent theoretical entities (like space–time region, classes of space–time regions, properties of these regions), whose meaning is no further defined. Logical, causal and other modalities are admitted as needed, and appropriate rules of deduction are introduced. Finally there are a number of axioms (or postulates) formulated in L_T, and their conjunction is called T.

Then CORRESPONDENCE-RULES are added. They serve to derive certain sentences in L_0 from particular sentences in L_T, or vice versa. They also serve indirectly to derive certain conclusions in L_0 from premisses in L_0 (or to derive the probabilities of conclusions in L_0). Such conclusions are understood as predictions of observable events. Let C be the conjunction of all correspondence rules: the whole theoretical system then consists of T & C.

The empirical meaningfulness of theoretical concepts is explicated by means of a CRITERION OF SIGNIFICANCE. A particular theoretical term M (an expression in L_T) is significant relative to the class K of other theoretical terms with respect to L_T, L_0, T and C

if there is a sentence S_M in L_T which contains M as the only descriptive term;
if there is a sentence S_K in L_T which contains descriptive terms from K, but not M;
if the conjunction S_M & S_K & T & C is consistent (i.e. not logically false);
if there is a sentence S_0 in L_0 such that S_0 is logically implied by the conjunction S_M & S_K & T & C, but is not logically implied by the conjunction S_K & T & C (Carnap 1956a: 51).

Theoretical terms are thus significant relative to a class of other theoretical terms which are necessary, but not sufficient by themselves, for the derivation (prediction) of observation-statements in L_0. In addition – along with L_T, L_0, and C – we have to refer to the theoretical axioms T, i.e. a particular theoretical concept can be meaningful (significant) in reference to one theory, but meaningless in reference to another. This requirement is therefore essentially weaker than that of direct correspondence (definability or translatability) of a theoretical term to an observational term. Significance refers only to the derivability of observation statements, not their verification, i.e. a theoretical concept is meaningful (significant) even if the observational predictions it makes possible are falsified.

Carnap also discusses the status of the concept of disposition (cf. 3.2 above). In general the following definition holds (Carnap 1956a: 63):

An object possesses the property D_{SR} just in case the following regularity holds: whenever the condition S holds for the thing or its environment, the event R occurs to the thing.

The so-called PURE DISPOSITION TERM belongs to an extended observations language L'_0, and is characterized as follows:

1. It can be reached from predicates of L_0 by one or more steps of the procedure described in the definition.

2. The specified relation between S and R constitutes its whole meaning.

3. The regularity involving S and R, on which the term is based, is understood as exceptionless.

Carnap also allows a THEORETICAL DISPOSITION TERM, where S and R can also be formulated by means of theoretical terms. This means that these concepts of disposition attain a further meaning through additional theoretical axioms or additional correspondence-rules. Obviously most dispositions of objects are to be described from the scientific point of view through the theoretical disposition concept.

Carnap's procedure is open to the following main criticisms:

1. For Carnap there is EXACTLY ONE SCIENTIFIC LANGUAGE, and therefore only ONE theoretical language and ONE observation-language for all sciences. All theoretical entities in empirical science are spatio-temporal regions specified in a particular way, all observations are made relative to spatiotemporal events (including spatial objects in events of this kind). This is too general: it does not include the specific peculiarities of individual scientific languages. It is because of these peculiarities that we have to develop special logics (modal, deontic, etc.), so that we can formulate adequate theories; and consequently we also need specific theoretical languages. Similarly, observation-languages have to be developed for experimental situations RELATIVE to a theoretical language. The relation of L_0 to L_T is thus not an absolute, as Carnap would have it; a given language (say that of perceptual psychology) can be at the same time a theoretical language (in relation to psychology) and an observation-language in relation to other theories.

2. Carnap's observation-language is oriented toward uniform requirements (e.g. it has to be reconstructed in a predicate calculus without modalities), without considering the needs of individual scientists. Above all, it is supposed to be immediately comprehensible. But OBSERVATIONAL CONCEPTS in general are NOT SIMPLY IMMEDIATELY AND UNPROBLEMATICALLY GIVEN: they are rather always the result of perceptual procedures involving generalization and abstraction. These

concepts stand in a language-dependent relation to others – a connection that we can already call (pre)theoretical, since it expresses implicit knowledge of perceptions, experiences and observations. All primary experiential and observational concepts are constructed, controlled, and reflected on, in contexts of experience; they are chosen with an eye to their relevance (i.e. in relation to particular goals), and this is in terms of a particular theoretical orientation in the empirical sciences. Only in the long-continued argumentative and experimental context of scientific practice does the use of such concepts become relatively stable.

3. For Carnap, the only empirical question is the content of a theory, the axioms and (derived) theorems that mediate between theoretical concepts – not their form. Since the possible form of a body of knowledge also determines its content, this is problematical, and especially so because it is in the form of theories that we define their generalizing character (in relation to experience). If we assume that scientific theories are partially obtained by the explication of pretheoretical knowledge or concepts, then their FORM is EMPIRICALLY DETERMINED by the relations of these concepts (cf. 7.5 below).

In this connection Carnap's CONVENTIONALITY PRINCIPLE, which derives immediately from his view of the one scientific language and the character of theories, is especially questionable. He writes (1956a: 46):

For L_T we do not claim to have a complete interpretation, but only the indirect and partial interpretation given by the correspondence rules. Therefore, we should feel free to choose the logical structure of this language as it best fits our needs for the purpose for which the language is constructed.

Theories are always set up, as we have seen, in relation to an existing preliminary understanding. The failure of the Vienna Circle's original programme can therefore not be taken as a justification for proposing totally free theory-construction in relation to any goal whatsoever: the first aim is always the facilitation of empirically oriented arguments and designs for action. Every theory must achieve this kind of adequacy.

It is not clear whether all theoretical terms must be significant in Carnap's sense. Theoreticians like Hempel allow a greater freedom on this point: in Hempel's view the question of meaningfulness ought not to be raised for particular terms or sentences, but only for a whole theoretical system.[1] He therefore only speaks of the significance of

[1] According to a procedure of Ramsey (1951) one can represent the whole empirical content of a theory in a so-called Ramsey sentence; this of course allows the evaluation of the significance of a theory as a whole, and only this. See also Stegmüller (1970).

theories, not terms: and he also allows degrees of significance (according to degree of confirmation by observational data and power to predict or explain observable events). For Carnap, the evaluation of theories is a point-by-point procedure, i.e. in terms of significance of particular terms; for Hempel it is global. The first view is certainly heuristically useful; the second is better for evaluating theoretical progress as a whole. An evaluation in terms of observable events is problematical at least in the social sciences, where we are dealing with things like convictions, social values and norms, and where it is also by no means certain what would count as observable events and how these are to be evaluated.

6.5 Deduction: summary

Let us try, in closing, to see how far we have succeeded in answering the questions about the process of deduction raised at the beginning of chapter 4.

1. From an empirical point of view, axiomatization is not a direct source of new knowledge; but it does produce new information about the INTERNAL STRUCTURE OF OUR KNOWLEDGE (Which sentences can be derived from which others? Are different parts of our knowledge compatible, i.e. is our knowledge consistent?) It can also tell us something about GAPS IN OUR KNOWLEDGE (especially with respect to defective premisses for derivations or inferences), and about POSSIBLE NEW EXPERIENCES (Which sentences are newly derivable or logically inferrable, and can therefore be taken as predictions?). In essence, then, an axiomatization allows us to put empirically relevant questions (What knowledge should be checked again? What directions should we look in for new knowledge?), as well as theoretically relevant ones (How do we attain consistency and (approximative) completeness of knowledge? Which abstractions, idealizations, and generalizations seem to be meaningful, and which ones are merely obstructive?).

2. The choice of a logical language permits precise definitions of the relation between syntactic aspects (especially derivability) and semantic aspects (especially logical consequence). In this way our knowledge is subjected to particular constructive standards; but at the same time it becomes possible to CLARIFY PROBLEMS OF FORM AND CONTENT TOGETHER.

3. The explanatory requirement bound up with theories largely follows the Hempel–Oppenheim schema (cf. 3.8 and the modifications

discussed there): either the explanandum E is derivable from the explanans (antecedent conditions $C_1, ..., C_n$; general laws $L_1, ... L_r$) or it is a logical consequence of the explanans. The concept of explanation is thus reconstructed as deducibility in its syntactic or semantic form. Explanation is to be understood as a relation between sentences and NOT as a relation between actions and sentences (the way this would be possible in the case of justification), i.e. as a syntactic–semantic relation. The use of the Hempel–Oppenheim schema of course allows two different interpretations:

(a) Theory-internal. All sentences of the explanans and explanandum are regarded as theoretical sentences; the distinction is solely that $C_1, ..., C_n$ are singular sentences and $L_1, ..., L_r$ are universal. E.g. in $C_1, ..., C_n$ and in E we attribute certain predicates (represented by predicate constants) to certain individuals (represented by individual constants), whereas in $L_1, ..., L_r$ we attribute certain predicates to ALL individuals of a certain domain (i.e. we use the universal quantifier).

(b) Theory-external:[1] We assume a particular interpretation of the theory T in terms of the observation-language L_0 (or in terms of another theory T′); there must thus be correspondence-rules between the two sets of expressions. The explanatory schema then relates sentences formulated in different languages (theories): e.g. $C_1, ..., C_n$ and E could be in L_0 or L_T, and only $L_1, ... , L_r$ in L_T. Of course we must add that the explanatory schema in the strong sense is usable where the same logic holds for L_T and L_0 (or $L_T′$).

4. In order to clarify the connection of theories, methodologies, and theory-oriented practical actions, we must develop a logic for normative sentences, and try to understand the mutual relations of descriptive, evaluative, and normative sentences, in particular contexts of argument. This is why the pragmatic concept of the defensibility of statements is so important.

[1] Carnap obviously had this interpretation in mind; cf. 6.4 above.

7 Explication

7.1 Reprise: theories and problems

We have examined the relationship between theories and their empirical subject matter in general terms, and also looked at some aspects of our central concern, the empirical status of linguistic theory. We will discuss this issue again from a different point of view in this chapter. Not that we will be able to arrive at any definitive solutions: given the conflict of theoretical approaches that characterizes linguistics at present, this is impossible. (And every solution is in any case relative to particular goals.)

Let us first briefly review the function of a theory. It should enable us to understand some problem and everything directly (and perhaps even indirectly) connected with it; i.e. we should be able to come to terms with it cognitively, clarify it, analyse it into its components and discover and apply specific problem-solving strategies. We have already touched on two kinds of theoretical understanding:

1. A theory describes and explains particular factual connections in a general and abstract way, and predicts additional ones. Explanation of course transcends simple description, since it involves stronger argumentation, provides systematically coherent and general higher-order descriptions and, in some appropriate way, connects our knowledge of a particular empirical domain to other knowledge.

2. A theory provides a general, systematic and explicit reconstruction of an existing preliminary understanding or knowledge, and our relation to it. It thus reconstructs cognitive operations which we can present in a linguistic form *vis-à-vis* our knowledge in relation to other men; and these operations in the last analysis have a claim to be explanatory, and to alter the relations between man, nature and society.

Starting from a given problem-situation, we have to deal with the following questions:

1. What is the source of the problem? There are at least three distinct types of answers to this:

(a) It arises from the need to justify certain non-communicative as well as communicative acts (like assertions, reproaches, proposals for action).

(b) The need for a new understanding of ourselves, for the expansion of our intellectual horizons; because some aspect of the way of life (including the conduct of science and other institutions) that we have previously taken as unproblematical is so no longer.

(c) We are aiming at particular goals, but the strategies for attaining them are still unclear; at the moment we can only follow paths toward solutions blindly and without being in control, without being able to say whether they are sensible, or have a chance of success.

2. What are the participants' needs and interests ? What is the nature of the existing preliminary understanding and knowledge of a given domain, what are the criteria of relevance ? What kind of initial abilities do we have, to what extent have we learned to handle language, arguments, instruments of various kinds ? What are the recognized standards and norms for solving problems ?

3. What are the overall goals, and the individual partial goals ? What decisions and actions lead to what consequences ? The systematic working out of a problem assumes that these questions have been answered – and the answers should contain anticipations or predictions of results. We justify actions we intend to perform by stating what consequences are to be expected and whether, and on what grounds, they are to be desired. (Thus there can also be problem-situations where we do not try for a solution because it could bring other undesired consequences along with it.)

7.2   The elucidation of concepts

The elucidation of problems is largely achieved by the elucidation of concepts, and this is true in all three areas mentioned above. With a certain amount of exaggeration we could even say that the elucidation of a problem consists in reducing it to ONE CONCEPT. The elucidation of this one concept is then the elucidation of the problem. But this is put very globally: the individual concepts must be elucidated in a consistent context, and this whole context then represented by an individual concept. Conceptual elucidation with respect to the three points mentioned above also requires clarity about the linguistic and argumentative forms in the concepts, to make them intersubjectively comprehensible.

In what follows I will speak of concepts only as linguistically presented; 'concept' will always mean 'conceptual expression'. We must now ask why elucidation of concepts is necessary and how it can be done.

Concepts in everyday usage are often VAGUE, AMBIGUOUS, and INCONSISTENT. We learn them in certain contexts, and we have to be able to generalize in order to transfer them to others. The same concept will be used in slightly different ways in different contexts, and will thus be learned in different ways. Each individual also connects private experiences with concepts: social value and private value cannot (and in general should not) be kept strictly separate, and social value varies from group to group. However, communication is still possible: each participant exerts himself with a certain 'good will' to understand the others, and their shared experience allows them to find the appropriate conceptual interpretation on the basis of context. Where this fails, or where disputes arise, we can attempt a conceptual elucidation, i.e. clarification or stabilization of the meaning of a concept for this situation. This is one of the reasons natural language is so versatile: it is not definitively fixed for any of its particular purposes, but can be appropriately changed and made more precise. This kind of refinement is also necessary for the scientific use of language.

There are various kinds of CONCEPTUAL VAGUENESS: the contents of a concept may be relatively obscure, i.e. the number of unclear usages may be very large; concepts may not be sharply distinguished from related ones, i.e. their range (in an extensional sense) and their value may not be precisely known; or the intension may be only partly known, i.e. only determined for a few contexts.[1]

CONCEPTUAL AMBIGUITY is generally due to the fact that concepts can have different meanings in different contexts. CONCEPTUAL INCONSISTENCY means that concepts are not always mutually compatible; they are not compatible in their different contexts of use (this is described above as ambiguity), or they are used by different persons with different meanings, different vaguenesses and different ambiguities.

There are several complementary types of conceptual elucidation. I will mention three, the third of which is especially important, as it leads to a sharpening of concepts, and transcends the possibilities of everyday language.

---

[1] These properties of concepts will be elaborated in 9.9 below, under the notion of partial intension. Note that this kind of vagueness is not in principle neutralizeable: concepts have to be usable at once in new, as yet unknown situations; and even theoretical concepts are generally only partially interpreted (or interpretable).

1. COLLOQUIAL ELUCIDATION. This requires the clarification, through more detailed and explicit paraphrases, of an individual concept or its use in typical sentential contexts. In this procedure we use with particular frequency certain linguistic forms which thus assume the character of standardized forms, within which all concepts and their uses are reinterpreted. The subsequent construction of conceptual (theoretical) languages is usually based on just such standardized paraphrase-forms.

2. CLARIFICATION BY TRANSLATION. Here we assume that we have available a language which is particularly well known and comprehensible, e.g. because it is especially rich and highly differentiated, or accessible to a great many groups of people (thus Latin used to be the scientific language one translated into). But this approach has its problems: do we really have any natural language at our disposal which is more highly differentiated and comprehensible than our own everyday one? If such a language did exist, would it not be a construct that we had developed for special purposes (the way scholarly Latin was extensively developed by the scholars themselves, and the way every standardized language also contains constructed elements)? And finally, what exactly does 'translation' mean here?[1] Is there any procedure for guaranteeing the adequacy of a translation? Probably not.

3. ANALYTICAL CLARIFICATION. This covers a set of procedures which have in common an attempt to understand concepts independently of their contexts of use, i.e. to work out their invariant properties. At the same time concepts are analysed by reduction to certain basic or primitive concepts, through categorization and the attendant precise definition of the primitive concepts, and through the attempt to establish all concepts by definition. Concepts are grouped, for instance, as classificatory, comparative and metrical: the first can be understood as predicates of a particular kind (e.g. 'black'), the second as relations of a particular kind (e.g. 'bigger than'), and the third can be analysed into expressions of metrical function (e.g. 'long' in '20 cm long'). The analysis at this point is obviously incomplete, since the predicates forming the concepts

---

[1] The correspondence of observational statements to theoretical ones is sometimes regarded as translation – though this is hardly possible according to Carnap's notion of correspondence (cf. 6.4 above). Occasionally the representation of colloquial statements in a constructed language is called translation. According to an idea of Montague's, the meaning of expressions in English, for example, can be obtained through a translation of these expressions into a particular form of intensional logic: provided that the semantics of intensional logic is to be interpreted as the semantics of English (so-called indirect meaning-correspondence). In this case we are dealing with translation into a constructed explication-language, i.e. an explication (cf. 7.4 below).

'black', 'good', 'normal', 'grammatical', etc., are not all of one type; and the same holds for the relations forming the concepts 'bigger than', 'related to', 'to hope', etc. The programme of conceptual analysis should lead in the end to all relevant concepts in a certain connection being analysed as – or, better, reconstructed as – expressions in a constructed conceptual language (theoretical language); this obviously assumes a corresponding richness in the constructed language.

7.3   Definition of concepts

We shall now look briefly at the problem of conceptual definition. In the traditional theory of concepts, going back ultimately to Plato, there is already a distinction between nominal and real definitions. A concept introduced through NOMINAL DEFINITION is chosen relatively arbitrarily, and can easily be replaced by another. In a REAL DEFINITION, however, it is the essence of a concept that is analysed, and this procedure cannot be arbitrary. We will be concerned here mainly with real definitions. On closer consideration nominal definitions are seen to be meaningful only in relation to an already precisely established set of concepts: they are used in the construction of languages, not in the analysis of languages and their concepts – especially when a complex concept is made easier to handle by introducing a new, simpler one in its place.[1] So the essence of a concept can be worked out in various ways: and correspondingly there are a number of kinds of real definition:[2]

   I. MEANING-ANALYSIS. A conceptual expression in a natural language (or one of its modified, e.g. standardized, forms) will be defined relative to other conceptual expressions in the same language; thus no new concept will be introduced without a statement being made about its relation to others. Relations of this kind (like synonymy, antonymy, incompatibility, etc.) can be called sense-relations; they can include either the concept as a whole, only individual components of the concept (in which case we speak e.g. of partial synonymy), or only contextual use of the concept (here we would speak of context-relative synonymy,

---

[1] This new concept is merely a technical aid for working in the constructed language; it does not provide any new information, and in principle can be eliminated again. An axiom introduced into a theory, on the contrary, always provides new information: an axiom is therefore never a nominal definition, but at most a real definition in the second sense, given further below. On the definition of new concepts within already existing constructed (logical) language cf. e.g. Essler (1970).

[2] Cf. Stegmüller (1958: 327–53, 329ff.). Stegmüller takes up some arguments of Hempel's here.

for instance, i.e. at least a three-place relation). In the transition to a constructed language we can, for example, represent the sense-relations existing between two constructions in the form of meaning-postulates; this means that no further ANALYSIS of meaning is to be performed, but rather that a particular meaning-relation is to be *fixed*, and this will count as a restriction on all interpretations in which one of the expressions involved in the relation appears.[1]

2. EMPIRICAL ANALYSIS. Here a conceptual expression is analysed according to what experiences (especially observations) it represents: we try to define the concept in relation to our experiential environment, for example the objects or classes of objects associated with it. This analysis is thus not intralinguistic, but is an analysis of a language's factual reference. An empirical scientist will first try for an empirical analysis of colloquial concepts in his science.[2] This procedure and meaning-analysis are interdependent: concepts are never isolated, but are always applied in a particular context representable through sense-relations; at the same time every concept is also related in a particular way to the world of experience.

3. EXPLICATION OF CONCEPTS. We set up a relation between an explicandum (i.e. a possible vague, ambiguous, inconsistent concept) and an explicatum (i.e. a clear, unambiguous, consistent one). The explicatum only encompasses some particular aspect of the explicandum, but it does this as precisely as possible. Thus one explicandum may have a whole series of explicata; these are not simply to be judged as better or worse, but rather as complementary elaborations of different aspects of the explicandum. These different explicata thus constitute a full solution of the possible ambiguity of the explicandum (e.g. with respect to different contexts of application). Every explication is goal-oriented, i.e. it is aimed at developing a theory of this or that aspect. To this extent the

---

[1] Cf. Carnap (1956b: 222–9), Schnelle (1973a: 15–25). I will consider sense-relations in more detail in connection with the explication of the concept of meaning (9.11 below).

A statement that two expressions stand in a particular sense-relation can also be seen as an analytic statement of a particular kind; but I will not go into the problems connected with this.

[2] A statement about the empirical analysis of a concept could be seen in a certain sense as synthetic. The interdependence of meaning-analysis and empirical analysis then shows that there is no operational criterion for distinguishing analytic from synthetic statements; correspondingly, logical and empirical theories cannot be precisely separated, so long as we allow expression-constants in the logic, since these always have an empirical sense. (I ignore the fact that the argument-forms reconstructed in logic also have an empirical sense.) On the theory of possible factual reference (referential semantics) cf. 9.1 below.

procedure of explication already assumes a particular (including linguistic) theory-form. Explication is not ultimately reducible to operations, nor can we give any strong criterion according to which an explication is to be judged adequate (though there have been attempts to discover such a criterion).

While meaning-analysis attempts to find precise sense-relations between concepts, and empirical analysis tries to find precise designation-relations (or at least interpretations) for concepts, the goal of explication is to replace an unclear concept by a clear one.

7.4 Explication of concepts

Every explication is a constructive procedure. But it is neither completely arbitrary nor solely dependent on the assumed goals of the theory. It is not just any concept that is to be constructed, but rather a particular aspect of one concept occurring in colloquial or standard-language use. Conceptual explication is clearly at the centre of any project involving the development of theories of some already existing knowledge; and this must be guided by specific ideas of what we will regard as an adequate explication, and what we will not (cf. Schnelle 1973a: ch. IIC, 100ff.).

The first attempt to set up uniform requirements for explications was made by Carnap, in connection with his explication of the concept of probability:[1]

1. The explicatum must be SIMILAR to the explicandum, i.e. we must be able to use the explicatum instead of the explicandum in all relevant cases.

2. There must be rules that establish the EXACT use of the explicatum (in connection with other scientific concepts).

3. The explicatum must turn out to be FRUITFUL for the formulation of general statements.

---

[1] Cf. Carnap & Stegmüller (1959: 15). Essler (1970: 58f.) gives a slightly different formulation: he says that '(2) the explicatum must be MORE PRECISE than the explicandum..., (3) the explicatum should be MORE FRUITFUL than the explicandum..., (4) the explicatum must be SIMPLER than the explicandum, and indeed (a) simpler in the definition of concepts and (b) in the formulation of the lawlike statements that are formulated in these concepts'.

Here 'precise', 'fruitful' and 'simple' are understood as comparative concepts, whereas in Carnap's formulation 'exact' and 'fruitful' are to be understood in an absolute classificatory sense; thus Essler obviously assumes that there is a scale of preciseness, according to what linguistic form an explication is directed toward. For simplicity there is a restriction that excludes, for instance, simplicity with respect to the possible deductions within the theory; this seems to me unjustified.

4. The explicatum must be as SIMPLE as possible (consistent with requirements 1–3 being met).

Only the first requirement concerns the relation of the explicatum to the explicandum – though it is not a strong criterion; the rest only concern the explicatum and its role in theory-construction. We are thus really dealing here with requirements on theories, not on the adequacy of explications. The sense of the first requirement will be clearer if we consider how we would proceed if we were being guided by it. Let us assume that a particular explicandum exists (whether in everyday language or standardized language). In general then we will find some cases in which it is clearly usable, and others where it is clearly not; in addition, there will be cases where it is not clear whether the concept is usable or not: these can be regarded as its vagueness-zone. The aim of the explication is to get the unclear cases to fall into one or the other category of clear cases, i.e. to get rid of the vagueness-zone. The similarity requirement can now be understood as follows: IN ALL CLEAR CASES the use of the explicatum should give the same results as the use of the explicandum.

In the description just given we already assume the consistency of the explicandum, at least with respect to the clear cases. This does not however create any difficulty, since wherever we have inconsistent application of concepts we can speak of unclear cases. We must of course ensure that clear, consistent cases are in the majority. In this connection Schnelle speaks of PRELIMINARY STABILIZATION OF AN EXPLICANDUM (1973a: 113). He suggests four ways of achieving this:

1. Stabilization on the basis of simple observational connections.

2. Stabilization already given in everyday language.

3. Stabilization because the explicandum becomes clearly recognizable through systematic correspondence with everyday language examples.

4. Stabilization through appropriate standardization of the everyday language.

The first kind of stabilization assumes that there exist relatively clear and consistently applicable observational concepts; this may well be the case in observing static constellations of objects, but hardly in observing processes or – as in linguistics – observing utterance-tokens and their contexts. Schnelle refers, thirdly, to a systematic presentation of examples and counter-examples in everyday language, as is commonly done in transformational syntactic arguments.[1]

---

[1] Cf. the reflections in 10.10 below on the structure of a typical transformational argument.

Schnelle adds a fifth kind of stabilization, which consists of performing certain SYSTEMATIC TESTS after obtaining an explicatum – tests where the explicandum is applied. These serve as an ADDITIONAL SUPPORT FOR THE EXPLICANDUM, and thus indirectly for the explicatum.[1]

These reflections on explication can be summed up as follows:

1. According to Carnap's requirements 2–4, we must always explicate WITH REFERENCE TO THEORIES; either we explicate central concepts (like 'meaning') in such a way that whole theories correspond to the explicatum, or we explicate different concepts interconnectedly.

2. We always explicate WITH REFERENCE TO CLEAR CASES, so that we can substitute precise arguments for our intuitions about them. But theories can also give answers for borderline cases; or we can explicate separately what a clear borderline case is.[2]

3. The explication-language is OF THE SAME ORDER as the explicandum-language (e.g. everyday language or some standardized language derived from it); we are therefore not dealing here with a descriptive language or a metalanguage relative to the language of the explicandum (the explicatum does not describe the explicandum).

Conceptual explication can best be demonstrated by examples. In that way we can judge as quickly as possible the extent to which the requirements for explication are actually to be considered as guiding principles for scientific activity, or where they should be modified.

Chomsky and Carnap are two authors who expressly construct at least part of their work as an explication programme. I will discuss some of their work in detail, not only to demonstrate a scientific procedure, but also to throw some light on the discussion of the content of linguistic concepts. In chapter 8 I will describe Chomsky's procedure in *Syntactic structures* (1957b), which can be summed up as the attempt to explicate the concept 'grammatical in L' (where 'L' = any language: in this case English). The result is the design of a new type of grammatical theory, exclusively concerned with the syntactic aspect.

In chapter 9 I will consider (among other things) Carnap's explication of the concept of meaning (constructed in a logical semantics); I will also look at competing concepts of meaning. From the standpoint of an example for explication I will show that a pre-theoretical concept (here 'meaning', though others like 'content', 'sense', etc., go along with it)

---

[1] Carnap proposed tests of this kind for the concepts of synonymy and analyticity (cf. Carnap 1956b: 238ff.; also Carnap 1963: 919ff.). Such tests are refined by Naess (1953).

[2] Cf. the discussion in 9.9 below on the explication of conceptual vagueness.

can be worked out in totally different directions, without it being clear at the outset how – or whether – these explications can be integrated.[1]

A single, relatively clarified concept of meaning (out of a horde of possible variants) usually suffices for special scientific purposes. In order to take account of the pretheoretical concept in all its various fields of application we would have to outline a general theory, in which all the different explicatum-concepts are laid out side by side. Such a general and integrative theory of meaning is not yet in sight; so I can only inquire into the various strands of development that go into the construction of a semantic theory. The concept of meaning is fundamental outside of linguistics as well – e.g. in logic and philosophy of language (not to mention psychology and social psychology); so its explication is a central task for a number of sciences.

7.5   On the empirical interpretation of linguistic theories

Explication is supposed to give a theoretical elucidation of particular experiential concepts, so as to make possible more precise argument and inference. An explication must reflect what is empirical in a science, i.e. how it will interpret everyday experience. Thus we cannot choose our explication arbitrarily; it has to be general and adequate to experience, and has to give coherent results in various empirical contexts. This is a necessary requirement – even in the absence of firm criteria – and we often find out only in a roundabout way that one explication is superior to another. Not even the theoretical form can be chosen arbitrarily: from the point of view of generality at least the forms of theories have to be empirically established.[2]

In what follows I will discuss the RELATION OF THEORETICAL LANGUAGE TO EVERYDAY LANGUAGE from the standpoint of explication. We will distinguish the domains A–D:

A. Facts, selected relative to problem-situations; goals; etc.
B. The language of the explicanda; the pretheoretical concepts (e.g. everyday language).

---

[1] Thus we could even take logic as a whole as an attempt to work out a theory of the concept of inference: as a result we find alongside material implication, strict implication and logical consequence, still other concepts of inference (cf. 5.5 above).

[2] Carnap's conventionality-principle allows arbitrary theory-forms and only requires subsequent justification of particular theoretical contents through correspondence to everyday explicanda. This overlooks the empirical character of the conceptual context; reconstructs only individual concepts in arbitrary preassigned forms, and says nothing about how these concepts are already expressed in everyday experience in particular connected forms.

C. The explication-language or theoretical language.

D. Interpretations (or models) of the theory (explicit statements of the extensions and intensions of the explicata).

In language B we speak about the domain A. The domain D belongs to a metalanguage relative to C (namely semantics), i.e. in D we speak in particular about C. In D we also speak indirectly about A, because the concepts of B are explicated in C. We can establish the following connection:

The relation holding between B and A gives us the pretheoretical understanding for setting up a theory in C; we formulate our previous knowledge of and relations to A in B. The theory C is now set up precisely for the purpose of explicating this knowledge. Therefore the relation between C and D must be able to be 'transmitted' to the relations between B and A; our understanding of a problem-situation will be subsequently stabilized, modified and clarified, to the extent that we can transmit certain interpretations in D to sentences in C in such a way that we can assume the same relation between the facts in A and our language in B.

Our artificial constructs in C and D thus co-determine our everyday-language understanding of the facts in A. We will in future also use our language B in a modified way, differentiate more sharply with respect to particular circumstances in A, and classify, generalize and abstract differently. According to the properties of the (more or less formal) explication-language C we will also organize and understand our use of language B differently. This can even lead to assertions about the language B which in fact can only hold for the language C: e.g. that a grammar is a recursive procedure for enumerating all the sentences of a language, or an automaton that generates particular sentences, or that it can decide whether a given string is or is not a sentence of the language, or that language is a set of relations between stimuli and responses.

The relation between the construct-language C and its interpretation in D sHows us something about the relation between the language B and the facts in A; it demonstrates our knowledge of A, though only certain aspects of our preliminary understanding. The requirement of explicitness in one aspect leads to other competing requirements (e.g. explicitness in some other aspect) having to be bypassed. The theory always serves only some purposes, but it serves them more precisely than ordinary language, while ordinary language can serve many more purposes, but less completely. Thus the theory, by fixing particular points of view or goals, becomes a substitute for our handling of B with respect to A. But the theory is always bound to fixed points of view, i.e. its assumptions, while ordinary language can always be developed in relation to other points of view or goals.

To avoid misunderstandings, I must emphasize two points:

1. There is NO EQUIVALENCE between the relations C to D and B to A: the expressions in C are not a direct translation of those in B, nor is there any strict procedure by which we can obtain corresponding expressions in C from expressions in B. Nor can we say generally that a language in C is adequate (adequacy can be measured only in relation to fixed goals).

2. D DESCRIBES the semantic properties of C, and similarly we can describe the syntactic and pragmatic properties of C;[1] it is nonetheless false to say that C describes B, or even merely that C describes A. For there are only a few cases in which we can be said to describe objects in A when we speak of them. Thus questions, requests, etc. relate to men's attitudes toward objects in A and to actions relative to A. In this way objects in A may be mentioned by means of descriptive expressions; thus descriptions are only presupposed (in the case of implicit reference we do not even do this) – but the act itself is not a descriptive act.

In general we can say that empirical theories capture, explain, demonstrate, show something relative to a bounded domain of facts in A; in this way they influence our understanding of and actions on A, insofar as we direct these according to our understanding of A and the imaginable consequences of the alternative actions at our disposal. Every empirical theory is thus a twofold reconstruction: on the one hand of the results of specially organized experimental situations relative to A, and on the other of the kind of linguistic argumentation procedures we use in B relative to A. The first aspect is primarily reconstructed in the semantics (understood as referential semantics) in D, and the second in the theoretical language C and the argumentations (e.g. deductions) permitted there.

We can set up an analogy between the reconstruction of these aspects.[2] We can understand either our EXPERIMENTAL SET-UPS or our FORMAL LANGUAGES (and logics) C as INSTRUMENTS which – applied to particular phenomena – lead to particular results (figure 6). In (a) we describe the structures of (b), as they emerge through the instrumental arrangement

---

[1] If we determine the interpretations of the expressions in C according to possible contexts of use, we can say that some of the pragmatic properties of C are described in D.

[2] I owe the idea of this analogy to a discussion with T. Potts.

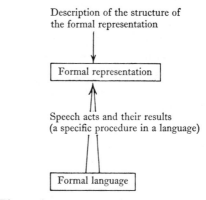

Figure 6

of (d) via (c); this does not however mean that (c) is now described in (a). But insofar as we describe the structures of (b), we show something about how (c) functions. (We could perhaps say that on the basis of the experimental set-ups we can see the structures of (c) AS structures of (b).) Now in order to represent the fact that in (a) we explicate our KNOW-LEDGE about (c), we must say in case I (speech-sounds): on the basis of our knowledge of (c) we have selected just this instrumental set-up, and from it we automatically get the result in (b). But this result must still be represented in linguistic form (described), in order for us to use it in our arguments; and for this we need a set-up according to case II. In case II (speech acts, and now also the representation of experimental results from case I), we can likewise say that on the basis of our knowledge about (c) we have selected the formal language in (d). But this set-up does not automatically yield results in (b); this would be the case only if we had an effective algorithm. In general we must consider our knowledge of (c) a second time, in order to obtain, as results, particular formal representations in (b). These results will be linguistic in form, and as such can be used in arguments; their description no longer represents an additional achievement. Description is necessary only if we have to discuss the properties of the formal representation.

Cases I and II, then, are not completely analogous. In case I we assume a set-up of type II, in order to reach level (a); we assume no such arrangement in case II. Our knowledge of linguistic procedure is available to us through reflection, and we can replace this only to a limited extent with algorithms. Our knowledge of speech sounds is available largely through observation; we can partly replace observation through apparatus such that we can observe the results of its automatic functioning. (This holds not only for phonetics, but also for psycholinguistic or neurophysiological experiments, e.g. during linguistic activities.) These results must however always be described. Wherever we need observations, we also need descriptions.

Now linguistics obviously employs instruments of types I and II;[1] according to the character of these instruments we can call linguistic descriptions either descriptive–empirical or explicative–empirical. Linguistics is descriptive–empirical insofar as we regard linguistic facts as belonging to the domain A referred to above: speech sounds, the activities of speech and perception, memory and the recovery of what is remembered, the phenomena of individual languages, the development and change of individual words and their representational functions. Linguistics is explicative–empirical in the sense that we reconstruct everyday language (i.e. our linguistic operations relative to the domain of facts) by means of a formal, explicit logical language. Thus it is a question rather of handling arbitrary facts, since we are not reconstructing the language of physics or mathematics, but ordinary language in all its essential functions. This kind of linguistics is not fundamentally different from logic. In formal logic we establish the presuppositions for explication, but from the point of view of content they are always applied to particular speech and argument forms. Actually, of course, the development of formal logic has always been oriented toward the language of mathematics, and has treated its subject matter as universal (and non-empirical); while linguistics has been concerned with a greater wealth of expressions, with variability in different languages, and with historical change. It is only in the highly developed (so-called 'non-classical') logics of modalities, obligations, etc., that the correspondence shows more clearly: these forms of logic can just as well be understood as theories of particular possibilities of expression in natural languages. Thus even the form of logics has an explicative–empirical character; it

---

[1] Something like what we have indicated by the two aspects of reconstruction may be the case for other empirical–theoretical sciences, like physics. Of course empirical understanding in physics has gradually been displaced on the observational side (naïve knowledge of physical processes and use of this knowledge outside type I set-ups hardly play any role for the physicist), and theoretical understanding has been displaced by formal reconstruction of such observational results (instead of reconstruction of procedures with observational results). There are also important physical theories (like special relativity) whose empirical basis is thought-experiments, and which rest in large part on the explication of concepts of everyday experience; in these observations at best play a secondary role.

allows the most general possible explication of the expressive possibilities of languages (without special reference to English, German, etc.).

Some linguists regard linguistics as mainly or even exclusively a descriptive–empirical science; and thus they take language exclusively as THE OBJECT OF OUR KNOWLEDGE, not as THE FORM IN WHICH IT IS REPRESENTED. This position is of course rarely held consistently, because the other one is often introduced by virtue of methodology. We begin from judgements IN language about linguistic correctness, normality, relatedness, similarities, etc., i.e. from a linguistic consciousness which is reflected in such judgements; not from observations OF a linguistic attitude which leads in particular (e.g. experimentally produced) situations to particular utterance-tokens; we also utilize explications of pretheoretical knowledge. Some linguists, however, use a misleading terminology. Schnelle for instance, considers that the factual reference of a linguistic construct-language resides in the fact that it describes natural languages. He sketches the relationship this way (1973a: 91):

Metalanguage: linguistic construct-language

$\downarrow$ Factual reference

Object language: ordinary language

This is open to the following objections:

1. The terms 'metalanguage' and 'object language' are introduced for constructed languages in order precisely to distinguish certain types of expressions in them; they have a precisely defined sense. One can speak in the metalanguage about all and only the properties of expressions and relations between expressions in the object language. If a linguistic theory speaks about constructed objects, it must first demonstrate the adequacy of its factual reference (in Schnelle's sense); it cannot introduce it by definition. So natural language ought to be understood here as an object of linguistic description, and not as a constructed object language.

2. Natural language already contains many possibilities for an 'object language'–'metalanguage' relation (in a transferred sense); we can generally speak in a natural language about parts of natural language and what we do with it. These relationships are directly represented in the construct-language as object language–metalanguage relationships, and not in ONE construct-language understood as a metalanguage (in Schnelle's sense).

3. It must be possible to speak in the natural language about the

linguistic construct-language; in this case the natural language would be a meta-metalanguage for itself. The special role of the construct-language relative to natural language would be lost, and the schema would be circular, if we did not stick to the notion that natural language plays two very different roles here.

On the basis of these objections I would rather propose the schema in figure 7. Here again we can distinguish the two interpretations that I will call descriptive and explicative:

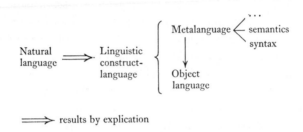

Figure 7

1. For each aspect of natural language we assume a separate linguistic construct-language (a phonology-language, a syntax-language, a semantics-language, etc.). These aspects are to be established within the factual domain (domain A in the schema referred to above). Thus the expressions of the phonology-language designate phonetic expression-forms, those of the syntax-language syntactic expression-forms, constructions, syntactic relations, etc., and those of the semantics-language meanings. On the phonological level this seems to make sense (notations in a phonetic, phonological, etc., 'script' are introduced for particular phonetic forms); and possibly also on the syntactic level (although syntactic expression-forms could just as well be reconstructed in the construct-language and then only designated by expressions in the metalanguage). On the semantic level however it is not at all clear what it would mean to say that meanings are designated; meanings can only be EXPRESSED, they are not objects that can be designated.

2. We assume a unitary linguistic construct-language for recording the syntactic–semantic (and perhaps also the pragmatic) aspects of a natural language – according to particular objectives we have in mind. The syntax and semantics (and perhaps pragmatics) of this construct-language, as they are describable in the corresponding metalanguage, show – according to the objectives – something about the syntax, seman-

tics (and possibly pragmatics) of natural language; but they are of the same order as it is. This means in particular that natural language meanings (e.g. concepts) are not described, but only somewhat differently (i.e. more explicitly) presented. Even in this version there are still various possible formulations, i.e. we can now develop different construct-languages with unequivocal translation-relations (e.g. Montague's grammatical theory).

A theory of grammar is accordingly nothing more than a linguistic construct-language, set up within certain limits and according to particular points of view, which in its most important aspects can serve for the reconstruction of the most varied individual languages. Insofar as the individual languages contain constants (lexical units), we need corresponding constants in the grammatical theory (or in the individual grammars).

8 On the explication of the concept 'grammatical in language L'

8.1 Presuppositions for explication

In this chapter I will not be concerned with different versions of the concept of grammar, but only with a particular and historically very important one: that developed by Chomsky in *Syntactic structures* (1957b).

In the first phase of an explication the main task is to achieve a relatively stable and unequivocal (standardized) explicandum, excluding other possible versions of the concept. This is the basis for the theoretical reconstruction. In the case of the concept 'grammatical in language L' there are several associated concepts that have to be explicated simultaneously – in any case the concept 'language L', which is part of the explicandum. We also have to make clear what this is to be applied to. These preliminary clarifications will have important consequences for delimiting the explicandum.

Chomsky begins his inquiry in chapter 2 with the following three assumptions (1957b: 13):

[a] I will consider a *language* to be a set (finite or infinite) of sentences, each finite in length and constructed out of a finite set of elements.

[b] ...each natural language has a finite set of phonemes (or letters in its alphabet) and each sentence is representable as a finite sequences of these phonemes (or letters).

[c] The grammar of L will...be a device that generates all of the grammatical sequences of L and none of the ungrammatical ones.

Clearly the concepts 'language L', 'sentence', and 'grammar of L' are already theoretically expressed, namely controlled by a strict constructive (set-theoretic) point of view. We can represent Chomsky's assumptions under (a) formally as follows:

Individual language	$L = \{s_1, s_2, ...\}$
Vocabulary of L	$V = \{e_1, e_2, ..., e_n\}$
(finite set of elements)	
Sentence in L (of length m)	$s = (e_1, e_2, ..., e_m),$
	where all $e_j \in V$

This represents a coherent theoretical position. We can criticize the following points:

1. THE LANGUAGE CONCEPT. The normal person hardly understands his language as a (possibly infinite) set of sentences; the explicandum chosen here should therefore be specially justified *vis-à-vis* alternative ones. Some alternative explicandum concepts might be: a language is the class of means of communication controlled in common by a group; a language is the class of conditions which the members of a group must observe in their communicative endeavours; a language is a special class of rules of social behaviour, etc.

2. THE SENTENCE CONCEPT. This is already theoretical; here it is not oriented toward the much more intuitively accessible concept of the utterance (production of temporally extended phonetic sequences or spatially extended graphic sequences in particular social situations), but only to the notion of finite construction out of elements or (in assumption (b)) that of an abstract sequence of phonemes.

3. THE STATUS OF THE ELEMENTS (vocabulary) is unclear. According to assumption (b), the elements can be identified with the phonemes (or letters) of a language. The concept of the phoneme again stems from particular theories (unlike 'language' and 'sentence', 'phoneme' is not a word in ordinary language); besides, phonemes have no meaning. Alternatively words (or word-stems or idioms), which all have meaning, could be taken as the basic elements.

4. We can infer from assumption (b), as well as indirectly from the others, that even 'sentence' and 'language' are taken only in the formal-syntactic sense, i.e. that sentences are NOT regarded as FORMAL CONSTRUCTIONS WITH MEANINGS. This concept of language is thus one-dimensional.

5. Assumption (c) appears to be circular: the grammar of L characterizes all those sentences that correspond to the grammar of L. In order to avoid this circularity we must know independently of the grammar which sentences are grammatical and which are not. Thus we need a pretheoretical concept of 'grammatical in L' that we can use in interrogations, observations, etc. The grammar of L should then reconstruct the results of empirical investigation.

What role does the CONCEPT OF GRAMMAR play in the theory? If we already had L available as an enumeration of sentences, then 'grammatical in L' would be trivially defined:

s_i is grammatical in L $=$ df $s_i \in L$

We must therefore assume that we do not already know L through enumeration, but must first construct it. A grammar of L is now just such a construction procedure (and thus a non-trivial enumeration procedure) for the set of all $s_i \in L$.

Every construction procedure unfolds in discrete steps; the sequence of steps that leads to a particular $s_i \in L$ characterizes at the same time a particular structure $t(s_i)$. A grammar of L thus generates pairs of sentences and the structures of these sentences:

$$G_L \Rightarrow L \times T = \{\langle s_1, t(s_1)\rangle, \langle s_2\ t(s_2)\rangle, \ldots\}$$

Every grammatical sentence in L must be constructable through G_L; this alone will yield, through a corresponding sequence of construction steps, a characterized structure for this sentence:

$$s_i \text{ is grammatical in } L = df\ (E\ t_i)\ (G_L \Rightarrow \langle s_i, t_i\rangle)$$

At this point we should add two notes:

1. A grammar is understood here as a CONSTRUCTION PROCEDURE for sentences. I will not discuss the alternative conception of a grammar as a DECISION PROCEDURE, i.e. one establishing in a finite number of steps whether a particular sequence of elements is or is not a sentence of L. This decision procedure would divide a given arbitrary set of element-sequences into two subsets: one contains exclusively the grammatical sentences of L, the other all sentences not grammatical in L (but grammatical in some other language, or another sociolect L'), as well as all those sequences which are not sentences in any language. A grammar designed as a decision procedure could also be called an analysis-grammar.[1]

2. Up to now the concept 'grammatical in L' has been applied only to SENTENCES. It might be extended to subsequences of sentences: every partial result reached in the construction of a sentence in L is likewise to be regarded as grammatical in L. Say that *I wanted to do a handstand on the grass* is a grammatical sentence of English. Then it makes sense to regard e.g. *I wanted, on the grass,* and *to do a handstand on the grass* as grammatical in English, as opposed to *a handstand on, to do a,* which are ungrammatical. Among other things, this serves to single out certain constructional procedures as against others.

The basis on which Chomsky wants to stabilize his explicandum concept 'grammatical in L' is the speaker's partial (intuitive) KNOWL-

---

[1] It is possible for a production-grammar to be understood simultaneously as an analysis-grammar, but this is not generally done.

EDGE about sentences and non-sentences (where non-sentence = ungrammatical in L).[1] The following other possible interpretations of 'grammatical in L' are excluded:

I. THE CONCEPT 'GRAMMATICAL IN L' IS NOT TO BE REDUCED TO CONCEPTS LIKE 'OBSERVED UTTERANCE IN L'. There are also observable utterances of ungrammatical sentences, i.e. utterance-tokens that the speaker himself would call 'incorrect', 'unfortunate', and the like; that is, they are classified as ungrammatical by the speakers themselves. On the other hand no collection – no matter how large – of grammatically acceptable utterances (e.g. a corpus assembled for some purpose) can exhaust the set of grammatical sentences (which may be infinitely large); there will thus always be sentences that are not in the corpus, even though they would be classifiable as grammatical. Literally this means (Chomsky 1957b: 15) that 'a grammar mirrors the behavior of the speaker who, on the basis of a finite and accidental experience with language, can produce or understand an indefinite number of new sentences.' Here I think that two questions remain unclarified:

(a) The purpose of the explication (or to put it another way the purpose of a grammar – understood as a theory of an individual language) is not made precise enough. There still remain THREE POSSIBLE INTERPRETATIONS:

A grammar reconstructs the speaker's (intuitive) KNOWLEDGE of his language (this was the definition given at first).

A grammar is a theory of the LINGUISTIC BEHAVIOUR of speakers; in particular a theory of what they utter and understand on specific occasions.

A grammar is a theory about what speakers must BE ABLE TO DO in order to communicate in a language.[2]

These interpretations are, to be sure, not independent of each other:

---

[1] In later work Chomsky uses the expression 'tacit knowledge', i.e. he emphasizes the implicit character of this knowledge. But 'knowledge' is possibly ambiguous, namely in the senses of 'knowing' or 'ability'. The problem then arises of the extent to which knowledge is a category accessible to empirical investigation (experiments, tests, etc.); in any case it is not an observable. Perhaps experiments in cognitive psychology (e.g. structure-recognition and structure-comparison) might help. Accordingly Chomsky classifies linguistics as a branch of cognitive psychology. If we wanted to follow up this idea, we could probably count all investigations in which some knowledge is explicated and reconstructed (e.g. in logic and philosophy of science) as cognitive psychology as well. This classification (which comes about only on the basis of particular experimental conditions) certainly does not seem to be very useful.

[2] The term 'competence' that Chomsky uses in later work is perhaps to be understood in this sense. Here it would be better to describe speakers' linguistic competence as dispositions for linguistic behaviour.

a person's linguistic behaviour depends on what he is able to do, and on what he knows about what he is able to do; and a person's knowledge of language depends on how he uses it or the contexts in which he uses it; the learning of a language involves reflection, and thus the acquisition of knowledge about language. However, these interpretations are not identical, and we therefore need some indication about which one should be taken as basic, or whether all three are to be developed together (in which case their mutual relations would have to be explored more exactly).

(b) The concept 'grammatical in L' is a theoretical concept, and not an operational one (even the explicandum is pretheoretical). Theoretical concepts cannot be fully reduced to observational ones; but it is possible to correlate observational concepts with them, if we set up a systematic procedure for doing so. Thus, for example, 'utterance in L' (or 'non-deviant utterance in L') could be the observational concept with which the concept 'grammatical in L' is to be systematically correlated. This would clearly establish the empirical basis: it would consist, not of experimental judgements about speakers' linguistic intuitions, but of observational judgements about speakers' utterance-tokens (in either natural or artificial situations). Linguistics would then not be a branch of COGNITIVE PSYCHOLOGY, but would be concerned with its own particular kind of observations and experiments. It would still, however, stand in a certain relation to psychology, since there are also psychological experiments concerned with the processes of speech-perception and production.

So with respect to both questions, Chomsky has not achieved the desired unequivocality in the explicandum: on the contrary, in the passage cited above, he hints at new and up to now undiscussed differentiations ('the BEHAVIOR of the speaker', the speaker's 'finite... EXPERIENCE', the fact that 'the speaker...CAN produce or understand an indefinite number of new sentences'). These must be discussed if we want to achieve the necessary clarity about the empirical status of the theory we are aiming for.

2. THE CONCEPT 'GRAMMATICAL IN L' IS NOT TO BE IDENTIFIED WITH THE CONCEPT 'MEANINGFUL IN L'. Thus both the sentences

(1) Colourless green ideas sleep furiously.

(2) Furiously sleep ideas colourless green.

are equally meaningless, but (1) is grammatical in English and (2) is not. As evidence Chomsky uses considerations which could relatively easily be checked experimentally:[1] (1) will be spoken with normal sentence intonation, but not (2); (1) will be more easily remembered and repeated after some lapse of time than (2); we can imagine contexts in which (1) might be uttered, but there are no such contexts for (2).

At this point it is clear that 'grammatical in L' is a SYNTACTIC CONCEPT, somewhat analogous to the concept of (syntactic) well-formedness in logical languages. Just as the class of well-formed sentences in a logical language also includes the logically false ones, so the class of grammatical sentences in a natural language also includes the meaningless, contradictory and nonsensical ones. The concepts 'logically true', 'logically false', 'true', etc. can only be applied to well-formed expressions in a logical language, just as – in Chomsky's theory – 'meaningful', 'contradictory', etc. can only be applied to grammatical sentences in the natural language. He does not raise the question of whether all sentences should perhaps be judged according to both syntactic and semantic criteria.

The nonsensicality of (1) can be demonstrated as follows: 'Something that's colourless can't also be green; nor can one say of ideas that they either have a colour or don't (colour predicates are not applicable to ideas); ideas can't sleep; something that sleeps won't be furious.' These are exclusively semantic arguments, and we assume that we know how we have to combine the meanings of the words in (1) in order to get the meaning of the whole sentence; we base our argument on the fact that we already accept (1) as grammatical in English. We behave differently when we want to explain why (2) is nonsensical: 'This is just "word-salad": I don't know what "colourless green" is supposed to be related to; maybe he means furious ideas, but that's not clear: maybe some ideas are supposed to be sleeping, but that's impossible.' Obviously most of these judgements are conditioned by the fact that we don't know how the words in this sentence should be combined; we only suspect that there won't be a meaningful combination.

Chomsky's programme here is first to work out the concept 'grammatical in L' as a pure syntactic concept, and only ADDITIONALLY to analyse the concept 'meaningful in L'. There are two main objections to this:

(a) we are often prepared to assign meanings even to utterances of

---

[1] Chomsky is obviously not referring to experiments on what speakers KNOW – except perhaps on the last point – but to experiments on speakers' BEHAVIOUR in appropriate novel situations.

ungrammatical sentences (e.g. to call an utterance in broken English contradictory). We must consider more exactly how we do this.

(b) Chomsky obviously thinks that 'grammatical in L' can be stabilized without recourse to semantic considerations.[1] This view gets some support through the reference to experiments concerning intonation and recall of sentences. But of course one might ask whether the singling out of the grammatical sentences in these experiments is not directly a result of the fact that we know how their meaning is to be built up out of the meanings of the individual words. The argument from the ability to think up possible contexts of utterance is much weaker: first, this can be done for a certain number of clearly ungrammatical sentences; and, secondly, it really means that even in these contexts one would be prepared to assign meanings to these sentences. It therefore seems to me that in defining the concept 'grammatical in L' we must appeal to semantic considerations in at least the following way (cf. the discussion of sentences (1)–(2)): only those sentences on which we can make judgements of meaning without special difficulties are grammatical; and this is because the meaning of the sentence derives from the combination of the meanings of individual words in it, and this combination is controlled by its syntactic structure.[2] If the syntactic construction is 'unsuccessful', then we do not know how to assign a total meaning (or several partial meanings, perhaps) to the sentence. If we explicate the concept 'grammatical in L' syntactically, then we must always do this with reference to the fact that this should make it possible to show how a particular sentence is interpreted (or understood).

3. THE CONCEPT 'GRAMMATICAL IN L' IS NOT TO BE UNDERSTOOD IN ANY STATISTICAL SENSE. Neither observations on the frequency of use of sentences nor assumptions about the degree of probability or improbability of the use of a particular sentence should be regarded as basic. Certainly Chomsky would admit that the linguistic experiences of speakers are so constituted that they have heard and produced particular sentences or syntactic constructions with different frequencies. But

[1] He remarks (1957b: 93) on the question 'How can you construct a grammar with no appeal to meaning?' that one could ask with equal justification 'how can you construct a grammar with no knowledge of the hair color of speakers?' This polemical position may be exaggerated, but it does indicate Chomsky's view that syntax does not simply provide the BASIS for a semantics, but should be developed completely INDEPENDENTLY of it.

[2] On the basis of constructional analogy we can now understand even sentences like *The bendates carulized elatically* as grammatical in English. When we know what the words *bendate, carulize* and *elatically* mean, we also know what the sentence means.

from this experience they extrapolate a CATEGORIAL KNOWLEDGE, and this knowledge is used for stabilizing the concept 'grammatical in L'. This means that even the average speaker will already treat 'grammatical in L' as a THEORETICAL CONCEPT. The question of correspondence with linguistic observations does not arise very often for the average speaker, which may justify our not overvaluing it in theory-construction. But since the speaker regards grammatical constructions as CONVENTIONAL PROCEDURES, it still remains open whether or not his grammatical knowledge is solely categorial. Conventions refer to the 'normality' of modes of action (and thus to particular socially stabilized contexts of expectation), transgressions of which are disadvantageous; they do not refer (at least primarily) to the frequency of modes of action. Even frequency and normality, of course, are not totally independent of each other; but we can properly leave this problem out of consideration when we are discussing only grammaticality.

8.2 Transformational grammar as an explicatum for 'grammatical in language L'

The explicatum for 'grammatical in English' should be a particular scientific grammar of English; the explicatum for 'grammatical in L' is a theory of grammar from which we can derive the grammars of all languages through the appropriate specification (cf 3.5 above). Each proposed grammatical theory GT is at least inadequate if for a language L_1 (e.g. English) it can be shown that the grammar of L_1 derived from GT is not an appropriate explicatum for 'grammatical in L_1'.

1. Whether or not a particular grammar of L_1 represents an appropriate explicatum for 'grammatical in L_1' will be judged in the first instance by whether it can reconstruct all clear cases of sentences in L_1, and none of the clear cases of non-sentences. According to this criterion of adequacy Chomsky claims (1957b: ch. 3)[1] that a FINITE-STATE GRAMMAR is not an appropriate explicatum for 'grammatical in English', because it cannot reconstruct sentences like

(3) If S_1, then S_2.
(4) Either S_3 or S_4.
(5) The man who said that S_5 is arriving today.
(6) If either (5) or S_4, then S_2.

(where S_1–S_5 can again be any of the sentences (3)–(6)).

---

[1] I give only the form of the argument; for details see Chomsky's full exposition.

But these are clear cases of sentences of English.

2. Chomsky uses simplicity (or generality) as a further criterion of adequacy. A particular grammar of L_1 is an inappropriate explicatum if it can represent a whole series of statements only in a complicated and non-general way: for example, statements about the structural similarity or ambiguity of sentences, which could be simply and generally reconstructed in some other way. The criterion is clearly applicable only when two different explicata are compared; so Chomsky formulates this as the task of a grammatical theory (ch. 6). In chapters 5, 7 and 8 the criterion is applied to PHRASE-STRUCTURE GRAMMARS, which construct sentences in a series of structure-expanding stages (and thus reconstruct the results of a stepwise analysis into immediate constituents); as a competing explicatum he uses a TRANSFORMATIONAL GRAMMAR (here outlined for the first time in book form); this also allows the construction of sentences from other sentences (or sentence structures from other sentence structures).[1] The result is that a phrase-structure grammar is not an appropriate explicatum for 'grammatical in English', because it is less simple (i.e. general) than a transformational grammar.

Chomsky adduces three types of arguments to support this:

(a) STRUCTURAL SIMILARITY OF SENTENCES. He proceeds from English examples: sentences which contain the conjunction of subordinated constituents (like *the scene of the movie and of the play was in Chicago*), and which can be systematically related to sentences without these conjunctions (*the scene of the movie was in Chicago* and *the scene of the play was in Chicago*); sentences with sequences of auxiliary verbs (like *the man has been reading the book*) which should receive a unitary treatment; sentences which stand in the active–passive relation to each other.[2] I will examine only the third example here, as it is perhaps the most illuminating.

Both (7) and (8) below will be regarded as grammatical sentences in English:

---

[1] The concept of transformation is taken from Harris – though he uses it in a more concrete sense. Chomsky has modified the notion in his later works: cf. 10.9 below.

[2] Chomsky (1957b: 42ff.). Chomsky is oriented here toward traditional grammatical ideas, insofar as he tries to formulate a unitary relation between active and passive sentences (the passive transformation). A closer analysis of all possible active and passive sentences in English (or a related language like German) will show that we are dealing here with at least two different relations: one between sentences in which the logical subject is in first position and sentences in which it is in a later position, and one between sentences in which the logical object is in a non-first position and sentences in which it is in first position. Thus the passive transformation can be split into two rules, each of which can be justified independently of the active–passive relation.

(7) John admires sincerity.

(8) Sincerity is admired by John.

But not all active sentences have corresponding passives (i.e. the passive structure has a more restricted use than the active). In addition, it is clear that all arguments that can be brought up to exclude sentences like

(9) Sincerity admires John

(formulated in selectional restrictions like 'the verb *admire* does not allow abstract subjects,' etc.) can be applied in exactly the same way to the corresponding passives, i.e.

(10) John is admired by sincerity.

A phrase-structure grammar must generate (7) and (8) independently of each other, but it must not – and especially not independently – generate (9) and (10); thus in each case the necessary restrictions have to be stated twice. The construction procedure can be simplified if the phrase-structure grammar only generates sentences like (7), and is prohibited from generating (9). Sentences like (8) can then be constructed by means of an added passive transformation:

If S_1 is a grammatical sentence of the form
$$NP_1 - Aux - V - NP_2$$

then the corresponding string of the form
$$NP_2 - Aux + be + en - V - by + NP_1$$
is also a grammatical sentence.

Sentences like (10) are automatically excluded as soon as (9) is marked as ungrammatical. The structural description of the active sentence automatically guarantees that passive sentences can only be constructed with transitive verbs, that *is admired* will automatically be followed by *by* NP_1, etc.

Chomsky seems to assume that the claim that (9) and (10) are clear cases of ungrammatical sentences can be justified by syntactic arguments. But it is not obvious why (1) should be regarded as a grammatical sentence, while (9) and (10) are ungrammatical. All the arguments that were proposed for the grammaticality of (1) must surely be applicable here. That verbs like *admire* do not take abstract subjects is a function of their meaning. In 1965 Chomsky introduced features like [+abstract] and [−abstract], which he understands as syntactic features of nouns (1965: ch. 2, §2.3). But this simply conceals the fact that arguments for or against the assignment of such features must be based on the meaning of the nouns (or on the meaning of the verbs that can be combined with them, or on the fact that sentences so constructed are either meaningful or not meaningful).

(b) STRUCTURAL AMBIGUITY OF SENTENCES. By means of a phrase-structure grammar we can represent the ambiguity of sentences like

(11) They are flying planes.

There are two constructional paths for obtaining (11); there are correspondingly two different structures for (11):

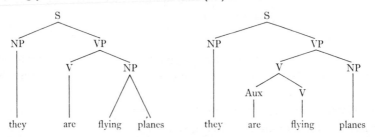

In the same way it should be possible to represent the ambiguity of phrases like

(12) the shooting of the hunters

i.e. through providing different constructional paths. This seems to be impossible using only a phrase-structure grammar, since (12) in both of its meanings has the same structure. With a transformational grammar, however, it is possible to provide two different constructional paths: in one case the sentence *the hunters shoot* is mapped into (12), while in the other the source is the sentence *they shoot the hunters*. There must thus be two different transformations, which when applied to different sentences will give the same result.

Even this argument goes beyond the original objective, which was solely a constructive enumeration of the set of grammatical sentences in English (including particular steps in construction that have grammatical phrases – i.e. sentence-constituents – as their output). Here it is required in addition that particular ambiguities in grammatical sentences (or phrases) be shown as ambiguities in the construction procedure. Possible ambiguity evidently plays a role in answering the question of how a sentence can be understood, i.e. how its meaning is to be reconstructed on the basis of the constructional steps employed. This problem however is clearly a semantic one.

(c) STATEMENTS IN TRADITIONAL GRAMMARS about sentence similarity and modality. Chomsky compares the following sentences (9off.):

(13) John ate an apple.
(14) Did John eat an apple ?
(15) What did John eat ?
(16) Who ate an apple ?

What criterion should we use for grouping these sentences ? According to intonation, (13), (15) and (16) belong to a group (falling intonation), according to word-order (13) and (16) belong together (NP-V-NP); but according to the traditional classification (14), (15) and (16) belong together (question sentences).

A grammar should reconstruct the speaker's knowledge about language: this includes paying attention to traditionally transmitted knowledge. Therefore sentences (13)–(16) should be classified according to their modality (declarative vs. interrogative). This argument is unconvincing for three reasons: (1) it is not clear that a phrase-structure grammar is incapable of providing this characterization; (2) contrary to the original intention, we now have recourse to semantic and not syntactic classifications: the modality of a sentence partly indicates what it can be used for (declaratives for assertions, interrogatives for questions); (3) the traditionally transmitted knowledge is also the result of particular attitudes (e.g. those that prevail in the schools). The argument thus runs the risk of circularity: today's linguistic theories only reconstruct yesterday's.

8.3 Grammatical theory

We have seen that according to Chomsky the concept 'grammatical in L' (for any arbitrary L) is to be explicated by a grammatical theory; while the different concepts 'grammatical in L_1', 'grammatical in L_2' (for fixed L_1, L_2, etc) are to be explicated by grammars of individual languages – which must be related in a particular way to grammatical theory. The grammatical theory fixes the conditions of universality (generality) of statements in the individual grammars (later called explanatory adequacy: cf. 3.5, 3.9 above); in addition the individual grammars must be externally adequate, i.e. with respect to data and facts (observational and descriptive adequacy). Chomsky discusses three possible versions of a grammatical theory GT:

1. The theory provides a practical and mechanical procedure for constructing a grammar on the basis of any corpus of natural-language sentences (utterance-tokens): it provides a DISCOVERY PROCEDURE for

grammars. According to this version there is no explication of, for example, 'grammatical in English' independent of grammatical theory; but there is a full independent establishment of what is a corpus in English. Chomsky makes clear enough that he does not accept this version.[1] The terminology however is somewhat misleading: there is no theory to be discovered, since it is given in advance, but a theory does have to be applied to a articular corpus of sentences in order to find a grammar for it. We are dealing here with the methodological problem of bringing independently obtained data into strict correspondence with a theory. But methodological procedures are never strictly applicable; they are applicable only in appraising the theoretical profit obtainable by their application. They do not guarantee the translatability of data into theoretical statements.

2. The theory provides a procedure for establishing, for every pair of corpus + grammar of the corpus, whether the grammar is adequate or not; it provides a DECISION PROCEDURE for grammars. Chomsky says 'the theory must provide a practical and mechanical method for determining whether or not a grammar proposed for a given corpus is, in fact, the BEST grammar OF THE LANGUAGE from which this corpus is drawn' (1957b: 51; emphasis mine). This problem is not soluble: first, the best grammar can only be discovered with reference to different competing grammars; second, the corpus has to be a representative one, which contains all relevant data – especially those cases that are critical for the theory. But there is no known criterion for such a notion of representativeness. We can only decide whether the grammar is adequate or not with respect to the sentences of the corpus.

3. The theory provides a procedure for establishing, for any corpus and any two grammars, which grammar is better: it provides an EVALUATION PROCEDURE for grammars. The role of the corpus is just as insufficiently established here as in the second version. But we now always begin with two competing grammars. This is the sense in which Chomsky undertakes the evaluation of phrase-structure grammars *vis-à-vis* transformational grammars. This version of grammatical theory particularly requires an explication of the simplicity criterion that is to be applied. Chomsky however fails to meet this theoretical requirement either here or in his later works. Most of his arguments do not have

---

[1] Chomsky often (incorrectly) identifies this version with the views of the American structuralists. But for them the problem was in general to LEGITIMIZE practical and mechanically applicable procedures, i.e. to provide them with some validity. Chomsky assumes the legitimation as given.

a clear enough structure to give us much hope of a result from a theoretical explication: for example we would have to clarify the extent to which they are to be taken as syntactic or semantic, what experimental or test results they should be based on, what kind of empirical interpretation the grammar should be given, etc.

The three versions we have discussed are illustrated in figure 8 (Chomsky 1957b: 51).

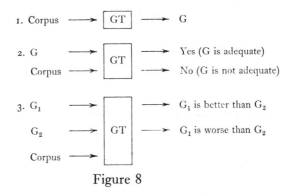

Figure 8

In all three versions the two following questions are still open:

(a) Are we dealing here with a THEORY THAT PROVIDES EFFECTIVE PROCEDURES in some strong sense? Then the corpus in every case must be formulated in the language of the theory, i.e. the natural-language sentences must be translated into appropriate representations; the translation itself will not be achieved within the theory. In addition, the procedures can be effective only if they are carried out RELATIVE TO THE CORPUS: it is impossible to carry them out relative to the language the corpus is taken from, because all we have is a knowledge of this language that is not yet explicated in this theory. We can also require that the corpus comprise all relevant data; but the selection of such a corpus already presupposes the grammar we are looking for.

(b) Are we dealing here with a METHODOLOGY, i.e. with the identification of research procedures (abstracting, explicating, etc.), which are to be used to develop explicit grammars (in the first version) or to check the adequacy of explicit grammars (in the second and third versions)? In both cases it is misleading to speak of a theory that can arrive at effective procedures. Chomsky rejects the first version, because there cannot be any strict operational procedures for the construction of grammars. The other two versions must be rejected on very similar grounds, because they simply attempt the same thing on a somewhat higher level. The decision as to whether a particular constructed grammar is adequate with respect to a WHOLE language (or more adequate than other grammars) presupposes our having this whole language available for basing a decision on. But we always have only a segment of the language available; we have selected it according to certain criteria and must evaluate according to certain criteria. It is only in relation to such criteria that we can say that 'G_1 is better than G_2'; 'better than' is thus not a global property of grammars, but a local one, namely relative to particular criteria. These criteria, which reflect the goals of our research procedures, can scarcely be turned into strict operational procedures; they can even change, for example on the basis of the results of particular constructive activities. The procedures provided by grammatical theory are frequently used, and they can be modified just as frequently. The explication of the concept 'grammatical in L' (for any arbitrary L) cannot therefore provide any strong criterion for whether the concept 'grammatical in English' is (compared to competing explicata) adequately explicated. In both cases the best we can do is give systematic guidance or orientation about how one should proceed in order to develop explicit grammars or evaluate ones already developed.

In his later work, Chomsky sees the task of a grammatical theory somewhat differently: he is concerned with an empirical theory that characterizes how human beings (especially children), confronted with particular linguistic data, learn an appropriate grammar in a finite amount of time. The three types of procedure we have discussed are then to be understood as HYPOTHESES ABOUT THE GLOBAL CHARACTER OF LANGUAGE ACQUISITION PROCESSES.[1]

[1] Cf. the discussion in 3.9 above, and the work of Peters discussed there. According to this view, a grammatical theory is in no sense a theory of linguistic description, which is what Lieb takes it to be (cf. 1.7 above).

9 On the explication of the concept of meaning

The concept of meaning is both one of the most basic and one of the most complex in linguistics. I will try to gather some of its many aspects[1] together in this chapter under three main headings,[2] and devote a section to each. (I will, however, exclude a number of possible ones : an earlier psychological concept, based on individual ideas and associations, as well as concept of meaning relative to arbitrary signalling situations.) I will also attempt to sketch out at least roughly the mutual relations of these three concepts, although the way the subject has developed prevents us achieving a real integration at present: the different lines of inquiry have been pursued too independently. The three sections of this chapter by and large merely present a critical inventory; though I hope this can serve as a basis for bringing the different positions more closely together. These three variants of the concept of meaning are:

I. THE EXTRALINGUISTIC MEANING OF LINGUISTIC EXPRESSIONS, or their factual reference, as treated in referential semantics (*Referenzsemantik*). What is the relation of linguistic expressions to the objects of our experience, what do we mean by them in particular contexts, how do we use them to constitute the domain we are talking about ? The development that I will outline here has in the past mainly been connected with logical semantics (Frege, Russell, Carnap, Model-theory); its relevance to linguistics has only been acknowledged recently. Of course there are older developments in linguistics itself in which the primary object of study is the factual reference of words and its historical change; but the aim here was not to achieve a systematic linguistic THEORY, and recent research has virtually abandoned this line of inquiry. I will not pursue it here.

---

[1] On this cf. for instance Ogden & Richards (1953), Schaff (1966: Part II, ch. 3).
[2] Cf. the distinction *Bezeichnung, Bedeutung, Sinn* in Coseriu (1973); the three variants to be treated correspond roughly to the traditional types of truth-theories (correspondence, coherence, pragmatic: cf. 5.4 above).

II. THE INTRALINGUISTIC MEANING OF LINGUISTIC EXPRESSIONS, as treated in conceptual semantics (*Inhaltssemantik*). What are the sense-relations between linguistic expressions? Here we deal with developments within linguistics itself (e.g. under the headings of 'lexical field theory' and 'componential analysis') which have only recently been introduced in the framework of logical languages, and in some cases partly explicated (cf. Lyons 1968: ch. 10; Brockhaus & Stechow 1971). The role of the sense-relations treated in this framework for a semantic theory of the first type is sketched out by Kemeny and Carnap under the term 'meaning postulates', and later by Schnelle under the term 'meaning constraints' (Carnap 1956b: appendix B, Schnelle 1973b: 15–25).

III. THE MEANING OF LINGUISTIC EXPRESSIONS IN COMMUNICATION SITUATIONS, as treated in speech-act semantics. What does an utterance mean for a speaker and for the addressee(s) and other possible hearers, in relation to the background of their social situation? This variant of the concept of meaning has been developed in particular by behaviouristically oriented philosophers of language (chiefly Morris), as well as within analytic philosophy (Wittgenstein, Austin, Hare, Searle, Grice). It is only recently that there have been developments that appear to open up the possibilities of a connection between theories of meaning of the first kind and concepts of meaning of this third kind; but research is still in its infancy.

9.I THE EXTRALINGUISTIC MEANING OF LINGUISTIC EXPRESSIONS (REFERENTIAL SEMANTICS)

9.1 Philosophical realism

The central attitude in most of the positions to be described here can be roughly characterized as philosophical realism: the assumption that beyond the speaker and his conceptual world there exist still other entities and processes, and that these are linguistically representable (THE REPRESENTATIONAL FUNCTION OF LANGUAGE). It is not only things that happen in extra-human nature that can be represented (whether on the basis of perception or memory or anticipation), but also what happens in our inner nature or the nature we construct artificially. Language can also represent our attitudes toward real facts of nature, or what we believe to be possible facts (knowledge, hopes, ideas of control, etc.). Since people communicate in connection with labour in the widest sense (production, consumption, planning, organization, etc.) we can assume that the representational function of language (or its factual reference) will play a special role: not only in assertions, descriptions and the like, but also in questions, demands, recommendations and so on. In the concept of meaning to be developed here, there is no consideration of the specific character of particular speech acts; in order to concentrate on factual reference, only declarative (or indicative) sentences are normally taken into account, as they are used, for example, in assertions, descriptions and explanations. (The strong orientation toward the needs of scientific communication may have contributed to this as well: claims of truth or falsity can be made about the content of an assertion, but not about that of a question or a demand.) Though it is assumed that the content of a question or demand is related in a specific way to the content of possible assertions, and can therefore be obtained by additional operations on these (e.g. a question should lead to an assertion of a particular kind, i.e. its answer; and a demand should lead to the establishment of a situation which is representable in assertions of a particular kind), there is still considerable uncertainty about how these 'additional operations' can be explicated. It is possible that this cannot be done within referential semantics at all, but only by means of speech-act semantics, i.e. by an explication of the relation of utterance-meanings to action schemata. This relation can then be extended in a similar way to the distinction between declarative sentence and act of assertion.

If we are to speak even generally of a position of philosophical realism, we still have to make distinctions (and, philosophically, not unimportant ones), for example with respect to whether or how far concepts are always linguistically presented: in general, what is the relation between facts, concepts and linguistic expressions ? There are of course also positions of mere CONCEPTUAL REALISM, which make no reference to a reality (nature) independent of human language and cognition. Where such a reference does in fact occur, it can be viewed in one of two ways – either statically (e.g. in the sense of Wittgenstein's '*Bild-theorie*' (Wittgenstein 1922: 4.01–4.2)): sentences represent reality and the structures of sentences display the structures of facts; or dynamically, as developing and changing in accordance with our relation to nature. It is only the more advanced versions of meaning-theory that allow different philosophical positions: the reason for this is that theoretical explication is understood at the outset as instrumental, not as a search for philosophical–ontological explanation. The advanced versions, however, also permit us to treat important differentiations, which are indispensable for a rational philosophical standpoint: for example, in the question as to what extent the worlds we speak about are themselves first linguistically and contextually established.

The less advanced versions, on the other hand, dangerously imply a static relation between language and reality (e.g. meaning-relations are understood as objectively given). This danger shows up especially in many semiotic discussions, which presuppose a very simple referential semantics. This is untenable on various grounds, but I will take such a simple version as my point of departure, and develop the criticisms as I proceed.

9.2   A very simple version of referential semantics

Let us assume that linguistic expressions have exactly one semantic function: namely DESIGNATING (or naming). Every linguistic expression of a certain (syntactic) category designates an extralinguistic entity of a certain type, e.g.:[1]

---

[1] Among proper names in the wider sense we can also include so-called definite designations. Thus alongside *Volker*, *Aristotle*, the following are also proper names: *Marianne's oldest brother*, *the Burgomaster of Coblenz* and *the next-to-last house on the left in Brentanostraße in Steglitz, when you come from Breitenbachplatz*.

Proper names designate objects.

One-place predicates (absolute adjectives, intransitive verbs, absolute general names) designate properties of objects.

Many-place predicates (relational adjectives, comparatives, transitive verbs, relational general names) designate relations of objects.

Sentences designate states of affairs (namely that objects have particular properties or stand in particular relations).

Many problems remain unelucidated in this simple version; they provide in the end a motivation for distinguishing at least two semantic functions (and thus two different concepts of meaning).

1. If we distinguish only between linguistic expressions and facts, then we must identify concepts with one or the other; and both these identifications are problematical.[1]

(a) The representation functon extends in the same way to the elements of states of affairs (or whole states of affairs) as well as to concepts. Concepts are identified with objects, attributes, or states of affairs. There is an objection to this: objects and attributes are (at least at times, or according to a particular idea that one can have of them) perceptible and observable; concepts are always learned, they are the result of perception and observation as well as further cognitive activity (generalization and abstraction). Objects can perhaps be pointed to, held in the hand, etc., while concepts are always presented linguistically. Particular expressions are relatively arbitrary labels for objects, but not for concepts – after a certain age, concepts can no longer develop independently of the command of a language; objects however can obviously change completely independently of a language.

(b) The designation function only extends to elements of states of affairs or whole states of affairs; concepts are identified with linguistic expressions. But now the question arises of how the theoretical (abstracting–generalizing) nature of concepts should be elucidated, if concepts are to be understood as designations of something in states of affairs. This holds especially for concepts like 'three', 'time', 'not red',

---

Examples of one-place predicates: *white, sleeps, ox*; many-place predicates: *big, bigger than, lies between, kisses, father of.* Properties and relations are often conflated as attributes: n-place predicates then designate n-place attributes.

Let $a_1, ..., a_n$ be proper names and let F be an n-place predicate; then the sentence $F(a_1, ..., a_n)$ designates the state of affairs that the attribute designated by F belongs to the n-tuple of objects designated by $a_1, ..., a_n$. If and only if this is in fact the existing state of affairs can we say that the sentence is true.

[1] Concepts that can have truth-values, sometimes also called 'propositions', are identified with sentences.

'phoneme', etc. We can indeed apply them to states of affairs, but can we say that we do so on the basis of their designating function?

2. We might perhaps use the following terminology: a predicate always expresses a concept, which in some way or another relates to a complex of properties; let this be the exact way of saying 'the predicate designates a property'. But what does it mean to say that a concept is related to a property? Let us suggest the following: the concept is APPLICABLE to objects with a particular property. But obviously we are now introducing a new terminology. First we are speaking of possible situations for the use of a concept. Second, we are speaking not only of properties, but also of classes of objects having properties in common. The attempt to differentiate between adjectives and general names as designations, respectively, of properties and classes of objects is similar. However both terminologies, can be used in any given case; *rose*, for example, can designate a property-complex of flowers or a class of flowers. We have to clarify the relationship of such terminologies, and what they tell us about the nature of concepts.

3. By confining ourselves to the designation function we conclude that a sentence that makes a false assertion (e.g. *Thomas is reading in the privy*) represents a state of affairs that does not exist; thus this sentence has no meaning. However, it does have a meaning, and only because it does can we dispute it. Similarly we can imagine proper names (like *Odysseus* or *the present King of Bavaria*) that do not designate anything in the real world, but nonetheless have a meaning. (The meaning of *the present King of Bavaria* derives from the meanings of its constituent expressions; the meaning of *Odysseus* derives from the use of this name in Greek literature.)

4. Expressions like *Cleopatra's lover*, *the Burgomaster of Coblenz*, can designate different people at different times (in different uses of the expressions); nevertheless in particular uses they are generally unambiguous: in each case they designate one person. This is even clearer with so-called deictic expressions like *I*, *there*, *an hour ago*, whose designation functions are determined exclusively by the situation in which they are used – but not arbitrarily, i.e. even these expressions have a meaning independent of every situation of use.

5. Frege treats the following case: *Morning Star* and *Evening Star* designate the same object, the planet Venus. Nevertheless the two sentences

(1) The Morning Star is identical to the Evening Star

(2) The Morning Star is identical to the Morning Star
do not have the same meaning: under certain conditions (1) can express
new knowledge, but never (2). Whether (1) is true can be shown only
on the basis of empirical information; (2) however is assumed to be
valid on logical grounds (tautological or *a priori* true); provided we
consider such sentences to be compatible with our use of 'identical'.

A first attempt to solve the problem indicated here consists of the
introduction of two different concepts of meaning: one is the FACTUAL
REFERENCE of an expression, the other its CONCEPTUAL REFERENCE. In the
table below I give a few of the terms that philosophers have used for
this distinction; though of course there are differences in the application
of these concepts from writer to writer (especially in the exact interpretation of conceptual reference).

	Factual reference	*Conceptual reference*
Mill (1843)	denotation	connotation
Frege (1966)	Bedeutung	Sinn
Russell (1956)	denotation	meaning
Black (1949)	reference	sense
Carnap (1956b)	extension	intension
Klaus (1966)	Bezeichnung	Bedeutung
v. Kutschera (1971)	Bezug	Bedeutung

In what follows I will briefly discuss Frege's explicandum concepts,
as well as Carnap's explication of 'extension' and 'intension'.

9.3 Reference and sense in Frege[1]

In his treatment of the two versions of the concept of meaning, Frege
restricts himself mainly to proper names and sentences; he treats
predicates as unsatisfied expressions that result when a proper name is
subtracted from a sentence. Nonetheless it is clear that in principle all
linguistic expressions should be treated analogously. The most important
points in Frege's discussion are:

1. Expressions with the same sense always have the same reference;
but expressions with the same reference do not always have the same
sense (e.g. *Volker's eldest brother, the eldest brother of Volker* have the
same sense; *Morning Star, Evening Star* have the same reference, but

---

[1] In keeping with usual English practice, I render Frege's *Bedeutung, bedeutet*, etc.
by 'reference', 'refers to', etc. [Trans.]

not the same sense). There are also expressions that have a sense, though it is questionable whether they have a reference (*Odysseus, come here*). AN EXPRESSION DESIGNATES (OR REFERS TO) ITS REFERENCE; IT EXPRESSES ITS SENSE.

2. The references of proper names (in the wider sense) are objects; these can be empirical or theoretical (thus even expressions like *the number 2, the concept 'man', truth,* designate objects). THE SENSE OF A PROPER NAME IS THE WAY IN WHICH IT IS GIVEN ['die Art seines Gegebenseins'].[1]

3. Frege's constructive orientation leads to the following definition: the reference of a complex expression derives from (is a function of) the references of its constituents. Sentences are the most important instances of complex expressions. Therefore we must correct our previous idea of what a sentence designates: A SENTENCE DESIGNATES A TRUTH-VALUE (either truth or falsity);[2] this notion is taken over by the whole tradition of logical semantics stemming from Frege. Truth is a theoretical object, which is very useful for the analysis of our speech, knowledge and perception; but it cannot be observed, and we should not attach any ontological interpretation to it:

Now if the truth-value of a sentence is its reference, then all true sentences have the same reference, and so do all false ones...We can thus never be concerned only with the reference of a sentence alone; but the mere thought of a sentence also gives us no knowledge; what counts is the thought together with its reference, i.e. its truth. (Frege 1966: 50)

It is clear from this passage that what a sentence expresses (its sense) is a THOUGHT. Thoughts for Frege are not subjective fancies, but 'objective contents', which can be the 'common property of men' (Frege 1966: 46). It is possible for different sentences to express the same thought; i.e. a thought can BE DECOMPOSED IN DIFFERENT WAYS, so that 'sometimes one thing, sometimes another can appear as subject or as predicate' (Frege 1966: 74),[3] e.g. *All mammals have red blood,*

---

[1] This needs clarification. Since Frege does not give it, he does not succeed in developing any criteria for sameness of sense. But we can assume that if Frege's concept of sense were narrowly conceived, expressions like *adult female swine* and *sow* would not have the same sense.

[2] Or the true or the false. 'We have seen that we should look for a reference of a sentence if the references of its constituents are the point; and this is the case if and only if we inquire about its truth-value' (Frege 1966: 48).

[3] The notions 'subject' and 'predicate' are used here in their traditional logical meaning; but they are also to be understood grammatically as functions of expressions in sentences. In *All mammals have red blood, have red blood* can easily be taken as a predicate (in the logical AND grammatical sense); but *all mammals* is only the grammatical, not the logical subject. Frege shows this by means of a negation test: the negation

Anything that is a mammal has red blood, If something is a mammal, then it has red blood. From these remarks we gather that Frege assumes an analytical standpoint: at the centre of his theory there stands, in addition to the category of proper names, that of sentences; and every sentence is taken as the expression of a thought as well as one of its possible decompositions.

4. Predicate expressions are for Frege chiefly a negatively defined category: when we 'take away' from the reference of a sentence the references of the proper names in it, what is 'left over' must be the reference of the predicate; otherwise the reference of a sentence would not be a function of the references of its constituents. Somewhat surprisingly however, a predicate expression for Frege designates (not expresses) a concept; thus the concept is not an entity like a thought but an entity like an object.

The unsatisfied part of a sentence, the reference of which we have called a concept, must have the property of becoming, when satisfied by any meaningful proper name, a proper sentence; i.e. of resulting in the proper name of a truth-value. (Frege 1973: 91)

5. The references of expressions are not the same in all contexts. Frege distinguishes between DIRECT REFERENCES (which we have already discussed) and INDIRECT REFERENCES, which expressions have in indirect discourse, as well as in other kinds of subordinate clauses (in a general way one can speak of intensional contexts). The characteristic of these contexts is that we cannot perform substitutions *salva veritate* (i.e. and still retain the truth-value of the whole sentence). Let us assume that Ottokar is the man who stole the Venus de Milo (*Ottokar* and *the man who stole the Venus de Milo* designate the same person). Nevertheless, in the following pairs of sentences one can be true and the other false:

(3) a. Nina $\begin{cases} \text{claims} \\ \text{believes} \end{cases}$ that she knows Ottokar.

   b. Nina $\begin{cases} \text{claims} \\ \text{believes} \end{cases}$ that she knows the man who stole the Venus de Milo.

of the sentence cannot be *All mammals do not have red blood*, but must be *Not all mammals have red blood*. Frege says that the predicative nature of the expression *mammal*, which is used here as grammatical subject, cannot be mistaken; neither *mammal* nor *all mammals* is a proper name. Later (9.8) I will outline a view according to which *all mammals* can be taken as belonging to a generalized category of proper names (terms or nominal phrases).

(4) a. Nina is looking for Ottokar.

b. Nina is looking for the man who stole the Venus de Milo.

The proper names *Ottokar* and *the man who stole the Venus de Milo* are used here in their indirect reference, which is identical to their sense. The same holds for sentences. Let us now assume that there are no Abominable Snowmen in the Himalayas, and that there is also no Loch Ness Monster. Nonetheless the sentences (5a, b) can have different truth-values:

(5) a. Nina$\begin{Bmatrix}\text{claims}\\\text{believes}\end{Bmatrix}$ that there are Abominable Snowmen in the Himalayas.

b. Nina$\begin{Bmatrix}\text{claims}\\\text{believes}\end{Bmatrix}$ that there is a Loch Ness Monster.

In order to 'compute' this truth-value on the basis of the references of the sentence constituents, we must obviously take account of the sense, not the truth-value, of the subordinate clauses: we are speaking about the content of a claim or belief of Nina's, not about Abominable Snowmen or the Loch Ness Monster. The indirect reference of a sentence (as in cases like (3) and (5)) is not always a thought. Frege discusses several other types of subordinate clauses as well, where the meaning of the subordinate clause is only part of a thought or simultaneously a thought AND a truth-value, or a thought AND a part of another thought, etc. It is clear that these considerations are still inexplicit (among other things they are not based on a reconstruction

	Designates	*Expresses*
Proper name a (direct use)	an object	the sense of a
Proper Name a (indirect use)	the sense of a	?
Declarative sentence (direct use)	a truth-value	a thought
Sentence A (indirect use)	(e.g.) a thought	the sense of the expression 'the idea that A'
Non-declarative sentence	nothing	a thought
Predicate P	a concept	the property of becoming a sentence, if P is satisfied by a designating proper name

of the formal nature of sentences); nevertheless they are stimulating and go far beyond anything but the most recent work in logical semantics.[1]

Frege's ideas can be summed up in the table on p. 204.

*9.4 Extension and intension in Carnap

Carnap's analysis in *Meaning and necessity* (1956b) differs from Frege's mainly on three points:

1. Carnap works with a constructed logical language, in which he explicates the two concepts of meaning as 'extension' and 'intension' respectively. Within this logical language he can establish by definition when two expressions have the same extension or intension. He thus obtains a concept of intension that is differently and significantly more broadly conceived than Frege's concept of sense; it will be necessary to look for further explicata.

2. Carnap begins with predicate expressions, i.e. he goes right to the point where Frege's analysis produces only a negatively defined notion. The results obtained here are then uniformly extended to individual expressions (proper names) and declarative sentences; other kinds of expressions are not considered, as they are not introduced in the logical language.

3. Carnap criticizes the notion that expressions can change their meaning in different contexts: he insists that meaning must be stable. In order to achieve this, it is necessary to restrict the substitutability of expressions for each other in particular contexts. Unlike Frege, Carnap does not analyse different sentence constructions in natural languages, but only one type of construction in a standardized language.

Ad 1. In order to obtain a criterion for sameness of extension and sameness of intension, Carnap first sets up two other concepts:

(a) Let the notion STATE-DESCRIPTION IN S (where S is a predicate logic language) be an explicatum for the notion 'possible world' as used by Leibniz and other philosophers. Let the language S contain a fixed number of individual constants (proper names) a, b, c,..., as well as

---

[1] E.g. we find the distinction between restrictive and non-restrictive relative clauses: in the latter (e.g. *Napoleon, who recognized the danger, led his guards against the enemy*), we can assume direct reference, i.e. substitution *salva veritate* is possible. For sentences with the verbs *recognize, know, imagine*, he proposes an analysis corresponding to the now common presupposition analysis: sentential complements designate a thought as well as a truth-value (i.e. according to the verb we presuppose the truth or falsity of the complement, just as when we use proper names we presuppose the existence of the designated objects: cf. Frege 1966: 46).

a fixed number of predicate constants of different numbers of places P^1, Q^1, ..., F^2, G^2, ... In this language then we can construct n atomic sentences:

$P^1(a)$, $P^1(b)$, ..., $Q^1(b)$, ..., $F^2(a, b)$, $F^2(b, a)$, $F^2(a, c)$, ...

A state-description in S is the complete description of a possible world-state, insofar as it can be given in expressions of S. More precisely, all individuals designated by expressions in S will be characterized with respect to all their attributes (properties and relations) that are expressible by means of predicates in S; a state-description in S is therefore a class of sentences which for every atomic sentence in S will contain either that sentence or its negation.

If there are n atomic sentences in S, then there are altogether 2^n different state-descriptions. The number 2^n may be very large: if we have three different individual constants and two one-place predicates, we have six atomic sentences, and therefore $2^6 = 64$ different state-descriptions. But whether in fact all of these state-descriptions also describe different world-states depends on the properties of the predicates. For instance, if F^2 expresses a symmetrical relation, the equivalences $F^2(a, b) \equiv F^2(b, a)$, $F^2(a, c) \equiv F^2(c, a)$, etc. (among others) will hold; i.e. in each case we could omit one of the equivalent atomic sentences, and thus get fewer 'relevant' state-descriptions. Similarly, let the following relation hold between P^1 and Q^1: $(x) (P^1(x) \supset Q^1(x))$; then all atomic sentences $Q^1(a)$, $Q^1(b)$, ..., could be omitted, without our losing the ability to represent actual different world-states by different state-descriptions.

According to Carnap, all such properties of predicates or relations between predicates are to be formulated in MEANING-POSTULATES; their function is to restrict the number of 'relevant' (non-redundant) state-descriptions, while simultaneously eliminating all state-descriptions which cannot describe any possible world-state. For instance, according to the relation of P^1 and Q^1 given above, a world-state captured in a state-description that includes both $P^1(a)$ and $\sim Q^1(a)$ is unthinkable.

For each atomic or complex sentence in S we can state a RANGE, namely a class of state-descriptions in which it holds. Each atomic sentence holds in exactly half of all state-descriptions (namely each one it belongs to), the conjunction of all atomic sentences holds in exactly one state-description, and the disjunction of all atomic setences holds in exactly $2^n - 1$ state-descriptions.

There is only one state-description that describes the present world-state: it contains all actually true sentences as well as the negations of all actually false sentences.

Carnap's concept of state-description is language-relative: the number of possible worlds is defined only by the richness of the language and not on the basis of any ontological considerations. Of course it remains problematical what kind of worlds these are that are described in state-descriptions: obviously they are not speakers' natural experiential worlds, but particular constructed interpretations in constructed language-systems. Thus the mutual interdependence of concepts expressed through predicates remains unconsidered, i.e. all predicates are regarded as independent. From a linguistic point of view this is extremely unsatisfactory. What should be in the foreground is how the number of possible interpretations of a class of sentences is restricted through the fact that particular sense-relations (e.g. explicated as meaning-postulates) hold between the predicates. This should not, however, be understood as saying that the number of 'relevant' state-descriptions should be restricted AFTER THE FACT, but rather that they should be restricted BEFOREHAND, on the basis of our knowledge of these sense-relations. (Only such possible worlds as agree with our linguistic knowledge can be stated; in this sense our linguistic knowledge, and the way we use it, is CONSTITUTIVE for the choice of possible worlds.)

(b) Let the notion 'L-TRUE' be an explicatum for the notion 'necessarily true'. Thus 'necessary' will be understood in the sense of 'linguistically necessary', and used exclusively in relation to a language.[1] The explicandum for 'L-true' is exemplified as follows (Carnap 1956b: 10):

A sentence s_i is L-true in S if and only if it is true in S in such a way that its truth can be established solely on the basis of the semantical rules of S alone, without any reference to extralinguistic facts.

The explicatum is defined by reference to the previously established explicatum 'state-description in S':

A sentence s_i is L-true in S = df s_i holds in every state-description in S.

From this we can derive other entirely plausible definitions:

---

[1] 'L' is to be understood as an abbreviation for 'logically'. The class of L-true sentences is substantially identical with the class of those sentences earlier called 'universally valid' (semantically). For 'necessary' the term 'analytic' is also used – in general however with respect to natural languages; and this leads to philosophical controversies which I cannot go into here.

s_i is L-false = df $\sim s_i$ is L-true.

s_i is L-equivalent to s_j = df the sentence $s_i \equiv s_j$ is L-true[1]

s_i is L-determinate = df s_i is either L-true or L-false.

s_i is factual = df s_i is not L-determinate.

A sentence is factual then if there is at least one state-description in S in which it holds, and one in which it does not. We can now define:

s_i is F-true = df s_i is true but not L-true.

s_i is F-equivalent to s_j = df the sentence $s_i \equiv s_j$ is F-true.[2]

The notion of equivalence can now be extended to non-sentential expressions. For example let '$P^1 \equiv Q^1$' be the abbreviation for '$(x)(P^1(x) \equiv Q^1(x))$'. We can then define, for arbitrary expressions r_i and r_j:

$$r_i \text{ is} \begin{Bmatrix} \text{equivalent} \\ \text{L-equivalent} \\ \text{F-equivalent} \end{Bmatrix} \text{with } r_j = \text{df the sentence } r_i \equiv r_j \text{ is} \begin{Bmatrix} \text{true} \\ \text{L-true} \\ \text{F-true} \end{Bmatrix}.$$

For every expression r_i we can specify an equivalence-class and an L-equivalence-class, namely the classes of all expressions that are equivalent or L-equivalent with r_i. The L-equivalence-class of any expression is always a subclass of the corresponding equivalence-class.[3]

After these preliminaries, Carnap arrives at the following definitions:

(E) Two expressions have THE SAME EXTENSION if and only if they are equivalent.

(I) Two expressions have THE SAME INTENSION if and only if they are L-equivalent.

Two intensionally identical expressions are accordingly always extensionally identical, but two extensionally identical expressions are not always intensionally identical. This fully reconstructs Frege's relation between sameness of sense and sameness of reference. In addition there is a criterion for sameness of intension and sameness of extension, insofar as we consider possible state-descriptions relative to a logical language S. This criterion, however, is *de facto* scarcely applicable,

[1] 'Equivalence' here is a SEMANTIC notion; the sign '$\equiv$' on the contrary belongs to the object language.

[2] 'F' is an abbreviation for 'factual'. The strict distinction of factual (empirical knowledge) and logical (linguistic knowledge) is of course problematical. It arises here from the introduction of a predicate logic language S and its semantic rules. The choice of particular semantic rules establishes what is to be understood as linguistic knowledge; we can make different choices if we want to set the boundaries differently.

[3] Obviously we can also construct F-equivalent classes; but these are uninteresting for Carnap, because the knowledge that goes into them is empirical, not linguistic.

(a) because the possible state-descriptions are only to be found when we already know the intensions of the expressions and their sense-relations, and (b) because – even if we assume knowledge of the state-descriptions – it will be clumsy in all richer logical languages. From this – practical – point of view Carnap's attempt is a failure.[1]

Ad 2. For Carnap there are always two ways of speaking about predicates like *mammal*: we can either speak of a CLASS OF INDIVIDUALS (i.e. of THE mammals) or of a PROPERTY shared by particular individuals (i.e. the property of being a mammal). We describe classes by enumerating their members; we describe properties by means of concepts, and concepts are linguistically determined. (Of course there are concepts – even empirical ones – that arise through processes of abstraction and generalization regarding previously established classes; this relation we do not consider here.)

For Carnap classes are identical if the corresponding predicates are equivalent; properties are identical if the corresponding predicates are L-equivalent. Together with the definitions (E) and (I) it is therefore sensible to assume that the extension of a predicate is a class, and the intension of a predicate is a property.

The concepts of extension and intension are now extended to declarative sentences and individual expressions: the extension of a sentence is its truth-value, and the intension of a sentence is the proposition it expresses. The extension of an individual expression is the individual (object) it designates, and the intension of an individual expression is the individual concept it expresses. We can now sum up the applications of Carnap's terminology:

	Extension	*Intension*
Predicate	a class	a property
Sentence	a truth-value	a proposition
Proper name	an individual	an individual-concept

Two critical notes are in order here:

(a) It is still relatively unclear what an individual concept is.[2] In descriptive designations like *the highest mountain on earth*, it must

---

[1] This also holds, by the way, for the theory of semantic information developed by Carnap and Bar-Hillel, which rests on the same foundations as this explication (cf. Bar-Hillel & Carnap 1964).

[2] There are only a few additional remarks in Carnap (1956b: 181ff.) which have also motivated a further development. Cf. 9.5 below.

obviously be a function of the intensions of the predicates used (*highest*, *mountain*, etc.); but what about proper names in the narrower sense, like *Carnap*? We could find an interpretation here that is itself extensional again, e.g. the intension of *Carnap* is the set of properties that Carnap possesses, and by means of which we can distinguish him from others ('born on...', 'died on...', 'author of...', 'father of...', 'lover of...', 'height...', etc.). Correspondingly the intension of *Hans Castorp* would be given as the set of characteristics of the person of that name in a novel of Thomas Mann. In the second case the intension is in fact determined within a semantic – even if very complicated – system; in the first case, in contrast, it is also conditioned by extralinguistic experience (especially for persons who have personally known Carnap).

(b) Carnap's system seems at first to contain an inconsistency: the intensions of predicates are properties and not concepts, but the intension of a sentence is a proposition (what Frege would call a 'thought'). This inconsistency, however, is only apparent. Carnap makes the following clear (1956b: 19f., 27f.): the properties of things are meant to be something physical that they possess; propositions are meant to be the circumstance that something or other physical is the case (assuming that we are concerned with physical objects). Carnap chooses this manner of speaking expressly in order to prevent us from understanding an intension as some kind of subjective mental image or representation; he wants to emphasize the fact that intensions are objective. Nevertheless he says that a property is also everything that can be meaningfully said, and a proposition is that which can be expressed in a declarative sentence.

Here, in my opinion, IS a contradiction: concepts are not identical with physical properties, and propositions (thoughts) are not identical with physical circumstances (even when we are speaking about physical objects). One cannot, on the one hand, introduce intensions under the concept of language-necessity (L-truth) if one is ready, on the other hand, to shift them back into extralinguistic nature. This is also totally unnecessary, if the point is only to emphasize the OBJECTIVITY OF INTENSIONS. It is much more important to work out, more clearly than Carnap has done, the CONCEPTUAL NATURE OF INTENSIONS, instead of indicating them naturalistically. (This will be achieved later, by regarding intensions as particular functions.)

Ad 3. Carnap points out that undesirable consequences arise if expressions can change their meaning according to context (he is not referring to ambiguous expressions). E.g. in the following sentences with iterated embedding, *Nina* would have a different meaning in each case (for details cf. Carnap 1956b: 130f.):

(6) a. Nina is lucky.
    b. It is possible that Nina is lucky.
    c. Hans believes it is possible that Nina is lucky.
    d. It is not necessarily the case that Hans believes that it is possible that Nina is lucky.

For Carnap each expression must have the same extension and intension in all contexts; only expressions with the same extension and intension cannot be replaced by another in such a way that the whole expression has the same extension and intension as before. Therefore the substitution principle must be constrained.

In the following we will be concerned only with expressions that have meaning (what Carnap calls 'designators'). Let us assume that the expression r_j occurs within the expression R_i, i.e. $R_i = \ldots r_j \ldots$ (where '...' stands for the context of r_j). Then we can define (cf. Carnap 1956b: 47f.):

> R_i is extensional with respect to r_j = df r_j can be replaced by an equivalent expression in such a way that the resulting expression $R_i{}'$ is equivalent to R_i.
> R_i is extensional = df R_i is extensional with respect to any occurrence of an expression within R_i.
> R_i is intensional with respect to r_j = df R_i is not extensional with respect to r_j but r_j can be replaced by an L-equivalent expression in such a way that the resulting expression R'_i is L-equivalent to R_i.
> R_i is intensional = df R_i is, with respect to any occurrence of an expression in it either extensional or intensional, but R_i is intensional with respect to at least one occurrence of an expression in it.

Now we can easily see that there are numerous complex expressions which in this sense are neither extensional nor intensional. This is because the notion of intension is very broadly conceived. Thus all L-true sentences are the same in intension: e.g. *Hans is either lazy or not lazy*, *Every pig is a pig*. This surely goes against our pretheoretical intuition, and even Frege would have said that the two sentences express different senses. Now consider these sentences:

212 The concept of meaning ı

(7) a. Emil$\begin{Bmatrix} \text{claims} \\ \text{believes} \end{Bmatrix}$that Hans is either lazy or not lazy.

    b. Emil$\begin{Bmatrix} \text{claims} \\ \text{believes} \end{Bmatrix}$that every pig is a pig.

According to Carnap's definition, these two sentences are not the same in intension, since the claim that (7a) ≡ (7b) would not hold in all possible worlds; they are not even the same in extension. Thus 'Emil $\begin{Bmatrix} \text{claims} \\ \text{believes} \end{Bmatrix}$ that...' is neither an extensional nor an intensional context. Carnap therefore attempts to find a narrower formulation for sameness of sense; he comes up with the notion of INTENSIONAL ISOMORPHY, more or less as follows (for the exact formulation cf. Carnap 1956b: 59):

> Two expressions are intensionally isomorphic if they are L-equivalent as wholes, as well as composed of a structurally isomorphic configuration of partial expressions, which for their part are L-equivalent.

It is clear that *Hans is either lazy or not lazy* and *Every pig is a pig* are not intensional isomorphs. However *7 is bigger than three* and *bigger than (7, 3)* are. But *7 is bigger than 3* and *3 is smaller than 7* are not, even if for Frege they would perhaps have the same sense; in this case the notion of intensional isomorphy would be too narrow. It is worth considering whether sentences that (in the Chomskyan sense) can be referred to a common deep structure are intensional isomorphs, or whether this would be a reasonable requirement on the formulation of deep structures. In this case, for instance, *Volker's eldest brother resides in Dresden* and *the eldest brother of Volker is resident in Dresden* should turn out to be intensional isomorphs.[1]

Carnap's search for a further specification of sameness of sense is especially problematical for contexts like 'Emil $\begin{Bmatrix} \text{claims} \\ \text{believes} \end{Bmatrix}$ that...':

indeed Carnap himself deals only with the belief contexts, though on at least one reading they correspond to the claim contexts (*Emil believes that...* = *Emil says that he believes that...*). Every attempt of this kind must founder on these cases; because it could be that Emil claims

---

[1] Note however that Carnap has explicated his concept of meaning relative to a logical language; we must still find appropriate translations between natural-language sentences and their analyses (e.g. in the form of deep structures) and a logical language.

The arguments for a deep structure analysis (and the corresponding analytical methods) have not up to now referred to intensional isomorphy; on the contrary, sentences for which a common deep structure is posited are often not the same in sense, though they have the same extension (cf. 10.10 below).

arbitrary, irrational and contradictory things. But even in belief contexts with the other reading ('On the basis of Emil's behaviour I have concluded that he believes that...') we must also assume that Emil's behaviour is such that we can draw factually consistent inferences from it. This means that a purely semantic analysis of such contexts is probably impossible.

In Carnap's explication several questions remain open (subsequent developments in logical semantics have faced them to some extent, and I will discuss this briefly in what follows):

1. What is the CONCEPTUAL NATURE OF INTENSIONS ? How are they related to extensions ? Are we dealing here only with two complementary terminologies, which emphasize different aspects (e.g. following Carnap, the property aspect or the class aspect) ? Or could we understand intension as a mediating notion, related to the way in which we can refer to objects with linguistic expressions (this would seem rather to correspond to Frege's view of sense) ? In this connection we also have to clarify further what should be understood by 'possible world' (comprehended in state-descriptions) and how this notion is connected to that of intension.

2. We must also clarify how the INTENSIONS OF COMPLEX EXPRESSIONS are to be put together from the intensions (and possibly extensions) of the constituent expressions. For this we must on the one hand refer more precisely to the syntactic structure of expressions, and on the other to a precise classification of the possible context-expressions. Carnap, as we have seen, has made only a very rough classification according to extensional and intensional contexts; but this is clearly insufficient.

3. The notion of intension has been introduced up to now only for a restricted class of sentences. It should be possible to make it usable at least for all declarative sentences, i.e. sentences with deictic expressions, ambiguous or vague expressions, expressions with temporally variable extensions – in fact for sentences in general whose truth-values depend on the situations in which they are used. E.g.

(8) I'm tired.
   It's raining.
   Odysseus has gone swimming.
   The castle is old.
   This house is bigger than that house.
   The weather in Newfoundland is mostly bad.

> Cleopatra's lover is tired.
> The Burgomaster of Coblenz is more conservative than his predecessor.

Finally, it would also be desirable to explicate the meaning of non-declarative sentences (interrogatives, imperatives, etc.), even though it is doubtful whether the notion of intension (in any version, even one different from Carnap's) is sufficient.

*9.5   The logic of possible worlds and reference-points

First let us look more precisely at the connection of the notion of intension with that of possible worlds. For this it will be best to start with a modal logic, in which expressions like 'possible' and 'necessary' are directly specified. Carnap in fact already enters on this path in chapter 5 of *Meaning and necessity*. Let us take a sentence like 'It is necessary that p' ('Np'). 'It is necessary that...' is an intensional context: a statement is made here about the intension of p, namely that the intension of p is such that the extension of p in all worlds is the truth. We can also formulate this connection as follows:

'Np' is true if and only if 'p' is L-true.

In the same way, for 'It is possible that p' ('Pp', where 'Pp' $= \sim N \sim p$) we can obtain:

'Pp' is true if and only if 'p' is not L-false.

This asserts that the intension of p is such that the extension of p in some worlds is the truth, though it may be falsehood in others. Such reflections can be generalized, and we can conclude that the intension of a sentence is identical to the distribution of its truth-values in different possible worlds.[1]

For Carnap, all individual constants that come into consideration will already be introduced in the logical language S. Accordingly all possible worlds also have the same domain of individuals D; they are distinct only in the assignment of attributes to the individuals in D. It is also possible, however, to introduce individual variables in the logical

---

[1] Carnap obviously aims at this interpretation, at least in the case of (non-definite) individual designators. Thus he explains that an individual designator (e.g. *the Burgomaster of Coblenz*) has the function of assigning exactly one individual constant to every state-description that describes a possible world (say *Kuno Müller* at one time, *Konrad Schmidt* at another). For the intension of the individual designator we can understand the corresponding function that assigns exactly one individual to each state (or possible world). These two functions correspond to each other, because each state-description uniquely designates one possible world, and each individual constant uniquely designates one individual (cf. Carnap 1956b: 181).

language – certainly variables of such a type that the variable domain is different with respect to different state-descriptions: in other words we can assume that the individual-domains D_w and $D_{w'}$ are distinct, if the worlds w and w′ differ. Similarly we can assume that the extension of predicates in the different worlds varies, as well as that an individual expression in different worlds designates a different individual in each case. Let W be the set of possible worlds, and let D be the union of the individual-domains of all possible worlds:

$$D = \underset{w \in W}{\cup} D_W$$

(D is sometimes also called the 'universe of discourse').

An interpretation (or a model) for a language-system S now specifies (a) the INDIVIDUAL-DOMAIN D; (b) an appropriate ASSIGNMENT-FUNCTION between the individual expressions and predicates in S (in general, the meaningful but non-sentential expressions in S) and certain individuals or classes of individuals in D; and (c) TRUTH-VALUE CONDITIONS for the sentences in S according to the assignments for the non-sentential expressions in S. In the extensional interpretation we do not consider differentiation according to different possible worlds; in the intensional interpretation however we do.

I. EXTENSIONAL INTERPRETATION

Extension of an individual expression = Element of D.

Extension of a one-place predicate = Subclass of D.

Extension of a two-place predicate = Subclass of D × D (i.e. class of pairs of elements of D).

2. INTENSIONAL INTERPRETATION

Intension of an individual expression = Function from W in D.

Intension of a one-place predicate = Function from W in the set of the subclasses of D.

Intension of a two-place predicate = Function from W in the set of subclasses of D × D.

Instead of this we could say (for example):

The intension of an individual expression – e.g. a – is the distribution of extensions of this expression in the different possible worlds.

$$\text{Intension of a:} \begin{cases} \text{Extension of a in world w} &= \text{Element of } D_w \\ \text{Extension of a in world w}' &= \text{Element of } D_{w'} \\ \text{Extension of a in world w}'' &= \text{Element of } D_{w''} \end{cases}$$

The notion of intension will thus be fully defined by the two notions extension and possible world; its conceptual nature stems from the fact that it deals with FUNCTIONS FROM POSSIBLE WORLDS IN THE EXTENSIONS RELATIVE TO THESE WORLDS.

Carnap assumes that there is EXACTLY ONE ACTUAL WORLD. All possible worlds are defined relative to this actual one (e.g. in statements like *If there weren't any airplanes, you couldn't get from Berlin to London in two hours, Peter couldn't catch any fish in the Main because it's so polluted no fish can live in it, If only rents were a little lower*). This is surely an unsatisfactory solution. Language is not an instrument that can only be used relative to ONE actual world, but it can be used on various occasions and for various times, i.e. the actual world can also be defined differently.

Basically there seem to be two ways of handling this problem:

(a) The actual world is defined in each case from the perspective of the context of use, corresponding also to which other possible worlds come into question from this perspective.

(b) The sentences of the natural language are understood in the logical sense as sentence formulae with free variables. The values of these variables are determined by the situations in which the sentences are used. (This way seems at first to be especially suitable for sentences like *I'm tired, Cleopatra's lover is tired, It's raining outside*, etc.).

Ad (a). This is the direction that recent developments in modal logic have taken. A two-place alternativeness relation A, representing a certain point of view, is defined over the set W of possible worlds: for each world w, then, only those worlds that stand in the relation A to w can be taken as POSSIBLE ALTERNATIVE WORLDS (under that point of view). All interpretations are made RELATIVE TO w and A. The relation A could of course be defined independently of any context of use, but then we would not be solving the original problem. We can now assume that each of the possible worlds is defined essentially by the individuals that appear in it, i.e. by establishment of the individual-domain D_w. Then we can define context-dependence (in a first approximation) as follows (cf. Kamp 1973): the actual world, as well as all alternative worlds to be considered in relation to it, contains all the individuals who in a sentence (or sequence of sentences) are referred to in such a way that the reference presupposes their existence; the actual world is singled out by virtue of the fact that the individuals there have particular attributes assigned to them. There are also further alternative worlds, which all contain the individuals referred to – regardless of whether or not their existence is presupposed by their being referred to.

EXAMPLE: *Peter couldn't meet Nina, because...*: both the actual world and the alternative worlds contain the persons referred to with *Peter* and *Nina*.

EXAMPLE: *If Nina had had a brother, then...*: both the actual world and the alternative worlds contain the person referred to with *Nina*; some of the alternative worlds (but not the actual world!) contain the person referred to with *Nina's brother*.

Ad (b). The direction sketched out under (a) is still unsatisfactory for sentences with deictic expressions, because the extension of *I, there*, etc. never derives from the VERBAL CONTEXT alone. Further developments in intensional logic attempt to handle this as well.

Intensions will now be understood generally as FUNCTIONS FROM POSSIBLE REFERENCE-POINTS (or indices) IN THE EXTENSIONS RELATIVE TO THESE REFERENCE-POINTS. A reference-point i is itself complex, i.e. it consists of several coordinates. Different versions of intensional logic define the relevant coordinates differently. For Montague, every reference-point is a pair of coordinates: a POSSIBLE WORLD w and a POSSIBLE CONTEXT OF USE j (cf. Montague 1968). In the context of use we can distinguish between verbal and extraverbal contexts (speech situations).[1] Among the extraverbal contexts the time of utterance is especially important; we can then say that the set of possible worlds is temporally ordered: the corresponding logics are called tense logics (and we can elucidate in them the distinction between past, present and future statements).

David Lewis (1972: 175ff., 213ff.) has proposed a relatively strong differentiation. He distinguishes at least eight coordinates of a reference-point:[2]

1. a possible world,
2. a time of utterance,

---

[1] Terminologically we can also fix this distinction through the notions 'cotext' (for verbal context) and 'context' (for extraverbal context). Note that the intension of an expression is here formulated as dependent on the possible EXTERNAL verbal contexts of the expression (this plays a role for instance in implicit relational expressions like *big*, *bad*, etc. (*big* relative to what standard?) and in all pro-forms or anaphors like *first, she, afterwards*, etc.) and not dependent on the INTERNAL structure of the expression. This internal structure is to be considered when the intensions of complex expressions are 'computed' from the intensions of the constituent expressions. In this sense Carnap's notion of intensional isomorphy, for instance, refers to internal structure.

[2] I have proposed similar differentiations of the reference-point from other points of view – though partly also on syntactic grounds and not within the framework of an explication of the concept of meaning; these coordinates of course are also needed there for an appropriate interpretation (cf. Wunderlich 1970: 82f.; 1971: 177ff.).

3. a place of utterance,
4. a speaker,
5. an audience,
6. the objects indicated by gestures,
7. the preceding verbal context, which can be referred to anaphorically,
8. an assignment for the variables (in expressions with free variables, e.g. pronouns).

These distinctions are not always sufficient; for example we often need a distinction of speaker's place, hearer's place and third places, and further distinctions between addressees and hearers. Lewis himself points out that it is possible for the coordinates time, place, audience, and object indicated by gesture to have different values within one sentence (e.g. *This house is bigger than this house*); further, that certain objects spoken about can be foregrounded by expectation; and finally that in some cases we have to consider a range of vagueness, etc. This shows that all we have at present is an enumeration of some factors that are obviously important for the meaning of expressions in particular situations of use. Neither Montague nor Lewis (nor any other logician or linguist) has explicitly formulated to the extent necessary, what precise influence the specified coordinates have for the meaning of linguistic expressions; in other words, we do not yet have a THEORY OF MEANING that really applies these coordinates, and does not merely assume them. Only in the case of counterfactual conditionals (*If elephants didn't have tusks, we couldn't buy ivory carvings*), where the coordinates of the possible world are significant, and in tense and time expressions, do we have the seeds of an explicit theory of meaning (cf. Lewis 1973; Kamp 1968; Wunderlich 1970: ch. 5).

There is still another problem, namely the (in principle) uniform treatment of verbal and extraverbal contexts. In the first case the important level is that of combined linguistic expressions, but in the second case that of pragmatics.

*9.6   Semantics on the basis of a categorial grammar

There is another problem which can be handled rather more satisfactorily in the present state of development of model-semantics and intensional logic: namely how the intension of complex expressions derives from the intensions of their constituent expressions. For this we invoke two different types of notions: on the one hand Frege's idea that there should be only a very few SEMANTIC PRIMITIVE TYPES (e.g. reference to objects and reference to truth-values), all others being derived from these; on the other hand the logicians' idea that the syntactic structure of sentences should clearly reflect their semantic structure (or, more formally, that semantic structure should be HOMO-MORPHOUS to syntactic structure). Categorial grammars seem to be especially suitable from this point of view for the explication of semantic–syntactic connections in richer languages (and natural languages are obviously richer than the logical systems treated so far). A particular version of categorial grammar is used in the work of Montague, Lewis, Cresswell and others; I will not discuss it in detail here, but simply demonstrate it with one example sentence. The fundamental assumption is that there must be exactly as many SYNTACTIC BASIC CATEGORIES as semantic primitive types and that every derived category must also correspond to a derived semantic type; this will guarantee homomorphism.

In our example

(9) Kuno believes that Nina loves him

the basic categories are N (the category of proper names) and S (the category of sentences). The expressions *Nina, Kuno* and *him* are of the category N; *believes* is of the derived category (S/N)/S; *loves* is of the derived category (S/N)/N. It is universally the case that an expression of the category X/Y in combination with an expression of the category Y yields a combined expression of the category X. The syntactic structure of (9) can then be represented in the following CATEGORIAL STRUCTURE TREE:

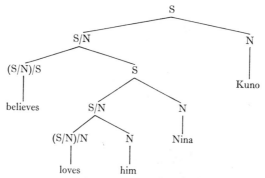

In the semantic interpretation, all basic syntactic categories are first assigned to the corresponding semantic types, in the form of intensions (i.e. for N: function from I in D; for S: function from I in the truth-values). For the derived categories the following should hold: from the conjunction of an X/Y-expression with a Y-expression we get an X-expression; correspondingly an X/Y-intension must be a function which takes a Y-intension as an argument and has an X-intension as its value. In an abbreviatory notation: $X/Y\text{-Int} = X\text{-Int}^{Y-\text{INT}}$ (with the argument-domain of the function as superscript). The interpretation of (9) then yields the following SEMANTIC STRUCTURE TREE (the terminal nodes represent the intensions of the individual expressions, and the other nodes the semantic types of these intensions or the combined intensions (after Lewis 1972):

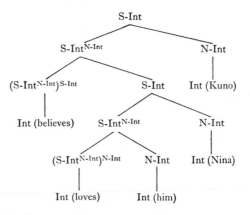

To 'compute' the INTENSION OF THE WHOLE SENTENCE we read the semantic tree from bottom to top: the intension of *loves* applied to the intension of *him* yields the intension of *loves him*; correspondingly in the next steps we obtain the intension of *Nina loves him, believes that Nina loves him,* and finally *Kuno believes that Nina loves him.* This procedure is INDEPENDENT OF WHAT THE INTENSIONS OF THE BASIC CATEGORIES ARE, i.e. whether they are understood as above as functions from reference-points in objects or truth-values, or any other way, e.g. as bundles of semantic features or as psychological representations in human brains.

The procedure is obviously simple; but the results do very much depend on what we regard as semantic primitives or syntactic basic categories, and what we regard as derived. Unlike Carnap's view, predicates are not regarded here as basic categories; and some difficulties now arise with such complex notions as the intension of *love,* which is a function from a function from reference points in objects in a function from a function from reference-points in truth-values (namely $(S-Int^{N-Int})^{N-Int})$. We could decide to regard such two-place predicates (or at any rate one-place predicates like *to love Kuno*) as basic categories, whose intensions are functions from reference-points in classes of pairs of objects (or classes of objects, corresponding to Carnap's procedure). But this is obviously only possible for some predicates, namely extensional ones like for example *married to, red, cackle* (perhaps *love* also belongs to this type, but this is not completely clear, at least in sentences like *Kuno loves Nina's charming ways, Kuno loves jazz*); and is not possible for non-extensional predicates like *fall* (in *the dollar is falling*), *charming, good,* etc. We must look around for another solution for these. The one outlined seems at least possible. Even the non-extensional and (in the Carnapian sense) non-intensional character of *believe* comes out immediately in this representation. For the extensional predicates we can state a procedure by which we can reduce the relatively complex intensions to simpler Carnapian intensions.[1] This is in any case the more general way, since extensional predicates can be understood as special cases.

The TOTAL MEANING OF A SENTENCE here is not to be identified with its intension (otherwise *Every pig is a pig* and *Volker is dreaming or not dreaming* might have the same meaning); nor is it to be identified with the intension plus the semantic structure up to the analysis into semantic primitives (otherwise *Every pig is a pig* and *Every woman is a woman* would have the same meaning); rather it is to be identified with the whole semantic structure tree, INCLUDING the intensions of the constituent expressions (the intension of *pig* is naturally different from that of *woman*). If two expressions have the same total meaning in this sense, then clearly we have found the narrowest possible notion of sameness of meaning (we have essentially reconstructed Carnap's notion of intensional isomorphy).

9.7 The context-dependence of intensions

In general we must start by assuming that the reference-points for the intensions of all expressions in a sentence are specified in the same way, since every situation of use of the whole sentence automatically represents a context for he constituent expression as well. Only in this case can we obtain an intension for the whole sentence that appropriately 'computes' the intensions of all its expressions. Likewise we can

[1] Such a procedure has been formulated by David Lewis (1972: 29).

generally assume that two occurrences of the same expression in a sentence have the same intension. This however leaves out of consideration the fact that at least one of the coordinates of the reference-point relates to the verbal context.

If we say that a sentence like *Every woman is a woman* is true with respect to all possible reference-points, then we take the intensions of both occurrences of *woman* as identical, and their different positions in the sentences are irrelevant. Nonetheless such sentences can in fact be uttered in a non-trivial sense: this presupposes that *Not every woman is a woman* could also be true. In this case the two instances of *woman* must be being used in different senses. In the second occurrence, *woman* is clearly being used predicatively; the intension of *woman* is taken as stable, possibly with an evaluative connotation. In the first occurrence, *woman* serves rather for an identification (subsumption under a class concept), and is to be regarded as having no evaluative connotation. For example, *Every person that I designate 'woman' is a woman*, or *Every woman in the biological sense is also a woman in the sociocultural sense* (i.e. *certain norms of social status, etc., must hold for her*). The possible differences of intension also show up in the adjectives *womanly* and *feminine*: *Every woman is womanly* (*womanly* connotes properties that not every person designated by *woman* necessarily possesses, e.g. housewifeliness, motherliness, etc.; so the sentence could be false); *Every woman is feminine* (even *feminine* connotes properties that not every woman necessarily possesses, e.g. lovingness, emotionality, etc.).

If we take the sentence *Every pig is a pig* in the sense of *Every pig is and will remain a pig* (or even *If something is at one time a pig, then it is a pig at any other time*), then it will be clear that in the first occurrence *pig* is being used in a momentary-identifying way (e.g. in the biological sense), while in the second it is being used, on the contrary, in a temporally invariant predicative (and possibly evaluative) way.

It is easy to find further examples. In the sentence *I dreamed that I kissed myself*, *I kissed myself* has the same intension as in isolated use (the extension of course is to be regarded as relative to the speaker's dream-world). Nevertheless the sentence *I dreamed I was Brigitte Bardot and I kissed myself* is ambiguous; and in both the obvious interpretations (*I myself kissed my other I, namely Brigitte Bardot*, and *My other I, namely Brigitte Bardot, kissed me*) the sequence *I kissed myself* has a different intension from what it has in the first sentence. This is because within the dream-world we assume an identification of two otherwise different persons; this shows that the intension of *I kissed myself* can change in different verbal contexts. The problem hinted at here is connected to that of so-called referential identity: do *I* and *myself* in *I see myself in the mirror* have the same intension ? Or do we have to distinguish the first *I* as a conscious perception, as against the second *myself* as an external appearance ?

*9.8 On the choice of semantic primitive types

We have so far distinguished only two semantic primitive types (functions in objects and truth-values), and correspondingly only two basic syntactic categories (proper names and sentences). This does not imply a claim that these elements and their combinatorial possibilities are enough to explicate all factual reference in natural languages. (It seems especially difficult, with these two primitives, to characterize reference to processes and their stages, including actions.) In general we restrict ourselves to a few basic types and categories because we want to see whether we can produce a consistent and formal explication of particular statement domains in natural languages. It is certainly even conceivable, according to an idea of Frege's, that we might admit only one semantic primitive, namely the function in a domain of objects; even truth-values will then be regarded as objects, and sentences as complex proper names. On the other hand there are proposals (e.g. by Lewis) which assume three basic categories: proper names, general names and sentences, and accordingly three semantic primitives: functions in objects, classes of objects and truth-values.[1]

Formulations are also possible in which the special category of proper names is entirely dispensed with. Given the syntactic parallelism of sentences like

(10) The dog next door barks
    Many dogs bark
    Every dog barks
    Fido barks

---

[1] The class of general names is smaller than the class of predicates: e.g. *man, dog*, etc., count as general names, but not *wail, blue*, etc. It is obvious that *dog*, for example, designates a class of beings; for *wail* this is less obvious. We do not intuitively understand a class of wailing beings, but rather a particular way in which beings behave. Likewise for *blue* we do not intuitively understand a class of blue things, but rather a property of things. This may explain Carnap's difficulty in defining the intensions of predicates (are they properties or concepts ?): he defines predicates so broadly that general names and verbs as well as adjectives all come under that heading.

we can collapse proper names like *Fido*, definite designations like *the dog next door* and quantified expressions like *many dogs*, *every dog* into a single category of 'terms' or nominal phrases. What would be an appropriate semantic type for the nominal phrase? Obviously we can say that in all cases certain CLASSES OF PROPERTIES ARE DESIGNATED.[1] In the case of *many dogs*, the properties do not all have to be compatible (e.g. some of the dogs that bark are male, while others are female); in the case of the proper names and definite designations they must be. One of the properties of Fido would be that this dog is normally called *Fido*; other properties would be that he belongs to the man next door, that he was born on 17 June 1970, etc.; these properties are obviously compatible. In such a representation we can also paraphrase *Fido barks* as *Barking belongs to the class of properties of Fido*, and analogously *Every dog barks* can be paraphrased as *Barking belongs to the class of properties of each individual dog*. Such an introduction of a unitary category 'nominal phrase' is however not to be regarded as ontologically motivated, but merely as a decision to allow certain theoretical generalizations. In every rational semantic theory the object-aspect and the class-of-properties-aspect should turn out to be equivalent, i.e. they must be derivable from each other and only count as two different terminologies emphasizing one or the other aspect.[2]

In general we can require that the form of syntactic–semantic linguistic analysis and explication should not depend on how we answer questions like 'What different kinds of things are there in the world and what different aspects do they have?', but rather on logical considerations ('Which aspects of our use of language do we want to elucidate, and from what point of view?'). Nevertheless, if we want to reconstruct linguistic reference with respect to its dynamic and processual characteristics, it is presumably necessary to assume that there are more semantic primitives than we have discussed, e.g. functions in times, places, causal relationships, etc., according to what we are primarily using language to talk about.

[1] On this cf. the discussion in Lewis (1972: 49ff.); likewise Kripke (1972: 252–5, 285). Instead of 'classes of properties' we could also speak of 'classes of subclasses of the object domain' (cf. Egli 1972).

[2] In the system developed by Montague (1973), the equivalence can in fact be shown; on this cf. Partee (1975).

9.9 Vagueness and partial intensions

We can give yet another and rather different interpretation to the intensions of linguistic expressions. Here we will emphasize their conceptual nature; though we will not identify intensions with concepts (insofar as by concepts we understand particular psychic representations or assume that concepts find their immediate expression in words or combinations of words, which is what makes them potentially objective). Obviously we identify intensions differently from Carnap – but also without any observable properties. We can understand intensions, however, as rules of a particular kind, namely as CONDITIONS FOR THE USABILITY OF AN EXPRESSION RELATIVE TO PARTICULAR CONTEXTS OF USE. Let the intension of a general name P be a function from I in classes of objects; then under the conditions of the reference-point i, P is usable of an object x where $i \rightarrow \{..., x, ...\}$ is an element of the intension of P. From this point of view we can also say that the intensions of linguistic expressions represent dispositions for their use (e.g. for the designation of objects) under the conditions of particular reference-points.[1]

Now we know that concepts very often have a VAGUENESS-ZONE, i.e. in some cases they are clearly applicable, and in others clearly not, while in still others their applicability is undetermined. If we represent the conditions for the applicability of a concept in the form of intensions, there are obviously two ways of explicating the VAGUENESS OF AN EXPRESSION (CONCEPT):

1. There are reference-points for which the value of the intension is not precisely determined, i.e. the intension is variable in a particular domain (e.g. the class of objects designated by a general name is not precisely bounded): either individual persons themselves are uncertain,

---

[1] Carnap (1955) attempts a similar interpretation of intensions (I quote from the reprint, 1956b: 233–47). He writes (242f.): 'the intension of a predicate "Q" for a speaker *X* is the general condition which an object *y* must fulfil in order for *X* to be willing to ascribe the predicate "Q" to *y*'. The characteristic difference from my interpretation is in the passage 'condition which an object must fulfil' (instead of condition which a communication situation must fulfil): this is connected with Carnap's naturalistic view of intensions. Thus a little later he expressly says that 'F [an intension or property: DW] is here always assumed to be an observable property, i.e. either directly observable or explicitly definable in terms of directly observable properties' (we thus find here a reductionist view in addition to the one we rejected earlier). Carnap's formulation of the concept of intension is in addition such that it should make possible an operationalization of the concept: we can devise test situations in which a speaker X must show his willingness to apply or not apply a particular predicate to a particular object. These tests should serve for a subsequent stabilization of the explicandum or an indication of the adequacy of the explication.

or different persons assume different value-assignments under the conditions of the same reference-point.

2. There are classes of reference-points for which no value is yet determined (e.g. because cases involving applications of this kind have never arisen); this kind of vagueness probably remains fundamental.

In the first case there is indeed a value 'defined' for the reference-point in question, but only within a particular domain; in the second case there is overall no value defined. We do not have to decide at the outset which of these two explications we should choose, or whether to take them as complementary. If we assume that it is possible to communicate in particular situations in a referentially unclear way, then we choose the first version; if we dispute this, then we choose the second.[1] Both versions correspond to the concept of RULE-VAGUENESS: either the results of a rule-application are not precisely defined, or the situations where the rule is to be applied are not precisely defined (though in any given case it can lead to a clear result), or only a few situations are defined, though there could be many more.

The following circumstances tend to favour the second version (or at least consideration of it): concepts (or the corresponding linguistic expressions) are LEARNED ON THE BASIS OF ONLY A FEW SITUATIONS OF USE (the intensions are gradually learned on the basis of extensions to particular reference-points); they cannot be fully learned in the sense of already being used in all possible contexts; there is always some generalization with respect to possible new situations. This generalization can leave certain new classes of situation unconsidered. Consider for example a child who has learned the expression *dog* in a city, and has learned it exclusively in situations where the animal so designated always appears accompanied by people on the street and in parks. How should he behave then, for instance on holiday, in a situation where a very similar animal is chasing a flock of sheep? Should this one also be called *dog*, or would not *wolf* perhaps be better? One could object here that the concept 'dog' is acquired mainly with reference to external

---

[1] Carnap seems to opt for the first version. Since he identifies intensions for instance with certain properties of objects, he can then propose the following explication of 'vagueness' (1956b: 242f.): 'In order to take vagueness into account, a pair of intensions F_1, F_2 must be stated: X has the disposition of ascribing affirmatively the predicate "Q" to an object y if and only if y has F_1; and the disposition of denying "Q" for y if and only if y has F_2. Thus, if y has neither F_1 nor F_2, X will give neither an affirmative nor a negative response; the property of having neither F_1 nor F_2 constitutes the zone of vagueness, which may possibly be empty.' Similarly those theoreticians who speak of 'fuzzy sets' in this connection would decide on the first version (e.g. Zadeh 1965, 1971).

appearance and similar properties; but then how should the child learn that both toy poodles and St Bernards are called *dog* – without still more criteria ? (On the other hand our child might also have trouble, if he saw a tame lion cub being taken for a walk, in NOT calling it *dog*.) It is perhaps clearer for concepts like 'love' that generalizations are made on the basis of several situations of use, and not on the basis of visible properties. With more theoretical concepts, e.g. 'communism', the verbal context plays the most important role; it may be that for such concepts we do not learn any intension at all, but rather the system of sense-relations in which they stand to other concepts.

If intensions according to the second version are defined only for some classes of reference-points, we can speak of PARTIAL INTENSIONS. Clearly the intensions of most expressions in natural languages are only partially determined – and this is the source of their vagueness with respect to new situations. Correspondingly the intensions of complex expressions are also only partially determined, and we cannot state a truth-value for sentences in every case. The same holds for semantic structures put together out of intensions, or the total meanings of complex expressions.

9.10 Three-valued logic

A totally different formulation of the vagueness-problem allows three truth-values, i.e. truth, falsehood and indeterminacy. (Indeterminacy here is thus a genuine truth-value, and not merely the absence of a truth-value for particular reference-points.) In this case we must reformulate the whole structure of logic, because this assumption has far-reaching consequences: we now have a THREE-VALUED LOGIC, instead of a two-valued logic, as before.[1] In this system we can express the truth-value 'undetermined' for a sentence, e.g. the application of a predicate to particular individual expressions must lie in the vagueness-zone of this predicate. In this way we can also explicate the vagueness of predicates. One possible advantage of a three-valued logic might be that it assumes as many truth-values as there are modalities in the various forms of modal logic (e.g. necessary, impossible, possible; verified, falsified, undetermined; proved, refuted, undecided; acceptable unacceptable, doubtful).

[1] The most convincing formulation of a three-valued logic I know is Blau (1973). But it remains to be shown how far his formulation is equivalent in principle to the concept of partial intensions, and what its advantages and possible disadvantages might be.

Under certain conditions these different modalities can be related to the different truth-values; it is conceivable that in principle we could work out the same kind of formalism. On the other hand, it seems to me that the concept of partial intension has a considerable advantage: it allows us to show more clearly, for instance, what the stepwise learning or refinement (or standardization) of a concept consists of. While in three-valued logic sentences must change their truth-values (true or false instead of undetermined), in intensional logic only the intensions of expressions have to be defined for new reference-points. For many problems a three-valued logic and an intensional logic with partial intensions achieve exactly the same results (e.g. in the problem discussed below).

9.11 Selectional restrictions and presuppositions

In addition to the possible vagueness of expressions, their possible MEANINGLESSNESS plays a role in semantics. A complex expression (e.g. a sentence) is meaningless if certain selection restrictions are violated, or if there are unfulfilled (false) presuppositions:

(11) a. Semantic theory snores.
    b. The sheep twittered in the morning.
    c. Frege wasn't interested in transformational grammar.
    d. Harold Wilson realized that he ought to leave the Liberal Party.
    e. Kuno has married his own widow.

These sentences cannot be used either in the positive or the negative sense; i.e. even their negations would be meaningless.

The meaninglessness arises – crudely – either on linguistic grounds (you can only say that living beings snore) or on the grounds of our extralinguistic knowledge (Harold Wilson is not a member of the Liberal Party).[1] In both cases however there are SYSTEMATIC TRUTH-VALUE-GAPS. In the framework of a three-valued logic the truth-value of all meaningless sentences is undetermined; in a two-valued logic we have to formulate restrictions on the class of admissible interpretations. In the case of SELECTIONAL RESTRICTIONS (e.g. *twitter* vs. *sheep*) we have to formulate appropriate special sense-relations between expressions of the language, which exclude combinations of this kind; in any

---

[1] I have already mentioned the problem of a strict distinction between linguistic and extralinguistic knowledge. We can however assume it for heuristic purposes (we argue against (11d) differently from (11a)).

case one version of this would be to define the intension of these expressions only for such contexts as stand in the sense-relation in question. (It would of course be possible to say that sheep twitter in reference to other worlds, like dream-worlds; but this would obviously involve an appropriate alteration of either the intension of *sheep* or *twitter*). In the case of PRESUPPOSITIONS we could speak of a sense-relation between sentences: *Harold Wilson realized that he ought to leave the Liberal Party* presupposes *Harold Wilson ought to leave the Liberal Party*, and this presupposes *Harold Wilson is a member of the Liberal Party*. In general, a sentence A presupposes a sentence B if B must be true in order for A to be assigned one of the two truth-values truth or falsehood. Somewhat more formally:[1]

Let A and B be sentences in L. A presupposes B in L where for every permissible interpretation V from L it is the case that:

If $V(A) = T$, then $V(B) = T$;
If $V(A) = F$, then $V(B) = T$.

The sense of this definition arises from the following consideration: for any arbitrary interpretation let $V(B) = F$; then by application of *modus tollens* according to the first condition $V(A) = F$, and according to the second condition $V(A) = T$. This is a contradiction; therefore $V(B) = F$ is excluded for any arbitrary interpretation.

For any sentence A there is a class of sentences which are presupposed by A; let us call it the presupposition-set PRES(A). The intension of A is then defined for those reference-points relative to which all elements of PRES(A) are fulfilled in the domain of interpretation (have the value 'truth'). A reference-point includes those possible worlds that are spoken of, as well as a particular argumentation context. If anyone asserts that A, and someone contradicts him by asserting not-A, then he has recourse to this same argumentation context; if however he contradicts him by saying that not-B (where $B \in$ PRES(A)), he destroys the context and opens up a new one.

---

[1] Cf. van Fraassen (1971: 154). On the whole problem of presupposition see the papers collected in Petöfi & Franck (1973).

9.II THE INTRALINGUISTIC MEANING OF LINGUISTIC EXPRESSIONS (CONCEPTUAL SEMANTICS)

9.12 Introductory remarks

In the structuralist view, single linguistic expressions essentially derive their meaning from their relation to other expressions, i.e. from their position in a whole field or network of expressions and structures available to users of the language. We cannot comprehend the meaning of a single expression in isolation (if we want to know what *hot* means we must at least know that it is used in the opposite way from *cold*). The total organization of the meanings expressible in a language is therefore a subject for linguistics. Many linguists either attempt to deal with this without paying attention to the theories of meaning developed in logic or reject them as inadequate for natural language. In addition it is often argued that the designation function of an expression can only be elucidated after its relations to other expressions are clear. But we could argue with equal justice that we can only elucidate relations to other expressions when we know the designating functions. For this reason we should not attempt to develop a conceptual semantics in complete isolation from referential semantics: the two must be regarded as complementary.

The proponent of the first position may argue that we can only speak about meaning in linguistic terms – with the aid of paraphrases, translations, comments, etc. If this is taken as an absolute, however, it leads to an undesirable quasi-autonomy: language is only to be understood by means of language. This clearly neglects at least three other factors:

1. Language is learned in practical surroundings which can be perceived and experienced without having to be mediated linguistically.

2. Language is used in daily social intercourse, which also includes non-linguistic contexts.

3. Language itself is not the only basis for our understanding of language; this also arises from logical/formal reconstructions, i.e. particular standards; explications would have no function if they were not developed with a specific view to the possibilities of ordinary language (regardless of the fact that they are only possible because we have already mastered a language, and can only be justified in it).

The relative interdependence of the meanings of linguistic expressions is shown by the fact that particular sentences (although syntactically well-formed) are meaningless or self-contradictory; and also by the fact that if particular sentences are meaningful and true, then certain others are meaningful, but not true (or the sentences are not usable at the same time), and others again are not meaningful. The meaning of each particular expression is determined by its RELATIVE POSITION with respect to neighbouring expressions within complex expressions (up to texts).

We can explicate the semantic relation of an expression a to other expressions b_j by means of particular sense-relations SR_i. In this case the total meaning of the expression a can be stated as:

$$\{\langle b_j, SR_i \rangle : SR_i(a, b_j)\}.$$

In principle the expression a naturally stands in particular relations to all other possible expressions in the language; we must then consider the totality of other expressions for the semantic explication of any individual one. Therefore the attempt is often made to invoke only primary (particularly fundamental) sense-relations; the remaining ones can then either be regarded as complex, or be derived by special inferential procedures. Reflections of this type are what underlie the frequent (and as yet unfulfilled) requirement for a recursive characterization of the set of sense-relations in a language.

This whole general domain has been neglected in recent linguistic research, and is consequently in serious need of development. Developments in logic have rarely been concerned with the problem of elucidating semantic connections within the vocabulary of a language; even the pragmatic aspect of situation-specific language use and the sociological aspect of group-specific and society-specific 'accumulation of knowledge' and 'accumulation of commonsense' within the vocabulary have been rigorously neglected. Because of the state of research, I will be able to refer in what follows only to a few quite unsatisfactory proposals which are hardly likely to lead to a satisfactory connection with the other concepts of meaning.

9.13 Paradigmatic and syntagmatic sense-relations

Two main types of sense-relations have traditionally been distinguished: PARADIGMATIC and SYNTAGMATIC. In the first case we are concerned with the replaceability of an expression a by other expressions b within a complex expression A, such that the total meaning is changed in a specific way (or retained). In the second case we are concerned with the total mutual relations of two expressions a and b that appear in different positions in a complex expression, e.g. a sentence. A theory of sense-relations must therefore be built on the syntax of sentences or similar complex expressions, and must also incorporate assumptions about the possible meanings of sentences. The concepts 'paradigmatic' and 'syntagmatic' themselves must of course be more precisely explicated; they will for the most part be used only informally, and related but theoretically more precise concepts will appear in their place.[1]

Dictionaries (along with descriptions of what a word designates) mainly represent paradigmatic relations, e.g. expressions synonymous with a given one (*wail*: *cry*, *tattle-tale*: *informer*) or what superordinate concepts an expression can be subsumed under (*grippe*: *acute virus disease*, *plane-tree*: *maple*). They often give syntagmatic relations as well (*crow*: *cry* [*of cock*], *whisper*:—*something in someone's ear*; *decipher*: —*a cryptogram*).

The idea that the meaning of expressions arises from their SYNTAGMATIC RELATIONS was first systematically developed by the structuralists. Bloomfield, for example, defines the concepts 'constructional meaning', 'functional meaning', and 'class-meaning', which he connects with a whole semantic programme (1926: §6):

> 23. **Def**. Such recurrent sames of order are CONSTRUCTIONS; the corresponding stimulus-reaction features are CONSTRUCTIONAL MEANINGS . . .
>
> 29. **Def**. Each of the ordered units in a construction is a POSITION . . .
>
> 30. **Assumption**. Each position in a construction can be filled only by certain forms.
>
> 31. **Def**. The meaning of a position is a FUNCTIONAL MEANING. That is, the constructional meaning of a construction may be divided into parts, one for each position; these parts are the functional meanings...
>
> 34. **Def**. The functional meanings in which the forms of a form-class appear constitute the CLASS-MEANING.

---

[1] Thus Schnelle (1973) distinguishes between 'meaning-relations' (paradigmatic, but related in some ways to meaning-structures in the sense of Lewis 1972) and 'meaning-conditions' (syntagmatic, namely in relation to different positions in meaning-structures of the Lewis type). Žolkovskij and Mel'čuk distinguish between lexical substitution (paradigmatic, with total or partial agreement of semantic features) and lexical parameters (syntagmatic, related to particular syntactic combination types, e.g. attribution): cf. the discussion in Apresjan (1971).

It is clear (especially from definition 31) that Bloomfield computes the functional meaning of expressions filling a particular position in a sentence on the basis of the part they play in the sentence's total meaning. It is this total meaning (here generalized as constructional meaning) and not the functional meaning that is to be described in stimulus-response terms, i.e. with reference to extralinguistic factors. At the same time it is clear that Bloomfield was attempting a programme largely corresponding to the approach to logic in 9.1 above, i.e. the establishment of a clear connection between intra- and extralinguistic meanings.

9.14 Components of meaning and semantic features

The traditional definitions of concepts according to *genus proximum* and *differentia specifica*, which were already common in antiquity, provide a clear example of the use of sense-relations. For example:

(a) A fish is a vertebrate [*gen. prox.*] that lives in the water, breathes with gills, etc. [*diff. spec.*].

(b) To wade is to walk [*gen. prox.*] over a surface covered with water or mud to a certain depth [*diff. spec.*].

The distinction between *gen. prox.* and *diff. spec.* however is often arbitrary; it depends on what aspects of the definiendum are foregrounded. Thus we could revise (a) above this way:

(a′) A fish is something that lives in the water [*gen. prox.*], has a vertebral column, and breathes with gills [*diff. spec.*].

We can therefore conflate the *gen. prox.* and *diff. spec.* under one concept: i.e. 'conceptual feature', 'semantic feature', or 'component of meaning'. The meaning-analysis of a single expression a would then consist of an enumeration of other expressions b, c, ... which are to be taken together as components of a. If we know the meaning of the components b, c, ..., we know the meaning of a.

This procedure raises problems if we do not know the meaning of the specified components, i.e. if it is a question of expressions in a language that we do not know sufficiently well (e.g. an *ad hoc* standardized language, a freely invented semiformal notation, or the like). This is the case with the following interpretations, when we confront them unprepared:

A is smaller than B = A is such that it could be as if a part of B. (Wierzbicka 1973: 623)

WINTER = a world a part of which is a sun causing creatures on earth to be warm. (Wierzbicka 1973: 625)

gießen: ⟨Kausation, ⟨Disposition [Person], ⟨Alteration: Raum [Flüssig], (⟨Partition [Richtung], ([Person])⟩)⟩⟩⟩ (Baumgärtner 1970: 70)

Obviously we have to be already familiar with the language for which the components are stated; otherwise the interpretation is worthless. If the language is not properly specified in advance for us, we have what might be called pseudonotations, which are unsuitable for explicating meaning (on pseudonotations see 9.18 below). From the examples cited it is also clear that there are at least two notions of the sort of language in which the components of meaning should be formulated. In the first two, expressions of English (though complex and standardized) are used to explicate expressions of English: the claim is that there exists a particular relation between expressions from in principle one and the same language (here expressed by the 'equals' sign);[1] in such a case we will speak of sense-relations.

In the third example an expression of German is assigned a bracket-notation, which very clearly does not belong to the German language. Certainly it uses German expressions like *Kausation, Raum*, but these are probably to be understood as theoretical concepts, and their meaning does not have to agree with that of the corresponding German words. In this case the colon certainly does not express a sense-relation, but rather the translation of a German expression in a theoretical language. (It is questionable whether, independently of logical procedures, we can find a plausible and comprehensible theoretical language for actually elucidating the meanings of individual expressions.)

We will not regard the selected expressions *Kausation, Raum*, etc., as components of meaning, but as semantic features. Components should thus belong to the language itself, while features belong to another (especially theoretical) language.

We can see from the examples that components as well as features are used in a particular syntactic configuration. In the first case relative clause constructions (among others) are used (i.e. *is such that, a part of which*); in the second, various kinds of bracketings, commas, colons. The traditional schema for conceptual definition is thus also inappro-

---

[1] It is not clear whether the 'equals' sign is to be understood as an expression of the synonymy relation or as an expression of the explication in a standardized form of English.

priate because it contains no definitions of how the *genus proximum* is to be syntactically combined with the various *differentiae specificae*. In a definition with a clear syntactic structure, for instance, like this:

> An uncle of X is either a brother of the father or mother of X, or the husband of one of the sisters of the father or mother of X

it is not at all clear what is to be taken as *gen. prox.* (surely not *brother*, but at best *male person*, i.e. one of the semantic components of *brother* or *husband*.)

9.15   Lexical fields

In German linguistics since the 1930s, the interdependence of meanings has primarily been treated under the concept of LEXICAL FIELD (*Wortfeld*, *sprachliches Feld*).[1] This is a holistic concept; the whole lexical inventory of a language is conceived as a systematically organized set of individual and interlaced lexical fields, each with its own internal organization, based on semantic relations. The meaning of individual words can only be understood in relation to the totality of one or more lexical fields. Unfortunately such relations are rarely formulated explicitly; they are rather at most intuitively illustrated by groups of words, e.g.:

(a)   very good – good – adequate – unsatisfactory – inadequate

(b)   white, black, yellow, blue, red
        |
        scarlet, carmine, vermilion

(c)   weise, klug, gescheit, gerissen, schlau, gewitzigt, listig

(d)   sin reda, wizze, redehaftî, fernumest, sinnigî, wizentheit, fruotheit, wîstuom, chunna, list (OHG: Notker)

(e)   evildoer, criminal, villain, scoundrel, bandit

(f)   patruus   amita   matertera   avunculus
        | | | |
     patruelis amitinus consobrinus avunculi filius

(g)   rooster   boar   stallion   man
        | | | |
       hen   sow   mare   woman
        | | | |
      chick   piglet   foal   child

---

[1] For information (even if somewhat biased) about the various versions of field-theory see Geckeler (1971); some of the most important discussions are in Schmidt (1973). An early explication of the idea of a lexical field in terms of Katzian semantics is given by Baumgärtner (1967).

(h)   roof   treetop   summit   apex
        | | | |
       house   tree   mountain   pyramid, cone

(i)   walk   grasp   see   hear   lick   kiss
        | | | | | |
       feet   hand   eye   ear   tongue   lips

(j)   dog   sheep   horse   rooster   bird
        | | | | |
       bark   bleat   neigh   crow   twitter

(k)   meeting   match   performance   exhibition
        | | | |
       hold   stage   give   stage

       journey   trial
        | |
       take   conduct

(l)   big   deep   high   broad   long   hard   fast   beautiful
        | | | | | | | |
       small shallow low   narrow   short   soft   slow   ugly

These sets are defined in terms of quite disparate aspects of meaning, and it must be admitted that in cases (c), (d), (e) the semantic relations are not easy to formulate. Trier (1931) wanted to use the concept of lexical field primarily for the analysis of abstract concepts (examples (c) and (d) are his); especially in documents from past ages (as here in Old High German) we can scarcely study the relationships of individual concepts to each other except via their different contextual functions in the existing texts; the question also arises of conditions on and directions of historical change in such fields of abstract concepts (*list* in OHG stands in a very different relation to neighbouring concepts than *List* in Modern German). A field of abstract concepts can perhaps be compared with a set of theoretical concepts within a theory; the values of concepts derive primarily from the way they are used in sentences together with other concepts (axioms or theorems in a theory, the statements of authors in the case of OHG literature).

In examples (f), (g), (h), and also to some extent in (i), (j), the words grouped together have clear designatory functions; in such cases semantic analysis is mainly directed, not toward connected statements in texts, but rather toward particular cultural, biological and other facts; here we have groupings not only on the basis of sense-relations, but often (sometimes primarily) on the basis of an analysis of factual reference – though without the necessary structuring in terms of an explicit theoretical framework. While most cases treat paradigmatic relations between words of the same syntactic category, examples (i), (j), (k) are based on syntagmatic relations; Porzig (1934), from whom these examples are taken in somewhat modified form, calls them 'substantial meaning relations' (*wesenhafte Bedeutungsbeziehungen*). These relationships are explicable under the concept of SELECTIONAL RESTRICTIONS: if the NP position in a simple sentence of the form NP–V is filled by *horse*, we cannot normally use *crow, bleat*, etc., in the V position; and if the V position is filled by *neighs*, we cannot normally use *rooster, sheep*, etc., in the NP position. Of course we must not ignore the fact that the relations in (j) are different from those in (k): the distinction between *bleat* and *neigh* is relatively easy to demonstrate by stating extensions (either of animals or particular typical sounds), while the distinction between *conduct* and *hold* can only be illustrated verbally. But some distinction is necessary for elucidating the semantic nature of selectional restrictions.

The mere grouping of expressions in a lexical field naturally does not represent an analysis (even if something of the sort is occasionally hinted at by the type of grouping); it is merely raw material for subsequent analysis on the basis of common or distinguishing components of meaning (or semantic features). The first of these types of analysis stems from the Copenhagen school. Hjelmslev for instance gives the following examples (1961: 70):

> ram = he-sheep
> ewe = she-sheep
> man = he-human being
> woman = she-human being
> boy = he-child
> girl = she-child
> stallion = he-horse
> mare = she-horse

Eight expressions are defined as combinations of six meaning-components. The sense-relation holding between *ram* and *ewe* is the same as that between *boy* and *girl* (we could call it the *he–she* relation); its first part is an element from the set of expressions designating male beings, and its second is an element from the set of expressions designating female beings. One common mode of analysis involves an attempt to recruit polar concepts as components of meaning, like 'male'–'female', 'human'–'non-human', 'concrete'–'abstract', etc.; this leads to a binary system, in which we can then mark one element of each pair with the coefficient ' + ' and the other with ' − ' (e.g. ' − male' instead of 'female'). Insofar as this can actually be done, it makes sense, since it is one way of establishing just what the simplest meaning differences are. But in the case of colour-terms or animal names, to take only simple cases, the procedure is unusable, and it is even worse when we come to complex abstract or theoretical concepts.[1]

*9.16   Meaning-postulates and componential analysis

Componential analysis, as we have seen, can make use either of expressions from the language being described (e.g. in Wierzbicka, Hjelmslev and perhaps Lakoff), or artificial terms which we will call semantic features (notably in Katz). In both cases the aim is to keep the number of components as small as possible, i.e. to take all other expressions as combinations of them. This attempt can also be reinforced by the desire to find a recursive procedure for the definition (or characterization) of sense-relations. There is a hint of this in some work of Lakoff (1972: ch. VII, esp. 615ff.) – though it is connected with other, untenable views. Lakoff suggests the following:

1. There is a set of ATOMIC PREDICATES whose mutual relations are established by MEANING-POSTULATES (where the sense-relations holding between specific expressions are defined), for example

$$\text{CERTAIN (S)} \supset \text{POSSIBLE} \quad \text{(S)}$$
$$\sim \text{NECESSARY (S)} \equiv \text{POSSIBLE} \sim \text{(S)}$$

and many others. (According to Lakoff's analysis we could add other atomic predicates, like CAUSE, COME ABOUT, SAY, GOOD, BAD, BELIEVE, INTEND, RESPONSIBLE FOR.)

2. Syntactic trees are generated (so-called logical structures) whose terminal nodes are exclusively atomic predicates; by means of particular transformations several such predicates can possibly be conflated under a common node. In this case they can be replaced by a semantically complex expression of the language in question (if the corresponding item exists).

---

[1] Cases like *hermaphrodite, ox* and so on can still be treated under certain conditions with features like ' ±male' or 'o male': in one case both components are present, in the other they are neutralized.

The need for a feature 'o male' (for 'castrated') is obviously explained on the basis of animal husbandry. Often a clear binary analysis of vocabulary is only possible because there are equally clearly structured facts. Of course it can be established for the classic case of domestic animals that the lexical distinctions do not rest only on distinctions of things, but also on pragmatic factors (e.g. the communicational relevance of the factual distinctions). Cf. Maas (1970).

For example, the tree

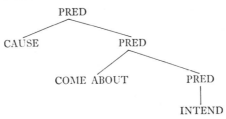

can be replaced by *persuade*.

The procedure for generating the syntactic trees is recursive; it permits all possible kinds of COMBINATIONS OF ATOMIC PREDICATES. The sense-relations between arbitrary semantically complex (derived) expressions are defined according to the sense-relations holding between the atomic predicates (which were established in the form of meaning-postulates) AND the complex structure the derived expression stands for.

This is only implicit in Lakoff's discussion, though it would be appropriate for justifying his distinction between lexical decomposition (return to atomic predicates) and meaning-postulates. Instead of this, however, Lakoff adds less convincing arguments of a totally different kind, for example, that meaning-postulates, since they belong to logic, must be universal; that the relation of CAUSE – COME ABOUT – INTEND to *persuade* is nonetheless specific for English, and thus should not be stated in the form of meaning-postulates; that CAUSE – COME ABOUT – BELIEVE can also be replaced by *persuade*;[1] that nonetheless the relationship of these TWO expressions *persuade* cannot be shown by meaning-postulates; etc. The most problematical of these is the notion that the atomic predicates are to be regarded as a UNIVERSAL INVENTORY OF ELEMENTS OF MEANING (realized in this or that selection and combination in all languages) – an opinion that he does not support and which cannot be supported so easily. We can note first that we are dealing with expressions which are taken from English (at a particular historical stage of its development), and that *come about* does not have a simple congener in German. In addition it is questionable whether those atomic predicates which prove to be useful in the analysis of one language (or even only particular lexical fields in this language) will turn out to be useful for the analysis of other arbitrary languages. The conception that all word-constants introduced into a logical language

---

[1] Incidentally, these two expressions *persuade* have different syntactic behaviour: ('...INTEND') counts as *persuade to*, ('...BELIEVE') as *persuade that*.

must therefore be universal is in any case false; and it is not clear what it could mean to say that the forms of a logical language (as a construct) as well as the arguments possible in it are universal. At best it can mean that it is possible to explicate all natural languages in the framework of this logical language.[1]

The assumption of fewer atomic predicates is not unconditionally necessary, anyhow, for explicating the meaning of expressions relative to other expressions in the same language. We can also take the aim of componential analysis to be that of relating each expression to others with minimal difference of meaning. For a minimal meaning difference we formulate an elementary sense-relation (the minimal difference can be null, in which case we have synonymy); all larger meaning differences can then be captured by means of compound sense-relations. A sense relation here is to be formulated over CLASSES OF EXPRESSIONS, which can also be syntactically complex (in this case we could refer for example to the corresponding semantic structure trees of the Lewis 1972 type). Thus to every sense-relation there correspond many meaning-postulates, while every meaning-postulate sets a few (often only two) SINGLE EXPRESSIONS in relation with each other. For instance: in order to state the sense-relation between *boar* and *mare*, we do not have to assume basic expressions like 'male', 'pig', etc.; instead of this we assume two elementary sense-relations R_1 and R_2. Given the two series *boar – stallion – mare* and *boar – sow – mare*, with a minimal meaning distinction between the members of the series, we get the compound sense-relation between *boar* and *mare* either as R_2R_1 or R_1R_2.

9.17   General remarks on meaning-analysis according to sense-relations

Every form of LINGUISTIC SEMANTICS (not to be identified with logical semantics) will crucially involve an analysis of meaning based on sense-relations; especially if we are investigating particular languages or dialects as well as their historical change and relation to other languages. But analysis of sense-relations is never enough: first, because we are also interested in the sense of individual expressions relative to particular situations of use (explicable for example as intensions and partial intensions); secondly, because, to return to a remark of Frege's, the

[1] One could say with almost equal justification that the bicycle or the refrigerator are universal: we can introduce these industrial products into any culture and correspondingly change its daily life.

meaning of a sentence is never given by its sense alone, but by its sense AND its truth-value. We are thus also interested in the meaning of expressions relative to totally determined situations of use. Now one could object that it is completely irrelevant for linguistics when and if sentences like *the dog is dangerous, you have lied to me*, etc., are true or not. This objection however is not valid. For the analysis of a concrete communication-situation (and this is to some extent the basis of every empirically oriented linguistic investigation) we must know throughout WHETHER true, false, undetermined, inappropriate, meaningless, etc., sentences are uttered. And in order to know how language is (or can be) used, we must also know WHEN particular sentences are true, false, meaningless, etc. In order to elucidate the conditions for speech and understanding, we must elucidate, among other things, the truth-conditions for sentences (and these depend on the extensions or intensions, as well as the syntactic positions of the expressions used in them). In this sense referential semantics is a necessary complement to conceptual semantics, and vice versa.

In addition we must note that the DEFINITION OF SENSE-RELATIONS in general is carried out on whole sentences containing the expressions concerned, and that therefore inferential and equivalence relations between sentences will be of special importance. So for the definition of sense-relations we must already assume a particular version of referential semantics. As an example, consider the DEFINITION OF THE SYNONYMY RELATION given by Lyons (1968: 450; note that he is concerned in particular with conceptual semantics):

If one sentence, s_1, implies another sentence, s_2, and if the converse also holds, s_1 and s_2 are equivalent: i.e. if $s_1 \supset s_2$ and $s_1 \supset s_1$, then $s_1 \equiv s_2$... If now the two equivalent sentences have the same syntactic structure and differ from one another only in that where one has a lexical item, x, the other has y, then x and y are synonymous.

In case either of the expressions x and y (or both) are ambiguous, we can define partial synonymy instead of synonymy. For example, *ball* is only partially synonymous with *dance*, since it can also designate a spherical object. In addition, given an appropriate consideration of intensions, we can investigate context-dependent synonymy. Thus *get* and *buy* are synonymous in some contexts of use but not in others (i.e. these verbs have different intensions, but the same extensions in certain contexts):

In front of a tobacconist's:
I must get some more tobacco.
I must buy some more tobacco.
At home:
I must get some coal from the cellar.
I must buy some coal from the cellar.

If, as in the case of synonymy above, all sense-relations are defined in terms of an established logical language, it is easy to understand what we mean in any particular case by saying that such-and-such a relation holds between two expressions (or even that an expression contains such-and-such components of meaning). We can base ourselves completely on the logical language and the arguments it allows, for example, in the statement of the possible logical consequences of permissible interpretations (in the sense of referential semantics). The sense-relations between two expressions x and y then most significantly represent a restriction on the interpretation of complex expressions in which x and y appear.

9.18   Pseudonotations

Many semantic analyses (field-analyses, componential analyses, or lexical decompositions) are neither simply colloquial (and thus comprehensible on the basis of our everyday linguistic knowledge) or based on one of the usual logical languages or some special one (and thus comprehensible by correspondence to that language). In these analyses we are confronted with formal descriptions that can at best be understood intuitively, but which precisely for this reason make the formalism superfluous. (The one advantage of these notations is their relative brevity.) I will call this kind of descriptive device pseudonotation and look here at three examples; this is not to say that there are not many still worse examples (e.g. inconsistent and in principle irreparable); or even that the examples cited are totally incomprehensible. My intention is mainly to advise caution: so long as a formal notation only serves to clarify things it is not pursuing any theoretical goals, and is to be taken exclusively in this illustrative function; we must not grant it independent status and suggest that it can provide new knowledge. If we intend to use a formal notation for theoretical purposes, we should first define the intended purpose and communicate it informally, and then provide an introduction to the formal notation – at least to those aspects of it that differ from other, already familiar notations.

1. In an analysis of German causative verbs like *fällen* 'fell', *schieben* 'shove', *gießen* 'pour', *streuen* 'strew', etc., and process verbs like *fallen* 'fall', *rollen* 'roll', *fließen* 'flow', *bröckeln* 'crumble', Baumgärtner (1970) uses the notation cited above (9.14) for *gießen*, which he later modifies as follows:

gießen: ⟨Kausation, ⟨Disposition [Person]$_0$, ⟨Alteration: Raum [Flüssig]$_1$, (⟨Partition [Richtung]$_4$, ([Person]$_2$)⟩)⟩⟩⟩

The subscript indices are supposed to designate the different 'actants' (i.e. syntactic neighbours) of the verb; the associated expressions like '[Person]' the necessary semantic features of these actants. On the basis of an example sentence *Der Polizist goß Wasser auf den Damm* ('The policeman poured water on the dam'), as well as additional diagrams of the syntactic structure of this sentence, it is clear that *der Polizist* occupies position 0, *Wasser* position 1, *auf den Damm* position 4, while position 2 remains empty. We can conclude from this that round brackets show that a given position may be empty. The angled brackets obviously display the syntactic construction in which the actants of the verb stand. For the cited sentence we obtain the following tree-representation:

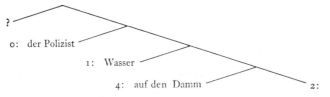

The highest position, indicated by '?', is presumably to be filled by the verb-form *goß*. We can see that Baumgärtner defines the meaning of a verb in a FUNCTIONAL perspective, i.e. according to the various sentence-meanings that the occurrence of *gießen* makes possible. He thereby attempts to reconstruct common paraphrases like 'pour means that someone empties a liquid in a particular direction', or 'pour means that someone brings it about that a liquid disseminates in a particular direction'. This intention certainly makes sense, but it is not sufficiently specified:

(a) He uses inadequately defined semantic features: '*Disposition*' must express the fact that the liquid should be in the 'relation of availability' to the person doing the pouring (a trivial assumption);

9-2

'*Alteration*: *Raum*' must mean that 'the relation of spatial alteration' holds (Bäumgartner 1970: 69) with reference to the direction (it is not clear to what extent spatial alteration represents a relation between an object and a direction). But how far are these relations reproduced in the bracketed expressions? We need to approach with good will in advance in order to recognize them there.

(b) Structures like those represented in the bracketed expressions should obviously be understood as semantic. But neither these structures in general nor the bracketed expressions in particular, nor the correspondence of these expressions to syntactic structure (Baumgärtner uses a version of generative syntax) are defined, or even introduced informally. In particular the place of the verb in the semantic structure remains unclear.

(c) It is not clear how one can interpret the given semantic structures, i.e. obtain the total meaning of a sentence like the one given (including its truth-conditions). This same objection can be levelled against Katz and Weinreich, whom Baumgärtner follows here (Katz & Fodor 1963; Weinreich 1966).

2. The following representation for the English verb *chase* comes from Katz (1966: 167); the variables X and Y refer to the beings involved:[1]

chase: ((Activity of X) (*Nature*: (Physical)) ((Motion) (*Rate*: (Fast)) (*Character*: (Following Y)))), (*Intention* of X: (Trying to catch ((Y) Motion)))

Unlike Baumgärtner's representation, this provides no coherent overall syntactic structure (as we can easily see if we try to convert the bracketing into a tree); the various semantic features are simply adjacent. This structure can thus not be expected to show how the semantic features combine to yield the total meaning of a sentence. Now we can remedy this somewhat by assuming a conjunction of features, which can be shown to be meaningful by an ordinary language paraphrase: 'Chasing is a physical activity of some X, in particular a fast motion, which consists of following some Y; and the X intends to catch the Y, who is likewise in motion.' Katz's notation achieves nothing more than this

---

[1] Katz's analysis is not exclusively conceptual semantic, since he considers reference as well. We can only read the representation this way: the variables stand for expressions that MENTION the beings (thus they are not simply designated by semantic features like [Person]); otherwise even the predicate-calculus reading, which Bierwisch assumes, would be erroneous.

paraphrase, because it has no explicit form. Bierwisch (1969) has discussed the weaknesses of this notation in detail. Assuming the same conceptual analysis of *chase* (which he does not take as definitive), he comes up with the following predicate-calculus notation:

chase: [[Physical] Activity & [Fast] Motion] X & [Following] XY & [Trying] X ([Catch] XY) & [Motion] Y

At the same time he defines:

$$[[P] \, Q] \, X \, = \, \mathrm{df} \, (EF) \, (F \subset Q \, \& \, P(F) \, \& \, F(X))$$

Predicates of predicates are contained in square brackets: F is contained in Q, F is predicated of X and P is predicated of F. There is a problem here: higher-order predicates are introduced without comment,[1] and a sentence, rather than say the intension of a sentence, is used as the second argument of 'Trying' ('X tries...' is not an extensional context).

The status of the predicate constants is also problematical: are they translations of English words, or theoretical concepts that will be justified elsewhere? Finally, we should note that when a translation into predicate logic is found, it remains open how this corresponds to the syntactic constructions in which *chase* can be used (unlike Baumgärtner, Bierwisch does not take account of position in a syntactic construction), and likewise how we are to obtain the total meaning of sentences with *chase*. Possibly the variables X and Y are to be replaced solely by proper names (X in subject position, Y in object position). But what happens in complex noun phrases with quantifiers? Even this improved notation still leaves a lot of questions open.

3. Most of the weaknesses referred to, as well as others, are found in the proposals of the so-called generative semanticists (e.g. Lakoff, McCawley, Postal). I will not consider McCawley here, since in his 'Program for logic' (1972) he treats a set of problems which are important for the explication of natural language (reflexives, coordination, quantifying expressions), but which fall into the domain of referential semantics; besides, he uses almost exclusively grammatical and not logical categories (NP, VP, V, S) and notations.

Lakoff on the other hand claims to represent a 'natural logic', i.e. the logic immanent in natural languages. If this is taken as a special requirement for linguistics, it is merely self-evident; on the other hand logical languages are always primarily modelled on natural languages, though

---

[1] On this cf. Bartsch (1971). On the problem of pseudonotation in general (with examples from Schmidt and Brekle) see Bartsch (1972).

of course they disregard certain aspects and properties. Lakoff's requirement thus means only that we should develop RICHER LOGICAL LANGUAGES, which allow us to explicate MORE ASPECTS of natural languages (to represent the logic of a language can only mean to RECONSTRUCT it in an explicit form). But in fact Lakoff uses one of these impoverished notations, so impoverished in fact that nearly all semantic distinctions disappear in it. It is really only structural differences that remain, and these are not sufficient for characterizing the syntactic forms of natural-language sentences. To this extent Lakoff's proposal is less capable of succeeding than Chomsky's generative grammar.

It is nonetheless this very impoverished notation that Lakoff uses to try to give the semantic representations of all possible complex sentences (with verbs like *say, believe, hope, know, cause*). The resulting representations (tree-structures) are therefore of necessity not well-formed in the logical sense; they do not yield any consistent interpretations. The lack of differentiation in Lakoff's notation shows up especially in the following points:[1]

(a) The only structures are predicate-argument structures. Negation, the various coordinators, sentential operators (like 'It is possible that', 'X believes that') and proper predicates appear without distinction simply as predicates. Variables (for proper names and probably also noun phrases) and sentences appear as arguments.

I have already referred to Lakoff's attempt at LEXICAL DECOMPOSITION of causative expressions like *persuade, convince*, etc. (9.16). He also treats *accuse* and *criticize* (where he considers additional presuppositions that make the analysis somewhat more complex) in a similar way. Now one would assume that in a semantic treatment, the sense-relations holding between CAUSE – COME ABOUT – INTEND and *persuade* would be more precisely clarified. The only statement on this, however, is that several transformations are to be applied to the structure on p. 247, (for 'x persuaded y to hit z') so that CAUSE – COME ABOUT – INTEND comes to stand under a single PRED node; and then the lexical unit *persuade* is substituted.

Now let us assume that the lexical decomposition of an expression is synonymous with the expression. This is however clearly false: from 'x persuaded y to do z' it does indeed follow that 'x caused it to come about that y intended to do z'; but the reverse does not hold. For if x

---

[1] For a somewhat more thorough criticism, with which I agree for the most part, see Bartsch & Vennemann (1972: 10–23).

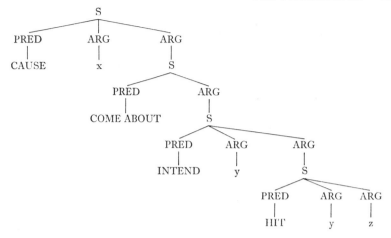

has persuaded y to do something, he has also spoken; but if x has only caused y to intend to do something, this could have happened any number of ways, and x does not have to have intended or even noticed what he did; in any case x does not have to have spoken. We could now conclude that lexical decomposition generally explicates, not the relation of synonymy, but that of hyponymy; as it is true in this case that:

persuade $(x, y, z) \supset$ CAUSE – COME ABOUT – INTEND (x, y, z).

But even this is false. For from 'x said that it was bad of y to do z' it follows that 'x criticized y for doing z'; but the reverse does not hold. For x could have criticized y in various ways, for example indirectly ('Why did you do that, you idiot?'); x does not have to have SAID that y's action was bad. So in this case we get the reverse of the relation above (cf. Lakoff 1972: 603f.):

SAY – BAD $(x, y, z) \supset$ criticize (x, y, z).

The result is that in most cases lexical decomposition obviously says nothing about the existing sense-relations; these have to be established individually in each case. Lakoff's proposed analytical procedure therefore does not yield a SEMANTIC analysis.

In my view this is not an accidental unfavourable result, but simply the consequence of using undefined structures. Given a careful introduction of corresponding structures, the idea of lexical decomposition might not be out of the way; and it could conceivably make the synonymy-relations between syntactically simple and syntactically complex expressions explicable.

9.19   On the explication of sense-relations

Sense-relations hold, to begin with, between expressions of everyday language, and we can provisionally elucidate them in that language by means of examples. But sense-relations, like other properties of ordinary language, can also be reconstructed or explicated in logical languages. By giving a DEFINITION OF A SENSE-RELATION IN A LOGICAL LANGUAGE we try to give an explicit characterization of ordinary-language sense-relations (i.e. simplify and standardize particular aspects of them from a single point of view). We assume a translation of the ordinary-language expressions into a logical language (= object language); the actual defining of sense-relations is done in the metalanguage. This is the sense in which Lyons' definition of synonymy (9.17), for instance, is to be understood. Most writers use a form of predicate calculus as the language of explication (e.g. Carnap 1956b; Lyons 1968); they thus formulate only sense-relations between classes of predicates. This restriction is justified only if we want mainly to emphasize particular simple and general sense-relations. But the problem of the context-dependence of sense-relations, in particular, is not taken care of this way. Schnelle (1973b) uses a richer logic, namely Lewis' (1972) intensional logic – though only in a general way; most of his attempt still remains programmatic.

There are two important ways of explicating the sense-relations between non-sentential expressions:

1. We first explicate sense-relations between sentences; we compare two structurally identical sentences s_1, s_2 which differ only in the occurrence of the expressions x in one and y in the other, in the same position. The sense-relation holding between s_1 and s_2 then holds for the two expressions x and y. Some typical sense-relations between sentences are:

NEGATION (in the semantic sense);

HYPONYMY (understood either as material or intensional implication ('entailment'));

SYNONYMY (understood as symmetrical hyponymy: s_1 and s_2 are synonymous where s_1 is hyponymous to s_2 and vice versa; we often speak here of equivalence, again to be taken in the semantic sense);

INCOMPATIBILITY (the conjunction of s_1 and s_2 yields a contradiction in the semantic sense; cf. the definition of soundness in an axiom system in 5.5 above);

PRESUPPOSITION (s_1 presupposes s_2 where s_2 is necessarily true while s_1 can be either true or false).

2. We compare two structurally identical sentences s_1, s_2, which differ only by having respectively the expressions x and y in the same position (all other expressions, since they are arbitrary, are replaced by variables which are quantified over). The sense-relation between x and y is then defined on the basis of the object-language relation holding between s_1 and s_2 (e.g. material implication). This is the procedure Lyons follows in defining synonymy.

Many writers take sense-relations exclusively as the explicanda. They stabilize the explicanda by operational definition, for instance:

The relation which for a speaker holds between two sentences s_1 and s_2 if and only if he would not, independently of the situation, assert s_1 in certain of its 'meanings' and deny s_2 in certain of its 'meanings', is the relation of partial hyponymy: s_1 is partially hyponymous to s_2. (Brockhaus & Stechow 1971: 8)

s_1 presupposes s_2 if and only if in every situation where the speaker is ready to affirm s_1 in one sense, he is ready to affirm s_2 in a particular sense, and if further in any situation where he is not ready to assert s_2 in this sense, he is not ready to use s_1 in the sense mentioned. (Egli 1971: 75)

Operational procedures of this kind naturally do not – as already suggested – automatically provide particular results; they only indicate a way of exploring some existing knowledge, for example, how we might develop appropriate tests for the stabilization of the given explicanda. Common formulations like 'A speaker would deny a sentence independently of any situation', or 'A speaker is not ready in any situation to use a sentence in particular sense' require clarification: they relate either to actual communication-situations or to situations in which communication is being reflected on. They are generally explicable mainly in a theory of pragmatics; here we can at least require a more precise account of the interrogation being assumed.

9.20 Examples of sense-relations

For simplicity's sake I will use predicate calculus here as the language of explication. Accordingly I will only mention a few simple sense-relations (cf. Lyons 1968: ch. 10 on this; under the appropriate conditions we could introduce more complex ones by compounding). This discussion is by no means conclusive; nor do I claim that the expressions introduced as examples are understood exclusively in the way explicated here.

The relations listed here are in fact fundamental: the synonymy relation leads to the analysis of an existing vocabulary into classes of equivalent expressions (these can for instance belong to different sub-languages, or domains of use, or be of different degrees of complexity); the hyponymy relation leads to a hierarchical analysis of the vocabulary (especially in the domain of general names – and depending on this it yields intersecting classifications of adjectives and verbs, according to the usability of adjectives and verbs with particular groups of nouns); the polarity relations lead to an analysis of the vocabulary (especially adjectives) according to particular dimensions and intradimensional classifications; only in the case of heteronymy does there normally exist a superordinate concept for the whole domain (also called a supernym).

I will formulate the sense-relations for simple predicating expressions, basing myself on the object-language relations between corresponding simple sentences (in the sense of procedure 2 sketched out in 9.19 above).

1. SYNONYMY
P is a synonym of $Q = df (x) (Px \equiv Qx)$ or $(x) (y) (Pxy \equiv Qxy)$, etc.
EXAMPLES: ⟨female horse, mare⟩
⟨privilege, prerogative⟩
⟨hide, conceal⟩

2. HYPONYMY
P is a hyponym of $Q = df (x) (Px \supset Qx)$
EXAMPLES: ⟨pheasant, bird⟩
⟨carmine, red⟩
⟨uncle, relative⟩

3. POLARITY (between one-place predicates)
(a) COMPLEMENTARITY
P is complementary to $Q = df (x) (Px \equiv \sim Qx)$
EXAMPLES: ⟨married, unmarried⟩
⟨male, female⟩
⟨dead, alive⟩
(b) ANTONYMY
P is an antonym of $Q = df (x) (Px \supset \sim Qx)$

EXAMPLES: ⟨tall, short⟩

⟨lazy, industrious⟩

(c) HETERONYMY

$P_1, ..., P_n$ are pairwise heteronyms (or belong to an antonymous n-tuple) = df (x) $(P_i x \equiv \sim (P_1 x \, v ... v \, P_{i-1} x \, v \, P_{i-1} x ... v \, P_n x)$ (for all i = 1, ..., n)

EXAMPLES: ⟨green, blue, red, ...⟩

⟨pig, horse, sheep, ...⟩

Complementary expressions are often said to be mutally contradictory, and antonymous expressions to be mutually contrary.[1] Complementary and antonymous expressions mostly belong to the class of adjectives; the complementaries are not gradeable, but the antonyms are gradeable (and intensifiable). The antonymous expressions designate poles of an entire scale; this explains why something that is not tall does not therefore have to be short. Of course one of these expressions is usually marked with respect to the other: we say *Otto is 1.70 metres tall* but not *Otto is 1.70 metres short*.[2] With the heteronymous expressions we are dealing either with more dimensions, according to which the designations are oriented, or the designation of various points within one dimension (e.g. *black, grey, white*). In all three cases the definition involves negation. In order for the definition to be meaningful, the negation must be restricted in a particular way. Mutually contradictory expressions and n-tuples of antonyms must fully encompass a certain domain; the expression cannot be used sensibly of objects outside this domain. Corresponding selectional restrictions must be assumed at the same time: *My dog is unmarried* is exactly as meaningless as *My dog is married*. In the case of *dead* and *alive* this is more problematical: think of a sentence like *Transformational grammar is dead*. It is especially problematical in the case of the domestic animal names mentioned above: *That's not a sheep; it's a moss-covered rock* is a normal English sentence; according to the definition given anything that is not a sheep must in any case be a domestic animal (or a living being); we must

[1] The distinction between 'contradictory' and 'contrary' comes originally from the theory of syllogisms, where it applies to sentences: *All men are lazy* is contrary to *No men are lazy*; *All men are lazy* and *Some men are not lazy*, as well as *No men are lazy* and *Some men are lazy* are mutually contradictory. This can easily be checked according to the given definitions (though naturally with no further quantification).

[2] For a detailed representation of the semantic properties of such adjectives see Bierwisch (1967), Teller (1969), Wunderlich (1973), Bartsch & Vennemann (1972: chs. 2–4).

therefore state in addition the superordinate concept under which the heteronymic expressions are subsumed (i.e. state particular hyponymy relations in the definition).

4. CONVERSENESS (also polarity between two-place predicates)

P is the converse of Q = df (x) (y) (Pxy ≡ Qyx)

EXAMPLES: ⟨younger than, older than⟩
⟨husband of, wife of⟩
⟨give, receive⟩
⟨buy, sell⟩

We can see that the two arguments reverse their positions: if Nina is older than Doro, then Doro is younger than Nina, and vice versa. Such expressions are especially common in three domains: comparatives (insofar as they are constructed from polar adjectives), kinship terms, and expressions for human exchange- relationships; here there is a third argument in each case that designates the exchanged object, but which remains unaffected in its syntactic function:

Nina gives Emil a $\begin{Bmatrix} \text{kiss} \\ \text{lollipop} \end{Bmatrix}$.

Nina gets a $\begin{Bmatrix} \text{kiss} \\ \text{lollipop} \end{Bmatrix}$ from Emil.

An analogous exchange of syntactic positions takes place in the transition from an active to a passive sentence:

Nina kisses Emil.
Emil is kissed by Nina.

We could also take ⟨kiss, be kissed⟩ as examples of lexical converses. But this would not make much sense, because there are so many passivizeable verbs, and passives are always formed with *be* and the past participle of the verb. The relation between active and passive sentences is thus more appropriately (i.e. generally, independently of particular verbs) treated in the syntax. Still we must not overlook the fact that there are analogies: not only in the similar inversion of syntactic positions, but also in the 'agent' and 'patient' interpretations.

On the matter of synonymy, there are three supplementary remarks that we should make:

1. In dictionary definitions (e.g. '*mumble*:...speak indistinctly;... bite, chew (as) with toothless gums' (*Concise Oxford Dictionary*)), it is often the case that we do not get two expressions of the same kind set in relation, but rather a simple one and a complex one. In the sentences

used for definition the syntactic position in the complex case must also be organized in a correspondingly complex way. The same holds for dictionary definitions that establish hyponyms (as in the case of the causative verbs: e.g. '*liquefy*: bring (solid or gas)...into liquid condition'; if one liquefies something, one causes it to become liquid, while the reverse does not always hold).

2. Synonymous sentences are often called paraphrases. In the narrow sense we will use the term SYNTACTIC PARAPHRASE for those sentences which in the main use the same lexical material, i.e. which differ only in word-order, function-words and perhaps the syntactic categories of similar lexical material. For syntactic paraphrase what is usually demanded is sameness of extension, not intension: in this case we assume a weaker notion of synonymy. Syntactic paraphrases occupy a special position in linguistic discussion: contemporary syntactic theory attempts to characterize such paraphrases as syntactically related; in particular, according to Chomsky's conception, each class of syntactic paraphrases is to be assigned exactly one deep structure, and the individual members of the class are constructed by means of transformational rules (cf. 10.9, 10.10 below). A deep structure thus does not, as is often assumed, characterize a paraphrase-class *in toto* (namely all paraphrases with common meaning), but only a subclass of paraphrases.

Example of a class of syntactic paraphrases:
It is to be hoped that the conference will be well attended.
The conference will, it is hoped, be well attended.
Hopefully the conference will be well attended.
The conference will, hopefully, be well attended.
Attendance at the conference will hopefully be good.
Good attendance at the conference is to be hoped for.

3. There are further paraphrase-types that can be handled relatively easily in grammatical theory, if this is extended to include indices for the interpretation of deictic expressions (cf. Wunderlich 1970: 69ff., 1971). We will speak in this case of DEICTIC PARAPHRASES. We can distinguish at least two types:

(a) Sentences which are used by two different participants, e.g.:
(S says to H): You're tired.
(H says to S): I'm tired.
(b) Sentences distinguished by direct vs. indirect discourse:

Peter promised: 'I'll be there on time tomorrow.'
Peter promised he would be here on time today.

I is replaced by *he, tomorrow* by *today, there* by *here,* i.e. it is really only the deictic expressions that change; though of course the replacements of *tomorrow* and *there* are not independent of the spatiotemporal contexts of utterance.[1] Significantly, it is sameness of extension (under the context in question) that is to be demanded in deictic paraphrases, i.e. we have here a typical case for referential semantics and not for conceptual semantics.

9.21   Sense-properties

Up to now we have dealt only with sense-relations that can be defined between sentences or on the basis of object-language relations between sentences. In a similar way we can also determine the SENSE-PROPERTIES of expressions. For example, the following distinction holds between *father of, older than,* and *similar*: *father of* is asymmetric, intransitive and irreflexive; *older than* is asymmetric, transitive and irreflexive; and *similar* is symmetric, non-transitive and reflexive. Let Adam be the father of Cain, older than Cain, and similar to Cain; and let Cain be the father of Noah, older than Noah, and similar to Noah. Then naturally Cain is not the father of Adam (and Noah is not the father of Cain); and further, Adam is not the father of Noah, and also not his own father. Cain is also not older than Adam (and Noah is not older than Cain), but naturally Adam is also older than Noah, though not older than himself. Cain is similar to Adam (and Noah to Cain), but it is not necessary that Noah be similar to Adam (the respective similarities could be in totally different features); but (in one sense of the word) Adam, Cain and Noah are similar to themselves.

The statement of the sense-properties for relational expressions has the same function as the statement of sense-relations: if the meaning of one sentence is fixed, then the meaning of other sentences is also determined.

$$\text{'P' is symmetric} = \text{df } (x)\,(y)\,(Pxy \supset Pyx)$$
$$\text{non-symmetric} = \text{df} \sim (x)\,(y)\,(Pxy \supset Pyx)$$

---

[1] The two following sentences might likewise be paraphrases of each other – in certain contexts; but they do not differ only in their deictic expressions:
Peter said: 'How come you're still here?'
Peter was surprised that I was still there.
Here we must assume that the interrogative sentence beginning with *how come* can be used with expressions of surprise (and is so used by Peter here); this can only be handled in a significantly extended theory of utterances in their contexts (cf. ch. 9.III below).

asymmetric $= \mathrm{df}\ (\mathrm{x})\ (\mathrm{y})\ (\mathrm{Pxy} \supset\ \sim \mathrm{Pyx})$
transitive $= \mathrm{df}\ (\mathrm{x})\ (\mathrm{y})\ (\mathrm{z})\ (\mathrm{Pxy}\ \&\ \mathrm{Pyz} \supset \mathrm{Pxz})$
non-transitive $= \mathrm{df} \sim (\mathrm{x})\ (\mathrm{y})\ (\mathrm{z})\ (\mathrm{Pxy}\ \&\ \mathrm{Pyz} \supset \mathrm{Pxz})$
intransitive $= \mathrm{df}\ (\mathrm{x})\ (\mathrm{y})\ (\mathrm{z})\ (\mathrm{Pxy}\ \&\ \mathrm{Pyz} \supset\ \sim \mathrm{Pxz})$
reflexive $= \mathrm{df}\ (\mathrm{x})\ ((\mathrm{Ey})\ \mathrm{Pxy}\ \mathrm{v}\ \mathrm{Pyx}) \supset \mathrm{Pxx})$
non-reflexive $= \mathrm{df} \sim (\mathrm{x})\ ((\mathrm{Ey})\ (\mathrm{Pxy}\ \mathrm{v}\ \mathrm{Pyx}) \supset \mathrm{Pxx})$
irreflexive $= \mathrm{df}\ (\mathrm{x})\ ((\mathrm{Ey})\ \mathrm{Pxy}\ \mathrm{v}\ \mathrm{Pyx}) \supset\ \sim \mathrm{Pxx})$

EXAMPLES:

symmetric: similar, same, contemporary of
non-symmetric: brother of, love
asymmetric: father of, younger than, follow
transitive: same, younger than
non-transitive: similar, brother of, friend of, see
intransitive: father of, give birth to
reflexive: same, contemporary of
non-reflexive: do away with, shave
irreflexive: father of, brother of, younger than

9.22   Other types of sense-relations

The concept of sense-relations can be extended still further. Under this heading, for instance, we could subsume special LEXICAL DERIVATIONAL RELATIONS (like those between *perform:performance*, *warm:warmth*, *rage:enraged*, *break:breakable*). In this case the relation does not hold between components of meaning or the total meanings of expressions, but between semantic types that correspond to syntactic categories.

From a syntagmatic point of view there exist among others the following sense-relations: (a) SELECTIONAL RESTRICTIONS, e.g. between a verb and its grammatical subjects and objects, between adjectives and nouns, etc.; (b) COREFERENCE between reflexive pronouns and their antecedents, between pronouns and noun phrases, verb phrases, sentences, etc.; (c) relations of VARIABLE SUBSTITUTION, e.g. in relative clauses of the form *anyone who...*, *everyone who...*; (d) relationships between conjuncts through COORDINATIONS like *both...and, even though...* Even here, however, the interpretations are not to be taken as mutually independent: if the verb has a particular meaning, then the grammatical subject depends on it; if a noun phrase has a particular reference, then a corresponding (anaphoric) pronoun depends on it, and so on.

9.III THE MEANING OF LINGUISTIC EXPRESSIONS IN COMMUNICATION-SITUATIONS (THE SEMANTICS OF SPEECH ACTS)

9.23 Introductory remarks

Speaking is an active and largely consciously controlled process; a speaker accepts responsibility for what he says and is also held responsible – unless he is ill, a social outsider, or incapable of responsibility in some other sense (e.g. judicially). On one level speech is of course the articulation of particular sounds which can be (and are) interpreted as words of a language in particular syntactic constructions of the language; at the same time they have meanings and social values bound up with them, relative to particular contexts of experience and the meanings of alternative constructions and expressions. But there is more to it than that. For speech to make sense, the uttered sentences (or quasi-sentences or texts) must not only be meaningful *per se*, but they must be relevant to some existing social situation and its further development. In this sense we can understand speaking (i.e. uttering sentences) as a form of human action. This action is primarily directed toward the social situation and its assessment, and only indirectly toward relation to the external environment. It is a symbolic action: human beings use it to express their relation to the environment and to each other, in the form of anticipations, demands, mediation of knowledge, as well as in problematizations, justifications, accusations and defences.

Every utterance-act has its 'prehistory' and 'posthistory': i.e. PRE-CONDITIONS, on the basis of the existing situation and its previous development (which must be appropriately 'conceptualized', i.e. grasped and evaluated, by the participants) and CONSEQUENCES, e.g. conclusions that each of the participants draws from it. Obviously there can be divergent assessments of the social preconditions, and the consequences can be other than intended: but not arbitrarily so, for the simple reason, in the first place, that communication would not then take place. A system of conventions and implicit as well as explicit institutions, in which each of the participants has an interest, will (if it is cooperatively controlled) guarantee that communication by and large will take place. Whoever transgresses against conventional and institutional procedures without sufficient reason not only risks being unable to achieve his individual aims, but may be severely sanctioned. Particular conventional expectations (based on the conventions and institutional procedures relevant to the situation) are also part of the preconditions of any speech act. These expectations are therefore not private: private expectations must rather be bound up with them, if they are to be comprehended (and perhaps fulfilled) by others.

The meaning of a speech act is judged by the CHANGE IT PRODUCES IN THE SOCIAL SITUATION RELATIVE TO THE ALTERNATIVE ACTS POSSIBLE IN THIS SITUATION. One of these alternatives will be the failure to perform the particular speech act (cf. von Wright 1963: 45ff.). That this is still an action can be seen from the fact that one must take responsibility for the forbearance of the act just as much as for the act itself. To be silent where an utterance is expected is therefore a communicative act, even if not a SPEECH act.

The situational change achieved through a speech act naturally depends on the sense the utterance expresses – but not on that alone: it also depends on the 'prehistory' of conventional expectations and very specific private, even unconventional, expectations, as well as the spatio-temporal circumstances (context of perception, etc.). As a first approximation we can define the MEANING OF A LINGUISTIC UTTERANCE, a speech act a, as:

$$\text{Mean (a)} = \langle Z_1, Z_2, \{Z_2^i\} \rangle$$

where

Z_1 = previously existing social situation,

Z_2 = subsequently achieved social situation,

Z_2^i = those social situations which would have been achieved on the basis of the alternative act a^i.

The class of alternative acts a^i is a function of Z_1.

The concept of SOCIAL SITUATION needs clarification. It has both a subjective and an intersubjective (or objective) component: the participants' various EVALUATIONS of the situation (their knowledge, beliefs, assumptions, wishes) are subjective; their OBLIGATIONS, among other things, are objective, at least to the extent that others can be called in to decide what obligations actually exist or have existed.

Given this preliminary clarification, we will discuss some attempts to develop a pragmatic concept of meaning, which refers to linguistic utterances (or utterance-types), and not to linguistic expressions.

9.24   Bloomfield's concept of meaning

A first opportunity for developing a pragmatic notion of meaning is provided for us by Bloomfield's famous story of Jack and Jill, together with his commentary (Bloomfield 1933: 22). The story goes as follows:

> Suppose that Jack and Jill are walking down a lane. Jill is hungry. She sees an apple in a tree. She makes a noise with her larynx, tongue and lips. Jack vaults the fence, climbs the tree, takes the apple, brings it to Jill, and places it in her hand. Jill eats the apple.

Bloomfield analyses this story into the following parts:

A. Practical events preceding the act of speech (Jill has a particular need; she knows that Jack is with her – she sees him; she experiences a particular need, which she has a chance of satisfying).

B. Jill's speech act.

C. Practical events following the speech act (a sequence of Jack's reaction acts, whose goal is to help Jill to satisfy her need; Jill satisfies her hunger).

Certain assumptions are necessary for the story to unfold as outlined; Jill must assume that Jack can understand her need and satisfy it; Jack must be ready to do so, etc. – i.e. Jack and Jill must judge the existing situation at least similarly.

So what role does speech play in this? Bloomfield says (1933: 24):

> Language enables one person to make a reaction (R) when another person has the stimulus (S). The division of labor, and, with it, the whole working of human society, is due to language.

Instead of Jill herself carrying out the reaction to the stimulus ($S \rightarrow R$), she replaces it by a linguistic act, which must be completed by the mediating action of another, i.e. Jack. For Jill an utterance is a linguistic reaction, for Jack it is a linguistic stimulus: $S \rightarrow r \ldots s \rightarrow R$. The utterance event $r \ldots s$ represents a means for dividing S and R between different persons. Normally every person is interested only in stimuli S and responses R. The meaning of an utterance-event is thus defined in reference to practical events of this kind; in short, 'the *meaning* of a linguistic form' is 'the situation in which the speaker utters it and the response which it calls forth in the hearer' (Bloomfield 1933: 139).

Meanings are specific forms of social behaviour; a child in a particular society learns them and can later reproduce them. More precisely, the child learns dispositions to behave in particular ways: under particular

conditions a stimulus of a particular type causes the utterance of a particular linguistic form, and this utterance in turn causes a particular type
of response. Utterances themselves (i.e. the articulatory processes and
the utterance-tokens) are the concern of physiology and acoustics; while
behavioural psychology is concerned with the effects of stimuli and
human reactions to them, i.e. with what Bloomfield calls the 'situation'.
In this sense meaning for Bloomfield is NOT a subject for linguistics.
This is of course a very broadly conceived notion of meaning, and the
idea that it should be analysed in an interdisciplinary context is not
unjustified. This is what lies behind Bloomfield's apparent hostility to
meaning. But there is another aspect of meaning, totally distinct from
this, which Bloomfield in fact sees as the central subject of linguistics:
namely constructional meaning and its parts, i.e. the functional meanings of the individual positions of a construction (cf. 9.13 above). These
meanings are socially mediated and language-bound; they are the
preconditions for the establishment and understanding of situations.

For Bloomfield, linguistics is oriented toward the analysis of acts of
utterance and response in a social context, and thus is primarily
materialistic. But there are various points that invite criticism:

1. Bloomfield describes dispositions, stimuli, speech acts and
reactions in a behaviouristically (physically or physiologically) reduced
observation-language. For example, 'She was hungry; that is, some of
her muscles were contracting, and some fluids were being secreted,
especially in her stomach' (1933: 23). But what really counts here is
Jill's perceptions and feelings: she does not investigate the contents of
her stomach, she FEELS hungry. This is still more important in her
assessment of Jack and her relationship to him. Jill has not simply
learned to set causal reactions in train, but to assess a social situation,
to expect it to continue in a particular way, and to act so that these
expectations are fulfilled. This cannot be worked out within a behaviouristic concept of meaning, but only within a linguistic and act-theoretical
one: Bloomfield, however, merely hints at this.

2. The function of language in COOPERATIVE ACTIONS (e.g. division
of labour) is certainly indicated in Bloomfield's remarks, but in the
Jack and Jill story it is left out of the picture. Jack and Jill have no
common problem to solve (at least no apparent one); Jack merely
contributes to the satisfaction of Jill's needs. He acts silently, he does
not define the situation from his point of view. It is not established that
in the situation in question Jill could not get the apple herself. It is only

in a situation where Jill is not capable of getting what she wants herself that it becomes NECESSARY for her to speak, so that she can extend her ability to get hold of what she wants (cf. Ehlich & Rehbein 1972: 229). If I cannot raise animals or hunt myself, and I want meat, then I have to prevail upon others – generally by means of language – to give me meat; and when I do this I must assume that they have the meat available (possibly also only through the intermediation of others); and I usually also have to provide some service in return. In this sense particular social situations develop through the division of labour, and at the same time control the necessary interactions.

3. We are not told WHAT Jill said. How did Jack find out that she wanted the apple? If Jill expected a particular result from her utterance, she could not have said JUST ANYTHING: she must have made use of a linguistic construction which conventionally served to request some-one to get something; in any case she must have acted so that her partner could understand her IN THIS SITUATION (e.g. considering specific common learning processes in her relationship with Jack, perhaps special agreements as well). But the situation is described in such a way that Jill could have said 'The sky is blue' or anything else, and Jack could ACCIDENTALLY have performed the response described, e.g. because he himself saw an apple and wanted to give it to Jill. This would scarcely be of any particular interest to linguistics. Bloomfield also ne-glects the fact that in this case the mere utterance of speech sounds would not have been enough; Jill must in speaking also have designated something that she saw in a particular direction, or done something simi-lar, so that Jack could know which apple she meant, and where it was to be got from. To a certain extent at least she must have mediated to Jack the same perceptual stimulus that moved her to her utterance.

4. Bloomfield's point of departure is an UNPROBLEMATICAL situation. But what would have happened if Jack had replied:

Why should I get you the apple?
Get the apple yourself.
I don't steal apples.
I don't want to get my trousers dirty.
What do you want from me, anyhow?
Eh?

These replies would make it clear that Jack does not accept Jill's assumptions about their common situation, or at least does not yet accept them, or has not understood her. The situational presuppositions at least have to be clarified. Even if we could imagine Jill getting Jack to fetch the apple by intensive pointing, we could not imagine how either of them could problematize the whole situation or clarify their own situations WITHOUT LANGUAGE.

Bloomfield treats his story as a pure situationally controlled inter-action: it is enough for each person to react to the other's behaviour and to the perceptible environment, and then to react to reactive behaviour, etc. In this way a social situation can neither be defined nor problematized; the existing situation is simply taken for granted, and there is no consideration of possible ALTERNATIVE ACTIONS. In addition, none of the participants has to clarify his behaviour or coordinate it with reference to potential others or their interests. If common action is to be anticipated and prepared for, it will be necessary to ensure the common interests of the participants and to elucidate the preconditions and expectable consequences of the action. Actions once begun cannot simply be carried on linearly; they have to be interpreted, while their preconditions and intentions are established and possible misunder-standings eliminated. Even corrections must be possible. Linguistic action must be guided by a plan of possibilities for communication and action, to which others can orient themselves linguistically. This notion of the RECIPROCITY OF THE SOCIAL SITUATION is completely missing in Bloomfield.

9.25 On Morris' semiotics

As far as utterances are concerned, Bloomfield utilizes a typical behaviourist concept of meaning, though he admits – in other contexts – a linguistic one, which cannot be reduced to the behaviourist concept. But in behaviourist philosophy of language, especially in Morris' semiotics, the concept of meaning is generally understood in the behaviourist way. (In principle it is open to the same objections as those levelled against Bloomfield above.) Actually for Morris the concept of meaning itself can in principle be eliminated; it is so complex that he prefers to introduce a separate explicatum for each dimension (syntac-tics, semantics, and pragmatics). Nonetheless he does give a general definition (1938: 47):

the meaning of a sign is exhaustively specified by the ascertainment of its rules of usage, the meaning of any sign is in principle exhaustively determinable by objective investigation.

262 *The concept of meaning* III

The first part of the definition is unexceptionable: it bears a striking resemblance to a remark of Wittgenstein's (1958: §43):

We can explain a *large* class of cases of the use of the word 'meaning' – if not *all* of them, this way: the meaning of a word is its use in the language.

But there is a fundamental distinction: for Wittgenstein the use in the language can be established only within a particular experience of life; we can experience as well as demonstrate use, but we cannot observe or define it from outside. Morris' 'objective investigation' however consists of a series of direct observations and experiments. He reduces the concept of 'rule' to modes of behaviour, and reduces these to reactions to particular stimuli. Morris distinguishes SYNTACTIC, SEMANTIC and PRAGMATIC rules, without analysing their connections in communication processes. The pragmatic rules thus constitute something like a 'residual category' (as is so often the case in linguistics):

The statement of the conditions under which terms are used, in so far as these cannot be formulated in terms of syntactical and semantical rules, constitutes the pragmatical rules for the terms in question. (Morris 1938: 35)

Of course Morris concedes that THERE IS A PRAGMATIC COMPONENT IN ALL RULES (simply because of the fact that they are applied):

Any rule when actually in use operates as a type of behavior, and in this sense there is a pragmatical component in all rules. (Morris 1938: 35)

But even here the specific distinction between a pragmatic rule and, for example, the pragmatic component of a syntactic rule remains unclear. According to logicians, every linguistic rule has a syntactic AND a semantic aspect,[1] and for cases (like the notion of intension) where reference is made to various contexts of application, also a pragmatic aspect: at least every rule controls a particular linguistic procedure. The different kinds of rules that Morris distinguishes would therefore not be linguistic rules, but metalinguistic rules, related to these different aspects.

---

[1] This is also pretty much the opinion of linguists. Of course there are some who think that there are linguistic rules with no specific semantic aspect, e.g. transformations which produce a constructional variant that has the same meaning and use as the input construction. Those linguists who regard a grammar as a descriptive theory of an individual language thus for the most part also distinguish Morris' rule-types (adding phonological rules): but they distinguish them in the theoretical descriptive language, not in the described language. Judging from Chomsky's strict distinction between 'grammatical in L' and 'meaningful in L', we must probably assume that he is also prepared to distinguish between syntactic and semantic rules in the described language. But it appears that he also makes use of semantic arguments in explicating 'grammatical in L' (cf. ch. 8 above).

It is clear from Morris' later reflections on the concept of the 'sign' that modes of behaviour (in which we can see the use of rules) are behaviouristically determined:

If anything, A, is a preparatory-stimulus which in the absence of stimulus-objects initiating response-sequences of a certain behavior-family causes a disposition in some organism to respond under certain conditions by response-sequences of this behavior-family, then A is a sign. (Morris 1946: 10)

In contrast to Bloomfield's view, a linguistic stimulus here does not necessarily call forth a response-reaction, but only a specific DISPOSITION TO REACT.[1] (To stay with Bloomfield's example, Jill could have said sometime previously. 'Jack dear, I'm so hungry, could you get me an apple?'; and when Jack sees an apple, he gets it for her.) But this disposition can be totally different for the different participants in a situation, and thus does not count as a property of a linguistic expression (as Morris suggests), but only as the specific effect in a given situation: if Jill says to Jack 'Don't step on the apple', then Jack has to be careful (he must not perform a particular action), while Jill can react with a reproach if he nevertheless does step on it. Kutschera (1971: 165ff., 363) has shown in detail that a definition of sign like the one quoted above is of very little use; so I will merely restrict myself to stating the fundamental criticism once again:

1. Morris does indeed say that every meaning is potentially inter-subjective; but in the stimulus–disposition–reaction form of reduction that he assumes he does not take account of the fact that an utterance only becomes intersubjectively meaningful if it follows conventional procedures, where conventions are social properties (comparable to institutions), and not the modes of behaviour of single individuals.

2. The behaviourist oversimplification does not express the fact that language is developed IN cooperative social practice FOR that practice.

3. We cannot explain the conceptual, abstract and anticipatory nature of language if we assume that human behaviour is based only on constellations of stimuli; linguistic activities are active and intentional.

---

[1] Note that this (behaviouristic) concept of disposition (similar to that of philosophers like Hempel) is not the same as the one I used earlier (3.2): I said there that an ability to speak or particular linguistic rules could be regarded as dispositions, which is not to say that these dispositions are simply 'on call' for external stimuli (i.e. that the external stimuli release purely causal processes). We must treat dispositions to intentional acts, not to causally induced reactions.

9.26 Descriptive, evaluative and normative statements in Hare

The idea that meaning derives from use has been approached in a fundamentally different way by some philosophers of language who have been – more or less – influenced by Wittgenstein (e.g. Austin, Hare, Grice, Searle). The aim of the analytical philosophers – clearly distinct from the behaviourists' – is to elucidate our KNOWLEDGE of language (which includes our knowledge of how we will behave in particular situations), rather than to reduce it to observations of linguistic behaviour that will ultimately be formulated in physicalistic (or naturalistic) concepts. Unlike the logicians, they do not investigate the simplest cases (e.g. the use of descriptive indicative sentences), but very complex ones; and they do this without the requirement of a formal explication.

I will look first at Hare's treatment (1952) of the use of *good* and *ought* (and *should*). According to Hare, we have to distinguish (a) what we use a particular word for, and (b) the criteria for its use, i.e. how we establish whether or not it is used correctly. We use *good* in order to commend an object or action, i.e. to single it out positively as against other comparable objects or actions (a commendation presupposes that the addressee has to make a decision, and that he is being given some kind of a guide). This USE-FUNCTION of *good* is what Hare calls its EVALUATIVE MEANING – and this remains constant in different uses:

That's a good car.
That's a good book.
He's a good lecturer.
It's a good thing to study logic.

But *good* also has a DESCRIPTIVE MEANING: it gives us information about CRITERIA FOR APPLICABILITY. These however are decided from case to case: a car is good for different reasons than a book or a lecturer. In order to single out alternative objects or actions in a given domain as good (or better than others), we must describe something that differentiates them; i.e. if two objects are identical in all respects we cannot call one *good* and the other *not good*. We will therefore answer the question why a particular car is good by expounding the assumed descriptive meaning of *good*, i.e. describing what makes a car a good one. Obviously standards of this kind can be very different. Hare therefore calls the evaluative meaning of *good* primary, and the descriptive meaning secondary. He gives additional grounds for this: we can use the evaluative content of *good* in order to alter its descriptive content for arbitrary classes of objects. (If a car-expert explains to me that a car with disc brakes is a good one, he may convince me – i.e. I will correct my standards for cars accordingly.)

We must criticize Hare's position on at least two grounds:

1. The meaning of *good* does not consist only of the fact that one can COMMEND with it.[1] We can perform many other speech acts with an utterance of the form 'X is good.' An utterance of *This is a really good wine* can mean, for instance:

a recommendation to buy the wine,
a request to agree with a judgement,
a justification of its high price,
a recognition of my host's conoisseurship,
an expression of my pride of possession,
a revocation of a previous judgement,
a request to enjoy the wine,
a devaluation of the wine tested just before.

If we add still more constructions in which we can use *good*, we multiply the number of speech acts accordingly:

'Your book is good' – praise of the addressee.
'Write a good book' – a demand.
'Is it a good book?' – a question.

It clearly makes little sense to describe the meaning of the sentence *This is a really good wine* in terms of the speech acts it can be used in: (a) the list given above can be extended, and more finely differentiated; (b) we can scarcely show that one of the specified acts is normal or central, while the others are only indirectly connected to it; this would be to claim that the sentence is many-ways ambiguous; (c) the meaning of an utterance of the sentence does not depend only on the sentence itself, but on the properties of the situation of utterance (and these in turn can be conventional, e.g. a question *Isn't the wine good?* could elicit the utterance); (d) we lose a possible generalization: the meaning of the sentence is that it expresses a value-judgement of a particular kind, and all the speech acts mentioned can be performed with value-judgements (not only *good*, but *beautiful*, *useful*, etc. express value-judgements). It makes even less sense to try to capture the meaning

---

[1] I.e. *good* is only partially synonymous with *worthy of commendation*, and not the same in intension.

of the demands, questions, etc., in which *good* is used, through the meaning of *good*. On the contrary, we can describe the specific meaning of these demands, questions, etc., by saying that they express and suggest to the addressee particular attitudes toward value-judgements.

Searle (1969: 136ff.) criticizes Hare's error under the heading of the SPEECH-ACT FALLACY.[1] First, it is a fundamental error to say that particular words define the type of performable speech acts. Secondly, possible speech acts should be analysed on the basis of the ILLOCUTIONARY FORCE INDICATING DEVICE of a sentence: the illocutionary force of a sentence is indicated for instance by explicit performatives like *I hereby commend...*, but not by the word *good*.[2]

2. Hare not only wrongly identifies the evaluative meaning of *good* with its frequent use in commendations; he distinguishes the so-called descriptive meaning as likewise a meaning of *good*. But we undertake a description only when we want to JUSTIFY having used *good*; not all criteria of this kind have to be considered part of the meaning. In addition, Hare himself calls our attention to the fact that the criteria of applicability for *good* can vary from case to case, and there are only a few cases where they are subject to particular conventions: so they must not be taken as intersubjective. We should therefore not speak of any descriptive MEANING of *good*. Hare himself also speaks of the supervenient or consequential character of the word *good*: it must be clear from the description of an object or action in what sense it can be judged to be good (cf. Hare 1952: ch. 5.2). The word *ought* also has a supervenient character which will be clear if we have to justify a prescription. We can demonstrate this with the following series of sentences:[3]

   (a) Logic clarifies what a strong argument is.
   (b) It's good to study logic.
   (c) 1. Anyone who wants to know what a strong argument is should study logic.

---

[1] For a discussion and criticism of Hare, including further arguments and reference to Austin, see Grewendorf (1971).

[2] On the concept of illocutionary force cf. Searle (1969: ch. 3); also 9.27 below. Searle's first objection is not entirely valid, since there are other individual words which indicate illocutionary force fairly clearly, especially in certain positions: *You will* PLEASE *close the window* is used in orders but not assertions, etc. Cf. Wunderlich (1972a: 18f.).

[3] Cf. Hare (1952: ch. 10). Hare believes that *right* can be substituted for *ought* in most cases (e.g. *it would be right for you to study logic* instead of (d1)); the two words thus have the same meaning in this respect. I think however that *right* should be understood as similar to *good*, but crucially applicable only to actions, not to objects.

    2. Whenever you want to know what a strong argument is, you
       should study logic.

(d) 1. You ought to study logic.

    2. You ought to have studied logic.

(e) Study logic!

A demand can be made with (e); advice can be given with (d1) (to my
mind a piece of advice comes very close to a commendation); (d2) can
be a criticism (in the form of retrospective advice); a value-judgement
can be made with (b), while (a) can be used to make a descriptive
statement. With (c) we can make a general judgement, which includes
descriptive elements of (a). If someone is asked why he utters (e), he
can justify it on any grounds whatever (e.g. 'I wanted you to get as fed
up with the formulae as I did'); but one of these grounds could be
cited from (b) or (c). If someone utters (d), he can obviously no longer
be doing this on any arbitrary grounds, but only on rational ones,
e.g. one of those given in (b) or (c). If anyone utters (b) or (c), he can
refer to (a) for justification. Instead of saying that (b) shows the supervenient character of *good*, i.e. its partly descriptive meaning, we might
better say that I can justify the statement (b) by means of (a). Thus we
can give descriptive criteria for the justification of value-judgements;
they characterize the extent to which I apply a criterion of value in this
particular aspect (cf. 5.8 above). The basic relationship so far sketched
out can be represented as follows:

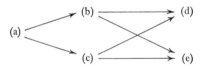

Justifications along this scale play an important role in pure scientific,
technological (political) and pedagogical activities.[1] But we should

---

[1] Reference to value-judgements or descriptive judgements is generally no longer
possible in the context of arbitrarily governed acts (e.g. board games or card games).
The statement

    (a) In this situation one ought to move the knight

can only be justified by statements like

    (b) If in this situation one doesn't move the knight, the queen and thus probably the
       game will be lost

where use is made of the expectation of subsequent moves according to the rules (as
well as the metarule 'one ought not to want to lose'). The statement

    (c) If trumps are played, then one ought – if possible – to follow suit

(in reference to the game of Skat) cannot be justified: it formulates one of the strict
rules that constitute the game of Skat (thus there are no alternative actions here; there
is only the possibility of setting up new rules – in which case one will be playing some

make it clear that the relations here are not relations of logical entailment: (b) does not follow from (a), etc. The use of terms like 'entailment' here is misleading.

9.27   Illocutionary acts in Austin and Searle

J.L. Austin's 1955 William James Lectures have had a profound influence on all subsequent discussion of speech acts and the concept of meaning stemming from them. Austin begins with a distinction between CONSTATIVE UTTERANCES, which can be true or false, and PERFORMATIVE UTTERANCES,[1] which can be successful or unsuccessful, without there being any question of truth or falsehood: what could it mean to say that *I hereby demand*...or *shut up !* were true or false ?[2] Later on, Austin shows that the criteria for performative utterances can be applied in the same way to constative utterances (he deals with assertions, which can fail just like all other kinds of speech acts).

He therefore develops, starting with lecture VIII, a new theory: that of LOCUTIONARY, ILLOCUTIONARY, and PERLOCUTIONARY acts. The 'constative'/'performative' distinction no longer serves to characterize different sorts of utterances, but to reconstruct different aspects of one and the same utterance. He distinguishes the following aspects of a speech act (1962: 92f., 101, 114):[3]

To say anything is:

other game, not Skat). To a certain extent this streatment can be carried over to linguistic rules. The statement

(d) If something is hot, one ought not to call it *cold*

can only be justified on the ground that otherwise we lose the basis for communication (and we can adduce descriptive statements about the particular uses of *hot* and *cold*).

[1] The term 'performative utterance' is somewhat unfortunate, since every utterance is the performance of an act (at least an articulatory act). We must distinguish further than between PRIMARY PERFORMATIVE UTTERANCES (e.g. *shut up*) and SECONDARY PERFORMATIVE UTTERANCES (e.g. *I hereby demand*...).

[2] There are of course logicians who would want to assign a truth-value to the utterances of such sentences (e.g. Lewis 1972: 210). An utterance in this case is true if the speaker really means (or does) what he says. But Austin's problem is not solved this way: how can an utterance be unsuccessful or, to put it another way, what are the conditions for success ? Obviously more conditions than the truth-condition above have to be stated: for if a speaker who speaks nonsense really means it, he runs the risk of not being understood. On Austin's various kinds of infelicity see 1.1 above.

[3] The term 'act' used in this way is misleading: we are not dealing with adjacent acts, but with the different (and naturally theoretically differentiated) ASPECTS OF ONLY ONE ACT. The individual acts are also not to be regarded as consequences of one another, e.g. the illocutionary act as a consequence of the locutionary, because this would presuppose the speaker's having to bear such a relation in mind. Only the results of the perlocutionary act are to be regarded as consequences.

(a) Always to perform a PHONETIC ACT: the utterance of certain sounds.

(b) Always to perform a PHATIC ACT: the utterance of certain vocables or words (i.e. sounds of a certain type that belong to a certain vocabulary) in a certain construction (i.e. in conformity to a certain grammar) with a certain intonation.

(c) Generally to perform a RHETIC ACT: the results of the phatic act and its constituents are used with a certain more or less definite meaning – namely sense and reference.

(d) Always to perform an ILLOCUTIONARY ACT: a certain force is exercised on the hearer in a conventional way, with reference to the special circumstances of the situation.

(e) Often to perform a PERLOCUTIONARY ACT: as a result of the illocutionary act certain non-conventional effects are achieved on the hearer with respect to his feelings, thoughts, and actions.

The acts (a)–(c) can be taken together as a LOCUTIONARY ACT. It is clear that Austin does not want to use the concept of meaning for the illocutionary act. Thus questions, warnings, promises, condemnations, criticisms, identifications, etc., are not regarded as the meanings of utterances, but as their ILLOCUTIONARY FORCES. The distinction between illocutionary and perlocutionary acts is probably the most problematical: Austin makes it FROM THE POINT OF VIEW OF CONVENTIONALITY. Certain effects of speaking may possibly be essentially outside conventional control (e.g. amazing, persuading, encouraging, humiliating, offending: none of these has an explicit performative formula, i.e. * *I hereby amaze you*..., etc.). Insofar as effects are conventionally produced, they belong to the illocutionary act. Thus (Austin 1962: 115ff.):

the illocutionary act as distinct from the perlocutionary is concerned with the production of effects in certain senses:

(1) ...the performance of an illocutionary act involves the securing of *uptake*.

(2) The illocutionary act 'takes effect' in certain ways, as distinguished from producing consequences in the sense of bringing about states of affairs in the 'normal' way, i.e. changes in the natural course of events...

(3) ...many illocutionary acts invite by convention a response or sequel...

So here are three ways in which illocutionary acts are bound up with effects; and these are all distinct from the producing of effects which is characteristic of the perlocutionary act.

Under (1) I understand that the speaker has to be secure that the utterance will be understood and accepted; under (2) that the hearer's attitude with respect to the social situation as a whole is altered in some way, which would not have been the case if the utterance had not been made; under (3) that particular obligations are imposed with respect to following acts.

Searle follows Austin fairly closely, though he attempts to be more systematic. He tries to provide in the first place a more precise analysis of the STRUCTURE OF ILLOCUTIONARY ACTS. To this end he formulates necessary and sufficient conditions for the utterance of certain sentences in the sense of performing particular illocutionary acts: the general form is this (Searle 1969: 57):

Given that a speaker S utters a sentence T in the presence of a hearer H, then, in the literal utterance of T, S sincerely and non-defectively promises that p to H if and only if the following conditions...obtain...

Searle's analyses are still unsatisfactory for a number of reasons: in part because they are very incomplete; in part because they isolate the individual speech acts from their preconditions and above all from their (expected, because conventional) consequences; and finally (and connected with the above) because he scarcely considers the hearer's role. I will not, however, go into these criticisms in detail here.[1]

The following table compares the different terminologies:

	Austin	*Searle*	*Hare*
locutionary act	⌠phonetic act ⌡ ⎰phatic act ⎱ ⌊rhetic act	utterance act propositional act	 phrastic
	illocutionary act	illocutionary act	neustic

*9.28 Intention-analysis in Grice

Grice's explication of a pragmatic concept of meaning is especially pertinent to our discussion here. Even though the scope of his analysis is very narrow (he largely ignores the preconditions of the social situation and the achieved alteration of this situation), he does achieve some significant clarifications of both philosophical and linguistic problems. These are problems that are usually not distinguished, but which receive, in Grice's analysis, a new differentiation that demonstrates the complexity of communication-processes. As in other analyses of this type, the explication is in a standardized natural language and not

---

[1] I have done this elsewhere: cf. Maas & Wunderlich (1972: 141–6), Wunderlich 1972a: 49–52). For more exhaustive criticism see Ehlich (1972).

a logical language. Grice published a first, relatively simple, analysis in 1957; since then, under the stimulus of numerous objections and the discussion of much more subtle examples, he has undertaken a significantly more detailed one; I will base this account mainly on this later work (Grice 1968, 1968, MS: chs. v–vii, 1969).

1. Grice suggests that since the various concepts of meaning are interdependent, they should be explicated together. He takes as his central concept that meaning which a speaker intends on a particular occasion of utterance ('utterer's occasion-meaning'); the other concepts of meaning can be derived by particular abstractions. Grice assumes, for instance, the following degrees (cf. the abstraction-grades in 4.3 above):

A. UTTERER'S OCCASION-MEANING
In doing X (articulating particular sounds or other signals), S meant that *p ('*' is a dummy mood-operator).
B. UTTERANCE-TYPE OCCASION-MEANING
In producing an utterance of type X, S meant '*p'.
C. TIMELESS MEANING FOR AN UTTERANCE-TYPE
An utterance of type X means '*p'.
D. APPLIED TIMELESS MEANING FOR AN UTTERANCE-TYPE
The utterance of type X here meant '*p'.

We see that these abstractions do not neglect the pragmatic dimension; in the transition to B we find instead a typification, on the one hand on the level of utterances, on the other, that of meaning. In the transition to C we abstract away from all the circumstances of the utterance-situation; the result is however to be used again in particular utterance-situations and to be confronted with the special meaning (intention) in each situation. This leads us to level D, which is a concretization *vis-à-vis* C and permits us to stabilize the abstraction process. What is primarily available to us on level A is experiences. Knowledge of what is possible in a language can only be obtained by abstraction and generalization and subsequent stabilization. To this extent Grice's orientation is empirical; though it is not based primarily on what one can observe in a communication-situation, but on the participants' assessments and intentions.

The main objection to Grice's procedure is that he does not make a clear distinction between what is conventionally expressed by means of language and what someone actually intends by his utterance (e.g. Searle

1969: 43f.). I think that Grice's neutralization of this distinction is fully intentional. The conventions of a language do not exist independently of the numerous situations in which one could communicate in the language; conventions are established, stabilized and modified in them, especially when what somebody intends by his utterance is clearly not what is generally intended, and thus causes misunderstandings. Then there must be discussion about what someone actually intended and what he reasonably could have (ought to have, should have) meant. Such discussions move along the scale of abstraction that Grice suggests.

For Grice the concept of the conventional is relative on still other grounds: often the convention is grounded in the form of the utterance, often in the contextual (e.g. institutionally given) frame of the utterance-occasion, often only in the fact that the participants observe the general principle of cooperation or conversational maxims derived from it and undertake that they will be observed. Even on this scale CONVENTION-ALITY IS VARIABLE. In particular contexts we can conventionally make a request by saying *Can you close the window?*, ask for agreement with *Isn't linguistics simple?*, and produce a reproach with *Aren't you funny?* – even though none of this arises directly from the interrogative form of the utterances.

In this connection Grice formulates a GENERAL PRINCIPLE OF COOPERA-TION, which everyone should (and indeed does) follow, if he sees in an exchange of speech a common goal (or in any case, if he accepts that the conversation should move in a particular direction (Grice 1975: 45)):

Make your conversational contribution such as is required, at the stage at which it occurs, by the accepted purpose or direction of the talk exchange in which you are engaged.

In agreement with this principle, or derivable from it, there are specific conversational maxims, like (Grice 1975: 45f.):

QUANTITY:
    1. Make your contribution as informative as is required (for the current purposes of the exchange).
    2. Do not make your contribution more informative than is required.
QUALITY: Try to make your contribution one that is true.
    1. Do not say what you believe to be false.
    2. Do not say that for which you lack adequate evidence.
RELATION: Be relevant.
MANNER: Be perspicuous.

1. Avoid obscurity of expression.
2. Avoid ambiguity.
3. Be brief (avoid unnecessary prolixity).
4. Be orderly.

Now it is quite possible for a speaker to intend something by his utterance that in a literal sense is not forthcoming from it; but the intention can be inferred by all the participants, solely on the assumption that the speaker is saying something sensible in the given context, i.e. something relevant and conducive to cooperation. The hearers carry out, in Grice's terminology, a CONVERSATIONAL IMPLICATURE (Grice 1975: 50):

He has said that p; there is no reason to suppose that he is not observing the maxims, or at least the cooperative principle; he could not be doing this unless he thought that q; he knows (and knows that I know that he knows) that I can see that the supposition that he thinks that q IS required; he has done nothing to stop me thinking that q; he intends me to think, or is at least willing to allow me to think, that q; and so he has implicated that q.

The general definition of a conversational implicature is (Grice 1975: 49f.):

A man who, by (in, when) saying (or making as if to say) that p has implicated that q, may be said to have conversationally implicated that q, PROVIDED THAT (1) he is to be presumed to be observing the conversational maxims, or at least the cooperative principle; (2) the supposition that he is aware that, or thinks that, q is required in order to make his saying or making as if to say p (or doing so in THOSE terms) consistent with this presumption; and (3) the speaker thinks (and would expect the hearer to think that the speaker thinks) that it is within the competence of the hearer to work out, or grasp intuitively, that the supposition mentioned in (2) IS required.

Assuming that conventionality is to be measured primarily by the cooperative aim of speech, it is clear why Grice does not set up a distinction between what can be intended in a literal sense (corresponding to the words and constructions used) and what a speaker can intend in a particular situation. In order to avoid restricting the concept of meaning at the outset, we should make such distinctions subsequently, if at all.

2. What a speaker has intended by a particular utterance is described by Grice in terms of the SPEAKER'S INTENTION. In the original analysis this was split into THREE PARTIAL INTENTIONS (Grice 1968, MS: ch. v, 15–16):

10   WFD

'S meant something by uttering x' is true if and only if S uttered x to an audience H, thereby intending
(1) H to produce a particular response r (or to induce a certain response in H);
(2) H to think/recognize at least in part from the utterance of x, that S intended (1);
(3) H to fulfil (1) on the basis of fulfilment of (2).

We can paraphrase this briefly as follows: the speaker has meant something if he has intended (1)–(3); and indeed he has then intended that the hearer should recognize that he, the hearer, should display the reaction r and that this recognition should at least partially be for him the reason for in fact displaying r.

We can notate the three partial intentions formally as follows:
(1) $I_S\ R_H$
(2) $I_S\ E_H\ I_S\ R_H$
(3) $I_S\ (E_H\ I_S\ R_H\ //\ R_H)$

Where:

I_S is the sentence-operator 'S intends that';

E_H is the sentence operator 'H recognizes that';

R_H is the sentence 'H displays a reaction of type R';

$A\ //\ B$ stands for 'B (partly) on the basis of A'.

Various objections have been raised against this original analysis, which I think have been taken care of in the later one:

(a) Strawson (1964) has noted that in many cases we must consider a HIGHER-ORDER INTENTION. The hearer must not only recognize that he should display the reaction r, but he should also recognize that the speaker intends this recognition:

(4) $I_S\ E_H\ I_S\ E_H\ I_S\ R_H$

This holds for allusions or for indirect utterances, in which an intention is to be recognized, without being expressed (e.g. because it would be rude to express it).

(b) Searle objects that Grice speaks simply of RESPONSES, without distinguishing whether these are achieved by illocutionary acts or are to be regarded as extra perlocutionary effects; i.e. the important illocutionary vs. perlocutionary distinction is lost. This objection is connected with the one cited above, that there is no clear distinction between the conventional and the non-conventional (Searle follows Austin here). In fact according to the Gricean analysis there are still further arbitrary intentions of the speaker that have to be considered (intention to impress someone, etc.). This objection was removed when Grice replaced the notion of response by the requirement that the hearer take a propositional attitude of the same kind as the speaker's.

(c) Gricean complex intentions can be misunderstood as a speaker's SUBJECTIVE INTENTIONS, which makes a theory of meaning based on them incomprehensible. How can purely subjective intentions be represented except in terms of meanings in a private language? But a hearer can easily recognize the speaker's subjective meaning if this is expressed in intersubjectively valid forms: i.e. the speaker must communicate in the common language. His subjective intentions will become intersubjectively communicable only when they are expressed in this language; this does not mean that they are totally exhausted by this expression, as Grice makes clear through the relativity of his concept of convention.

3. On the basis of these and other considerations Grice introduces (1968, MS) a series of stepwise differentiations. The hearer must recognize the intention on the basis of particular linguistic features of the utterance; these are correlated in particular ways (conventionally, restricted-conventionally, iconically, associatively, etc.) with the speaker's propositional attitude; each propositional attitude ψ is correlated with a mood operator *. The most significant clarification is what the intended reaction of the hearer is supposed to be. Up to this point Grice proceeded from the idea that an assertion should not produce belief (conviction) in the hearer, but request an action. Now however, only specific PROPOSITIONAL ATTITUDES are in general elicited; in a request this is the hearer's intention to act, not his action itself. Grice demonstrates this by means of dialogues like:

'The machine has stopped.' – 'Yes.'
'Stop the machine!' – 'Yes.'

In the first case the 'yes' designates a belief of the hearer's, in the second case an intention; we can say that in both cases it represents acceptance of the alterations of the hearer's propositional attitude intended by the speaker. The speaker's intention is then fulfilled: indeed his intentions may reach further (that the machine actually be stopped), but they then extend to a later period of time; the fulfilment of these intentions can in any case no longer be achieved linguistically. It now requires a decision of the hearer's, and this can depend on many other factors.

According to Grice, we can distinguish in many utterances the following meaning factors:

(a) AN EXHIBITIVE FACTOR: the hearer should recognize that the speaker has a particular propositional attitude;

(b) A PROTREPTIC FACTOR: the hearer should make this attitude his own.[1]

We can paraphrase the first as: the hearer should understand; and the second as: the hearer should accept. (On this distinction cf. the non-Gricean reflections in Wunderlich 1972c: 286ff., 1972a: 22f.) One of Grice's later versions of meaning analysis goes like this (1968, MS: ch. VI, 9):

Let f = a set of linguistic features,
     p = propositional content,
     ψ = propositional attitude,
     c = type of correlation.

'S means by x that $*\psi p$': '(Ef) (Ec): S utters x intending H:

(1) to think that x has f

+ (2) to think S intends (1)

(3) to think f is correlated in way c with the state of ψ-ing that p

+ (4) to think S intends (3)

(5) to think S intends H, via (1) and (3), to think that S ψ's that p

(6) on the basis of the fulfilment of (5), to think that S ψ's that p

+ (7) to think S intends (6)

(8) on the basis of the fulfilment of (6), to ψ that p.'

(8) does not hold in all cases; the same is true for (2), (4) and (7). In our chosen formal notation we can now write:

(1) $I_S E_H (x \rightarrow f)$

(2) $I_S E_H I_S E_H (x \rightarrow f)$

(3) $I_S E_H (f_c \rightarrow \psi p)$

(4) $I_S E_H I_c E_H (f_S \rightarrow \psi p)$

(5) $I_S (E_H (x \rightarrow f) \& E_H (f_c \rightarrow \psi p) \; // \; E_H I_S E_H \psi_S p)$

(6) $I_S (E_H I_S E_H \psi_S p \; // \; E_H \psi_S p)$

(7) $I_S E_H (E_H I_S E_H \psi_S p \; // \; E_H \psi_S p)$

(8) $I_S (E_H \psi_S p \; // \; \psi_H p)$

---

[1] The protreptic factor plays no role for example in the following situations: an examination candidate answers the examiner's question (the examiner does not usually want to know the answer – he knows it already – but wants to know whether the candidate knows it); someone reminds someone else of something (here we only have the reactivation of existing knowledge); someone gives a closing summary.

The symbol '→' indicates the assignment of a value to a particular argument of a function: this assignment is possible only through acquaintance with the language. The assignment $f_c \rightarrow \psi p$ characterizes a semantic interpretation.

We must add a few critical notes to this brief outline:

(a) The introduction of complex intentions can in principle be carried still further. Is there any reason to stop at intentions of the second order, or is the way open to an infinite regress? Since communication processes do in fact work, an analysis that allows an infinite regress can hardly be correct. Grice discusses this point, though without taking an unequivocal position. In his view it is only clear that the analysis is (1) non-circular ('S intends p' is not described in terms of 'S intends q' or the like), and (2) that the problem of regress cannot be settled as simply as in cases like 'S thinks that he thinks that he thinks that...' or 'It is true that it is true that it is true that...' It is clear in the formal notation that an operator with an S-index must always alternate with one with an H-index. This is an expression of the reflexivity of communication: a speaker anticipates the hearer's expectations, the hearer's expectations with respect to his own expectations, etc. Grice's analysis is not merely speaker-centred; on the contrary, it specifically claims that the comprehension of this complex intention is the hearer's achievement (he shows his understanding in this way); so is his following of it (i.e. in order to fulfil the step intended in (8) – he shows his acceptance in this way). The speaker intends the hearer to make certain cognitive inferences (indicated by the value-assignments ' → ' and recognition on the basis of another's recognition, specified with '//'); but the hearer must carry out these inferences. (Correspondingly conversational implicature is described from the hearer's perspective.) We can probably interpret this as follows: whenever the speaker follows the existing conventions relatively strictly, the hearer can already understand him on a lower level of intention-analysis (which he is determined to do); there is no need then of higher-order intentions. But if no clear sense arises for the hearer on this lower level, he has to consider further degrees; on the basis of these he can then perform the appropriate reductions – for example from (2) to (1), from (4) to (3), etc. (This presupposes that a different function-value f is to be obtained than if (1) alone were being considered.)

(b) The analysis is incomplete. The situational alteration that a speech act is supposed to achieve consists solely in the hearer's adopting a propositional attitude of the speaker's. (Whether this actually happens naturally depends on the hearer; he can also misunderstand, intentionally misunderstand, want to make the presuppositions into a problem, etc.) For every propositional attitude there is obviously a corresponding speech-act type, which allows it to be mediated (expressed by the mood operator '*'): for the questioning attitude ('Is it p or something else ?') there is the erotetic act, for the ordering attitude ('Let it be p'), there is the directive act, etc.[1] Grice does not differentiate other ways of carrying out the act of questioning, besides use of the interrogative mood (e.g. 'You must surely be hungry', 'I just don't know when our appointment is for') – and similarly for the other speech-act types. The intention of an erotetic act is fulfilled if the hearer adopts the questioning attitude, of an order if he adopts the ordering attitude. But the hearer must also understand these attitudes as directed toward himself: the ordering attitude must be at least 'Let p be brought about by H', to which the hearer must add 'H – that's ME.' Questions should lead to answers, requests to advice or promises, reproaches to justifications, orders to actions. Every speech act stands in an at least partially conventional connection with other (preceding and following) speech acts, as well as with certain non-communicative actions. Insofar as these connections are conventional, it follows that a speech act leads not only to the adoption of propositional attitudes, but also to the ESTABLISHMENT OF SPECIFIC RELATIONS OF OBLIGATION: if someone does not answer a question or try to answer it, he violates the communicative obligation imposed on him by the question. The speaker of course can impose this obligation on the hearer only to the extent that it belongs conventionally to the nature of the question; measures like threats or the use of force, etc., can compel particular behaviour on the part of the hearer – but without imposing obligations in our sense.

(c) Grice always uses only a few examples to illustrate his analysis, though the analysis itself is extremely general. In no place does he systematically investigate specific types of speech acts (or utterances); the necessary differentiations are therefore lacking. The role played by particular linguistic constructions in the explicit or implicit expression of propositional attitudes remains undefined. (Linguistic constructions and means of construction are assigned a very general place within the

[1] The distinction between mood operator and propositional attitude does not correspond to Hare's distinction between 'phrastic' and 'neustic' (Hare 1952: ch. 2), since the phrastic is to be identified with the proposition rather than the propositional attitude.

complex intention, but their value is not precisely characterized.) In addition, the concepts that Grice uses, like 'think', 'recognize', 'believe', etc., are not precisely defined; a spectrum for the use of one or the other of these remains open.[1] Finally, the type of cognitive procedures that the hearer is supposed to carry out (drawing inferences on the basis of something already known, etc.) remain undefined. For example, are we to distinguish different kinds of inferences, like those explicated in logic? Which factors are to be considered in detail?

9.29 Outline of a theory of speech acts

In what follows the concept 'speech act' will include those aspects defined by Austin and Searle as illocutionary acts. But I will not make a strict distinction between 'illocutionary' and 'perlocutionary', since conventions are not always precisely defined.

The production of utterance-tokens is part of every speech act; but any speech act cannot be performed with just any utterance. (For example one can *inter alia* make a promise with an utterance of 'I'll come tomorrow', but not with 'I came yesterday'.) The relation between speech-act type and utterance type can be summed up in two complementary assertions:

1. SPEECH-ACT TYPE CAN BE CONVENTIONALLY INDICATED BY THE FORM AND CONTENT OF THE UTTERANCE-TOKENS. This purpose is served by sentence-modalities, performative formulae, individual indicator words in special positions (*please, you know*, etc.), forms of address, intonation, etc.

EXAMPLES:
'What time is it?' → Question
'I assure you that I wasn't.' → Assurance
'Would you please close the window.' → Request
'I missed the train, you know.' → Justification
'You idiot!' → Insult
'I WILL come to your seminar tomorrow.' → Promise

2. SPEECH-ACT TYPE IS NOT EXCLUSIVELY DETERMINED BY THE FORM AND CONTENT OF THE UTTERANCE-TOKENS, BUT IN CERTAIN RESTRICTED CONTEXTS ALSO BY
(a) INSTITUTIONAL EXPECTATIONS AND OBLIGATIONS TO ACT;
(b) PERSON-SPECIFIC ASSESSMENTS OF THE COMMUNICATION SITUATION.

[1] In his later analyses Grice uses 'think' fairly systematically – though he sometimes also uses 'recognize'. These concepts are hardly identical; I get the impression that 'think' is often to be taken in the sense of 'recognize'.

EXAMPLES: (without differentiation according to (a) or (b))
'You may close the window.' → Permission, Command
'I advise you to shut your mouth.' → Threat
'Why did you do that ?' → Reproach
'You're the friendliest person I've met here.' → Complaint

These two claims together express a particular knowledge. In addition we can derive from them a set of regulative principles for two complementary research directions:

1. Grammatical theory should be developed with a view toward discovering which speech-act types are indicatable (indicated) by which forms and content.

2. There are classes of restricted contexts that should be studied with a view to discovering which obligations hold in them, and how these obligations are correlated with person-specific assessments of communication-situations.

From the point of view in 1, the two sentences *I'll come tomorrow* and *I promise you that I'll come tomorrow* are to be treated as different; only the second INDICATES an act of promising. The fact that a promise can also be made with the first sentence (as well as a threat, the expression of a presumption, etc.) can only be settled from the point of view 2.

Searle's procedure is thus unsatisfactory, because it is oriented exclusively to 1. He writes (1969: 17f.):

There are, therefore, not two irreducibly distinct semantic studies, one a study of the meanings of sentences and one a study of the performances of speech acts. For just as it is part of our notion of the meaning of a sentence that a literal utterance of that sentence with that meaning in a certain context would be the performance of a particular speech act, so it is a part of our notion of a speech act that there is a possible sentence (or sentences) the utterance of which in a certain context would in virtue of its (or their) meaning constitute a performance of that speech act...Therefore, it is in principle possible for every speech act one performs or could perform to be uniquely determined by a given sentence (or set of sentences), given the assumption that the speaker is speaking literally and that the context is appropriate.

Searle formulates his 'principle of expressibility' still more explicitly (1969: 20):

for any meaning X and any speaker S whenever S means (intends to convey, wishes to communicate in an utterance, etc.) X then it is possible that there is some expression E such that E is an exact expression of formulation of X.

Searle restricts this in two ways: first, there will not always be an expression for all effects (e.g. emotional, poetic) that one wants to produce in the hearer; second, just because something can be said does not mean that it must be able to be understood, i.e. he explicitly allows for a PRIVATE LANGUAGE as well. Now (leaving aside the fact that private languages are problematical for other reasons), it is not clear what a meaning X would be in such a context. Above all it is not clear how it would be possible for private-language meanings to have exact expressions in a socially valid language. There are three possible interpretations of the principle:

(a) A speaker can only mean something that also has an exact expression in a non-private language. But this would contradict not only Searle's assumption of a private language, but also the position I have been arguing for, that social conventions develop implicitly; this presupposes that private meanings are not always congruent with social meanings.

(b) Everything that can be conventionally meant by a speaker is also exactly expressible. This would be circular if 'conventionally' means that there are corresponding expressions in the language, or it would be a definition of the use of 'conventional' (the conventional is only what is exactly expressible) that I do not accept.

(c) This is really a PRINCIPLE OF POSSIBLE EXPRESSIBILITY, in which it is again either nonsensical or superfluous to consider the possibility of a private language: if particular implicit conventions have developed, then situations will exist (e.g. the justification of sanctions) where they will be talked about. These situations require explicitness, and thus under certain conditions the extension of a language; and such extensions are always possible.

Only the third interpretation is acceptable; but it leads necessarily to the second of the research directions mentioned above. For at present certainly not all speech-act types and propositional attitudes can be unequivocally, i.e. literally, indicated in utterance-tokens (assuming that there are general standards enabling us to establish literalness or non-literalness). And even if this were so, the assumption that all men at any time speak literally goes against experience. It incorporates an ideal, which may be valid in certain domains like science, legislation, or jurisprudence, but which we can hardly set up as a regulatory principle for everyday communication. We know that in general we can perform different speech acts by the utterance of a given sentence, and that we generally have different sentences at our disposal for carrying out a given speech act.

I will not define precisely what I mean in assertion 2 (a) by an 'institution', but merely illustrate it. I think that the elucidation of the CONCEPT OF AN INSTITUTION presupposes, among other things, an investigation into what specific expectations or obligations hold with reference to the course of communication, what authorities are to be consulted, who has what status, who is right, etc. (these authorities guarantee the social validity of obligations). When we recognize particular institutions, we also recognize the specific obligations within them. But we already recognize institutions in part by virtue of the way we conduct our daily lives within them, and this cannot depend on our own decisions. We do not have to justify each of our speech acts individually, because they are already justified in the institutional context of our language; we only have to justify, now and then, our failures to perform them, or transgressions of some other kind. (We do not have to justify greeting someone, but under certain conditions we may have to justify not doing so. And similarly for all institutionally prescribed speech acts, especially rituals.) To this extent there is also a 'relief' in communicative intercourse, bound up with our relative freedom from having to justify individual speech acts in specific institutional settings.

EXAMPLE:

The following dialogue can be performed in various contexts:

(9)   x: 'What do you want ?' ('May I help you ?')

(10) y: 'Nothing, thanks.' ('No thank you.')

(11) x: 'Then please leave the $\begin{cases} \text{A. restaurant} \\ \text{B. shop} \\ \text{C. aeroplane} \\ \text{D. house} \end{cases}$ at once.'

Context A: x is a waiter, y is looking for a table. The reply (10) is obviously not allowed; therefore (11) is allowed as a notification of sanction (and expected, if one has replied with (10)).

Context B: x is a clerk in a bookshop, y is a customer. The reply (10) is probably not allowed, but the reply 'Nothing, thanks; I'm just looking around' is allowed here (though not in context A), and therefore (11) is not to be expected in any case.

Context C: x is a stewardess, y is a passenger. The stewardess comes down the aisle and utters (9). The answer (10) is obviously allowed, and therefore (11) is not. (Even if the passenger has rung, so that (10) is hardly expected by the stewardess, (11) is still not allowed – on other grounds: the difficulty of leaving a moving plane, etc.)

Context D_1: x is a carpet salesman who has rung the bell of a flat, y is the occupant. (9) is not allowed, because it is x who wants to claim y's attention; therefore not only (10), but also a notification of sanction is allowed (expectable).

Context D_2: as above, only this time x is the occupant and y the carpet salesman. (10) is not allowed, therefore (11) is.

In all four contexts introductory utterances like *I know what you want* (*I can help you*) would be quite abnormal and in fact barely tolerable (except for example toward frequent visitors or the like). On the other hand this is often the form in which – explicitly or implicitly – advertisements claim the reader's attention, which gives us some insight into the unique status of advertising.

Under aspect 2(b) we treat those communication sequences in which it is not the institutional context (and its attendant obligations) that dominates, but rather the remaining context, including the participants' particular familiarity with each other. Here we can often get utterances whose meaning is some speech act other than the one ('literally') indicated by the utterance-token.

EXAMPLES:
'Dinner is ready.' → Statement + request
'I'm sure that we can toboggan on the Teufelsberg now.' → Statement + proposal
'Could you close the window before you leave.' → Question + request
'I'm out of petrol.' → Statement + request

The speaker (unless he is being deliberately ambiguous) surely intends either to make a statement or a request. But the hearer can interpret it in either way. I assume here that the hearer first understands an utterance as a statement act, but since he does not see the communicative point of this act, and nonetheless assumes that the speaker had a communicative intention, he infers that it is a request (cf. Grice's notion of conversational implicature: 9.28 above). It seems to me however to be characteristic of these speech acts that the conventions for, say, meaning and understanding a request rather than a statement in a particular context, are not so clear that one of the participants could justify sanctions on the basis of his having intended one speech act, while the other participant understood a different one. In general this will merely be treated as a case of misunderstanding, and an attempt will be made to explicate it.

We must now ask about the FORM in which we should state our knowledge about which utterances mean which speech acts in which contexts. As a first approximation we can talk of speech acts in the way as we do in ordinary language, i.e. use those verbs (and verb-like expressions) that serve to designate particular speech-act types. (If we're talking about questions, we can use the verb *ask*, namely (a) when we recapitulate question-situations, (b) represent future or possible question-situations, and (c) explicate an interrogative act as such: *I hereby ask you whether…, that was meant as a question.*) On this basis we can formulate necessary and sufficient conditions for the adequacy of descriptions, e.g. in the form:

> (A) 'S has performed a speech act of type A with respect to H' is true if and only if ****.
> (Under '****' we state the particular conditions.)

We can imagine different variants of this, e.g.:

> (B) 'S has, by uttering the sentence T, performed a speech act of type A with respect to H' is true if and only if ****.
> (C) With the utterance of the sentence T in a situation of type K one performs a speech act of type A if and only if ****.

The strict observance of such forms requires us to have reflected precisely about our knowledge. We will have learned a great deal if we have performed this kind of analysis for a large number of speech-act types.[1] But there are some problems:

1. It is not clear how, in the strict form of the schema, we can distinguish between conventional conditions and (more or less accidental) non-conventional circumstances. Can we say for example that S has asked H a question if S intended to ask and H recognized the intention correctly – even if S has only uttered very indirectly (e.g. in the 'literal' sense has made a statement)? Should we use this descriptive form for speech acts like boasting, even if it is fairly certain that no-one 'literally' boasts?

---

[1] Searle's (1969) programme points in such a direction, though with the restriction that the principle of literalness of utterance is to be observed. This is precisely what has turned out to be problematical.

2. We can certainly perform more speech acts than we can talk about. If we only used those verbs (or verb-like expressions) that appear in particular languages, to what extent could we say anything about the speech acts possible in a society? Would we not merely be saying something about the lexical items available for designating speech acts? Does not a formal set-up like (A)–(C) merely establish precise definitions of the use of particular verbs (or verb-like expressions)? I.e. we are studying the semantics of the verbs used in the description, and not the speech acts themselves. We do not learn about what people do when they speak, but only how they talk about what they do when they speak.

3. Conventions and the obligations (and possibly sanctions) bound up with them do not remain fixed for all time: since we are usually dealing with implicit conventions, their latitude of freedom is often first narrowed (i.e. fixed) within communication-situations by the participants – with reference to possible authorities that can be invoked (other persons, everyday experiences, etc.). Descriptions of the form (A)–(C) are from a certain point of view also establishments (regulations) which do not allow common 'bargaining' about the meaning of utterances (as speech acts of this or that kind).

4. It is not very useful for the elucidation of the respective similarities and differences of speech-act types to use the totality of verbs (or verb-like expressions) that a language has for the designation of speech acts. We must therefore ask whether there might not be a small number of basic and perhaps universal speech-act types (as indicated for instance by the grammatical moods – indicative, interrogative, imperative, optative), which can be freely differentiated and combined along different dimensions. Can we encompass all speech acts in terms of such basic speech acts, together with the appropriate parameters of differentiation? Could we finally introduce a theoretical vocabulary for this purpose, which does not necessarily correspond to certain lexical items of a particular language?

5. In the descriptions (A)–(C) the individual speech acts are taken in isolation, not in their relation to preceding and possibly following speech acts, or to possible alternative acts. The first point could be taken care of by referring in the conditions to other speech acts; the second point by analysing alternative speech acts in conjunction with one particular act (e.g. in a recursive schema). It may also make sense to select a dynamic schema ('What consequences follow from a speech act of type A?') rather than a static one ('Under what conditions do we

have a speech act of type A ?') – even if they ultimately turn out to be equivalent.

6. Is THE DESCRIPTION OF SPEECH ACTS really the right way to treat them ? Could not we proceed as we do in logic, where we do not describe particular argument-types, but explicate them by means of specific rules of deduction ? Or by analogy to programming, where commands are explicated as programming instructions (Rescher 1966 treats various kinds of commands this way). Can we even RECONSTRUCT some speech acts – at least some of the basic ones – in a similar way as FORMAL ACTIONS, instead of describing them in sentences of a formal system ?

In general, we must distinguish in every speech act:

(a) The speaker.

(b) The set of addressees; for these there are acts of addressing, i.e. acts which specially orient the attention of the person concerned to the utterance (e.g. expressions like *Your Majesty. . . , listen to me, you, hello*).

(c) The total set of hearers, which can include persons other than the addressees. In many speech acts there are possible or even fully determined (non-addressee) hearers intended, i.e. people who ARE SUPPOSED to hear without being directly addressed – especially in public meetings, on TV, in Parliament, etc. The speech-act type in fact can be dissociated according to addressees and hearers:

EXAMPLE:

Someone says in Peter's presence: 'I'll defend you against Peter.'
→ Promise to the addressee
→ Threat to Peter

(d) The possible public: those persons and authorities to whom it is assumed that the content of utterances could be transmitted. Very often a speaker comports himself with a view toward a possible public: persons in this realm can be called on in cases of conflict (i.e. the possible public represents the basis for justification); in institutional contexts the possible public often extends to the institution as a whole.

Speakers' propositional attitudes play an important role in all discussions of speech acts: a speaker expresses his own propositional attitude and intends the hearer to assume a similar or corresponding one. For example in the following utterances there is in each case a different attitude to the proposition 'that Peter comes to the cinema with us' (or 'Peter's coming with us to the cinema'):

Peter is certainly coming to the cinema with us.

Is Peter coming to the cinema with us then ?

Let Peter come to the cinema with us!

Peter must come to the cinema with us!

The objects of the attitudes are thus propositions and not sentences. If we are only speaking of propositions, we usually use *that*-S or nominalized forms; this shows that propositions are obviously particular time-independent objects (but propositional attitudes are not). We therefore cannot identify propositions with the intensions of sentences in referential semantics. There the intension of a sentence is taken as a function from the set of possible reference-points in the set of truth-values; a reference-point includes one of the possible worlds as well as the elements of possible situations of utterance. In order to maintain for speech-act theory the important notion of proposition (and also to set referential semantics and speech-act theory in the proper relation), Stalnaker (1972: 385) proposes the following scheme:[1]

1. Let the INTERPRETATION of a sentence be a function from the set of possible reference-points in the set of propositions.

2. Let a PROPOSITION be a function from the set of possible worlds in the set of truth-values.

The one function is now divided into two, whose character can be different. A further advantage of the proposal could be that the constitution of possible alternative worlds in situations of utterance is now to be captured in such a way that the first function also singles out the alternative worlds which come into question as arguments of the proposition. Though we might now imagine how different propositional attitudes are to be represented by different functions of type 1, we still lack a proper interpretation of non-declarative sentences. How could the value of a particular interpretation of an interrogative sentence be a proposition ? And how should we understand formally the fact that a speech act is, after all, a kind of action that determines in a particular way the future of an interaction, or is determined by its history ? In order to make this question answerable I will discuss some preliminary points.

Every speech act effects an alteration in the social situation existing between the speaker and the addressee (and possible other hearers). We have to distinguish two kinds of alterations:

---

[1] If we regard a proposition as a conceptual correlate of a state of affairs, then this makes precise the notion that sentences designate states of affairs.

I. EVERY SPEECH ACT EFFECTS ALTERATIONS IN THE PROPOSITIONAL ATTITUDES OF SPEAKER AND HEARER.

2. EVERY SPEECH ACT FULFILLS AND/OR ELICITS PARTICULAR OBLIGATIONS FOR SPEAKER AND HEARER.

Among the alterations in propositional attitudes we include especially alterations in the assessment of the interaction (assumptions, knowledge, beliefs about the partners and their relationships). Not all actually occurring changes are in fact conventionally bound. For instance, a speaker may wish to use the utterance *I find your book extremely abstract* to convince the hearer that he admires his exposition; but the hearer actually feels himself not complimented but criticized or even offended. (The reverse is also possible: the speaker wants to criticize, but the hearer takes it as a compliment). The speaker's intentions are EXPRESSED as his intentions only if this happens conventionally or restricted-conventionally (or at least comprehensibly in the common situation). Obviously it cannot be a task for speech-act theory to discuss the actually (and often accidentally) occurring alterations, nor the actual acceptances and following acts; rather the task is to treat these only to the extent that they are conventionally (in the absolute or restricted sense) expectable, and thus ought to take place.

Every SOCIAL RULE bound up with an obligation can be described in the following form:

(R) When the conditions G exist, one ought to perform (or omit) an act of type A; otherwise one can expect a sanction from the domain T.

The strength of the obligation (measured by the extent of the set of conditions G and the degree of sanction) as well as the type A of the obligated act depend on the character of the institution as well as the personal relations between speaker and addressee.

Most speech acts are preceded by other acts; in any case there already exists a social situation (and this in turn is first set up by an act of addressing). Such acts (in general, the existing social situation) REALIZE CERTAIN INITIAL CONDITIONS (in the sense of the rule-form given above) according to existing social rules; they thus ENGENDER PARTICULAR OBLIGATIONS for the case in question. Let us call these INITIATIVE SPEECH ACTS. Thus interrogative acts engender the obligation to answer, requests engender the obligation to perform the requested action (or at least to take a position) – all assuming that this would not transgress an already existing obligation (namely the obligation not to act). Even acts of assertion engender obligations – generally the following:

1. The speaker undertakes to authenticate the content of the assertion if necessary, and to act in future in conformity with the content of the assertion (semantic presuppositions also count here as part of the content).

2. The addressee is obliged to direct his future actions so that they conform to the fact that the speaker believes (knows) the content of the assertion.

If speech acts take place under the conditions of a (possibly institution-specific) social rule whose initial conditions are realized beforehand, they may FULFIL the engendered obligations, or possibly TRANSGRESS against them. Let us call these REACTIVE SPEECH ACTS. Besides these there are possible substitute acts, delaying acts, problematizing acts, etc. At the same time these can engender new obligations. Of course not all speech acts that fulfil an obligation necessarily engender new obligations (e.g. if someone returns a greeting).

For every obligated act of type A there is a conventionally tolerated CLASS OF ALTERNATIVE SUBSTITUTE ACTS, defined by the type of the obligated act. For instance, the speaker's assessment of the addressee, especially of his knowledge, may be factually false; in this case the obligated action cannot be performed, but one of the alternatives has to be instead in order to meet the obligation.

EXAMPLE:

Request for information → Informative answer

or

$$\left.\begin{array}{l} \text{'I don't know.'} \\ \text{'I don't understand exactly} \\ \text{what you want to know.'} \\ \text{'You'd best look it up in} \\ \text{the dictionary.'} \end{array}\right\}$$

These replies all fulfil the obligation, even if the question is not answered. Replies that question the obligation itself (e.g. *Why do you want to know?* – which of course can also mean that it's not clear what kind of answer is expected) are to be judged differently, as are those that fundamentally dispute the very existence of the obligation to answer. (One HAS THE RIGHT to answer the question *Who did you sleep with last night?* with *You can't ask me that.*)

The obligations arising from many speech acts are conditional (e.g. one only has to authenticate an assertion when asked to); but the obligations arising from others are unconditional, partly for the hearer, partly for the speaker himself. With a question I commit my audience to an answer; if I cite a premiss or begin an enumeration with 'first', I commit myself to continuing. Where there are unconditional obligations to continue I will speak of SPEECH-ACT SEQUENCES; where a dialogue or monologue is continued without such obligations (e.g. after an answer or an argument) I will speak of SPEECH-ACT CHAINS. (Obligations are thus in a special sense 'text-forming.')

EXAMPLES OF SPEECH-ACT SEQUENCES:

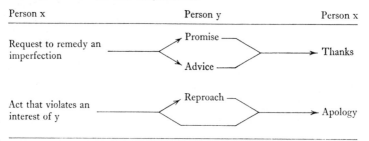

In addition, other sequences can be subordinated to a conventional sequence:

EXAMPLE:

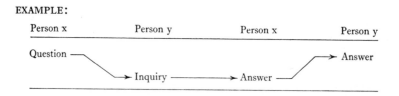

Monologic speech-act sequences can also be interrupted at various places by other subordinated sequences, e.g. in conducting an argument. Dialogues and monologues in general consist of concatenations of individual sequences. The concatenations themselves arise non-conventionally, out of specific alterations in propositional attitudes, degree of attention, through associations, etc.

In order to develop a theory of speech acts, we need (a) more precise insights into and specification of propositional attitudes, and (b) the assistance of deontic logic, developed on the basis of logics of action. This is in any sense the minimal presupposition, provided we accept the two points which constitute the alteration effected through speech acts.[1] In the first domain we must specify the most important BASIC TYPES OF PROPOSITIONAL ATTITUDES.

As a first approximation the following are probably absolutely necessary:

1. 'to know that' (recognition can probably be described as that which leads to knowing, but we must still distinguish this from perception);
2. 'to believe that' (often to be taken in the sense of 'suppose unquestioningly that');
3. 'to assume (presume) that';
4. 'to wish that' (on the basis of interests and preferences);
5. 'to will (intend) that' (on the basis of decisions);

For wishing and willing (and also partly for assuming) we must describe not only the alterations of these attitudes in time, but also the operands in each case (wishing and willing relate to the future); we must assume a LOGIC OF CHANGES as well as a TENSE LOGIC. If we want to consider the embedding of speech acts in other, non-communicative acts, then we need additional operators, like 'to be able', 'to need'.

The framework of propositional attitudes and engendered or fulfilled obligations serves for the pragmatic interpretation of utterances in their respective contexts. Besides this, we can envisage a semantical interpretation of non-declarative sentences not depending on the context, i.e. one that gives their literal meaning, within the framework of model-theory. Then we can answer the question above of how we should formally understand the fact that speech acts are actions, even on the level of semantics. But in any case, to get the full interpretation, we have to base ourselves on the context as well, i.e. we have to reinterpret the semantic interpretation on the level of pragmatics.[2]

For each grammatical mood we have a characteristic outcome function which yields, at a certain reference point, a set of possible futures. For example, the outcome function for the imperative sentence *Shut the door* yields that set of possible futures for each of which it is true that the addressee will shut the door. (Thus, the addressee knows

---

[1] There are already some basic works in both these areas. On propositional attitudes (especially knowledge, belief and perception) see the works of Hintikka (1962, 1969). For deontic logic I would recommend Iwin (1972), Kalinowski (1972), the papers in Hilpinen (1971) and the works of von Wright (1963, 1968).

[2] I have worked this out in more detail in Wunderlich (1976a) and Wunderlich (1976b: ch. 3).

from the uttered sentence alone which restrictions on his future behaviour are induced, and when he wants to comply with the command he
will always try to remain in the respective set of possible futures.)

The outcome function for the interrogative sentence *When does the
next train leave for Oxford* yields that set of possible futures for each of
which the addressee (or possibly someone else) will serve with an answer
such that some time-expression t can be derived, and the open formula
The next train for Oxford leaves at . . . can be satisfied. (Again, the addressee knows from the uttered sentence alone which restrictions on his
future behaviour are induced.)[1]

In the light of the foregoing discussion, we can get an abstract semantical interpretation in this way only for initiative speech acts, whereas
reactive speech acts are always related to the preceding context. For
example, whether or not *At ten thirty* will yield an answer, and which
one, depends on the circumstance whether a question was posed before,
and which one.

Finally, there are two special problems that we should discuss:

1. Stalnaker (1972: 387f.) distinguishes correctly between SEMANTIC
and PRAGMATIC PRESUPPOSITIONS. From a semantic point of view,
presupposition is a relation between sentences (or, if we adopt propositions, as Stalnaker assumes, between propositions). From a pragmatic
point of view, it is a special type of speaker's propositional attitude. We
can say, roughly:

In an utterance S makes the presupposition p where:

(a) S believes that p.
(b) S assumes that H believes that p.
(c) S says that q; but S does not say that p (both in the literal sense).
(d) For S the truth of p is necessary if q is to be interpretable.

If PRES is the class of presuppositions p_1 made by S in his utterance,
then the class of possible worlds is defined by PRES (they must be
consistent with p_1), in respect of which q is to be understood. From
every presupposition p_i made by S there arise the same obligations for
S as if he had asserted that p_1. (In assertions S can also express what he
believes; but if he assumes that the hearer believes it too, it is generally
a violation of the principle of relevance if he nonetheless asserts it.)

---

[1] I give here only a very brief outline of the main idea that I have elaborated in
Wunderlich (1976b: chs. 4 and 5).

If in his utterance S expresses a semantic presupposition (and that implicitly: e.g. by the non-generalizing use of the definite article he expresses the existence and uniqueness of an object in this context), he is also naturally making a pragmatic presupposition; S does not however express all his presuppositions implicitly (so that they can be inferred from the utterance-token alone); this means that not all pragmatic presuppositions have to be reconstructable as semantic presuppositions as well.

2. The attempt has often been made to characterize lies and deceptions as special speech acts. This however shows a misunderstanding of the nature of DECEPTIVE SPEECH ACTS. All these speech acts make use of conventional procedures and can thus be classified accordingly: a lie is an act of assertion. Anyone who lies wants to maintain the appearance that he believes (or knows) what he is saying; therefore he will also submit to the obligations stemming from the assertion (as far as he can while keeping up appearances).

The specific distinction between deceptive and non-deceptive speech acts is to be defined solely on the level of propositional attitudes. If S asserts that p but knows that not-p, he behaves conventionally as if he believed (knew) that p. Insofar as the hearer does not suspect that S knows that not-p, he will behave in conformity to S's believing (knowing) that p (contrary to what is actually the case); and this is precisely what S intends. The subsequent development of the interaction may naturally provide new grounds for assuming that the speaker's propositional attitude is different from what he pretended. We can make the following rough distinctions:

S ASSERTS THAT p:

sincere assertion	S knows that p (S believes that he knows that p).
lying assertion	S knows that not-p.
deceptive assertion	S doesn't know whether p.
erroneous assertion	S believes that he knows that p; and: not-p.

IO *Systematic operations*

10.1 Operations between perception and theory

Much of the linguist's activity consists of the systematic confrontation of linguistic data with theories or theory sketches. As I have already pointed out, there are no strict procedures for deriving theories from data, i.e. every programme that claims to do anything of the sort already incorporates (without admitting it) theoretical premises – or it achieves nothing at all. Still less, of course, can we derive data from theories; all we can do, assuming particular, clear initial data, is predict new data and make decisions in the unclear cases. But even if methodical–heuristic procedures cannot be taken as strict, unequivocal, or complete, we still cannot do without them; we have to compare and evaluate individual perceptions, experiences and judgements in order to establish meaningful theoretical concepts; and theorizing is meaningful only if it is adequate to the facts and our knowledge of them. The individual datum itself, i.e. a linguistic observation, is the product of (pre)-theoretical orientations; acquisition and selection of data, as well as their subsequent processing (especially classification and generalization) are based on theoretical premises. And in general we can only stabilize and explicate concepts if we already have an extensive collection of analysed data at our disposal. ALL SYSTEMATIC OPERATIONS ARE GROUNDED IN THIS DIALECTIC OF EXPERIENCE AND THEORETICAL EXPLICATION. This means that we do not have to start out by setting up, as a basis for further work, particular concepts of both experience and data. A linguistic datum can be the result of a directed observation as well as of an interrogation or an intuitive presentation of our linguistic behaviour (i.e. it can mirror our linguistic knowledge). Insofar as data express the results of perceptions, we can say that the systematic operations on them are already laid down in perceptual processes; and in turn they affect the nature of our perceptions. Insofar as data are theoretically reconstructed, we can say that operations on the data also correspond to particular theoretical operations: and we select our methods according to these.

All PERCEPTUAL PROCESSES are guided by the relevance of the percepts for our activities. We isolate and compare individual objects (which among other things presupposes memory), and we discriminate 'sames' and 'differents'. 'Sames' are objects that fall under a single classificatory concept; 'differents' are objects that fall under different ones. A large enough set of concepts allows us to discover that the objects of perception are partially the same and partially different.We can in other words assign to the objects of perception a structure consisting of individual features, and we can establish RELATIONSHIPS AND ANALOGIES between objects according to shared features.

Speech sounds, for instance, have a quite complex structure for the speaker; they can be compared with one another on the basis of numerous features, even if we consider only those relevant for communication. Anyone who controls (or only partly controls) a language has learned the distinction between such features; though this does not mean that he must also know it consciously. Even in the establishment of linguistic data, on whatever basis, some of the distinctive criteria remain unconscious – as long as we assume that the data are established by persons who themselves speak or at least understand the language in question. It is only in analysing data that we use the criteria consciously. The primary procedures thus correspond by and large to processes of perception.[1] Units (e.g. sounds, words, sentence-constituents, sentences) are abstracted, isolated and classified on various levels; the combination of units on a lower level produces the internal structure of higher units; and these units can be seen, according to their internal structures and structural elements, as related or analogous.

In ordinary language we already use certain more or less systematic operations based on relatedness: deviant utterances are either silently or explicitly corrected by the hearer, and often corrected by the speaker himself. Utterances that remain as a whole not understood are paraphrased and discussed.

[1] Thus Bloomfield (1926) begins his exposition of the basic principles of linguistics with statements like: '**Assumption** 1. Within certain communities successive utterances are alike or partly alike...**Assumption** 4. Different morphemes may be alike or partly alike as to vocal features...**Assumption** 8. Different non-minimum forms may be alike or partly alike as to the order of the constituent forms and as to the stimulus–reaction features corresponding to this order.'

10.2   Analogy, comparison, and historical reconstruction

In earlier linguistics the establishment of ANALOGIES was considered to be one of the most important methodological steps. Hermann Paul speaks in this connection (1909: ch. v) of 'proportion groups' (*Proportionsgruppen*): *sage* is to *sagte* as *frage* is to *fragte*; *erziehen : Erzieher : Erziehung = entdecken : Entdecker : Entdeckung*; etc.

From such 'concrete models' we can derive 'abstract rules' (so that the linguist in principle proceeds like the language learner). The explicatum for the concept of analogy is thus the concept of linguistic rule: if the elements of a proportion group behave analogously to each other, this means that the same rules (word-formation rules, inflexional rules, phonological rules, etc.) will apply to certain input elements. One of the most important motivations for linguistic change is analogical innovation: a missing member of a proportion will be introduced according to the existing proportion; this can be described as an extension of the applicational domain of a particular rule.

The whole of historical–comparative linguistics rests on the principle of COMPARISON of sound- and word-forms in different languages (known either as spoken languages or through documents). This is the basis for the RECONSTRUCTION OF COMMON PARENT LANGUAGES: from a set of corresponding data in different languages we can infer common parent elements, from which the data (according to language-internal principles of change) can be uniformly derived.[1] This process involves two assumptions, each of which has its quite sensible restrictions.

1. There really exists a common parent language (there must accordingly have been a corresponding speech-community; according to this procedure we must for example introduce a relatively unitary Proto-Indo-European people).

2. The processes of language change can be separated into language-external (e.g. lexical borrowing) and language-internal aspects; the latter can be reconstructed on the basis of linguistic data alone.

Language change is only part of historical change as a whole. Thus the claim for the existence of a real common parent language spoken in a historical community must in any case be supported by other historical facts as well as ethnic, cultural, mythological, etc., evidence. If such

---

[1] For a brief recent exposition of the historical–comparative reconstructive method, together with (even if not very precise) theoretical assumptions, see Hoenigswald (1960); also Anttila (1972); Sturtevant (1968).

support is lacking, one has to give up the claim and look for other possibilities for language-comparison, for example on typological grounds.
There are also linguists who are ready to relativize this notion insofar as
they regard the common parent language merely as a theoretical construct, which only has to represent what the compared data have in
common. This may have methodological advantages with respect to an
attempt to isolate the possible internal basis for linguistic comparison,
but it remains problematical *vis-à-vis* the historical concern.

Historical facts show that some cultural groups and accordingly their
languages are rather isolated for centuries, whereas others are involved in
continuous contacts: though wars between neighbouring tribes, occupa-
tion, development of agriculture and administration under foreign
influence, trade, etc. In accordance with those facts the linguist can set
up hypotheses as to which processes are externally induced or triggered
and which are regular on internal grounds. He can likewise start with
the linguistic data and try to separate out those processes that can
regularly be explained on internal grounds, provided he supports his
findings later on with the data from language contacts.

10.3 Presuppositions for data-exploration

The task of systematic methodical operations is:

1. To translate data which has been rather unsystematically obtained
relative to a problem into linguistic arguments, or to bring it into such
arguments in a clear way. For the explication of particular concepts and
rules the METHOD OF EXAMPLE AND COUNTEREXAMPLE is particularly
important: the one furnishes the clear cases of the application of the
concept (rule), the other the clear cases of non-application. By adducing
as many examples as possible we try to make generalizing statements; by
adducing counterexamples we try to find the precise limitations on
generalizations, to prove that generalization is unobtainable on a given
point.

2. To extend the data-base systematically, i.e. to obtain data bearing
on a problem as comprehensively as possible, and to use it in arguments
for or against particular theoretical decisions.

For each more precise data-exploration there are four main points to
discuss: it is only from this discussion that we can find out what systematic operations it makes sense to use, and what position we should take
vis-à-vis the data we already have or the acquisition of new data.

1. Detailed discussion of the problem, definition of the goals of the investigation.

2. Definition of the data-type and data-base.

3. Setting up of general scientific standards.

4. Setting up of a special theory-form – at least in broad outline – and the theoretical operations to be employed in it.

Ad 1. DEFINITION OF GOALS. Here we must consider empirical, application-oriented and theory-oriented goals. Obviously one investigation cannot achieve all goals; the goals are to be ordered according to their relevance, or one is to be given pre-eminence, while others are neglected.

(a) We may want to discuss and explicate – theoretically – some particular domain of phenomena or individual phenomenon in language and language-use; we can concentrate more on the use of language or more on the possibilities of use (that are systematically laid down in a language). We can call this the SETTING OF EMPIRICAL GOALS.

(b) We may be aiming for particular practical applications: for example, working out therapeutic language pedagogy or methods of language teaching (especially foreign languages) – in both cases the basis is an attempted causal analysis of errors or disorders. Or we may want to work out methods of machine data-processing and machine communication – here the point of departure is a precise analysis of machine capabilities, as well as possibilities for language-standardization. Or we may be interested in outlining strategies for media criticism, education about deceptive language-use, development of consciousness in the public and educational spheres – here we strive for very detailed analyses against a broad theoretical background, without wanting to achieve completeness of data in any one aspect: we are much more interested in typical demonstration-cases, which under the appropriate conditions can be translated into stylized teaching/learning situations. This is the SETTING OF PRACTICAL GOALS.

(c) We may be interested in deciding particular theoretical questions; here too the emphasis is not on breadth or completeness of data, but only on the ability to make decisions in controversial cases. Here we will also have to translate the data into arguments; but they do not lead to a strict and unique decision-procedure. This is the SETTING OF THEORETICAL GOALS.

(d) We may be interested in investigating possible link-ups with neighbouring theories: for example, semantic theory and syntactic theory, semantic theory and psychology of language, semantic–pragmatic theory and sociological theory, synchronic and diachronic grammatical theory, etc. The data should be of such a type that they motivate a unitary interpretation (or at least compatible interpretations) of different theories; the different aspects of the data treated in different theories should be represented for the interpretation of the theories as mutually complementary: i.e. every theory should be developed in regard to the other(s). This is the SETTING OF INTERTHEORETICAL GOALS.

Ad 2. DATA-TYPE AND DATA-BASE. I will treat only a few kinds of data here, mainly those that are relevant for the setting of theoretical and empirical goals (and only contingently for practical purposes, insofar as these are based on empirical or theoretical discussions of a general character):

(a) Statements (perhaps in terms of degree) about the GRAMMATICALITY of complex expressions, especially sentences. For example *Peter is drinking sulphide of mercury* is grammatical in English, *Peter is drinkable sulphide of mercury* isn't; the following sentences are decreasingly grammatical in German:

Du hast ihn doch kommen sehen müssen.
Du hast ihn doch kommen sehen gemußt.
Du hast müssen ihn doch kommen sehen.
Du hast gemußt sehen ihn doch kommen.
Du kommen gemußt ihn doch hast sehen.
('You must have seen him come.')

(b) Statements about the STRUCTURAL ANALYSIS and constituency of individual parts of an expression. For example in *Du hast ihn doch kommen sehen müssen*, *hast* and *müssen* belong together more closely than *kommen* and *müssen*.

(c) Statements that certain expressions are MEANINGLESS (*My linguistics snores*), while others have TRANSFERRED MEANINGS (*That's a lame excuse, What a delicious surprise*), that expressions have SEVERAL well-distinguished meanings (*Visiting relatives can be boring*).

(d) Statements (possibly in terms of degree) about the ACCEPTABILITY of expressions. For example *the monster on the table by the bat-cage's neck-bolt* is less acceptable than *the neck-bolt of the monster on the table by the bat-cage*).

(e) Statements about RELATEDNESS OF MEANING; paraphrase, entailment, presupposition, as well as other sense-relations.

(f) Statements about close or distant relatedness of expressions on the basis of sameness or similarity of structure, similar vocabulary, etc. (i.e. phonological, lexical, morphological, syntactic relatedness).

(g) Statements (possibly in terms of degree) about the ACCEPTABILITY or non-acceptability of utterances in particular contexts (the primary concern here is whether the speaker does or does not fulfil the conventions and obligations arising from the language, the preconditions for action, the institutional context, the perceptual context, the general conditions for cooperation, etc.).

(h) Statements about the FREQUENCY of use of particular expressions or constructions, or about the frequency of certain speech-act types and sequences in particular social contexts.

(i) Statements about the type and frequency of particular linguistic MISTAKES and corrections, typical translation-errors, etc.

(j) Statements about typical CHANGES in the repetition of previously heard utterances, in retelling of stories, etc.

Ad 3. SCIENTIFIC STANDARDS. We must establish the extent to which the investigation is to be regarded as descriptive (including classification and partial generalization) or explanatory (of the facts or the data they represent).

How much abstraction and idealization is allowed ? What degree of explicitness (and perhaps formalization) do we want ? How can we find the most economical (simple) formal notation, what kind of logical language should we choose ? How can we guarantee the testability of theoretical statements ? The more empirical work there is in a given domain, the higher the claims to scientific status that we can make. It would not be expedient to make equally strong theoretical claims for all investigations, because we can often justify them only at the expense of the empirical claims, e.g. with a degree of idealization that makes the original problem unrecognizable. Different theoretical requirements can thus conflict, so that we have to find a reasonable pragmatic compromise. Not all investigations require that we make the highest claims to explicitness and formalization. The particular claim that is to be made depends on the goals, the type and complexity of the data, and the steps that are necessary for acquiring and exploring the data.

Ad 4. SPECIAL THEORY-FORM. In most areas of linguistics the appropriate theory-forms still have to be found, i.e. we cannot presuppose a particular one for the investigation. Only in the very narrow area of grammatical and phonological research is the contemporary situation such that we can choose between competing theory-forms, according to the aspect of primary interest. In the framework of TRANSFORMATIONAL GENERATIVE GRAMMAR, what is primarily to be explicated is the syntactic relatedness of sentences belonging to a syntactic paraphrase-class; subject and object sentence-embeddings are especially easy to treat, while there are difficulties with adverbials, comparatives, nominalizations, quantified noun phrases and relative clauses. In the framework of a MIXED ADJUNCTION-GRAMMAR (Joshi 1969) we can easily distinguish different kinds of syntactic expansions of sentences (e.g. expansions inside noun phrases as well as relative clause embeddings, as against subject and object complements). With a CATEGORIAL GRAMMAR we can easily capture the role of syntactic constructions for the constitution of sentence meanings. If we want to compare construction-forms according to the syntactic (and indirectly, the semantic) roles they play in the positions they appear in, certain forms of DEPENDENCY GRAMMAR, for example as proposed by Fillmore (1968) or Anderson (1971) are preferable. Of course, if we are interested in the interpretation of sentences, these grammars can probably be formulated still more explicitly in the form of a categorial grammar.

I will not go into the advantages and disadvantages of the recognized types of grammatical theories, but only note (a) that they do not make identical theoretical claims and (b) that they cannot all capture all syntactic–semantic phenomena and relations equally well. We can only compare grammatical theories point by point,[1] even if we can show in individual simple cases that they represent in principle equivalent formalizations (equivalent with respect to the sentences treated, but not in terms of the structures assigned to them). We are thus fully justified in preferring one of these theories for particular purposes, even if it is less useful for others. Partee (1975) has recently tried to extend Montague's grammatical theory (which permits a clear assignment of semantic interpretation, and basically represents a modification of categorial grammar) with transformations; this could combine the advantages of Montague grammar and transformational grammar.

On the basis of discussions like those cited, we obtain more precise criteria for conducting methodological–heuristic arguments, for the direction and criteria for extending the data-base, and for what systematic operations we should carry out in order to make the data available for particular arguments. There are as yet only a few investigations that expressly reflect this methodological–heuristic process, mainly in reference to transformational grammar (e.g. Postal 1974; Huber & Kummer 1973; Botha 1970, 1973; Itkonen 1976).

[1] See for example Hirschman (1971) for a comparison of categorial grammars, phrase-structure grammars, mixed adjunction grammars and a Harris-type operator grammar. She compares them from several points of view, but mainly how and to what extent transformations can be formulated in them.

10.4   Data-collection and data-processing

I will mention five important types of data-collection and processing, which are distinguished mainly by their theoretical orientation:

1. SEGMENTATION AND CLASSIFICATION: the two most important procedures in American structuralism. The theoretical claim here is comparatively small; the goal is a coherent description of expression-classes and their combinatory possibilities in the sentences of a given language.[1] We begin with a collection of data in a corpus (the manner of collection is irrelevant: we can treat utterance-tokens of particular speakers, or a number of grammatically classified sentences or text-fragments). Then we segment the material, i.e. establish units and identify them by position on the various distinguishable levels (sound, morpheme, sentence-constituent, sentence). In order to group the units into classes, we check them for substitutability in identical environments. (Substitutability means in the first instance that the result of a substitution likewise occurs in the corpus; but it can also mean that even if the result does not occur in the corpus, it could, e.g. if it is a grammatical sentence of the language.) If two units are mutually substitutable, they are equivalent; all equivalent units are grouped in classes. The classes can still be extended, insofar as we can adduce combinations of expressions substitutable for individual expressions (units). Every sentence (text) finally represents a sequence of units from particular classes; it can thus be represented by a sequence of the corresponding class-symbols. In testing for substitutability the point of departure is the data collected in the corpus: later this is expanded, under certain conditions, in order to discover further combinatorial possibilities (i.e. the classification procedure itself motivates an extension of the data-base); in addition the corpus is often normalized, in order to achieve meaningful results (i.e. mainly normalizations from the morphological point of view, or on the basis of permutation, which lead to a normal word-order). Segmentation and classification are generally not to be understood as strict procedures, but as controlled within a set of further criteria. This establishes the intersubjective validity of the results; though of course these further criteria are often left to the linguist's intuition.

2. SYSTEMATIC ARRANGEMENT AND MODIFICATION OF DATA ALONG THE

---

[1] There is so much literature on the methods of American structuralism (and its European variants) that it would be superfluous to mention it here. I will mention only one paper of Harris' (1946), which demonstrates the method clearly on English and Hidatsa, in such a way that its value can be seen from a comparative point of view.

LINES OF THEORETICAL ARGUMENTS. In this case our basis is not a pre-existing corpus, which is (putatively) to be described completely; rather we normally adduce only those data – often produced on the basis of the investigator's linguistic knowledge – that are relevant to a particular empirical–theoretical question. The set of data can be freely expanded at every stage. The modifications of the data (e.g. in reference to the question of whether the results will be grammatical forms of the language) are completely directed by the theoretical operations provided for in the grammar. Later on (10.8) I will discuss a few such operations in reference to example sentences. In addition (10.9) I will briefly discuss Harris' different versions of the concept of transformation, which will furnish a good example of the extent to which theoretical developments influence systematic operations. Finally (10.10) I will discuss one of the typical arguments used by Chomsky and other grammarians to justify a level of syntactic deep structure.

3. SYSTEMATIC DEVELOPMENT OF A GRAMMAR OF A LANGUAGE-FRAGMENT. The various components of a grammar (i.e. its phonological, syntactic and semantic rules) are interdependent. The transformational grammarians (cf. especially Chomsky & Halle 1968) first did away with the autonomy of phonological rules by making the input to the phonological component the output of the syntactic component. Then the generative semanticists and Montague abolished the respective autonomies of syntax and semantics. In order to make the study of interdependencies more comprehensive, and eliminate possible gaps in our knowledge and sources of inconsistency, we want to explicate the rules as fully as possible. Since it is senseless (if not impossible) to try and reconstruct the whole grammar of a language in all its aspects, we base our investigation on a certain bounded fragment; but this has to be studied exhaustively. The choice of the fragment is directed by the theoretical goal, and by the extent to which particular phenomena can be successfully handled within the theory. Thus the set of data depends on the possibilities of theory-construction, though in principle it can be freely expanded. Syntactic and semantic data relevant to a common core of phenomena are always involved; phonological data usually are as well.

4. COMPUTER-SIMULATION OF THEORETICAL RULES. A theoretical grammar will claim for example that it characterizes all and only the grammatical (or meaningful) sentences of a language; i.e. the theoretical operations must be so constrained as to produce only the desired results. The discussion of examples and counterexamples, together with the

corresponding systematic modifications of the examples, does not easily lead to a comprehensive test of whether or not this claim is fulfilled. Therefore we simulate the theoretical rules in a computer program, which randomly generates arbitrary artificial data.[1] We can then check to see whether this corresponds to naturally obtained (or obtainable) data. If we translate it back into the language in which our data originated, we can handle it like any other data. If an artificial datum says 'According to the rules r_1, ..., r_n the sentence A is derivable', we can for instance ask whether 'Sentence A is grammatical in L' represents a datum that we would accept on the basis of our linguistic knowledge. If not, then the theoretical rules are clearly in need of revision.

5. COMPREHENSIVE ANALYSIS OF A COMPLETE DOMAIN OF RELATED DATA. It is a common practice of theoretically oriented linguists to neglect all those data which cannot be treated within a given framework. If one wants, however, to search for new theoretical insights and to fill hitherto existing knowledge-gaps, it is useful to base the analysis on an almost complete domain of related data, e.g. all the utterances of a three-year-old child during a week, or all the utterances produced in a school class for a day, or within the first five minutes of a collection of interviews, or all verbs in a language (cf. Gross 1975, in French), or all speech-act designating verbs in a language (cf. Berliner Gruppe 1975, in German). Clearly, this kind of work involves a quite extensive corpus, and cannot usually be done without the aid of a computer. The aim is to categorize each entry in the light of a particular theoretical purpose.

10.5   Excursus 1: General remarks on formal languages

Theoretical operations in linguistics are to be understood in the formal algebraic sense. What is meant is operations defined on special algebraic structures, called FORMAL LANGUAGES. Formal languages are merely sets of uninterpreted strings of symbols; a corresponding grammar specifies which strings constructed out of a particular vocabulary of symbols belong to the formal language, and which do not: in other words, the grammar establishes the structure of those strings belonging to the language. In a somewhat more general notion of formal language, we could also regard other ABSTRACT CONCATENATION STRUCTURES as elements of a formal language: e.g. strings of matrices, labelled trees, or

---

[1] There is a program for testing transformational grammars, formulated on the basis of Chomsky's (1965) version: Friedman (1971).

labelled bracketings. Reference to appropriate formal languages plays a considerable role in linguistic notation: strings of matrices are used for example in phonology and syntax for the combination of particular feature-complexes; labelled trees or (essentially equivalent) labelled bracketings are used in syntax and semantics; even logical languages are formal languages in this sense. Nonetheless formal languages can be developed at the outset with no reference to the requirements of linguistics or logic; there is no specific interpretation initially bound up with the formal strings of symbols. It is rather the case that arbitrary interpretations are possible in all domains where such concatenation-structures play a role (e.g. musical notation, machine-codes, organization programs, gene structures, etc.).

I must therefore emphasize that formal languages and the grammars that go with them cannot count as explications of the linguistic notions of 'language' and 'grammar': particular forms of notation developed in this connection represent NEITHER A CONCEPTUAL EXPLICATION NOR A LINGUISTIC RECONSTRUCTION NOR A THEORY in any sense whatever. The distinction between formal languages and, for example, logical languages is however often insufficiently observed; in particular some linguists have mistakenly assumed that a formal grammar in the above sense is already a reconstruction of a natural-language grammar. This is to take a purely formal-syntactic position: the function of a grammar of a natural language is simply to characterize which combinations of expressions are well-formed from a syntactic (and only syntactic) point of view. This position as we have seen is taken by Chomsky, for instance,[1] as well as other mathematically oriented linguists. The other grammar types mentioned above (adjunction grammars, categorial grammars) are also frequently interpreted in this formal-syntactic sense. I want to take a different position here: by GRAMMAR OF A NATURAL LANGUAGE I understand the totality of those rules which allow us to understand which meanings can be expressed in which expressions, i.e. what relations exist between (abstraction-)classes of sound-forms and possible meanings (in all the various versions of this concept).

In order to make my position clearer, I will return to some earlier reflections. I have argued that the processes of natural-language argumentation can be at least partly reconstructed in a logical system. Every logic presupposes a particular logical language; particular logical

---

[1] Cf. ch. 8 above. I attempted to show there that Chomsky cannot manage his explication of 'grammatical in L' without recourse to semantics.

languages likewise induce particular logics, i.e. particular types of inference. I have argued further that conceptual explications are generally carried out within a theoretical language, so that under particular assumptions a theoretical language can be identified with a logical language. We can indeed understand a logical language as a special instance of a formal language; but this is only a partial characterization. I have argued that we always mean by a logical language one that has, from the outset, both a syntax and a semantics; we can understand these languages, i.e. they are not initially uninterpreted. Only in syntax and semantics (as parts of metalogic) are these aspects treated separately. The most characteristic property of logical languages is that the notion of syntactic derivation (a purely formal operation on expressions) largely corresponds to the notion of logical consequence (in simple logics it even corresponds in a strong sense). In order to talk about semantic connections, it thus suffices to some extent to discuss the corresponding formal operations on the sentences of the language. ALL MEANINGFUL FORMAL OPERATIONS IN LOGIC HAVE THEIR SEMANTIC EQUIVALENTS; this is precisely the way these languages are constructed. The situation in formal languages is different: here formal operations generally have no initial semantic equivalent, and even for particular interpretations of the language it is not necessary to state a semantic equivalent.

Natural languages presumably differ from logical languages in having ALTERNATIVE EXPRESSIONS, namely syntactic paraphrases, which are distinct neither in meaning nor in the relevant lexical material (except for pure function-words), but are distinct in syntactic form; there are no such alternatives in logical languages (mutually equivalent expressions contain different constituent expressions, e.g. connectives or quantifiers). This however only justifies the use of purely syntactic means of explication FOR THESE CASES: e.g. syntactic transformations which are not semantically meaningful. It does not justify regarding formal languages as appropriate explications for natural languages.

In linguistic reconstruction there are two important goals that have to be distinguished: (a) reconstruction of a particular SCIENTIFIC LANGUAGE (and with it the logic of scientific arguments), and (b) reconstruction of particular PARTS OF THE NATURAL COLLOQUIAL LANGUAGE. In the first case the richness required in the construct language depends on the goals of the scientific language. Thus for instance we can often restrict ourselves to very simple indicative sentences, like those representable in the predicate calculus. In the second case, the richness of the construct language must be such that all important aspects of natural languages can in fact be represented. Now one could object that even in linguistics it is primarily only the scientific language, in which for example the linguistic data are reconstructed, that has to be reconstructed; if we keep only to the syntactic aspect of natural languages, then we only have to reconstruct the observations we make of it; if we deal with other aspects, then likewise only those observations we make there. We could however formulate those observations themselves in a simple language, for example one that the predicate calculus would explicate satisfactorily.

This of course misses two points: first, we cannot formulate complex linguistic relationships in a FUNDAMENTALLY simpler language, although it might succeed, via standardization and more explicit means of expression, in restricting somewhat the richness of natural language; in other words, certain extensions of the predicate calculus (in the directions described earlier) appear to be indispensable. Secondly, our main aim is to elucidate the interdependence of individual aspects of language, especially how the possible meanings of sentences are expressed in various construction forms. If we consider the different aspects in isolation, we achieve this only partially: for we also make observations about ambiguity, relatedness of meaning, etc. These can only be explicated in a language that has both a syntax and a semantics, or by developing together from the outset different formal languages (each for the treatment of one aspect).[1]

Formal languages thus always explicate only the FORMAL SIDE of an aspect of language; the prime candidate for this is natural language syntax, which is obviously already formal. The key to the proper use of formal languages in linguistics is to keep this distinction in mind, i.e. refrain from taking them *per se* as appropriate explications for natural languages. We can then also use formal languages as a means of stating what we want to regard as theoretical operations.

*10.6 Excursus II: Important operations in formal languages

First, a clarification of some algebraic concepts.

A two-place RELATION is a set of ordered pairs (likewise an n-place relation is a set of ordered n-tuples). The domain D of the relation comprises the set of those elements which appear as first coordinates, the

---

[1] Thus even Montague grammar is a system of mutually connected concatenation algebras, i.e. a system of formal languages in our sense, which interpret one another.

range E the set of those elements that appear as second coordinates. A relation is unique if it assigns to every element in the domain exactly one element in the range. Such a relation is also called a FUNCTION from D in E, or a MAPPING from D in E.

A two-place CONNECTION is a function from the product set A × B in the set C (thus a three-place relation); correspondingly an n-place connection is a function from the product of n sets in a further set (thus an (n + 1)-place relation). These are also often called OPERATIONS or TRANSFORMATIONS. We speak of an OPERATOR FUNCTION IN THE STRICT SENSE when we are dealing with a function from A × B in B: we say then that the set A operates on the set B, and A is the operator domain.[1]

Every mapping (or function), as well as every operation in the stricter or looser sense, can be given two fundamentally different interpretations:[2]

1. As RELATIONS between sets of objects which we think of as already present.

2. As INSTRUCTIONS FOR FORMING the objects of a set out of those of another set or sets.

If our goals are constructive, we generally emphasize the second interpretation.

We now consider the simplest case, where the elements of the formal language (its 'sentences' and 'sentence-constituents') are strings consisting only of simple symbols, taken from a particular vocabulary (the set of 'words'). Every language of this type is a subset of the SEMIGROUP (MONOID) over the given vocabulary; the way this set is bounded is determined by the particular grammar we assume. A semigroup S over the vocabulary V is the set of all finite strings of symbols of V, with very simple algebraic properties:

(a) S is closed under the operation of concatenation: if $x \in S$, $y \in S$ and $z = x\,y$, then $z \in S$.

---

[1] In this sense for example adjectives and adverbs can be regarded as operators: an adjective operates on a noun phrase and the result is a noun phrase; the same for adverbs and verb phrases, or adverbs and sentences:

$\langle \text{old}_{Adj}, \text{ my car}_{NP} \rangle \rightarrow \text{my old car}_{NP}$

$\langle \text{quickly}_{Adv}, \text{run}_{VP} \rangle \rightarrow \text{run quickly}_{VP}$

$\langle \text{hopefully}_{Adv}, \text{Karen will come}_{S} \rangle \rightarrow \text{hopefully, Karen will come}_{S}$

We can see, by the way, that these operations cannot be understood purely syntactically because of the different kinds of results we get: the operator can be preposed, interposed, or postposed (cf. the possible reorderings in the last example).

[2] To take a simple example: we can understand multiplication as a relation between the pair of numbers $\langle 2, 3 \rangle$ and the number 6, or as an instruction for constructing a further number, 6, out of the pair $\langle 2, 3 \rangle$.

(b) Concatenation is associative: (x y) z = x(y z).

(c) There is a null string o as identity element: xo = ox = x.

x, y, and z are variables over strings.

The algebraic properties of formal languages are obviously more complex; so we can use these properties as the basis for a partial ordering of the types of formal languages.[1]

In many formal grammars we can distinguish two types of rules:

1. PRODUCTION RULES, which state how certain simple strings ('basic strings') can be formed out of the vocabulary elements.

2. TRANSFORMATIONAL RULES, which state how other strings can be formed out of simple ones by alteration and expansion.

In Chomsky's transformational grammar, this distinction is made in its strict sense; though a wider range of phenomena are treated as the output of the production rules in 1965 than in 1957 (which shows that the decision criteria can vary). Chomsky's production rules are the rules of a phrase-structure grammar: he also uses an auxiliary vocabulary, consisting of symbols for grammatical categories. The production of basic strings also establishes their internal structure.

The production rules of a phrase-structure grammar are either of the form a → x (context-free) or y a z → y x z or equivalently a → x/y __ z (context-sensitive); here a is a single symbol and x, y, z are strings (perhaps null). The symbol on the left always belongs to the auxiliary vocabulary, the one on the right either to the auxiliary vocabulary or the (terminal) vocabulary proper.

EXAMPLES:

1.

Auxiliary vocabulary: {S, NP, VP, Pred, PP}
Vocabulary: {V, N, Art, P, Adj, Cop}
Initial symbol: S
Production rules: 　S → NP Pred
　　　　　　　　　S → NP VP
　　　　　　　NP → Art N
　　　　　　　VP → V
　　　　　　　VP → V NP
　　　　　　　VP → V PP

[1] One of these orderings is called the 'Chomsky Hierarchy' (cf. Chomsky 1959). The standard work on so-called context-free grammars (the most important class of formal languages) is Ginsburg (1966). For a much more detailed account of formal grammars than I can give here, with many linguistically motivated examples, see Kratzer *et al.* (1973).

$$PP \rightarrow P\ NP$$
$$Pred \rightarrow Cop\ NP$$
$$Pred \rightarrow Cop\ PP$$
$$Pred \rightarrow Cop\ Adj$$

The rules are unordered. The first rule to be applied must be the one with 'S' on the left: if there is more than one such rule we have to make a choice. The other rules can then be applied whenever the symbol on their left-hand side has been produced by a previous rule and has not yet been replaced by another symbol. The production of a string is terminated when there are no more symbols left that occur on the left-hand side of a rule.

The sample grammar allows, among others, these productions:

S	S
NP Pred	NP VP
Art N Pred	Art N VP
Art N Cop PP	Art N V NP
Art N Cop P NP	Art N V Art N
Art N Cop P Art N	

The terminal strings contain only vocabulary symbols. The structure of these strings can be represented either by labelled bracketings or tree structures, which can themselves be interpreted from the productions: e.g. the production on the left above can be represented as:

[[Art N]$_{NP}$ [Cop [P [Art N]$_{N\bar{P}}$]$_{PP}$]$_{Pred}$]$_S$

or

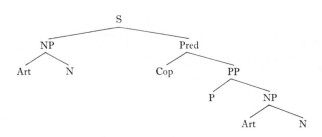

If we interpret the symbols appropriately (e.g. 'Art' as article, 'N' as noun, etc.) we can establish the fact that the grammar characterizes the structures of simple sentences. We can substitute appropriate expressions from a natural language for the symbols, so that the two productions above can be understood as formal characterizations of sentences like *The chicken is in the pot* or *The dog bites a child*.

2. We can take the word (or morpheme) categories as belonging to the auxiliary vocabulary, and the words (or morphemes) themselves as belonging to the terminal vocabulary. In this case the terminal strings produced by the grammar are not the structures of sentences, but the sentences themselves:

Auxiliary vocabulary: {S, NP, VP, Pred, PP, V, N, Art, P, Adj, Cop}
Vocabulary: {the, a chicken, dog, pot, smells, ...}
Initial Symbol: S
Production Rules: as in 1, plus: Art → the

$$\vdots$$

$$V \rightarrow smells$$

$$\vdots$$

$$N \rightarrow chicken...etc.$$

It is obvious that this grammar will produce many ungrammatical sentences (e.g. *A pot smells the child*). Further distinctions have to be introduced, in order to handle (first) case, number and other morphological categories and (second) selectional restrictions, e.g. between *pot* and *smells*. This is why Chomsky (1965) proposed syntactic features and special subcategorization rules to introduce them.

The constructive use of production rules, as described above, represents only one way of formally characterizing a sentence. The following are in principle equivalent formulations for a production rule like S → NP VP:

1. A string of symbols NP VP IS TO BE DESCRIBED AS AN S.

2. Assuming that we understand NP, VP, S as SYMBOLS FOR SETS, there is a function from the product set NP × VP in the set S.

3. If the symbols NP, VP and S are taken as PREDICATE CONSTANTS, then it is the case that: $(x)\,(y)\,(NP(x)\,\&\,VP(y) \supset S(x\,y))$.

4. We can write the rules in the form of SYMBOLS OF A CATEGORIAL GRAMMAR; then the formulation of a single metarule will suffice to establish which concatenations are allowed and what category the resulting string belongs to. This metarule might have the form: an expression of the category X/Y can only be concatenated with an expression of the category Y to its right, and an expression of the

category Y/X only with an expression of the category Y to its left; the result is an X. If we select NP and S as basic categories, then the content of the production rule above can be represented by the statement that NP/S is a category (it stands in place of VP); if we choose VP and S as basic categories, then it suffices to say that S/VP (instead of NP) is a category.

In order to translate the whole sample grammar into a categorial grammar, we must of course introduce further basic categories, since otherwise the structure of NP, for example, would not be expressible. If we take N as a further basic category, we cannot treat an NP to the left of a V in the same way as an NP to the right of a V. This shows that it is impossible to translate the given grammar in this form (i.e. rule for rule) into a categorial grammar. The conditions on a categorial grammar are different from those on a phrase-structure grammar. The basic categories of a categorial grammar are selected partly on semantic grounds; likewise the formal sentence structures represent forms on the basis of which the total meanings of the sentences are to be obtained. Such considerations generally play no role in the justification of the rules of a phrase-structure grammar; therefore it is not surprising that we cannot reformulate an arbitrarily constructed phrase-structure grammar as a categorial grammar.

Productions like those of our sample grammar give the forms of simple sentences, often called KERNEL SENTENCE STRUCTURES (or the kernel sentences themselves). TRANSFORMATIONAL RULES must be applied in order to obtain complex sentence-forms. Every transformation can be understood as a RELATION BETWEEN LABELLED TREES or a RELATION BETWEEN LABELLED BRACKETINGS.[1] In certain cases we can disregard the structure of the strings; then we can regard transformations as relations merely between strings of symbols. (Every relation of one of these kinds can, as already suggested, also be taken as a direction for construction.) If the result of a transformation must be uniquely defined, we must have functions (or mappings); if we have to be able to get back from the result of a transformation to its input structure or string, we must have reversible functions, i.e. bi-unique relations.

Many transformations effect different changes or expansions of an initial string simultaneously. We can take the active–passive transformation as an example: *I saw him* ⇒ *He was seen by me*. There are reorderings, morphological changes and expansions. The attempt has often

---

[1] The first notion (trees) has been mathematically investigated by Ginsburg & Partee (1969); the second (bracketings) by Peters & Ritchie (1969). It turns out that they are not fully equivalent for the formulation of transformations.

been made to take transformations of this kind as composed of elementary transformations; some of the most important of these are:

1. UNARY TRANSFORMATIONS (to be understood as two-place relations).
(a) DELETION: a part of a string (structure) is deleted, e.g.

   a b c d → a b d
(b) PERMUTATION: two parts of a string (structure) change position, or all parts change their positions (whereby some parts can also retain their original positions), e.g.

   a b c d → d a c b
(c) REPETITION (copying): a part of a string (structure) is repeated in a particular position, e.g.

   a b c d → c a b c d
   a b c d → a b b c d

2. BINARY TRANSFORMATIONS (to be understood as three-place relations).
(d) SUBSTITUTION: a portion of a string (structure) is replaced by something else; special case: the substituendum is of the same category as the substituens, e.g.

   $\langle$e, a b c d$\rangle$ → a b e d
   $\langle e_B, [a\ b\ c_B\ d]_A \rangle$ → $[a\ b\ e_B\ d\ ]_A$
(e) ADDITION: two substrings (substructures) are concatenated, e.g.

   $\langle$a b c, d e f$\rangle$ → a b c d e f
(f) CONJUNCTION (a four-place relation): two substrings (substructures) of the same category are conjoined by means of an additional symbol, e.g.

   $\langle g, [a\ b\ c]_A, [d\ e\ f\ ]_A \rangle$ → $[a\ b\ c\ g\ d\ e\ f]_A$
(g) EXTERNAL ADJUNCTION (operator function in the strict sense): the addition of a substring yields a total string of the same category, e.g.

   $\langle d, [a\ b\ c]_A \rangle$ → $[d\ a\ b\ c]_A$
(h) INTERNAL ADJUNCTION, e.g.

   $\langle d, a\ b_A\ c \rangle$ → a $[d\ b]_A$ c

All these transformations are still insufficiently characterized from the mathematical point of view (e.g. we still have to state which position is to be deleted or replaced, formulate conditions for reversibility, etc.; with respect to structures there are obviously many more possibilities of alteration, each dependent on what initial structures can appear). The enumeration is merely an illustration.

*10.7   Recursiveness in formal grammars

It is said that natural languages can make infinite use of finite means; we can reconstruct this property formally by means of rules that can reapply to their own outputs (i.e. a particular kind of recursive definition). The following examples make it clear that an object complement sentence can be added to another object complement, a relative clause to another relative clause, a noun to another noun (possibly with preposition), a conjunction to another conjunction:

> I asked him whether he knew that Peter had said that he believed that...
> I saw a man go up to the house that stood on the corner where...
> I was tired, which meant that I couldn't work, which led to...
> I will begin the preliminaries to the discussion about the implementation of the measures for the prevention of...
> I see a man and a woman and another man and...

(there can also be mixed forms).

In logical languages recursiveness is achieved for example in the following way:

> If p and q are sentences of L, then p & q is also a sentence of L (and now if r is a sentence of L, then so is p & q & r, etc.).

In a phrase-structure grammar with transformations we can introduce recursiveness either in the production rules or the transformations:

$$S \to S \text{ and } S \qquad \text{OR} \qquad \langle \text{and, S, S} \rangle \to S \text{ and } S$$

Harris, and Chomsky in his earlier works (e.g. 1957b), chose the second way, and not only for this case, but generally (thus we get ternary transformations; Harris divides them into further classes – differently in his various works – while Chomsky introduces them unitarily as GENERALIZED TRANSFORMATIONS). The basis in both cases is a very restricted set of kernel sentence-forms, which Harris introduces by enumeration, and Chomsky by production rules.[1]

On the basis of the above, it is clear that transformations can CHANGE MEANING, since every sentence expansion introduces new lexical items and new meaningful connections. Only later (1965) – following Katz & Postal (1964) – did Chomsky introduce a new restriction, with the aim of stabilizing his concept of deep structure (as representing a paraphrase

---

[1] I will consider additional – and more important – differences between Harris' and Chomsky's ideas in 10.9 below.

class): only paraphrastic (i.e. non-meaning-changing) transformations were admitted. Recursivity must now be introduced in the production rules.

In order to characterize SUBJECT and OBJECT COMPLEMENTS, we could for instance use the following rules:

(1) $S \rightarrow NP\ VP$
(2) $VP \rightarrow V\ NP$
(3) $NP \rightarrow S$
(4) $NP \rightarrow Art\ N$

Rule (3) contains the symbol 'S' on the right, which appears on the left in (1); thus the first rule must always be applied again if (3) is applied. This obviously opens the way to arbitrary repetitions of rule-applications; the iteration is broken only when all NPs are expanded by rule (4).

In a similar (but formally distinct) way we must also produce other kinds of iterable sentence embeddings (and in general iterable sentence expansions) in the base structures. In the case of RELATIVE CLAUSES, to take only one example, the following versions have been proposed, which differ with respect to the treatment of the internal structure of the clause (especially the relative pronoun: cf. Partee 1972):

EXAMPLE: *The child who is playing in the garden = A.*

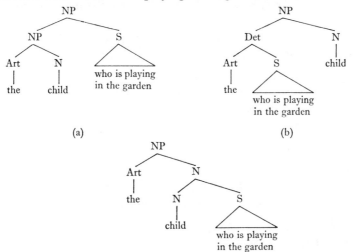

From a semantic point of view these versions each express something different. In (a), the meaning of *the child* is part of the meaning of A (this could hold for the non-restrictive reading *the child, who by the way*

is playing in the garden); in (b), the meaning of *the, who is playing in garden* is part of the meaning of A (whatever this means); in (c), the meaning of *child who is playing in the garden* is part of the meaning of A (this could hold for the restrictive reading *that child who is playing in the garden*; the article can be freely combined in this version, which would allow parallel cases like *all children who . . ., several children who . . .*, etc.).

Even if we find some way of distinguishing formally between subject and object complements on the one hand and relative clauses on the other, how do we treat cases like *the fact that the child is playing in the garden*, or iterable constructions like *the preliminaries to the discussion about the implementation* ? There is a whole set of problems of this kind in phrase-structure grammars with transformations that are barely explicable formally, or explicable only with great difficulty; especially if we require that the formal structures also be consistently interpretable.

10.8　An example of the systematic modification of a sentence

It is clear that we can derive a number of operations for the systematic alteration and expansion of expressions from the formal operations we have considered. The systematic operations however must be performed on the expressions of a particular language, not on uninterpreted strings of symbols; the results must also be interpretable in a particular way, i.e. we have to consider not only the formal change achieved by the operation, but also the change in content. We can classify the operations according to what syntactic and/or semantic changes they effect (e.g. meaning-preserving vs. meaning-changing, where the former could mean that the expression of particular facts remains unchanged).

We can illustrate the role of systematic operations briefly by a few alterations of the sentence

(5) Nina kisses me.

The factual content that (5) expresses naturally depends on the interpretation of *me*, which in turn depends on the situation of utterance. By deletion we get (6) below, by permutation we get (7), by substitution (8)–(10):

(6) Nina kisses.
(7) Me, Nina kisses.
(8) Nina kisses Emil.
(9) Emil kisses me.
(10) Nina bites me.

(5) is partially hyponymous to (6); the reverse naturally does not hold. (Along these lines we could test to see under what conditions deletions yield expressions which are semantically entailed by the original expression.) (7) is synonymous with (5) where there is contrastive stress on *me* in (5); otherwise (7) in any case expresses the same factual content as (5), i.e. both sentences are extensionally the same just in case the extension of *me* is the same. (Along these lines we could test the extent to which permutation yields syntactic paraphrases, and what intensional changes it produces.)[1] (8) and (5) are extensionally the same just in case (5) is uttered in a particular situation by Emil; of course he could not utter (8) in that situation (so it is somewhat difficult to take both sentences as synonymous here). (9) designates a very similar factual content to (5), but not identical in the two cases (assuming that Nina and Emil are not the same person). (10) in special situations can designate the same state of affairs as (5); though from another point of view: thus they are in no case synonymous.

Substitution represents one of the most important systematic procedures in the structuralist programme; the aim of course is solely to discover classes of expressions corresponding to their possible syntactic positions (thus e.g. *kisses* and *bites* belong to the same expression-class). We can however go further and test for semantic relationships. In the case of substitution these are of course different in each of the examples.

Further interesting alterations of (5) lead to the following:

(11) It's Nina who kisses me.
(12) The one who kisses me is Nina.
(13) Nina does kiss me.
(14) I am kissed by Nina.
(15) Nina gives me a kiss.
(16) I get a kiss from Nina.

Given constant extension for *me*, (11)–(16) express the same factual content; under certain assumptions (11)–(14) can be regarded as syntactic paraphrases of (5), but hardly (15) (the verb is *give* instead of *kiss*, the semantic content of *kiss* is transferred to the direct object), and certainly not (16) (the lexical material again is changed in a similar way). (11) is synonymous with (5) if *Nina* bears contrastive stress in (5). (12) and (13) are to be understood similarly to (11), but presuppose a different context. Whether passives like (14) are synonymous to the corre-

---

[1] This holds particularly for languages like German that allow free word-order.

sponding actives is at least disputable. In any case however (15) and (5) as well as (16) and (14) are respectively synonymous, though (16) is not a passive of (15) but rather contains a lexical converse (*get* instead of *give*). None of the sentences (11)–(16) stands in any of the elementary formal relations to (5); to produce (11)–(13) we need certain repetitions, as well as still further substitutions (*who* or *the one* for *Nina*), and in cases like (12) we also need permutation. The active–passive relation in (14) vs. (5) and the converseness-relation in (16) vs. (15) are expressed partly by permutation, though there is morphological change as well, etc.

There are many possible expansions for simple sentences like (5); none of these however is either synonymous to or a syntactic paraphrase of (5) – though some of them, under certain conditions, retain the same extension as (5). Let us consider some of these possible expansions:

(17) Nina kisses me and not Peter.
(18) Nina kisses and bites me.
(19) Your friend Nina kisses me.
(20) The Nina who is kissing me is sweet.
(21) Nina kisses me on the forehead.
(22) Nina kisses me sweetly.
(23) When Nina kisses me, she often bites.
(24) Nina kisses me to cheer me up.
(25) Nina kisses the boy she met yesterday.
(26) Nina kisses me, which astonishes me.
(27) Nina kisses me astonishingly.
(28) Nina wants to kiss me.
(29) Nina has promised to kiss me.
(30) I perceive that Nina is kissing me.
(31) The way Nina kisses me is beautiful.
(32) Nina's kissing (me) cheers me up.

The formal alterations can be described in terms of conjunctions, additions and adjunctions; we also have permutations and occasional morphological changes. Most of the alterations are formally very complex; it is not easy to describe them in terms of elementary alterations (especially if the result of each elementary operation has to be interpretable). This has led (among other things) to the search for 'normalized' forms for sentences of this type, which are theoretically easier to handle (e.g. for (17), if *me* and *Peter* are stressed: *Nina kisses me, and/but Nina doesn't kiss Peter*; for (26) *Nina kisses me. This astonishes me*; for

(29): *Nina has promised that she will kiss me*). But it is still not clear which of the expansions should be explicated by production rules and which by transformations. Explication of the whole set of possibilities for alteration in an interconnected and open system is obviously not to be achieved at one go. Therefore the first thing to do is look at only a few possibilities, not only on the grounds of their formal relatedness (which would tempt one to treat (21) and (22), (24) and (26), (29) and (30) together, even though the problems they raise are in part quite different); but rather also on the grounds of conceptual relatedness. For example (20) and (30)–(32) partially presuppose (5), but (28) and (29) do not; (17)–(19), (21), (22), (24), (26) and (27) are partially hyponymous to (5); in (21) *on the forehead* is to be understood extensionally, but in (22) *sweetly* is to be understood intensionally (we could also say *Nina kisses me. In this way she is sweet*, but nothing like this in the case of (21)); the second part of (24) mentions an intention of Nina's, but the second part of (26) is a speaker's comment, and so on.

10.9 Harris' concept of transformation

The systematic development of methodical operations in syntax is partly due to Harris' work in the 1950s and 1960s.[1] But this work, from the beginning, shows hardly any evidence of a precise theoretical position. In any case Harris does not develop operations on the basis of theoretical notions, in order to serve with the help of data in making particular theoretical decisions, but rather the reverse: he states his operations as heuristic procedures. They are used for the analysis of sentences, so that the analyses can serve as a basis for discovering corresponding theoretical operations. In addition, certain practical tasks are foregrounded from the beginning.

The University of Pennsylvania's *Discourse Analysis* project plays an important part in this: its task was to provide a systematic characterization of texts on the basis of their information-content (no doubt the background to this is practical problems of document storage and information retrieval). The basic idea of the procedure is described in Harris' paper 'Discourse analysis' (1952: cf. the criticism of its theoreti-

[1] Harris' most important papers are collected in Harris (1970). There is also a selection of his later papers, with commentaries and various works influenced by him and proposing applications, in Plötz (1972). In his introduction Plötz gives a good outline of the development of Harris' position. The more systematic compilation of the different kinds of operations in Plötz (1971) is also useful.

cal defects in Bierwisch 1965). In order for the classical methods of segmentation and classification to be carried out, the sentences of a text have to be regularized in certain ways: this is to reduce the complexity and irregularity of the sentences, conditioned for instance by particular kinds of textual connections. Harris called these procedures TRANS-FORMATIONS. The requirements imposed on transformations derived primarily from the practical task: (a) the morphemic content was to remain unaltered; (b) the result of a transformation had to be substitutable for the original sentence in the text; (c) the grammatical relations had to be essentially preserved (this requirement is the one most in need of explanation: what was meant, rather, was that the role of particular expressions for the constitution of sentence-meaning was not to be changed, e.g. the logical subject in the original sentence should also appear as logical subject in the transform, etc.).

In other works Harris has modified and specified the general requirements on transformations as SYSTEMATIC PROCEDURES; he has also undertaken a series of theoretical clarifications, in which transformations come increasingly to be regarded as THEORETICAL OPERATIONS. On the basis of such clarifications Harris was able to distinguish a number of classes of transformations – though the theoretical form of a grammar as a whole was still unclear. He first proposed a very simple STRING GRAMMAR, which however failed to capture important structural connections. A further development by Joshi led to the adjunction-grammars mentioned earlier. The concept of transformation was taken up in a very different way by Chomsky: for him transformations are theoretical operations which can be defined on the basis of a phrase-structure grammar.

In the development of Harris' concept of transformation we can trace four further positions:[1]

1. Transformations are defined as RELATIONS OVER CLASSES OF SENTENCES. Since only sentences that have the same form (grammatical structure) comprise a class, every individual transformation can be regarded as a relation between particular sentence forms. The criteria are:

(a) The corresponding sentences of the domain and range must display the same selectional (co-occurrence) restrictions between their constituent expressions.

(b) Difference in meaning is allowed only insofar as it is effected by the different grammatical constructions.

---

[1] These are represented in the following papers: 1. in Harris (1957); 2. in Harris (1957, 1965); 3. in Harris (1964); 4. in Harris (1969).

(c) Any ordering of the sentences of a class according to their acceptability (naturalness, normalcy, deviance, marginality) must be the same for the domain and range (this is clearly a pragmatic criterion).

2. The basis is a FINITE SET OF KERNEL SENTENCE-FORMS; all other sentence-forms can be obtained by transformations (taken here as constructional directions). The set of kernel sentence-forms in English is variously defined; in Harris (1957) it contains the following: N v V, N v V P N, N v V N, N *is* N, N *is* A, N *is* P N, N *is* D (where 'N' = noun phrase, 'V' = verb, 'P' = preposition, 'A' = adjective, 'D' = adverb of a particular kind, and 'v' = the tense morpheme).

3. All transformations are regarded as PRODUCTS OF particular ELEMENTARY TRANSFORMATIONS.

4. The basis is an information-bearing semantic system of predications and operator functions (which is used in a rather problematical way that does justice neither to logical requirements nor to the richness of natural language). Three kinds of transformations are distinguished: (a) INCREMENT or OPERATOR TRANSFORMATIONS which derive complex predicate expressions from simple ones (they are thus relations between proposition-like objects); (b) MORPHOPHONEMIC TRANSFORMATIONS, which can derive the sentences of the language from predicate expressions; (c) a set of PARAPHRASTIC TRANSFORMATIONS, which can derive a set of paraphrase sentences from sentences. In a derived sense, then, there are particular transformational relations between sentences which are not paraphrases of each other, namely (a' in the example below) if the predicate expressions in them are related by increment transformations:

EXAMPLE:

I will leave this brief discussion here. It must be clear now that Harris finally regarded his concept of transformation as theoretical. The theoretical claim is of course much weaker than Chomsky's: Harris gives an outline rather than an explicit formulation of a theory. Thus the concept of transformation is not precisely defined, but only formulated in various ways by means of examples; the degree of generalization and abstraction remains slight; Harris is concerned almost exclusively with the grammar of English, and does not discuss linguistic universals and the general form of grammatical theory; he remains essentially on a descriptive level, and does not attempt to formulate and apply (as operational criteria) criteria for empirical adequacy. For this reason the style of argument is very informal, e.g. there is no discussion of examples and counterexamples to justify particular theoretical explications.

On the other hand Harris' conception is superior to Chomsky's in a number of ways: he avoids ambitious theoretical speculation (which always runs the risk of vacuity); his point of view is consistently descriptive; he proceeds from observations or test-results rather than from an analysis of speakers' intuitive knowledge; the basis (at least in the last modification) is a system of semantic information (even if wholly extensional), and not an abstract syntax. In addition, Harris can handle many problems better with increment or operator transformations than Chomsky can with the production rules of a phrase-structure grammar (e.g. adverbial constructions, comparatives, nominalizations). And finally Harris develops numerous test-operations (represented as special transformations) which are both heuristically and pedagogically useful.

The most important difference between Chomsky's concept of transformation and Harris' is that for Chomsky transformations are RELATIONS BETWEEN STRUCTURES (or classes of structures), but never between sentences. Let us assume that sentences a and b are syntactic paraphrases. Harris would represent this relation in the form of a transformation (let us call it an H-transformation) which operates on the sentence-forms of a or b. Chomsky would try to formulate a common deep structure, from which both the sentence-forms of a and b would be derivable (a C-transformation). Let this common deep structure be P_1. The most important requirement on P_1 is that it must explicitly represent certain information common to sentences a and b. (In addition P_1 must be producible by means of the production rules of a phrase-structure grammar.) Now if from this point of view sentence a is already more explicit than b, then P_1 is to be so defined that its form is more similar to that of a than that of b; the form of a is then derivable in fewer transformational steps than that of b. Let the form (or surface structure) of a be P_n^a, and that of b be P_m^b. Then for each one we must formulate a sequence of transformations that will convert P_1 stepwise into P_n^a or P_m^b; the first parts of these sequences can be identical:

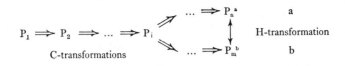

10.10 A Chomskyan argument for deep structures

Finally I will discuss one of Chomsky's central arguments, which has been used in a number of forms to establish the need for deep structures.

1. Given two sentences with the same constructional form (surface structure) – which may under certain conditions differ minimally in lexical material – we cannot draw any conclusion as to how these sentences are related to others that derive from them by the same kind of alteration of form: in one case we might get paraphrases, in another we might not. In general: TWO SENTENCES OF THE SAME FORM CAN BELONG TO TOTALLY DIFFERENT PARAPHRASE-CLASSES.[1]

2. The surface forms of sentences often contain only implicitly information needed to decide which other sentences are paraphrases of them. This information must be made explicit in the corresponding deep structures.

Along with this argument there is a similar one which Chomsky used as early as 1957: there are ambiguous sentences, whose ambiguity cannot be traced either to the ambiguity of the lexical items in them or different analyses of the surface constituent structure (e.g. *Flying planes can be dangerous*: either the planes are flying, or they are being flown). This ARGUMENT FROM CONSTRUCTIONAL AMBIGUITY is of course not very fruitful from a systematic point of view, because it gives us no indication of what form the corresponding deep structures might have. In the other argument a deep structure is defined from the outset as a representative of a paraphrase-class, in which all important information is explicit and from which all members of the paraphrase-class should be derivable by as few general transformations as possible.

Chomsky's example sentences (1965: 22) are:

A. I persuaded a specialist to examine John.
B. I persuaded John to be examined by a specialist.
C. I expected a specialist to examine John.
D. I expected John to be examined by a specialist.

---

[1] The argument could also be carried out so that in the one case the result is a paraphrase, and in the other an ungrammatical sentence. In the following longer example I will treat this modification as well.

The argument can be divided into three steps:

(a) The sentences A and C, B and D have the same surface forms, with different lexis; the same relation R holds between A and B, and between C and D.

(b) C is true if and only if D is true; A and B however can be true or false independently of each other. It follows from this that the relation R has no unitary semantic function (in one case it is – extensionally – meaning-preserving, in the other it is meaning-changing). The relations between the surface forms of the sentences can thus not be elucidated satisfactorily.

(c) The different semantic functions of R come about as follows: in A and B the grammatical subject of the complement of *persuade* is the same as the logical subject (*specialist*, *John* respectively), while in C and D the logical subject is the same in both cases (*specialist*). The deep structure must show which expression fills the role of logical subject: C and D have the same deep structure, but not A and B. The role of grammatical subject is determined by particular transformations (here passivization in the complement). This naturally assumes that the complements of *persuade* and *expect* are regarded as embedded object sentences; since it only makes sense to speak of grammatical and logical subjects and the application of the passive transformation with respect to sentences. The likeness of the respective surface forms is to a certain extent merely an accidental result of the reduction of the embedded sentence. But on the basis of the semantics of *persuade* and *expect* we nevertheless understand (in the sense of deep structure) the same surface forms as having different meanings.

This argument, which I give here in more detail than Chomsky does, uses explicitly semantic considerations, which naturally depend on prior theoretical decisions, among others these: an important intersentential relationship, to be explicated in the grammar, is PARAPHRASE (of course this is explicated here only insofar as we are dealing with SYNTACTIC PARAPHRASES); we must distinguish between GRAMMATICAL and LOGICAL subject, and we can even do this for the verbal complement, which does not itself have the form of a finite sentence; transformations must be EXTENSIONALLY MEANING-PRESERVING; ALL THE GRAMMATICAL INFORMATION necessary for establishing the extensions of sentences is to be made EXPLICIT in deep structure.

One can raise objections to these theoretical decisions. The strongest objection is to the notion that only the extensions of sentences are to be taken as their meanings. But in C and D the intension of the verbal complement also plays a role in determining the extensions of the sentences: *expect* is an intensional verb, not an extensional one. That in this case the intensions of the verbal complements are probably the same is due entirely to the restriction to syntactic paraphrases. These two prior theoretical decisions – at first motivated separately – are thus interdependent. Another objection must be levelled against Chomsky's failure to identify his argument as semantically oriented. The status of a logical subject (as distinct from a grammatical subject) is not clarified; it is simply assumed that any speaker will know what a logical subject is. This is however hardly the case; the most we can assume is that some speakers have learned what a logical subject is in school. The linguist however ought to clarify the assumptions behind his explication more clearly. If we want to be able to speak of deep structures making logical subjects explicit, then we must assume that deep structures are expressions in a logical language. But this is not the case.

I will pursue Chomsky's argument a bit further still, but in a basically parallel way, on the basis of the following sentences:[1]

(33) Der Agent scheint den Demonstranten auszufragen.

(34) Der Agent versucht den Demonstranten auszufragen.

(35) Der Demonstrant scheint vom Agenten ausgefragt zu werden.

(36) Der Demonstrant versucht vom Agenten ausgefragt zu werden.

(37) Es scheint, daß der Agent den Demonstranten ausfragt.

(38) *Es versucht, daß der Agent den Demonstranted ausfragt.

(39) Es scheint, daß der Demonstrant vom Agenten ausgefragt wird.

(40) *Es versucht, daß der Demonstrant vom Agenten ausgrefragt wird.

(41) *Den Demonstranten auszufragen wird vom Agenten geschienen.

(42) Den Demonstranten auszufragen wird vom Agenten versucht.

(43) *Vom Agenten ausgefragt zu werden wird vom Demonstranten geschienen.

(44) Vom Agenten ausgefragt zu werden wird vom Demonstranten versucht.

---

[1] (33)–(6) are from Huber & Kummer (1973: §1.5). The argument from these four sentences would run parallel to Chomsky's. [Since some of what follows hinges on properties of German syntax (e.g. there is no English equivalent to (44), literally 'By the detective to be questioned was by the demonstrator attempted'), I have left the examples in German. Sentence (33) translates as 'The detective seems to be questioning the demonstrator', (34) as 'The detective is trying to question the demonstrator'. Trans.]

We can argue as follows:

1. The sentences are pairwise constructionally identical; there are particular relations holding between their constructions, e.g. as follows:

$$\{33, 34\} \longrightarrow \begin{matrix} \{37, 38\} \\ \{41, 42\} \end{matrix}$$

$$\{35, 36\} \longrightarrow \begin{matrix} \{39, 40\} \\ \{43, 44\} \end{matrix}$$

2. (33) and (35) are syntactic paraphrases of each other, but not (34) and (36).

3. (38) and (40) are ungrammatical, as are (41) and (43). In this case the formal relations between the surface forms not only have a different semantic function, but they are only partially definable in relation to grammatical sentences.

4. From the previous observations we can conclude that *scheinen* is possible with the abstract subject *es*, but not *versuchen*; on the other hand *versuchen* is passivizable, but not *scheinen*. We can now therefore use these observations as indications for how the deep structures are to be defined, without any consideration of grammatical and logical subjects: the information we have so far should be explicit in the deep structures.

5. We find three paraphrase-classes altogether, namely {33, 35, 37, 39}, {34, 42}, and {36, 44}; so we have to find three distinct deep structures.

6. The deep structures not only have to characterize the paraphrase-classes, they also have to correspond to certain generalizations. Further, the transformations must also be formulated in the most general way possible.[1] The abstract subject *es* (e.g. in (37)) is a pure form-element without any proper semantic function; it can be replaced by a subject complement identical to the subordinate clause in (37). Just as there are paraphrases *Es ist notwendig, daß p* and *Daß p, ist notwendig*, we can suggest for (5) the slightly deviant paraphrase *Daß der Agent den Demonstranten ausfragt, scheint* (this is the price we pay for the generalization). The deep structure should be (relative to the others) most similar to this paraphrase.

The question of how to handle the complement of *versuchen* is more

---

[1] For this reason among others Huber & Kummer (1973: ch. 10) – following a proposal of Chomsky's – dispense with a unitary passive transformation. In their view passivization can only be captured by a sequence of two transformations, each in itself significantly more general (these are NP-preposing and NP-postposing); in addition it is also possible to capture the form of the mediopassive (here only one of these rules applies).

difficult. In cases like *glauben, hoffen* ['believe', 'hope'] etc. there are *daß*-S paraphrases; with *versuchen* we get these only if the embedded logical subject is not identical with the subject of *versuchen*: e.g. *Der Agent versucht, daß er vom Demonstranten ausgefragt wird* is grammatical, as against **Der Agent versucht, daß er [der Agent] den Demonstranten ausfragt*. Therefore we can assume that the form of this last sentence is most similar to the deep structure: on the one hand on the grounds of generalization, on the other because it is not a requirement that the deep structure must in all cases correspond exactly to a grammatical sentence. The idiosyncracies to be observed here (which indeed vary in different subsystems of German and can easily change) can be neglected in the abstract formulation.

We can now formulate the three deep structures (omitting inflexion) as follows (in the third the embedded passive should perhaps be replaced by an active – depending on what we think about the active–passive relation):

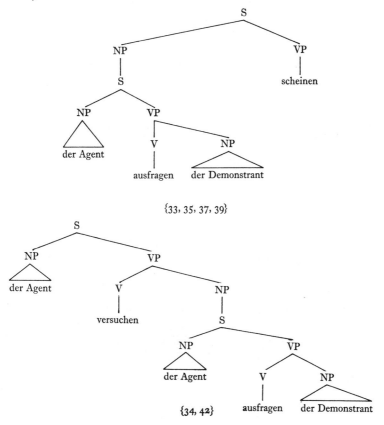

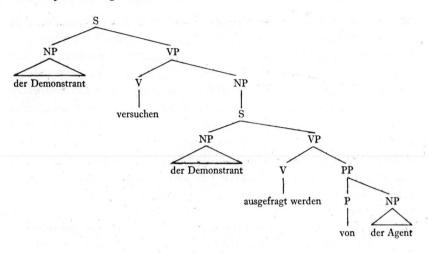

{36, 44}

II Language-families and grammar-families

11.1 Problems with the concept of a language-system

In the preceding chapters I have often spoken rather casually about individual languages and their grammars (e.g. THE German language, THE English language), as if these were unitary phenomena. But as I argued in 4.4 above, this manner of speaking always involves a degree of abstraction and idealization – which is permissible only from certain points of view. I distinguished there between different degrees of abstraction:

- A. Linguistic system of an individual person.
- B. Homogeneous linguistic system for a group, relative to particular situations of use (sociolect).
- C. Dialectal and diatypic characteristic varieties of a language at a given time.
- D. Individual language at a given time.

We can regard a language as the sum of the conditions controlling verbal communication in a speech-community. Every linguistic system encompasses a class of intersubjectively acknowledged conventions or rules which the speakers follow in their speech acts; when they do this they produce particular utterance-tokens (manifestations of the language), which, as participants, they also understand. But language is not merely the result of the maturation processes of individual persons; it is the result of a social learning-process of persons in a group (or even in several different groups), or of a learning-process of a group as a whole. For these reasons it is impossible to regard a language (or a linguistic system) as a mere collection of individual systems, or a speech-community as a mere collection of persons. This is why I emphasized the centrality of the concept of the SOCIOLECT (and not that of the individual's linguistic system). A sociolect comprises the relatively similar linguistic activities of a (sociologically) relatively similar group of persons with frequent communicative contacts. Individuals can possess part of a sociolect (we can call this an idiolect), or even several different sociolects. But a sociolect is defined independently of which persons possess which parts of it; the population of a sociolectal community can vary constantly.

The components of any LINGUISTIC SYSTEM can be roughly characterized in terms of the sketch in 3.10, p. 91 above. In general only that part of the system excluding utterance-tokens and situational meanings is regarded as the speaker's GRAMMAR. This demarcation of the concept of grammar of course poses problems: e.g. intensions are defined relative to possible situations of utterance; the type of speech act is only partly indicated in the utterance-tokens; and the utterance-tokens only have to correspond partially to the rules of the grammar in this narrower sense. I will not however go into the possibilities of a conceptual demarcation of grammar and linguistic system here. In what follows I will assume that we can identify a grammar with a linguistic system (or even with an abstraction-structure of a linguistic system or parts of it). In particular we can regard a grammar G as the grammar of a sociolect – though this is not necessary at the outset. Let a speech-community M be the class of persons who (as speakers and hearers) partially command a grammar G and at least follow it at times when they communicate (in fact, they belong to M only when and insofar as they do this).

This notion must now be relativized and expanded:

1. Those persons who follow a grammar G in common by and large do so UNCONSCIOUSLY: they generally have no explicit knowledge of it. Only in cases of communication- or norm-discrepancy do they reflect on and explicate parts of G, and thus obtain the corresponding knowledge.

2. From the learner's standpoint, the learning of G is partly a process of accommodation to existing practices. From the teacher's standpoint (insofar as there are teachers) it is partly a training in existing practices. At the same time the learning of G also represents, for each individual, a process of abstraction and generalization, namely orientation only to the relevant conventional practices and internalization of rules on the basis of only a small number of communicative experiences. For those persons who follow G, then, G is always a PRODUCT OF ABSTRACTION. If they want to make G conscious, they have to make this conscious as well.

3. Many rules of G (since they are only implicit) have no firmly circumscribed domain of strict application (and no correspondingly circumscribed complementary domain of non-strict application).

(a) The APPLICATIONAL RANGE of a rule shows itself in the fact that the speakers in M use certain rules to different extents; one rule is extended to another's cost. On the levels of sentences and utterance-tokens there are generally always several alternatives with the same semantic function.

(b) These differential extensions of rules are tolerated by other speakers and hearers, i.e. they do not occasion communication difficulties or reprimands because of incongruous utterances. To every applicational range there thus corresponds a RANGE OF TOLERANCE.

(c) The speakers' communication procedures are NOT WHOLLY CONVENTIONAL; there are always some that are newly produced by analogy to existing ones, and these are also understood and accepted (at first only in special situations).

4. Within a speech-community M there are differences in the command of rules in G, which result, among other things, from the fact that not all speakers use them with the same frequency. This DIFFERENCE IN COMMAND often shows up in uncertainty about the applicational range of a rule, or about the choice of rules from a class of very similar ones. This difference will generally be tolerated by others, and is thus externalized in a range of tolerance. A typical difference is that between active command (production of utterances) and passive command (understanding of utterances). This latter is of course mainly relevant not within a speech-community, but rather across its boundaries.

5. Those persons who belong to a speech-community M_1 can easily belong simultaneously to another community M_2 – since a speech-community is here defined only in relation to a linguistic system or a grammar G, and not to a collection of persons in all their activities and communicative relations.

6. It is clear that linguistic contact is also possible between persons from different speech-communities M_1 and M_2, especially if we are dealing with sociolects of the same language.

In the explicit reconstruction of languages the linguist must achieve at least the degree of abstraction that the speakers' linguistic capabilities and linguistic knowledge already have. But he often abstracts and idealizes beyond this: thus he may neglect the applicational range of rules, the corresponding range of tolerance, variant command, etc., since they are difficult to formulate precisely. But the most important idealization is this: the linguist isolates and throws into relief one linguistic system as against a number of related and neighbouring ones, and tries to capture only this – and not at the same time the processes of interaction with related and neighbouring systems (which nonetheless have a profound influence on the particular formation of this system). This idealization must be at least partly undone; that is, RELATIONS BETWEEN LINGUISTIC SYSTEMS must become an object of investigation.

11.2 Language-families

As soon as we look systematically at a national language like German, two very important points attract our attention. First, there is a set of particular VARIETIES existing at a given time: the worker speaks differently from the civil servant, the school-child from the actor, the man from Hamburg from the man from Passau; the man from Hamburg does not speak the way he writes. Secondly, there is a set of TEMPORAL PHASES of the individual varieties as well as of German as a whole, and these are also distinct from each other in many ways: the man from Cologne in 1973 speaks differently from the way a man from Cologne spoke in 1750, and he in turn spoke differently from one in 1400, etc. So what we have to elucidate here is both the relationship of the individual contemporary varieties to each other, and their historical mutability. But these aspects are not completely separable; they are rather, in fact, mutually illuminating. Many of the varieties are explicable as historically developed divergences (different kinds of contacts with neighbours, slight mutual contacts); many historical changes of a language are explicable as the result of the mutual influences of its varieties.

The investigation of the relations between linguistic systems must of course cover more than the internal groupings or developments of a national language – because this national language itself is only a relatively late result of a historical development (the European national languages began to develop at the end of the Middle Ages) to which contact with other languages as well as demarcation have contributed. We thus have to consider any language (i.e. what can sensibly be called a language on its own) as consisting of several varieties, and the historical development of this language as partly determined by the internal relations between these varieties.

We can group different neighbouring or partly similar sociolects, dialects, professional dialects, national languages, etc. into LANGUAGE-FAMILIES; their grammars can correspondingly be grouped into GRAMMAR-FAMILIES.

The size of a family can be conceived on a large or a small scale:

A NATIONAL LANGUAGE like German can be regarded as a FAMILY OF

ITS DIFFERENT VARIETIES. Various factors can be invoked to justify this, and each one can be differentially weighted: e.g. what the members of the family have in common is greater than their differences, or in any case what they have in common with the members of other comparable families – i.e. here national languages. In spite of all the differences the speakers are mutually comprehensible; where they do not understand each other they can change their speech in such a way that they can, without feeling that they have to learn a new language; the speakers share a common cultural, historical, social and/or political background.

German can be placed, along with Danish, Dutch, Swedish, Norwegian, English, etc. in a FAMILY OF GERMANIC LANGUAGES. We can justify this by invoking facts that verify a genetic relationship; or we can show that the vocabulary, syntax and morphology of this group have many things in common *vis-à-vis* other languages.

The Germanic languages can be placed, along with Romance, Slavic and others, in a FAMILY OF INDO-EUROPEAN LANGUAGES. Here we can also invoke historical facts, evidence for a common ancestral language as well as frequent contact. In addition to this, there are purely typological and structural reasons for grouping at least some of these languages in one family.

In general, we have to say that each grouping we make is relative to a certain purpose; and there are clearly different purposes. A man identifies himself by his own language as opposed to those of other people (who were in ancient times called barbarians). There are several distinct cultural and political reasons for grouping; and the socio-historically oriented linguist can take these as the subject of his investigation. On the other hand, the linguist may follow up different theoretical aims when he investigates relations between linguistic systems. From his point of view subjects can be:

1. TYPOLOGICAL GROUPINGS, for example the family of SOV languages (with a subject-verb-object order), the family of inflexional languages, the family of languages with postpositions, etc.

2. LOCAL GROUPINGS, for example the family of languages in the Indian subcontinent, the family of languages in the Baltic area, several 'contact-families' (e.g. Indic and Dravidian, which have become typologically similar over time).

3. GENETIC GROUPINGS, for example the families of Germanic languages, of Semitic languages, of Turkic languages.

11.3   Criticism of the homogeneity assumption

If we want to develop a theory-form for the description or explication of grammars, it is extremely useful to begin with the idealizing assumption that ALL SPEAKERS OF THE LANGUAGE IN QUESTION FOLLOW THE LINGUISTIC RULES PERFECTLY, AND THAT THE SPEECH-COMMUNITY IS COMPLETELY HOMOGENEOUS.[1] What are the implications of such an assumption ?[2]

1. We must first clarify what we mean by 'language' and 'speech-community'. Empirically the assumption seems to be defensible only under a very narrow definition of both, e.g. 'language' in the sense of 'sociolect', though perhaps this concept can also be applied to the dialectal and diatypic varieties. The homogeneity assumption would naturally be justified if we were dealing only with standardized languages, e.g. scientific languages. This suggests that homogeneity of a language and ideal following of linguistic rules basically imply a claim (not always met even in scientific languages) which requires more justification than it is usually given.

Thus we could for instance even regard High German as homogeneous – at least in a normative sense; but this kind of standardization can only hold for the public use of a language in teaching, administration, etc., and not for private use among colleagues, in the family, etc.; this normally escapes such standardization. Dictionaries and similar works, and the institutions (like academies) connected with them (e.g. Duden in Germany) can also count as standardizing authorities; but Duden, for instance, in its recent editions, concedes a good deal of range of tolerance, so that we can no longer speak of strict homogeneity.

But the idealizing homogeneity assumption is not generally intended as normative (e.g. by Chomsky, whose goals are descriptive and explanatory). The idealization is generally supposed to help in working out a clear notion of a linguistic system or a grammar; simultaneous consideration of all the different variants of a language would simply get in the way. To this extent it is the expression of a certain theoretical helpless-

---

[1] Many linguists have made this basic assumption; it is explicitly formulated for instance by Chomsky (1965: 3): 'Linguistic theory is concerned primarily with an ideal speaker–listener, in a completely homogeneous speech-community, who knows its language perfectly and is unaffected by such grammatically irrelevant conditions as memory limitations, distractions, shifts of attention and interest, and errors (random or characteristic)...'

[2] For further criticisms of the homogeneity assumption see Weinreich, Labov & Herzog (1968), and the various works on linguistic variation by Labov (1972), De Camp (1970), Bailey (1973), Bailey & Shuy (1973), Carden (1973), Klein (1974), etc.

ness with respect to the richness of linguistic variation. This is in fact precisely the reason that it would be disastrous for language-teaching in the schools to be guided by a linguistic theory that assumes such idealizations. There the descriptive idealization would simply function as a NORMATIVE FIXATION (not only causing misunderstanding, but providing the whole framework for reflection on language). Schools should provide opportunities for the discussion of linguistic hetero-geneity and the concomitant need for linguistic tolerance.

The homogeneity assumption is no doubt justified, at least to a certain extent, by the overall converging or normalizing tendency that we can see in the development of individual languages since the Middle Ages. It is especially clear in the European states that commerce, printing, industrialization, and most recently radio and TV, have prompted a development of 'common languages', which increasingly transcend regional boundaries. In general either the dialects of regions surround-ing national capitals, or – often in connection with this – the speech-styles of particularly well-known writers have prevailed. (For example, Dante in Italy with a Florentine dialect, Luther in Germany with a dialect stemming from the East Central German administrative lan-guage – though certainly neither of these 'common languages' remained unchanged in later times. But they did contribute significantly to the stabilization of a supraregional standard language.) These supraregional languages, however, should not be equated with the many regional and social varieties; the differences are merely diminished. Of course, in a centuries-long tradition the language of a country tends to be largely identified with a relatively stable (and stabilizing) literary and admini-strative language – and comparatively little attention is paid to the 'folk languages'. The idea of linguistic homogeneity may after all rest at least partially on the after-effects of such a tradition.

2. The assumption that a language is homogeneous also implies that it DEVELOPS HOMOGENEOUSLY. Every language is indeed something socially objective, even if only to the extent that individual speakers have internalized its rules and follow them. For language development to be homogeneous it would be necessary for all speakers to change the rules and lexical items in the same way and at the same time. This is certainly extremely improbable (it is conceivable mainly in very small groups, where actual arrangements can be made by speakers). A more realistic picture would be that at the outset some speakers change their linguistic behaviour, and eventually the other members of community accommo-

date to the new rules and lexical items. But there would then be at least some intermediate stages of the language which are not fully homogeneous. Beyond this there are no obvious reasons why such a homogeneous language should change at all, other than there being some conflict between generations of speakers or accommodation to new social and cultural circumstances. The only question is how this could come about without at least partial simultaneous alterations in the conditions for communication, and to this extent in the language. One of the most important reasons for language change, namely compromise between contemporary and competing forms of a language, cannot be captured under the homogeneity assumption.[1]

If the homogeneity assumption is permissible only for sociolects or similar varieties of a language, what is the proper DEFINING CRITERION FOR A LANGUAGE ? There are two possibilities (or a third, i.e. a combination of the two):

1. Internal criteria: linguistic relatedness of the individual sociolects, etc. of a language.

2. External criteria: nationality, culture, history, etc. Do the inhabitants of Austria speak German (possibly Bavarian) or Austrian ? Do the East Germans and the West Germans speak the same language or two different ones ? On historical (and possibly cultural) grounds we would claim one; on national grounds the other. Clearly the question does not make very much sense, even if no-one can deny that in fact everybody (linguists included) does begin with the assumption that certain languages and not others are spoken. The answer in any case should probably not be given descriptively, but as a postulate – according to the purposes in question. There can be a linguistic purpose; but there can also be purposes of national demarcation, or the demarcation of a national minority within a state.[2]

---

[1] A typical consequence of the homogeneity assumption is the oversimplification of the notion of history in the dominant schools of nineteenth- and early twentieth-century linguistics: the history of a language was not regarded primarily as a continuous process of innovation, but as a sequence of more or less clearly distinguished language-states, without consideration of social factors controlling linguistic innovation.

[2] For similar reasons even languages that are hardly spoken any more can be elevated to the status of national languages, in order to document independence (e.g. Irish in Eire after independence).

11.4 On the construction of a language as a whole

If it is relatively arbitrary to demarcate THE German language (e.g. as against Swiss German or the language of the Siebenbürgen, then the definition of tasks like 'write the rules for the grammar of German' remains relatively obscure, while 'write the rules for the colloquial speech of Stuttgart' is rather clearer. The consequence is that we can regard the German language solely as a construct, or more precisely, as a family of all the sociolects of German. It still remains an open question, of course, whether there exists a procedure for constructing 'German' out of this set of individual sociolects.

There have been various proposals for doing just this. Most of them reduce to one of the following (where G = the individual language in question (e.g. 'German') and g_i its individual sociolects):

1. G is the set-theoretical intersection of all g_i.
2. G is the set-theoretical union of all g_i.
3. G is a complex set-theoretical structure from g_i.
4. G is a transformation from a superior (dominant, central) sociolect or dialect out of g_i.

We can choose either a 'weak' or a 'strong' interpretation for G and g_i: the weak interpretation takes G or g_i as a set of sentences or utterance-forms; the strong interpretation takes G or g_i as a linguistic system or grammar (including a lexicon).

Obviously procedure 1 leads to a minimal form, procedure 2 to a maximal form, which we can still regard as an 'individual language' or a 'grammar of an individual language'. A language consisting only of what all its sociolects have in common is probably too poor; a language that includes everything its individual sociolects include is probably too rich. The overall question is: would it still be a language? Is there anybody who speaks it?

In order to avoid these two extremes and their attendant problems, 3 is often chosen; this aims at a 'middle way'. A typical example is the procedure of Althaus & Henne (1971). They take the individual linguistic competence of the speaker–hearer as the union of a set of available linguistic symbols and a set of available linguistic rules. In a dialogue only that portion of the linguistic competence common to both speakers is used. The set-theoretical intersection of two individual linguistic competences is called a linguistic code; it is defined relative to the two partners in the dialogue. The union of all pairwise constructed competence-intersections yields the linguistic system:

Linguistic system $= \underset{i,j}{\cup}$ (Linguistic competence$_i$ ∩ Linguistic competence$_j$)

where i, j are independent variables ranging over the values 1 to N, and where N is the number of individuals in the speech-community; the intersection where i = j is not considered.

That this way of defining a linguistic system is in fact a 'middle way' can be seen from figure 9 illustrating the simple case where N = 3. Such

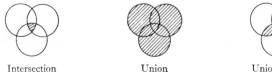

Intersection   Union   Union of all
                                           pairwise intersections

Figure 9

a set-theoretical construction of a linguistic system on the basis of individual competences must nonetheless remain essentially unsatisfactory, despite further improvements of the Althaus and Henne formula:

1. It is not clear – and it is even beyond clarification – how the individual competences develop on the basis of numerous communicative acts within social groups.

2. The definition assumes that we know in advance which persons belong to a speech-community and which do not. If only one person dies or one enters the community, according to the formula the linguistic system can change. (In larger speech-communities the number N can change every hour or even every minute.)

But if we did not restrict it to the speech-community, the formula would make no sense at all; since it would then allow us to consider for instance the 'common code' of a Japanese and a German – whatever this might look like.

3. The Althaus and Henne formula reduces the social aspects of a language to a number of two-sided (dialogic) relations; but in this framework there is no way of explaining how the authority of a pre-existing colloquial language (which each of the partners can relate to) is to have effect in such relationships. In merely two-sided relationships we can get arbitrary communicative arrangements, which are obviously free from the requirement that they belong to the colloquial language; but here

such two-sided arrangements are by definition constituents of a linguistic system.

4. The three objections raised so far concern the construction of a linguistic system out of INDIVIDUAL COMPETENCES. These difficulties of course vanish if we refer at the outset to SOCIOLECTS; then only the number of sociolects is relevant, and not the number of speakers or the number of possible contacts between them. The chief objection still remains; however we visualize the set-theoretical procedure for constructing a language out of its sociolects, it suggests that the result is a language spoken by individuals. But this is false: no one communicates only by means of all the important features of German, but everyone communicates by means of particular portions of German, as he has learned them (under certain circumstances several important portions of German can be missing, but other, unimportant ones immediately available).

The fourth procedure poses the question rather differently, and at the same time it escapes the difficulties arising from a pure set-theoretical model. The fundamental question here is this: is there a DOMINANT dialect within a larger speech-community, which is especially prestigious, regarded by most of the members as central or supraregional, or spoken by particularly influential or powerful groups? Is the language as a whole to be constructed relative to this dominant dialect? This procedure attempts to mirror somewhat the process through which national languages develop, i.e. it attempts to equate a prestigious supraregional dialect with the language of a larger community as a whole. But this procedure too makes the same mistake of neglecting the existence of other dialects (sociolects), or even reconstructing only one particular dialect, and not the language as a whole.

*11.5 Kanngiesser's theory of grammar-families

To my mind Kanngiesser (1972) has chosen the most reasonable way out:[1] he essentially denies that languages are homogeneous objects that can be obtained by any process whatever from the class of their sociolects; the heterogeneous character of language is part of its definition. A language can no longer be characterized by a single grammar, but only

[1] When I wrote this book I was not aware of the famous article of Weinreich, Labov & Herzog (1968), who present empirical work that supports and adds concrete detail to Kanngiesser's rather abstract outline. I also became acquainted with Bailey's work on polylectal grammars (e.g. Bailey 1973) too late to include discussion of it here.

by means of a FAMILY OF COEXISTING GRAMMARS. If we apply the first procedure above (the intersection model) to the members of this family, we get its GRAMMAR-STANDARD (*Grammatikstandard*);[1] if we apply the second procedure (union) we get its GRAMMAR-POTENTIAL (*Grammatik-potential*). Grammar-standard and grammar-potential, however, are not themselves grammars, but only grammar-aggregates: they are sets of elements and rules, which even taken together still do not characterize any language or even any sociolect. The grammar-standard (which in the extreme case can even be the empty set) plays a role for a language only insofar as it remains by definition untouched by intralinguistic compensatory tendencies.

The grammar-potential gives a more significant characterization of a language; this set contains everything that could potentially (on the basis of intralinguistic compensatory tendencies) be taken as one of the constituent grammars. The grammar-potential thus sets the upper limit on what can be expressed in a language at a given time; but it is in principle not attainable by any speaker or group of speakers – or attainable only insofar as the speaker avails himself of the whole family of grammars: and this would presumably be prevented by the limitations of his memory.

In accordance with Kanngiesser's procedure we can introduce a set of theoretically important notions concerning a family of grammars $F(G_i) = \{G_1, G_2, ..., G_n\}$. Here Kanngiesser makes an important – but not unproblematical – preliminary decision: the grammar-standard of $F(G_i)$ must be a non-empty set (and indeed all the individual intersections of all category sets, all lexicon sets, and all rule sets must be non-empty). According to Kanngiesser it is only if we make this assumption that we can show the coherence of any $F(G_i)$ convincingly; only in this way can we justify saying that $F(G_i)$ actually represents a language. But we can imagine a different notion, in which we minimally assume only pairwise relatednesses. Here we would rather be following Wittgenstein's notion of family resemblance (e.g. a child is related to both his parents, but his parents do not have to be related to each other). This is represented graphically in figure 10.

Kanngiesser's preliminary decision has further consequences: (a) the G_i within $F(G_i)$ form, in the mathematical sense, a ramifying ordering; (b) the G_i are not only pairwise related to each other, but are also related as a whole; this relatedness can therefore be set up as a transitive relation

---

[1] The grammar-standard is not to be confused with the grammar of a standard dialect or standardized language; these are instances of particular forms of a language.

(as well as an irreflexive and symmetrical one); (c) if sentences or utterance-forms are grammatical relative to one of the G_i, they are at least not ungrammatical relative to all other G_j (which is as much as to say that speakers of these other sociolects can understand them without having to control the sociolect of G_i actively, and further that they will or ought to tolerate them); Kanngiesser therefore introduces the concept of SEMIGRAMMATICALITY relative to these other G_j.

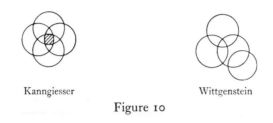

Kanngiesser   Wittgenstein

Figure 10

Now to Kanngiesser's exposition in detail (I paraphrase it somewhat freely):

1. Grammaticality evaluations of sentences (or utterance-forms: in the following we will only consider sentences, but this is not an essential restriction) are basically made relative to some G_i, not to $F(G_i)$. But beyond this we can state a DEGREE OF GRAMMATICALITY for every generally possible sentence in $F(G_i)$, which is identical to the number of G_i's relative to which it is grammatical. The higher the degree of grammaticality, the more central the sentence is within $F(G_i)$; the lower, the more peripheral. If the degree of grammaticality $m = 1$, the sentence is grammatical in only one sociolect of the language (Kanngiesser 1972: 91f.). If a sentence is grammatical relative to several G_i, this does not necessarily mean that it is also understood the same way relative to these G_i: in other words, it can have a different structural description, or the lexical elements used can be understood differently. If we pursue this notion, it becomes problematical to assign a sentence with a high degree of grammaticality to the centre from the beginning, insofar as by the centre we understand what most or all of the G_i's have in common. What turns out to be common here is not the structural properties of sentences, but only the evaluation of a particular sequence of word-forms.

A sentence which is grammatical relative to at least one G_i is then SEMIGRAMMATICAL relative to all other G_j. A sentence that is not grammatical relative to any G_i in $F(G_i)$ is UNGRAMMATICAL in $F(G_i)$. Nevertheless even such a sentence – some S^x – may be TOLERATED; though this will depend on whether some slight modification can transform it into another S_1 that is grammatical relative to one or more G_i; S^x will then be understood in the same way as S_1. This (silent or explicit) correction of S^x to S_1 may be possible for some sociolects (in which S^x is only trivially ungrammatical), but not for others. The possibility of toleration generally presupposes that there is only one expectable correction (to S_1), while other corrections to S_2, S_3, etc., are significantly less probable; otherwise S^x could be understood in a number of ways, and this would hardly be tolerable. For the speaker of a sociolect it is naturally not always necessary to decide whether a particular sentence is ungrammatical in $F(G_i)$ (but perhaps corrigible), or semigrammatical, i.e. grammatical in other related sociolects. One of the educational tasks of the schools should consist in the cultivation of precisely this ability to distinguish to a certain extent, so that children can develop a tolerance for semigrammatical utterances. They should learn to distinguish between sentences like

These dishes need washed
Will you can come ?

which are grammatical in some sociolects of English, while

Those dishes needing washed
Will you may come ?

are probably not grammatical in any.

There are two further phenomena of importance in reference to grammaticality (Kanngiesser 1972: 100, 58):

(a) In the utterances of an individual language (characterized by $F_1(G_i)$) we can use complex or non-complex expressions of another language (characterized by $F_2(G_j)$); these expressions have phonological, morphological, or syntactic properties that follow none of the G_i from $F_1(G_1)$, but rules from $F_2(G_j)$. This can be captured by means of the concept of EXTRAGRAMMATICALITY: in order to judge grammaticality we must draw on the rules of $F_2(G_j)$ in addition to those of $F_1(G_i)$:

EXAMPLES:[1]

Last but not least ist darauf zu achten, daß...

Die Diskussion verlief sine ira et studio.

Gehen wir lunch essen.

Das bleibt aber entre nous.

Bringen Sie mir eine Pizza mit Frutti di mare.

(b) Utterances like the following can be assigned without difficulty to English, and can probably be understood by most speakers of English – even though there can hardly be at present any G_i in the family of English sociolects that could judge these sentences to be grammatical:

Tragedy, as it was antiently compos'd, hath been ever held the gravest, moralest, and most profitable of all other Poems: therefore said by *Aristotle* to be of power of raising pity and fear, or terror, to purge the mind of those and such like passions, that is to temper and reduce them to just measure with a kind of delight, stirr'd up by reading or seeing those passions well imitated. Nor is Nature wanting in her own efforts to make good his assertion: for so in Physic things of melancholic hue and quality are us'd against melancholy, sowr against sowr, salt to remove salt humours. Hence philosophers and other gravest writers...frequently cite out of Tragic Poets, both to adorn and illustrate thir discourse. [Milton, preface to *Samson Agonistes*]

Grammaticality judgements are generally made with respect to particular historical stages of a language. The stages collectively constitute a family and not a mere temporal sequence of states. Sentences like those above have many features which are grammatical with respect to present-day English; but they have others which are grammatical only with respect to earlier stages. When we have to consider grammaticality judgements of elements of different historical stages, we can speak of TRANSGRAMMATICALITY.

2. Kanngiesser (1972: 102) defines at first only one form of relatedness holding between the individual sociolects of a language (or more precisely, their grammars). But actually he does not deal with a single relation, but a SYSTEM OF TYPES OF RELATEDNESS on all grammatical levels; and from the set of such systems of any pair of sociolects he assembles the whole system of relationships within the family of sociolects. The study of such relations is similar in many ways to the central

---

[1] In these examples we could still assume that the foreign elements in German are incorporated in frozen idioms (even though this would not explain their phonological structure and pronunciation); what is more striking is the common appearance of properties of two totally different languages in the so-called CODE-SWITCHING of bilinguals, which in fact shows determined regularities. E.g. *Before that wir haben gewohnt about vier Meilen von hier* (cf. Clyne 1972: 33).

concerns of contrastive grammatical theory (cf. Nickel 1972). It is to be noted that the numerous investigations of dialects, professional languages, special languages, as well as the languages of specific social strata are seldom laid out comparatively in terms of relatednesses within a grammar-family: either individual dialects, etc. are singled out and studied for their own sake, or are set in relation only with a prestigious standard; occasionally the geographical and other distributions of certain words (e.g. in the sense of dialect geography) or certain constructions are investigated.

On the basis of a detailed investigation of relatedness between sociolects, we could define a measure of degree of relatedness, which would state the extents of both similarity and difference.

Every one of these relatednesses can now be interpreted differently: either we regard two related sociolects as particularly integrated with each other (i.e. we assume a CONVERGING TENDENCY on the basis of contact), or we regard two dialects related in only certain aspects as nonintegrated in specific ways (i.e. we assume a DIVERGING TENDENCY, perhaps on the basis of a spatial, social or labour-defined separation, which led to a conditioned separation in development). Which of these two interpretations is to be chosen in a given case depends on further investigations, e.g. sociological studies of individual and group mobility. The second possibility can often be invoked in historical studies, e.g. for the explanation of the rise of several daughter languages from one original parent language (where relatively independent dialects developed at first, and then entered into contact with other languages). It can likewise be applied to the development of dialects within a language, if we assume that some have been relatively innovative, and others not. Thus under certain conditions we can regard different dialects of a language as representing historically different phases (as in fact is usual in traditional historical dialectology), and the narrowing divergences between them as an increasing historical agreement. In the same way the increasing distance between the dialects used in religious ritual and the colloquial dialects is clear (this is often true as well for administrative and legal language). In this century too there is an increasing distance between rural and village dialects and those of the major urban centres – so that the rural dialects often represent historically older forms; only in particular circumstances are they more innovating than the urban ones.[1]

[1] In the late nineteenth and early twentieth centuries dialect geographers attempted to use the rise of dialects as a basis for the reconstruction of the geographical expansion of medieval dialects (e.g. in the reconstruction of the so-called High German Sound Shift).

3. Among the requirements for a linguistic theory, Kanngiesser (1972: 118) includes the specification of possible extensions of constituent grammars. Every EXTENSION-RULE effects a modification in a subsystem of a grammar (especially in the vocabulary and phonological rules – though obviously syntactic, semantic and pragmatic modifications should be included as well). Kanngiesser distinguishes between conservative and non-conservative extensions. A CONSERVATIVE EXTENSION is one where a sociolect develops in the direction of a related one, or more precisely adopts grammatical possibilities from this sociolect. This designates in particular the tendency of sociolects to converge, e.g. under pressure for common communication. So-called 'compensatory language education' is understood by many of its advocates in such a conservative sense: as accommodation by 'lower class' speakers to the 'middle class' dialect taken as standard.

The NON-CONSERVATIVE EXTENSIONS of course are more important for the development of a language: for they consist in the innovatory development of new linguistic possibilities.[1] Thus the creation of a supraregional language must depend on non-conservative innovations, and still more the creation of special professional languages, where this is at least clear in the invention of special terminologies. Non-conservative innovations are also engendered by contact with neighbouring languages of completely different structure (which are only slightly related, if at all), since the new elements must (at least phonologically) be 'accommodated' to the grammar of the incorporating language.

4. The processes of extension of constituent grammars can again be seen from the point of view of convergence or divergence: conservative extensions support the tendency toward convergence of individual grammars; innovations that take place in some sociolects but not others support the tendency toward divergence. Later on such innovations can of course again come under the heading of the tendency toward convergence, insofar as they are taken up by other dialects.

Kanngiesser sees his model of coexisting grammars as an explicit attempt TO UNITE THE SYNCHRONIC AND DIACHRONIC ASPECTS OF LANGUAGE. He notes that a linguistic theory remains unsatisfactory as long as it is unable to explain (at least in principle) both variability within a language and the continuous development of this language (partly brought about by this variability). Exclusive emphasis on the synchronic

---

[1] The notions 'conservative' and 'innovating' have been worked out in some detail by Vaiana (1972) and Lass (1976: chs. 3 and 4).

aspect has led to the development of linguistic theories that in principle no longer allow a connection with diachrony, e.g. insofar as they postulate linguistic homogeneity. In consequence this aspect can never be correctly understood, because the history of a language at the present time should not merely be divided into a sequence of synchronic states.

Every language characterized by means of a family of grammars can be interpreted at the same time both synchronically and diachronically: synchronically as A CLASS OF MEANS OF COMMUNICATION USED AT A GIVEN TIME (or means of communication controlled by certain groups at a given time); diachronically as A CLASS OF DIFFERENT PHASES IN THE DEVELOPMENT OF THE MEANS OF COMMUNICATION (Kanngiesser 1972: 141). If we wish, we can relate the diachronic interpretation to the phases of child language, or to generation-specific languages, as well as to those sociolects that represent different phases in the development of the language as a whole. This might even permit us to separate, within the grammar of an individual sociolect, the creative rules (that can be used immediately for innovation) from those that only apply to a restricted class of linguistic elements, and are in many cases to be regarded as relics of past developmental stages of the language. This means that the simultaneity of different phases can even be captured in a homogeneous grammar by characterizing its rules as restrictedly or unrestrictedly applicable.[1] This is especially clear in the case of derivational affixes, some of which can be used almost without restriction (e.g. *-ung, -heit* in German), while others have a very restricted applicability (e.g. *-sam, -nis*).

11.6　Closing questions

After this very general exposition most of the questions one would want to ask about languages and language variants, their mutual interaction, and the social and political problems arising from them remain, as before, unanswered. I have merely outlined a possible theory form for dealing with them – and even this is extremely unsatisfactory. We still need to fill out and develop the theory in concrete terms, and discuss its utility for the solution of specific practical problems. I do not of course mean to imply that this is all unexplored country; on the contrary, there is a wealth of old and new work concerned in great detail with problems of bilingualism, language contact, social and political implications, and historical change – even if much of it is not guided by any very clear

---

[1] Such attempts have been made within generative phonology and the study of word formation, but not within generative syntax.

theory. The necessarily restricted purview of this book, and the emphasis on crucial issues in the foundations of linguistics do not allow the discussion of this literature in detail. Therefore in closing I would simply like to raise a few of the questions that I think are worth following up, and cite just a few works for further consideration.[1]

What are the conditions under which members of different speech-communities learn to communicate (supraregional cooperation, national integration, social, cultural, economic and political dependence, school-room introduction, situations involving immigration and migrant workers, etc.)? How do these affect the type of linguistic contact? What contacts, on what levels, in the use of what means of expression, actually do take place? How do they affect the change or stabilization of particular linguistic systems? To what extent can we observe interferences between systems, code-switching, formation of 'mixed languages', approximation of linguistic systems? Are these changes treated differentially according to the degree of relatedness between the systems? How do political, economic and social conflicts work out in linguistic terms? What special problems exist for instance in those European countries with multilingual populations (e.g. Switzerland, Belgium, Jugoslavia, the USSR), in countries with large numbers of immigrants (e.g. the USA, Australia, European countries with large numbers of migrant workers), or in those areas containing population groups with totally different languages (e.g. India, Africa)? What are the problems involved in language-planning (creation of supraregional languages, development of unified writing systems, pedagogical planning)? In what parts of the linguistic system are primary innovations to be expected, and how do they affect other parts? How do they affect converging or diverging tendencies relative to neighbouring systems? What are the arguments for genetic relationship of languages? What other arguments can be brought to bear on the possible future development of languages? How can such arguments be translated into rational language-planning (including teaching)?

[1] The basic work on problems of bilingualism and interference is Weinreich (1963). Important collections dealing with the whole area (excluding the more historical questions) are Gumperz & Hymes (1964, 1972), Fishman (1968, 1971, 1972).

For sociolinguistic research results in considerable detail see Labov *et al.* (1968), which lays out a set of research methods; Labov has published individual research results in numerous papers, some of which are collected in Labov (1972). See also Fishman *et al.* (1968).

For a general introduction to historical linguistics see Sturtevant (1968), Anttila(1972).

Many basic problems of language contact as well as historical change have been treated by Jespersen (1922, 1946).

References

Abbreviations of journals

LB	*Linguistische Berichte*
FL	*Foundations of Language*
IC	*Information and Control*
IS	*Information Sciences*
JL	*Journal of Linguistics*
JSL	*Journal of Symbolic Logic*
Lg	*Language*
TDP	*Transformations and Discourse Analysis Papers* (University of Pennsylvania)

Ackermann, W. (1958). Über die Beziehung zwischen strikter und strenger Implikation. *Dialectica* 12.

Althaus, H. P. & Henne, H. (1971). Sozialkompetenz und Sozialperformanz. Thesen zur Sozialkommunikation. *Zeitschrift für Dialektologie und Linguistik* 38.1–15.

Anderson, A. R. & Belnap, N. D. (1962). The calculus of pure entailment. *JSL* 27.

Anderson, J. M. (1971). *The grammar of case. Towards a localistic theory.* Cambridge.

Anttila, R. (1972). *An introduction to historical and comparative linguistics* New York.

Apresjan, J. D. (1971). *Ideen und Methoden der modernen strukturellen Linguistik*. Munich.

Austin, J. L. (1962). *How to do things with words*. Cambridge.

Bailey, C.-J. N. (1973). *Variation and linguistic theory*. Arlington.

Bailey, C.-J. N. & Shuy, R. W. (eds.) (1973). *New ways of analyzing variation in English*. Washington.

Ballmer, T. (1972). Einführung und Kontrolle von Diskurswelten. In Wunderlich (1972a: 183–206).

Bar-Hillel, Y. (1964). *Language and information*. Reading.
   (1971). *Pragmatics of natural languages*. Dordrecht.
   & Carnap, R. (1964). Outline of a theory of semantic information. In Bar-Hillel (1964: 221–74).

Bartsch, R. (1971). Semantische Darstellung von Prädikaten. *LB* 13.33–48.

(1972). Zum Problem pseudo-logischer Notation in der generativen Semantik. *Beiträge zur Linguistik und Informationsverarbeitung* 21.50–7.

& Vennemann, T. (1972). *Semantic structures*. Frankfurt.

Baumgärtner, K. (1967). Die Struktur des Bedeutungsfeldes. *Satz und Wort im heutigen Deutsch Jahrbuch 1965/66*, 165–97. Düsseldorf.

(1970). Konstituenz und Dependenz. In H. Steger, *Vorschläge für eine strukturäle Grammatik des Deutschen*. Darmstadt.

Belnap, N. D. (1973). Restricted quantification and conditional assertion. In H. Leblanc, *Truth, syntax and modality*, 48–75. Amsterdam.

Bennett, J. (1973). The meaning-nominalist strategy. *FL* 10.141–68.

Berka, K. & Kreiser, L. (1971). *Logik-Texte*. Berlin.

Berliner Gruppe (1975, MS). Sprachliches Handeln – Modelle und Listen. (Forthcoming Munich 1977).

Bierwisch, M. (1965). Review of Z. S. Harris 'Discourse analysis reprints'. *Linguistics* 13.61–73.

(1967). Some semantic universals of German adjectivals. *FL* 3.1–36.

(1969). On certain problems of semantic representations. *FL* 5.153–84.

Black, M. (1949). *Language and philosophy*. New York.

Blau, U. (1973). Zur 3-wertigen Logik der natürlichen Sprache. *Papiere zur Linguistik* 4.20–96.

Bloch, B. (1948). A set of postulates for phonemic analysis. *Lg* 3.3–47.

Bloomfield, L. (1926). A set of postulates for the science of language. *Lg*. 2–153–54.

(1933). *Language*. London.

Botha, R. P. (1970). *The methodological status of grammatical argumentation*. The Hague.

(1973). *The justification of linguistic hypotheses*. The Hague.

Brockhaus, K. & Stechow, A. v. (1971). On formal semantics: a new approach. *LB* 11.7–36.

Bühler, K. (1965). *Sprachtheorie* (1st ed. 1934). Stuttgart.

Čabnomme (1971). On concrete syntax. In *Studies out in left field: defamatory essays presented to James D. McCawley*, 151–5. Edmonton.

Carden, G. (1973). Dialect variation and abstract syntax. In R. Shuy (ed.), *Some new directions in linguistics*. Georgetown.

Carnap, R. (1955). Meaning and synonymy in natural languages. *Philosophical Studies* 7.33–47. Reprinted in Carnap (1956b: 233–47).

(1956a). The methodological character of theoretical concepts. In H. Fiegl & M. Scriven (eds.), *The foundations of science and the concepts of psychology and psychoanalysis*. Minnesota Studies in the Philosophy of Science, vol. 1, 38–76. Minneapolis.

(1956b). *Meaning and necessity*. 2nd ed. Chicago.

(1958). *Introduction to symbolic logic and its applications.* New York.

(1963). Replies and systematic expositions. In P. A. Schilpp, *The philosophy of Rudolf Carnap,* 859–1013. La Salle, Ill.

& Stegmüller, W. (1959). *Induktive Logik und Wahrscheinlichkeit.* Vienna.

Chomsky, N. (1957a). Review of Skinner (1957). *Lg* 35.26–58.

(1957b). *Syntactic structures.* The Hague.

(1959). On formal properties of grammars. *IC* 2.137–67.

(1964). *Current issues in linguistic theory.* The Hague.

(1965). *Aspects of the theory of syntax.* Cambridge, Mass.

(1970). Deep structure, surface structure, and semantic interpretation. In N. Chomsky, *Studies on semantics in generative grammar,* 62–119. The Hague & Paris, 1972.

(1972). *Language and mind.* New York.

(1976). *Reflections on language.* London.

& Halle, M. (1968). *The sound pattern of English.* New York.

Clyne, M. (1972). *Perspectives on language contact.* Melbourne.

Copi, I. (1968). *Introduction to logic.* 3rd ed. New York & London.

Coseriu, E. (1973). *Die Lage in der Linguistik.* Innsbrucker Beiträge zur Sprachwissenschaft. Innsbruck.

Cresswell, M. J. (1973). *Logics and languages.* London.

Davidson, D. & Harman, G. (1972). *Semantics of natural language.* Dordrecht.

De Camp, E. (1970). Is a sociolinguistic theory possible ? In J. E. Alatis (ed.), *Report of the 20th Annual Round Table Meeting on Linguistics and Language Studies.* Georgetown.

Diederich, W. (ed.) (1974). *Theorien der Wissenschaftsgeschichte.* Frankfurt.

Dray, W. (1957). *Laws and explanation in history.* Oxford.

Egli, U. (1971). Zweiwertigkeit und Präsupposition. *LB* 13.74–8.

(1972). Zur integrierten Grammatiktheorie. *LB* 21.1–14.

Ehlich, K. (1972). Thesen zur Sprechakttheorie. In Wunderlich (1972a: 122–6).

& Rehbein, J. (1972). Zur Konstitution pragmatischer Einheiten in einer Institution: Das Speiserestaurant. In Wunderlich (1972a: 209–54).

Essler, W. (1970). *Wissenschaftstheorie,* vol. 1: *Definition und Reduktion.* Munich.

Fillmore, C. (1968). The case for case. In E. Bach & R. Harms, *Universals in linguistic theory,* 1–88. New York.

(1971). *Some problems of case grammar.* Columbus.

Fishman, J. A. (1968). *Readings in the sociology of language.* The Hague.

(1971). *Advances in the sociology of language,* vol. 1: *Basic concepts, theories, and problems: alternative approaches.* The Hague.

(1972). *Advances in the sociology of language,* vol. 2: *Selected studies and applications.* The Hague.

Fishman, J. A., Cooper, R. C., Ma, R. *et al.* (1968). *Bilingualism in the Barrio, final report.* Bloomington.

Fraassen, B. C. v. (1971). *Formal semantics and logic.* New York.

Frege, G. (1966). Uber Sinn und Bedeutung (1st pub. 1892). In *Funktion, Begriff, Bedeutung,* 38–63. Göttingen.

(1973). Einleitung in die Logik (1st pub. 1906). In G. Frege, *Schriften zur Logik. Aus dem Nachlaß,* 75–92. Berlin.

Friedman, J. (1971). *A computer model of transformational grammar.* New York.

Geckeler, H. (1971). *Strukturelle Semantik und Wortfeldtheorie.* Munich.

Gentzen, G. (1934/5). Untersuchungen über das logische Schließen. *Mathematische Zeitschrift* 39.176–210, 405–31. Reprinted in Berka & Kreiser (1971: 192–253).

Ginsburg, S. (1966). *The mathematical theory of context-free languages.* New York.

Ginsburg, S. & Partee, B. H. (1969). A mathematical model of transformational grammar. *IC* 15.297–334.

Greenberg, J. H. (ed.) (1963). *Universals of language.* Cambridge, Mass.

Gregory, M. (1967). Aspects of varieties differentiation. *JL* 3.177–98.

Grewendorf, G. (1971). Untersuchungen zur Unterscheidung der deskriptiven und wertenden Komponente in der Bedeutung der Wertäußerungen. Mag. Arbeit. Munich.

Grice, H. P. (1957). Meaning. *Philosophical Review* 66.377–88.

(1968). Utterer's meaning, sentence-meaning, and word-meaning. *FL* 4.1–18.

(1968, MS). Logic and conversation.

(1969). Utterer's meaning and intentions. *Philosophical Review* 78.147–77.

(1975). Logic and conversation. In: P. Cole and J. L. Morgan (eds.), *Syntax and semantics,* vol. 3: *Speech Acts,* 41–58. New York.

Gross, M. (1975). *Méthodes en syntaxe. Régime des constructions complétives.* Paris.

Gumperz, J. & Hymes, D. (1964). *The ethnography of communication* (= *American Anthropologist* 66: 6, part 2).

(1972). *Directions in sociolinguistics.* New York.

Habermas, J. (1968). Erkenntnis und Interesse. In *Technik und Wissenschaft als 'Ideologie'.* Frankfurt.

(1971). Vorbereitende Bemerkungen zu einer Theorie der kommunikativen Kompetenz. In J. Habermas & N. Luhmann, *Theorie der Gesellschaft oder Sozialtechnologie – Was leistet die Systemforschung?* Frankfurt.

Hamblin, C. L. (1970). *Fallacies.* London.

Hare, R. M. (1952). *The language of morals.* Oxford.

Harris, Z. S. (1946). From morpheme to utterance. *Lg* 22.161–83.

(1952). Discourse analysis. *Lg* 28.1–30.

(1957). Co-occurrence and transformation in linguistic structure. *Lg* 33.283–340.

(1964). The elementary transformations. *TDP* 54.

(1965). Transformational theory. *Lg* 41.363–401.

(1969). The two systems of grammar: report and paraphrase. *TDP* 79.

(1970). *Papers in structural and transformational linguistics.* Dordrecht.

Hasenjäger, G. (1962). *Einführung in die Grundbegriffe und Probleme der modernen Logik.* Freiburg & Munich.

Heeschen, C. & Kegel, G. (1972). Zum Autonomiegedanken der Linguistik, oder: das Verhältnis von Psychologie und Linguistik im Selbstverstandnis der Linguistik. *LB* 21.42–54.

Heger, K. (1969). 'Sprache' und 'Dialekt' als linguistisches und soziolinguistisches Problem. *Folia Linguistica* 3.46–67.

(1971). *Monem, Wort und Satz.* Tübingen.

Hempel, C. G. (1965). *Aspects of scientific explanation.* New York & London.

& Oppenheim, P. (1948). Studies in the logic of explanation. *Philosophy of Science* 15.135–75.

Hilpinen, R. (1971). *Deontic logic: introductory and systematic readings.* Dordrecht.

Hintikka, J. (1962). *Knowledge and belief.* Ithaca, N.Y.

(1969). *Models for modalities: selected essays.* Dordrecht.

Hirschman, L. (1971). A comparison of formalisms for transformational grammar. *Transformations and Discourse Analysis Papers No. 87.* Philadelphia.

Hjelmslev, L. (1961). *Prolegomena to a theory of language.* Madison.

Hoenigswald, H. (1960). *Language change and linguistic reconstruction.* Chicago.

Huber, W. & Kummer, W. (1973). *Transformationelle Syntax des Deutschen. Syntaktische Transformationen,* vol. 1. Munich.

Itkonen, E. (1976). *Grammar and metascience.* Turku.

Iwin, A. A. (1972). Grundprobleme der deontischen Logik. In H. Wessel, *Quantoren – Modalitäten – Paradoxen,* 402–522. Berlin.

Jackendoff, R. S. (1972). *Semantic interpretation in generative grammar.* Cambridge, Mass.

Jakobson, R. & Halle, M. (1956). *Fundamentals of language.* The Hague.

Jespersen, O. (1922). *Language, its nature, development, and origin.* London.

(1946). *Mankind, nation and individual from a linguistic point of view.* London.

Joshi, A. K. (1969). Properties of formal grammars with mixed types of rules and their linguistic relevance. *TDP* 77.

Kalinowski, G. (1972). *La logique des normes*. Paris.

Kamp, H. (1968). Tense logic and the theory of linear order. PhD dissertation, UCLA.

—— (1973). Quantification and reference in modal and tense logic. MS.

Kanngiesser, S. (1972). *Aspekte der synchronen und diachronen linguistik*. Tübingen.

—— (1973). Aspekte zur Semantik und Pragmatik. *LB* 24.1–28.

Katz, J. J. (1966). *The philosophy of language*. New York.

—— & Fodor, J. A. (1963). The structure of a semantic theory. *LG* 39.170–210.

—— & Postal, P. M. (1964). *An integrated theory of linguistic descriptions*. Cambridge, Mass.

Kiefer, F. & Ruwet, N. (1973). *Generative grammar in Europe*. Dordrecht.

Klaus, G. (1966). *Spezielle Erkenntnistheorie*. Berlin.

Klein, W. (1974). *Variation in der Sprache*. Kronberg.

Klix, F. (1971). *Information und Verhalten*. Berlin, Berne, Stuttgart & Vienna.

Kratzer, A., Pause, E., Stechow, A. v. (1973). *Einführung in Theorie und Anwendung der generativen Syntax*. Frankfurt.

Kripke, S. A. (1959). The problem of entailment. *JSL* 24.324.

—— (1972). Naming and necessity. In Davidson & Harman (1972: 253–355).

Kuhn, T. (1962). *The structure of scientific revolutions*. Chicago.

Kutschera, F. v. (1971). *Sprachphilosophie*. Munich.

—— (1972). *Wissenschaftstheorie*. Munich.

Labov, W. (1972). *Sociolinguistic patterns*. Philadelphia.

Labov, W., Cohen, P., Robins, C., Lewis, J. (1968). *A study of the non-standard English of Negro and Puerto Rican speakers in New York City, Final Report*, vols. 1 and 2. Washington, D.C.

Lakoff, G. (1972). Linguistics and natural logic. In Davidson & Harman (1972: 545–665).

Lass, R. (1976). *English phonology and phonological theory*. Cambridge.

Lewis, C. I. (1914). The calculus of strict implication. *Mind* 23.240–7.

Lewis, D. (1969). *Conventions*. Cambridge, Mass.

—— (1972). General semantics. In Davidson & Harman (1972: 169–218).

—— (1973). *Counterfactuals*. Oxford.

Lieb, H. H. (1970). *Sprachstadium und Sprachsystem*. Stuttgart.

—— (1975). Universals of language: quandaries and prospects. *FL* 12.471–511.

—— (1976a). Zum Verhältnis von Sprachtheorien, Grammatiktheorien und Grammatiken. In Wunderlich (1976c: 200–14).

—— (1976b). Rekonstruktive Wissenschaftstheorie und empirische Wissenschaft. In Wunderlich (1976c: 183–99).

Lyons, J. (1968). *Introduction to theoretical linguistics*. Cambridge.

Maas, U. (1970). *Review of L. Wolf* (1968), *Sprachgeographische Untersuchungen zu den Bezeichnungen für Haustiere im Massif Central. Romanistiches Jahrbuch* 20.175–84.

& Wunderlich, D. (1972). *Pragmatik und sprachliches Handeln.* Frankfurt.

McCawley, J. D. (1972). A program for logic. In Davidson & Harman (1972: 498–544).

Matthews, P. H. (1972). *Inflectional morphology.* Cambridge.

Mead, G. H. (1934). *Mind, self and society. From the standpoint of a social behaviorist.* Chicago.

Mill, J. S. (1843). *A system of logic, ratiocinative and inductive.* London.

Montague, R. M. (1968). Pragmatics. In R. Klibansky (ed.), *Contemporary philosophy: a survey,* vol. 1. Florence, 1968. And in R. Montague, *Formal philosophy: selected papers,* 95–118. New Haven & London, 1974.

(1973). The proper treatment of quantification in ordinary English. In J. Hintikka, J. Moravcsik & P. Suppes, *Approaches to natural language,* 221–42. Dordrecht & Boston.

Morris, C. (1938). *Foundations of the theory of signs.* Chicago.

(1946). *Language and behavior.* London.

Naess, A. (1953). *Interpretation and preciseness.* Oslo.

Nickel, G. (1972). *Reader zur konstrastiven Linguistik.* Frankfurt.

Ogden, C. K. & Richards, I. A. (1953). *The meaning of meaning.* London.

Partee, B. H. (1972). Some transformational extensions of Montague grammar. *UCLA Occasional Papers in Linguistics* 2.1–24.

(1975). Montague grammar and transformational grammar. *Linguistic Inquiry* 6.203–300.

Passmore, J. (1962). Explanation in everyday life, in science, and in history. *History and Theory* 2.105–23.

Paul, H. (1909). *Prinzipien der Sprachgeschichte.* 4th ed. Halle.

Perelman, C. & Olbrechts-Tyteca, L. (1958). *La nouvelle rhétorique: traité de l'argumentation.* Paris.

Peters, S. (1972). The projection problem: how is a grammar to be selected? In S. Peters, *Goals of linguistic theory,* 171–87. Engelwood Cliffs, N.J.

Peters, S. & Ritchie, R. W. (1969). On the generative power of transformational grammars. Technical Report in Computer Science, University of Washington. Seattle.

Petöfi, J. S. & Franck, D. (1973). *Präsuppositionen in Philosophie und Linguistik.* Frankfurt.

Plötz, S. (1971). *Operationen in der Linguistik.* Hamburg.

(1972). *Transformationelle Analyse. Die Transformationstheorie von Zellig Harris und ihre Entwicklung.* Frankfurt.

Popper, K. R. (1972). *Objective knowledge. An evolutionary approach.* Oxford.

Porzig, W. (1934). Wesenhafte Bedeutungsbeziehungen. *Beiträge zur Geschichte der deutschen Sprache und Litteratur* 58.70–97.

Postal, P. M. (1974). *On raising: one rule of English grammar and its theoretical implications.* Cambridge, Mass.

Ramsey, F. P. (1951). Theories. In F. P. Ramsey, *The foundations of mathematics.* 212–36. London.

Rescher, N. (1966). *The logic of commands.* London.

(1973). *The coherence theory of truth.* Oxford.

Russell, B. (1956). On denoting. In B. Russell, *Logic and Knowledge.* London.

Schaff, A. (1966). *Einführung in die Semantik.* Berlin.

Schmidt, L. (1973). *Wortfeldforschung. Zur Geschichte und Theorie des sprachlichen Feldes.* Darmstadt.

Schmidt, S. J. (1968). *Sprache und Denken als sprachphilosophisches Problem von Locke bis Wittgenstein.* The Hague.

Schnelle, H. (1968). Methoden mathematischer Linguistik. *Enzyklopädie der geisteswissenschaftlichen Arbeitsmethoden*, 135–60. Munich.

(1973a). *Sprachphilosophie und Linguistik.* Reinbek.

(1973b). Meaning constraints. *Synthèse* 23.15–25.

Searle, J. R. (1969). *Speech acts.* Cambridge.

Sinowjew, A. A. (1970). *Komplexe Logik. Grundlagen einer Logischen Theorie des Wissens.* Berlin, Braunschweig & Basle.

Skinner, B. F. (1957). *Verbal behavior.* New York.

Sneed, J. (1971). *The logical structure of mathematical physics.* Dordrecht.

Stalnaker, R. C. (1972). Pragmatics. In Davidson & Harman (1972: 380–97).

Stegmüller, W. (1958). Wissenschaftstheorie. In *Fischer Lexicon Philosophie.* Frankfurt.

(1969). *Wissenschaftliche Erklärung und Begründung.* Berlin, Heidelberg & New York.

(1970). *Probleme und Resultate der Wissenschaftstheorie und Analytischen Philosophie*, vol. 2: *Theorie und Erfahrung.*

Strawson, P. F. (1964). Intention and convention in speech acts. *Philosophical Review* 73.439–60.

Sturtevant, E. H. (1968). *Linguistic change: an introduction to the historical study of language.* Chicago.

Tarski, A. (1935). Der Wahrheitsbegriff in den formalisierten Sprachen. *Studia Philosophica Commentarii Societatis Philosophicae Polonorum* 1. Reprinted in Berka & Kreiser (1971: 447–559).

Teller, P. (1969). Some discussion and extension of Manfred Bierwisch's work on German adjectivals. *FL* 5.185–217.

Thomason, R. H. (1970). *Symbolic logic: an introduction.* London.

Toulmin, S. (1969). *The uses of argument*. Cambridge.

Trier, J. (1931). *Der deutsche Wortschatz im Sinnbezirk des Verstandes. Die Geschichte eines sprachlichen Feldes*, vol. 1. Heidelberg.

Vaiana, M. (1972). A study of the dialects of the southern counties of Scotland. Unpublished PhD thesis, Indiana University.

Wang, J. (1968). Zur Anwendung kombinatorischer Verfahren der Logik auf die Formalisierung der Syntax. *IPK-Forschungsbericht* 68/5. Bonn.

(1971). Zur Beziehung zwischen generativen und axiomatischen Methoden in linguistischen Untersuchungen. In A. v. Stechow, *Beiträge zur generativen Grammatik*, 273–82. Braunschweig.

Weinreich, U. (1963). *Languages in contact. Findings and problems*. The Hague.

(1966). Explorations in semantic theory. In T. Sebeok, *Current trends in linguistics*, vol. 3, 395–477. The Hague.

Weinreich, U., Labov, W. & Herzog, M. (1968). Empirical foundations for a theory of language change. In W. P. Lehmann & Y. Malkiel (eds.), *Directions for historical linguistics*, 95–195. Austin.

Weisgerber, L. (1970). Muß die Linguistik die Sprachwissenschaft bekämpfen? *LB* 9.58–63.

Weydt, H. (1975). Das Problem der Sprachbeschreibung durch Simulation. In B. Schlieben-Lange (ed.), *Sprachtheorie*, 53–80. Hamburg.

Whitaker, H. A. (1971). *On the representation of language in the human brain*. Edmonton.

White, A. R. (1970). *Truth*. London.

Wierzbicka, R. (1973). A semantic model of time and space. In Kiefer & Ruwet (1973: 616–28).

Wittgenstein, L. (1922). *Tractatus Logico-philosophicus*. London.

(1958). *Philosophische Untersuchungen*. Oxford.

Wright, G. H. v. (1951). *An essay in modal logic*. Amsterdam.

(1963). *Norm and action*. London.

(1968). An essay in deontic logic and the general theory of action. *Acta Philosophica Fennica* 21.1–110.

Wunderlich, D. (1970). *Tempus und Zeitreferenz im Deutschen*. Munich.

(1971). Pragmatik, Sprechsituation, Deixis. *Zeitschrift für Literaturwissenschaft und Linguistik* 1/2.177ff.

(1972a). *Linguistische Pragmatik*. Frankfurt.

(1972b). Zur Konventionalität von Sprechhandlungen. In Wunderlich (1972a: 11–58).

(1972c). Mannheimer Notizen zur Pragmatik. In Maas & Wunderlich (1972: 279–94).

(1973). Vergleichssätze. In Kiefer & Ruwet (1973: 629–72).

(1976a). Towards an integrated theory of grammatical and pragmatical meaning. In A. Kasher (ed.), *Language in focus: foundations, methods and systems, Essays in memory of Yehoshua Bar-Hillel*, 251–77. Dordrecht.

(1976b). *Studien zur Sprechakttheorie*. Frankfurt.

(ed.) (1976c). *Wissenschaftstheorie der Linguistik*. Kronberg.

Zadeh, L. (1965). Fuzzy sets. *IC* 8.338–53.

(1971). Quantitative fuzzy semantics. *IS* 3.159–76.

Index of names

DATE DUE